Dracula
EVERLASTING

I

STORY BY
NUNZIO DEFILIPPIS
& CHRISTINA WEIR

ART BY
RHEA SILVAN

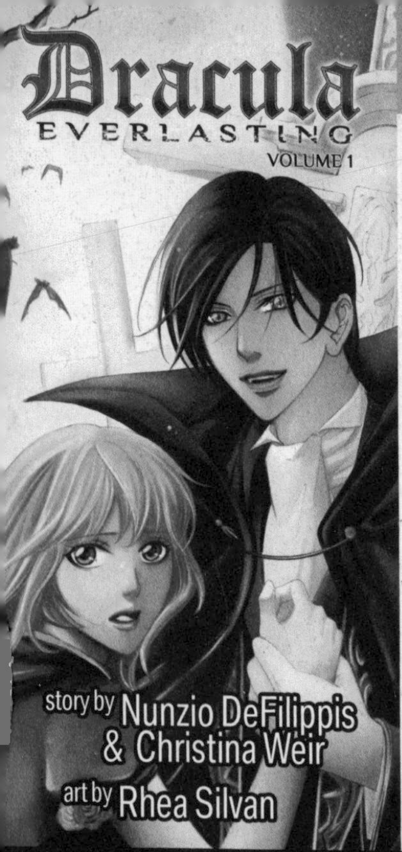
Dracula
EVERLASTING
VOLUME 1
story by Nunzio DeFilippis
& Christina Weir
art by Rhea Silvan

STAFF CREDITS

toning/art assists	Eirin
lettering	Nicky Lim
layout	Adam Arnold
design	Nicky Lim
copy editor	Shanti Whitesides
editor	Adam Arnold
publisher	Jason DeAngelis Seven Seas Entertainment

This is a work of fiction. Names, characters, places, and incidents are the products of the author's imagination or are used fictitiously. Any resemblance to actual events, locales, or persons, living or dead, is entirely coincidental.

ISBN: 978-1-935934-03-5

Printed in Canada

First Printing: October 2011

10 9 8 7 6 5 4 3 2 1

Seven Seas

READING DIRECTIONS

This book reads from ***right to left***, Japanese style. If this is your first time reading manga, you start reading from the top right panel on each page and take it from there. If you get lost, just follow the ... ards ... !!

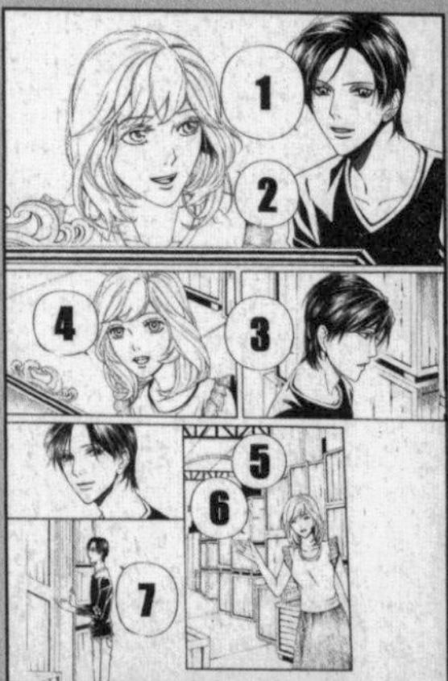
1
2
3
4
5
6
7

CHAPTER
1

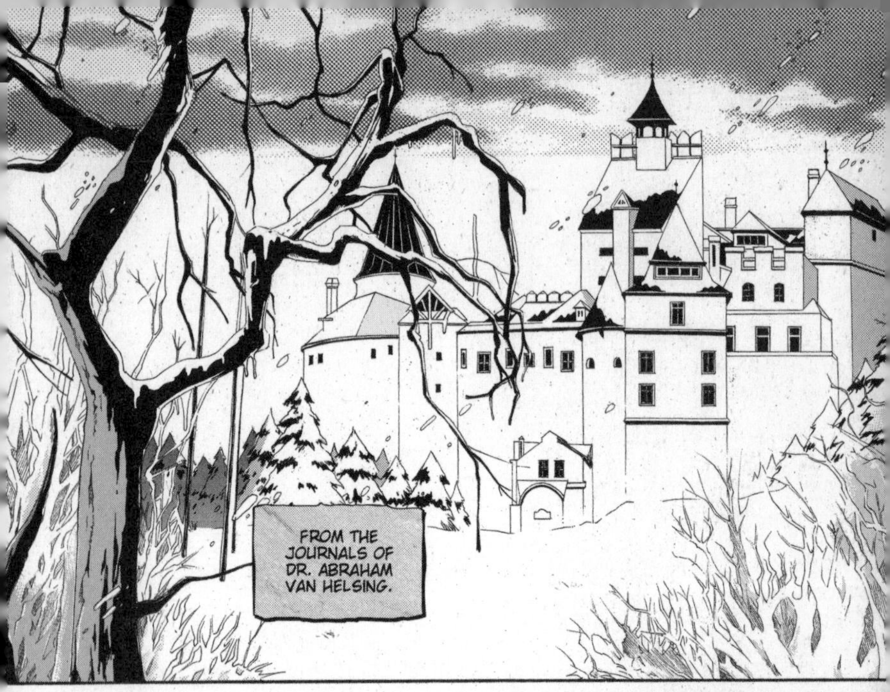
FROM THE JOURNALS OF DR. ABRAHAM VAN HELSING.

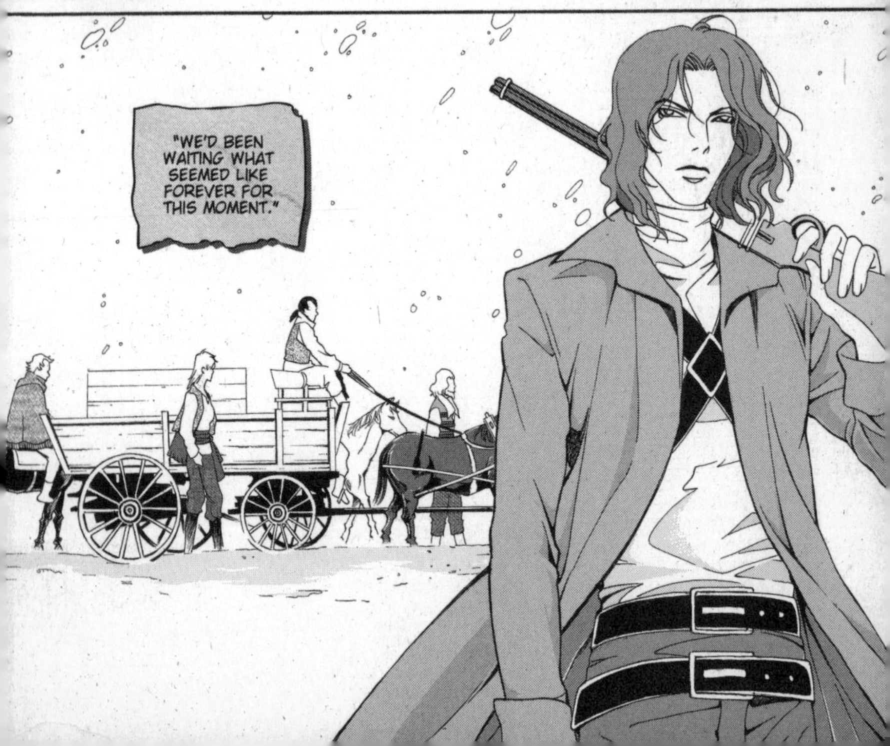
"WE'D BEEN WAITING WHAT SEEMED LIKE FOREVER FOR THIS MOMENT."

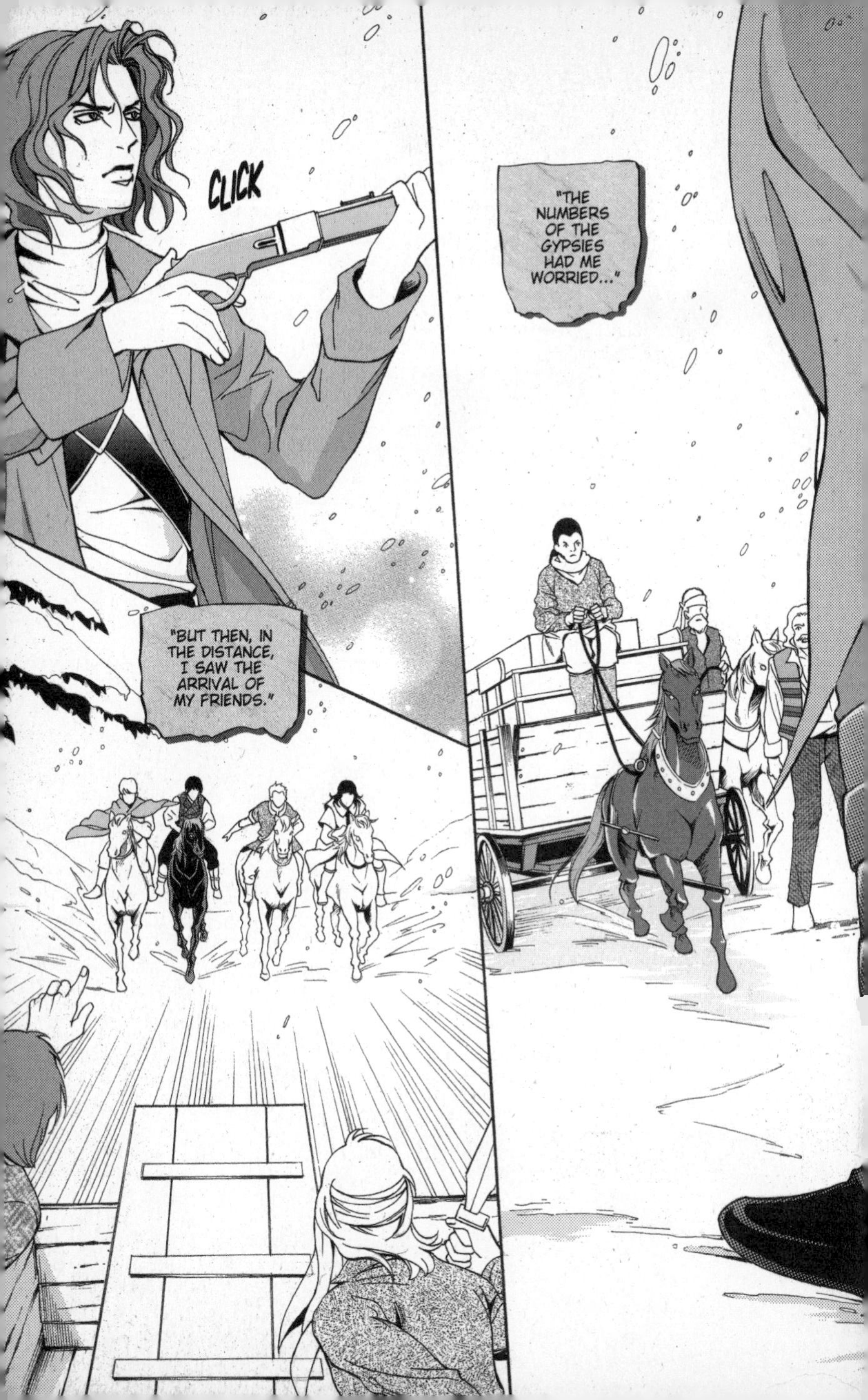
"THE NUMBERS OF THE GYPSIES HAD ME WORRIED..."
CLICK
"BUT THEN, IN THE DISTANCE, I SAW THE ARRIVAL OF MY FRIENDS."

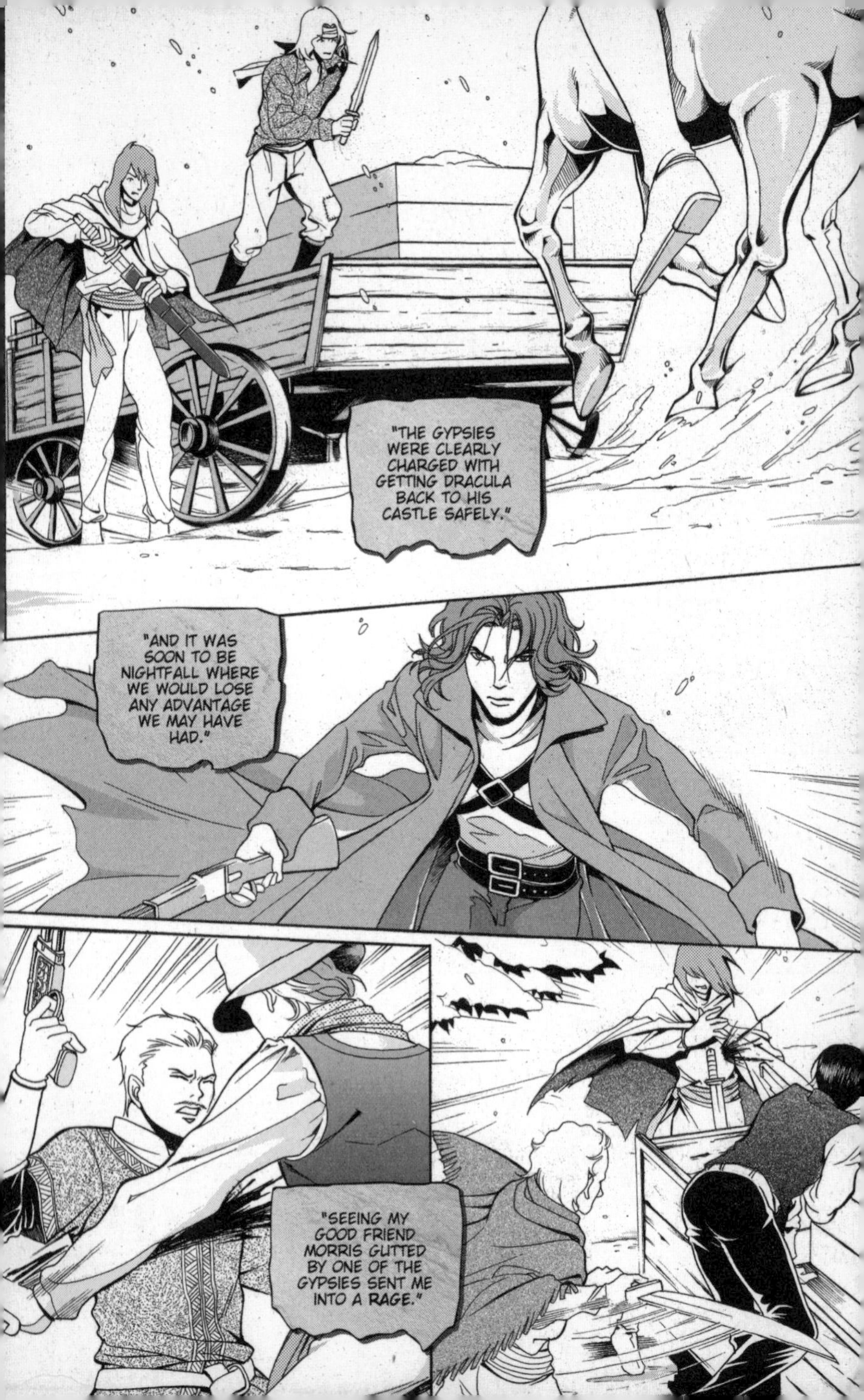
"THE GYPSIES WERE CLEARLY CHARGED WITH GETTING DRACULA BACK TO HIS CASTLE SAFELY."
"AND IT WAS SOON TO BE NIGHTFALL WHERE WE WOULD LOSE ANY ADVANTAGE WE MAY HAVE HAD."
"SEEING MY GOOD FRIEND MORRIS GUTTED BY ONE OF THE GYPSIES SENT ME INTO A RAGE."

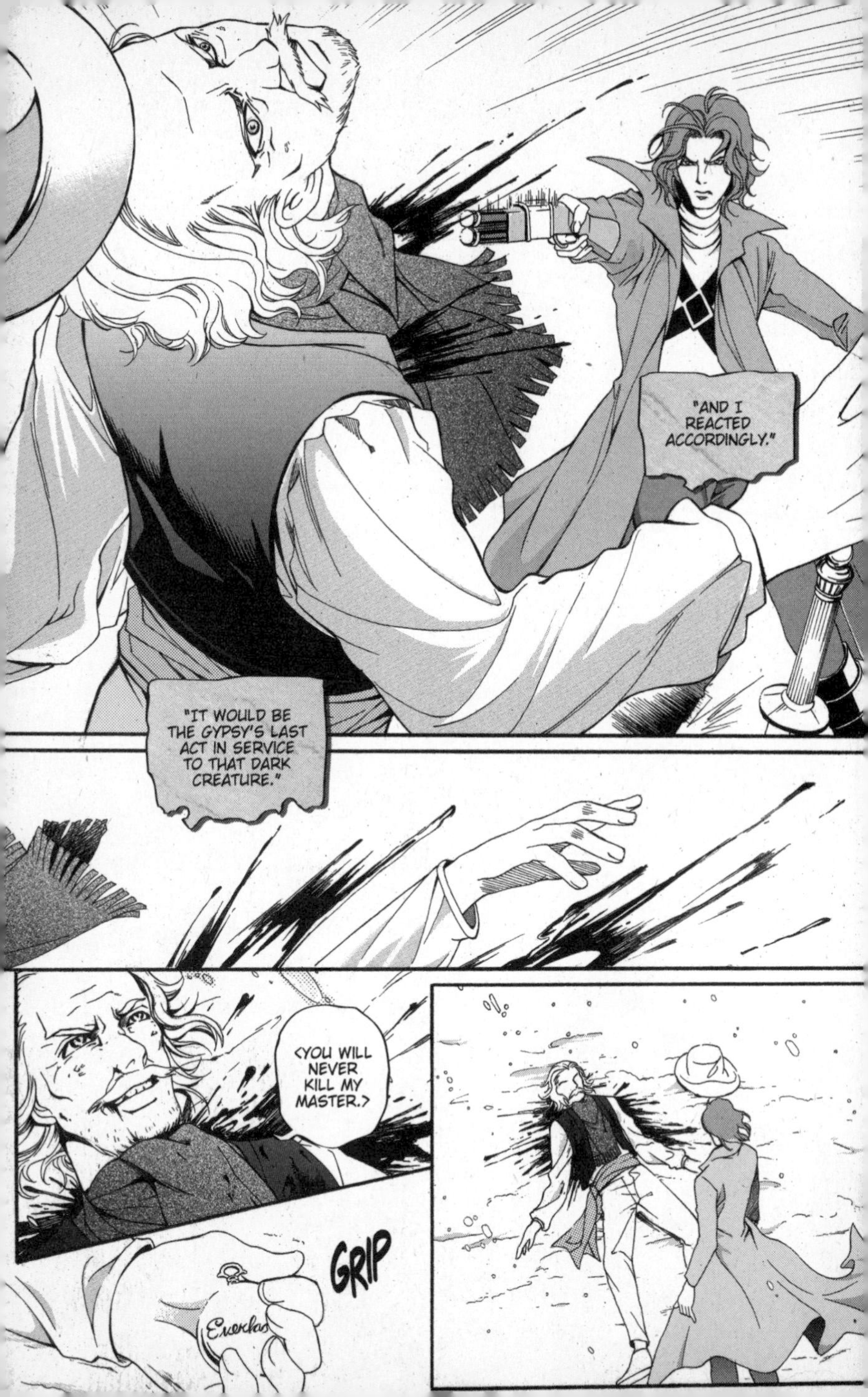
"AND I REACTED ACCORDINGLY."
"IT WOULD BE THE GYPSY'S LAST ACT IN SERVICE TO THAT DARK CREATURE."
<YOU WILL NEVER KILL MY MASTER.>
GRIP

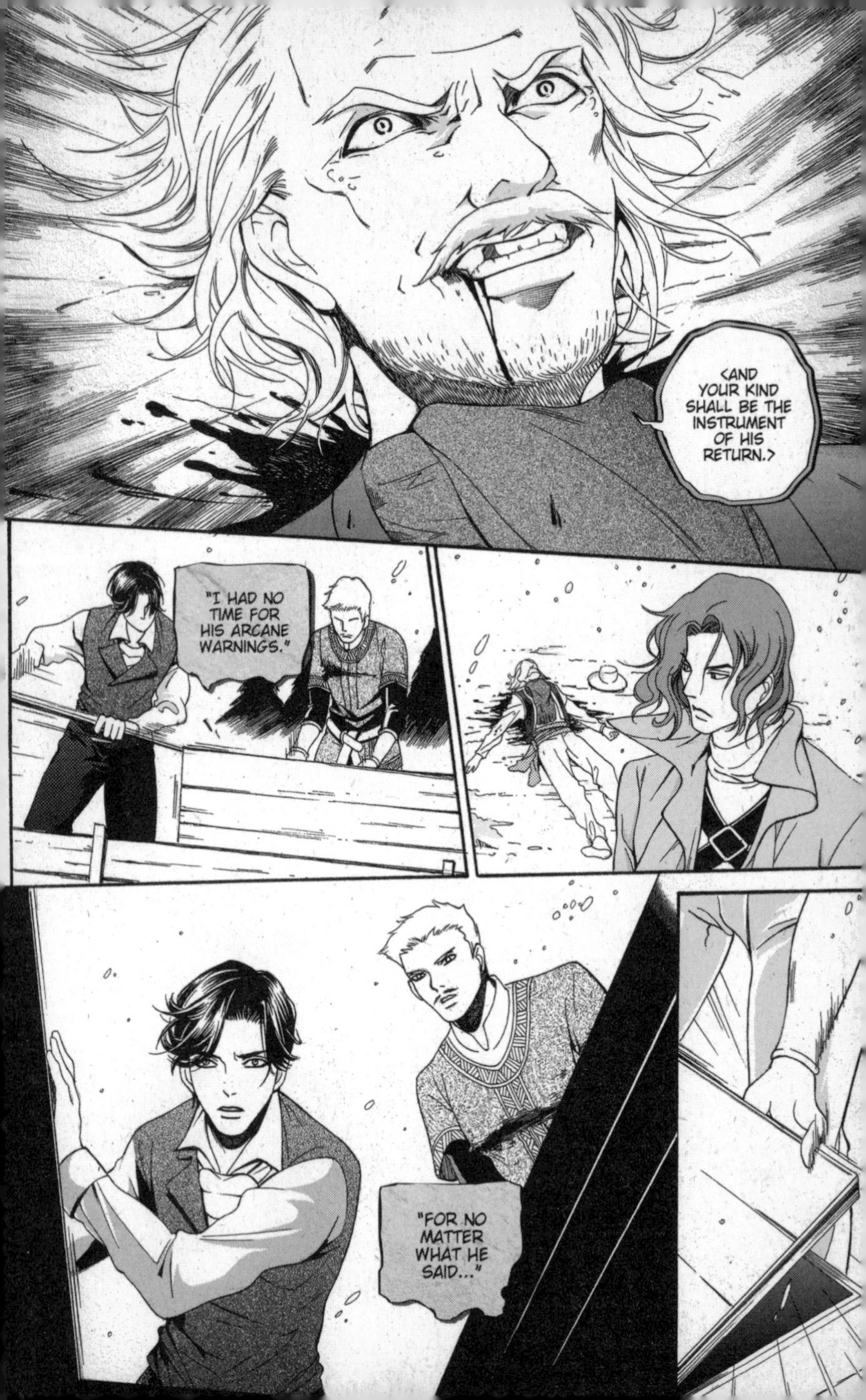
<AND YOUR KIND SHALL BE THE INSTRUMENT OF HIS RETURN.>
"I HAD NO TIME FOR HIS ARCANE WARNINGS."
"FOR NO MATTER WHAT HE SAID..."

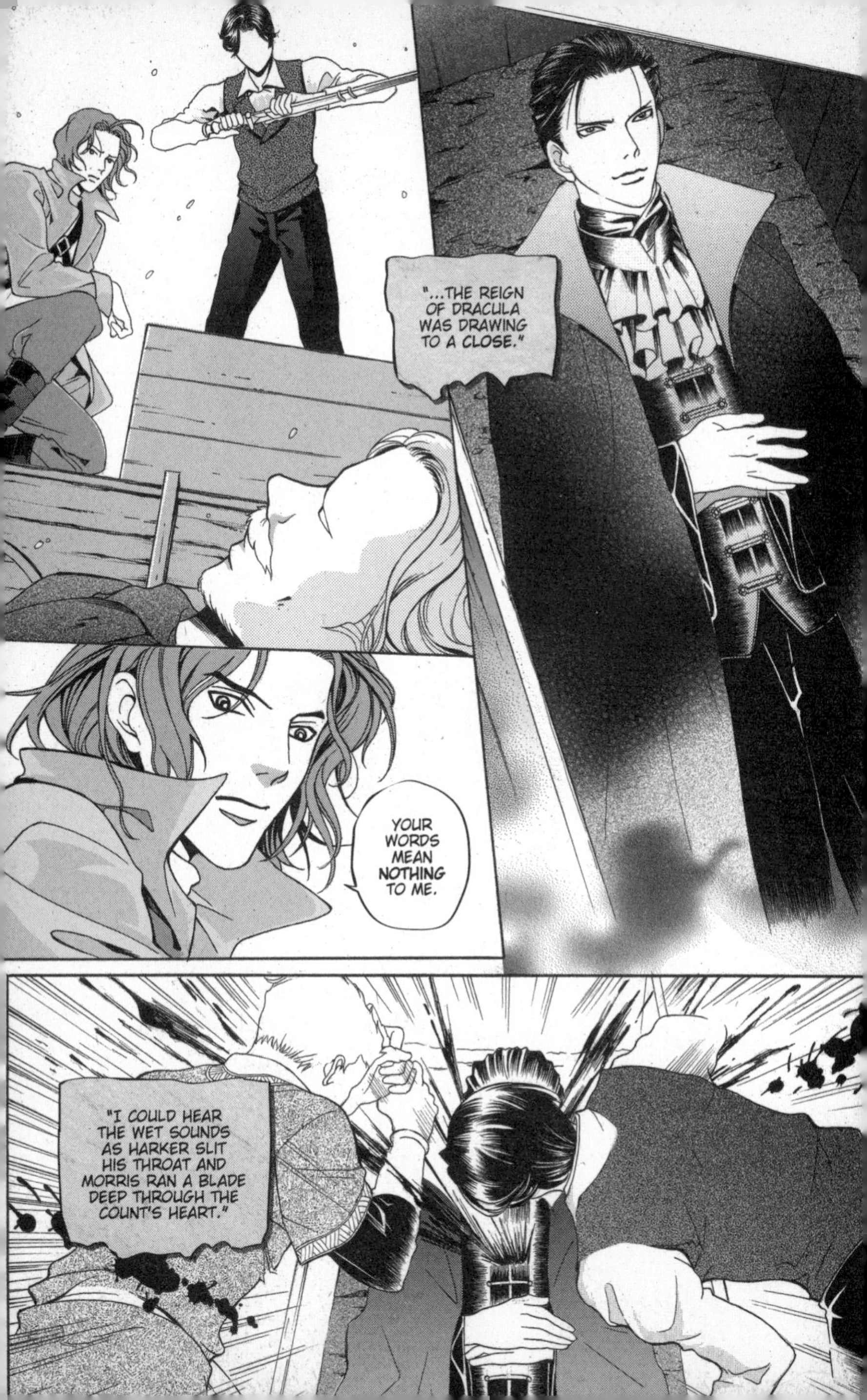
"...THE REIGN OF DRACULA WAS DRAWING TO A CLOSE."
YOUR WORDS MEAN NOTHING TO ME.
"I COULD HEAR THE WET SOUNDS AS HARKER SLIT HIS THROAT AND MORRIS RAN A BLADE DEEP THROUGH THE COUNT'S HEART."

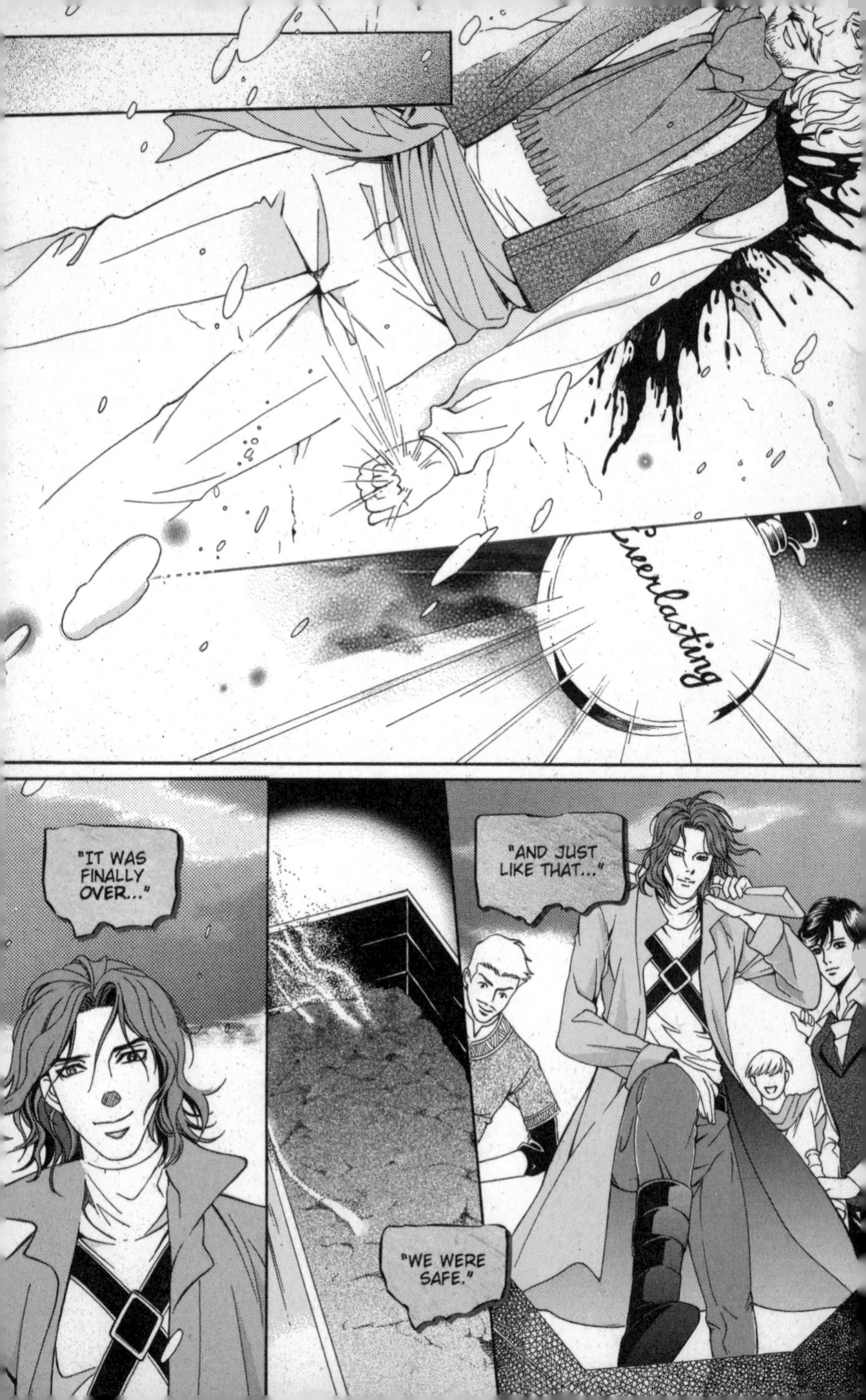
Everlasting
"AND JUST LIKE THAT..."
"WE WERE SAFE."
"IT WAS FINALLY OVER..."

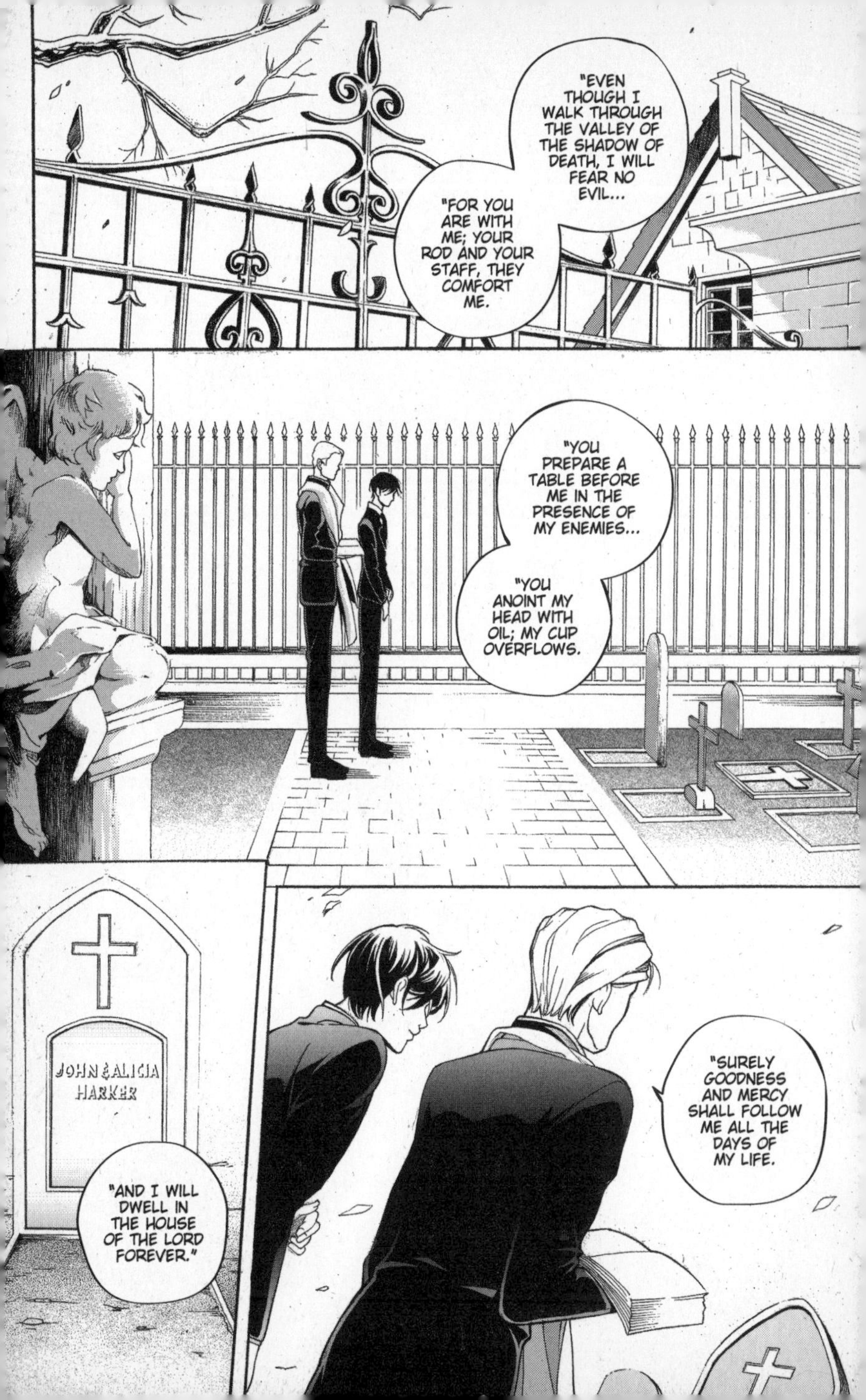
"EVEN THOUGH I WALK THROUGH THE VALLEY OF THE SHADOW OF DEATH, I WILL FEAR NO EVIL...
"FOR YOU ARE WITH ME; YOUR ROD AND YOUR STAFF, THEY COMFORT ME.
"YOU PREPARE A TABLE BEFORE ME IN THE PRESENCE OF MY ENEMIES...
"YOU ANOINT MY HEAD WITH OIL; MY CUP OVERFLOWS.
"SURELY GOODNESS AND MERCY SHALL FOLLOW ME ALL THE DAYS OF MY LIFE.
JOHN & ALICIA HARKER
"AND I WILL DWELL IN THE HOUSE OF THE LORD FOREVER."

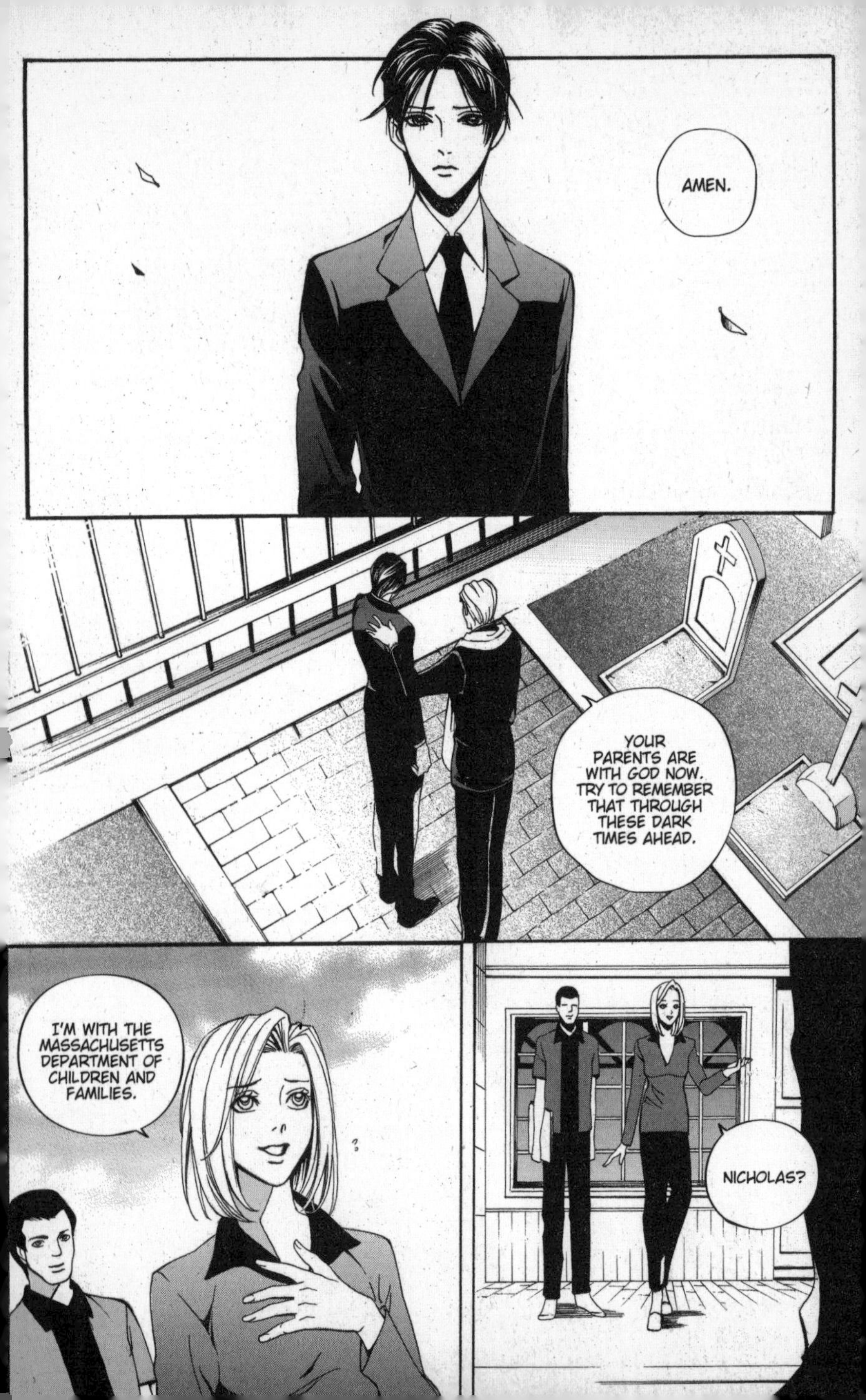
AMEN.
YOUR PARENTS ARE WITH GOD NOW. TRY TO REMEMBER THAT THROUGH THESE DARK TIMES AHEAD.
NICHOLAS?
I'M WITH THE MASSACHUSETTS DEPARTMENT OF CHILDREN AND FAMILIES.

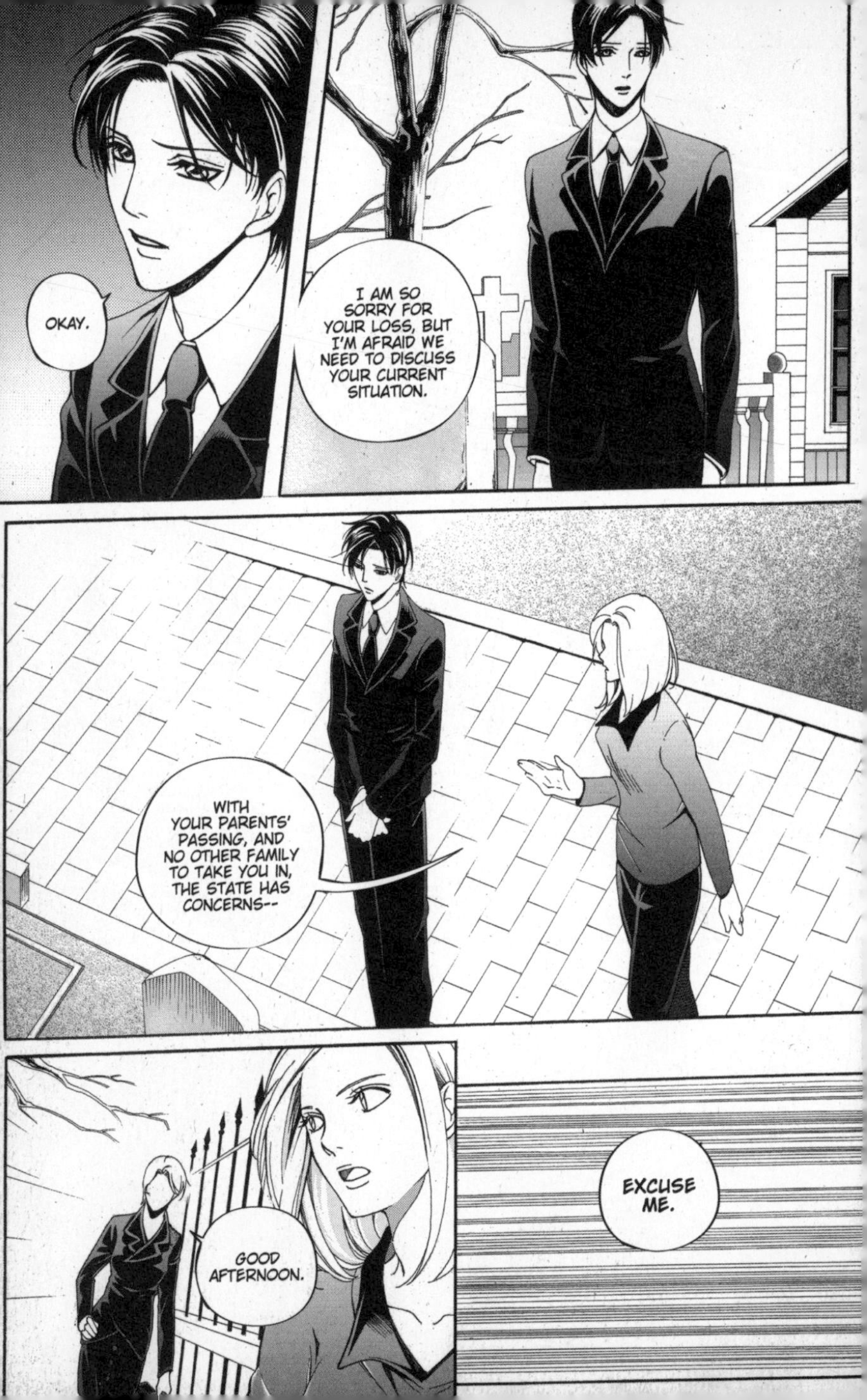
I AM SO SORRY FOR YOUR LOSS, BUT I'M AFRAID WE NEED TO DISCUSS YOUR CURRENT SITUATION.
OKAY.
WITH YOUR PARENTS' PASSING, AND NO OTHER FAMILY TO TAKE YOU IN, THE STATE HAS CONCERNS--
EXCUSE ME.
GOOD AFTERNOON.

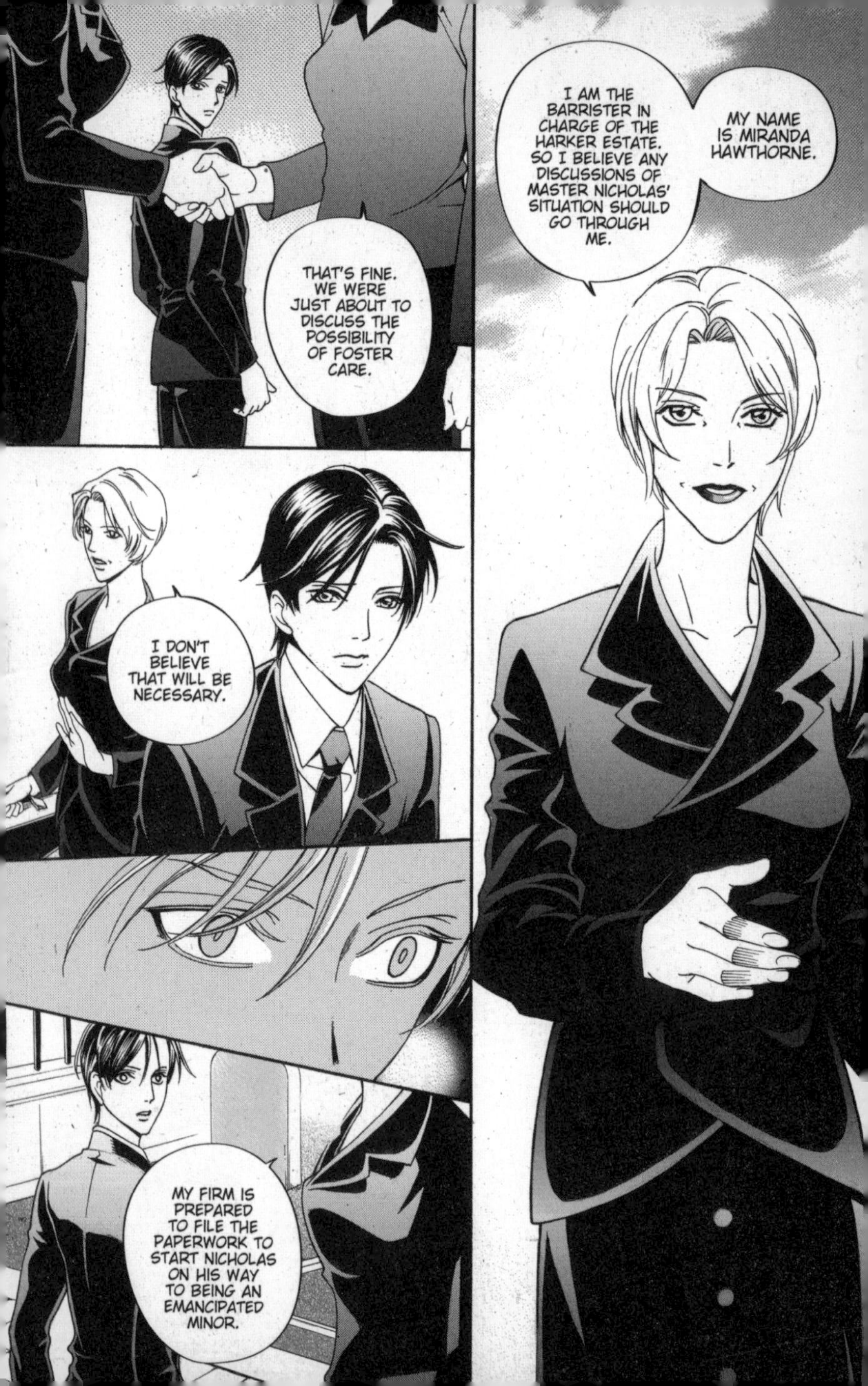
MY NAME IS MIRANDA HAWTHORNE.
I AM THE BARRISTER IN CHARGE OF THE HARKER ESTATE. SO I BELIEVE ANY DISCUSSIONS OF MASTER NICHOLAS' SITUATION SHOULD GO THROUGH ME.
THAT'S FINE. WE WERE JUST ABOUT TO DISCUSS THE POSSIBILITY OF FOSTER CARE.
I DON'T BELIEVE THAT WILL BE NECESSARY.
MY FIRM IS PREPARED TO FILE THE PAPERWORK TO START NICHOLAS ON HIS WAY TO BEING AN EMANCIPATED MINOR.

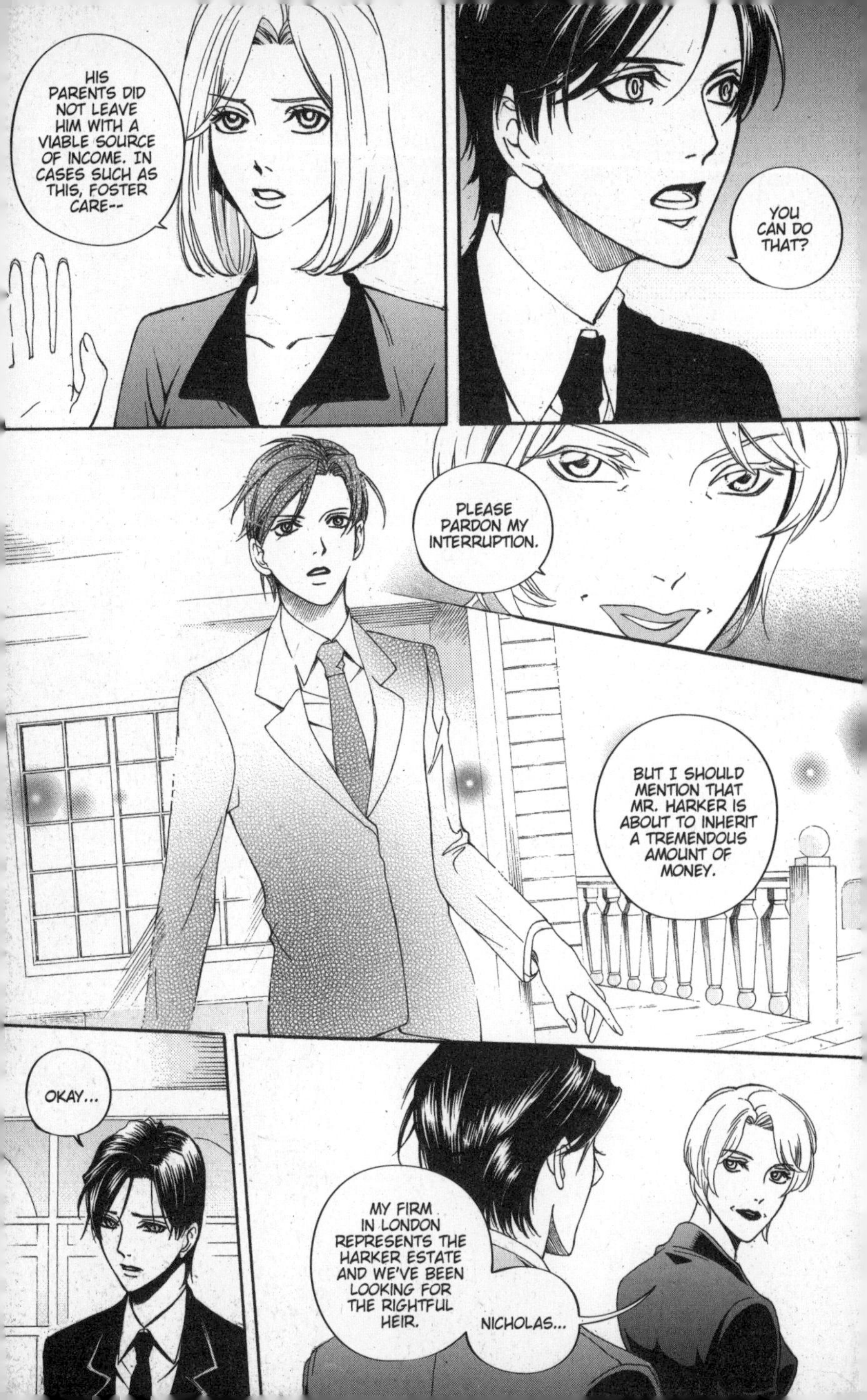
YOU CAN DO THAT?
HIS PARENTS DID NOT LEAVE HIM WITH A VIABLE SOURCE OF INCOME. IN CASES SUCH AS THIS, FOSTER CARE--
PLEASE PARDON MY INTERRUPTION.
BUT I SHOULD MENTION THAT MR. HARKER IS ABOUT TO INHERIT A TREMENDOUS AMOUNT OF MONEY.
MY FIRM IN LONDON REPRESENTS THE HARKER ESTATE AND WE'VE BEEN LOOKING FOR THE RIGHTFUL HEIR.
NICHOLAS...
OKAY...

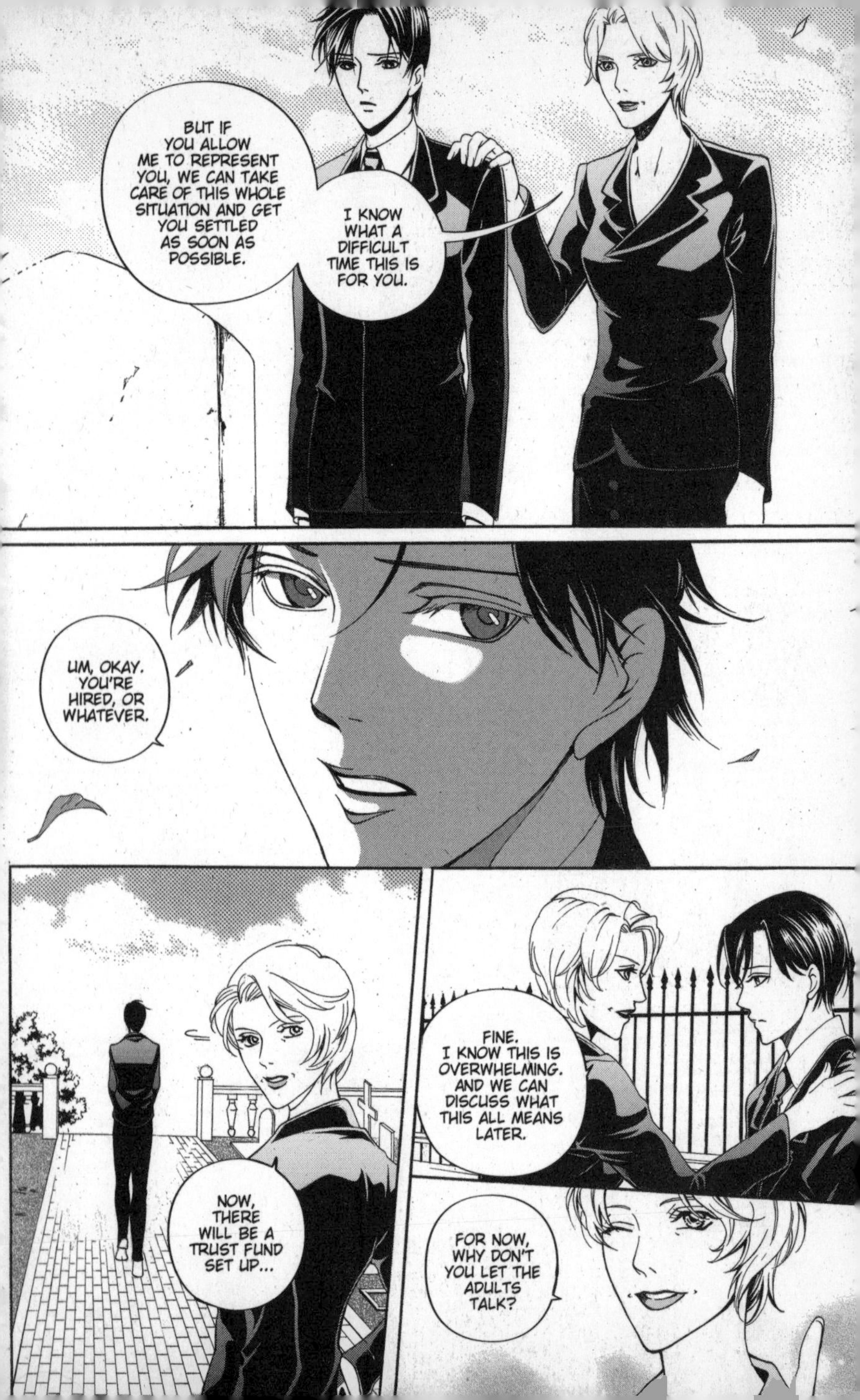
I KNOW WHAT A DIFFICULT TIME THIS IS FOR YOU.
BUT IF YOU ALLOW ME TO REPRESENT YOU, WE CAN TAKE CARE OF THIS WHOLE SITUATION AND GET YOU SETTLED AS SOON AS POSSIBLE.
UM, OKAY. YOU'RE HIRED, OR WHATEVER.
FINE. I KNOW THIS IS OVERWHELMING. AND WE CAN DISCUSS WHAT THIS ALL MEANS LATER.
FOR NOW, WHY DON'T YOU LET THE ADULTS TALK?
NOW, THERE WILL BE A TRUST FUND SET UP...

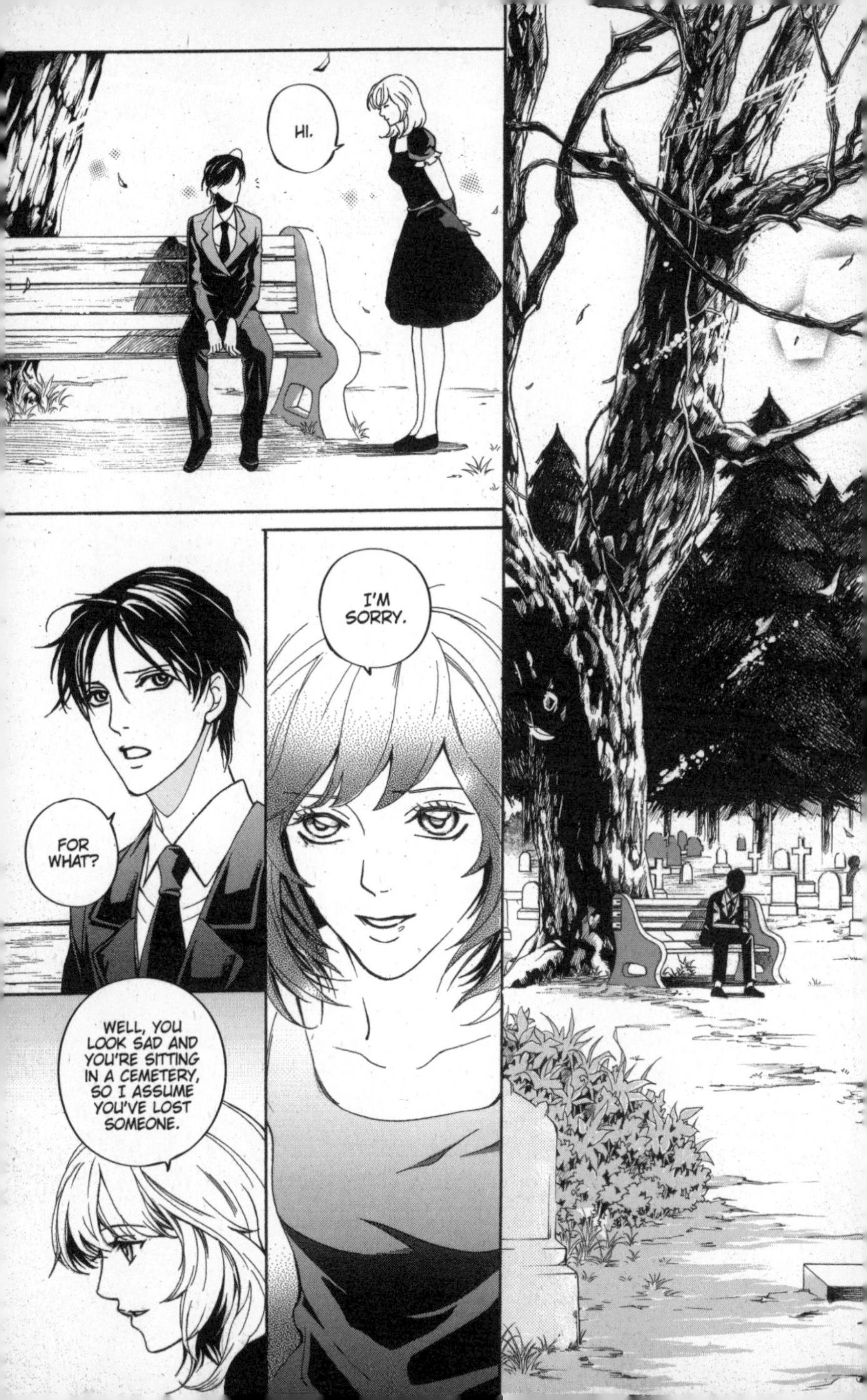
HI.
I'M SORRY.
FOR WHAT?
WELL, YOU LOOK SAD AND YOU'RE SITTING IN A CEMETERY, SO I ASSUME YOU'VE LOST SOMEONE.

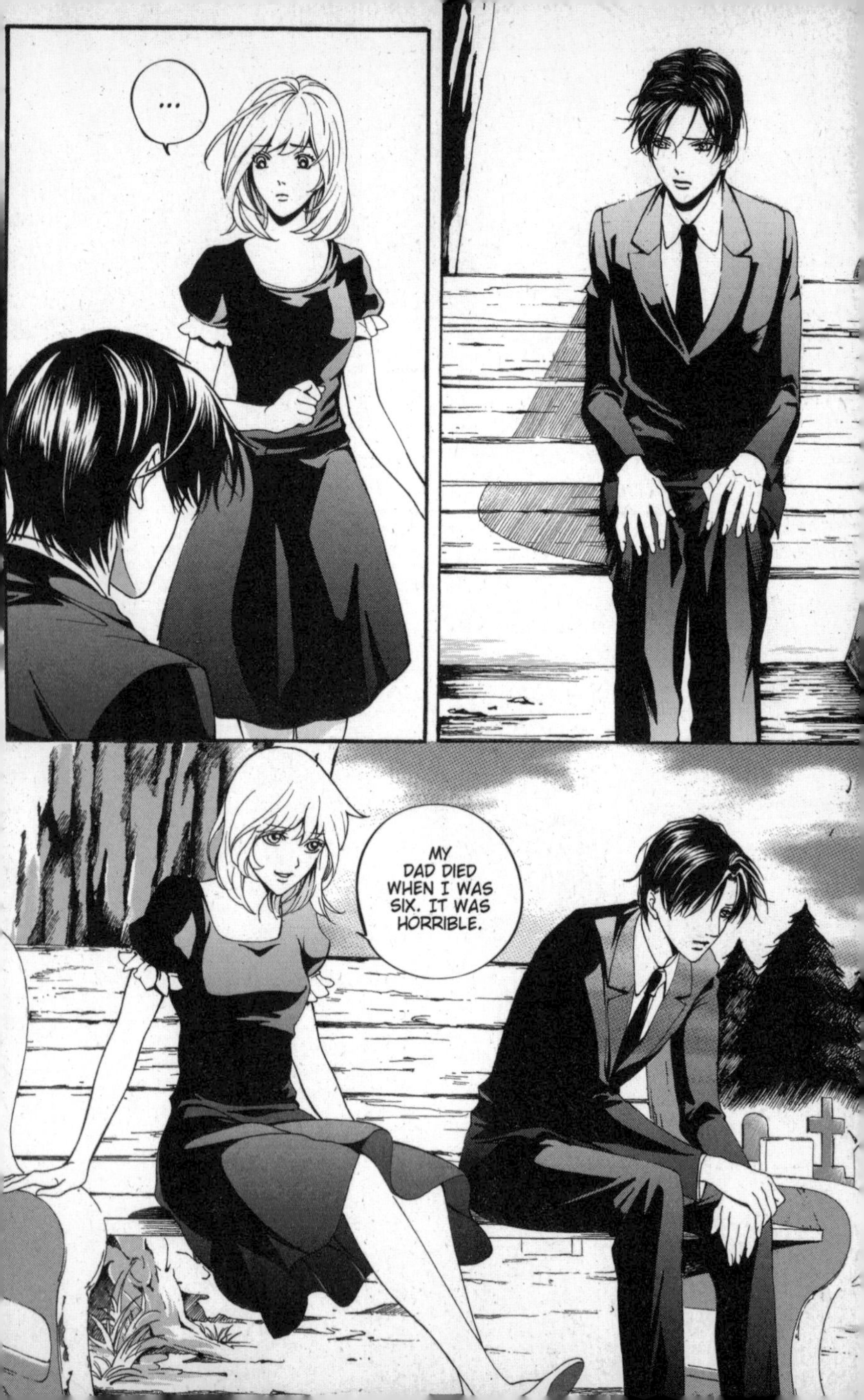
...
MY DAD DIED WHEN I WAS SIX. IT WAS HORRIBLE.

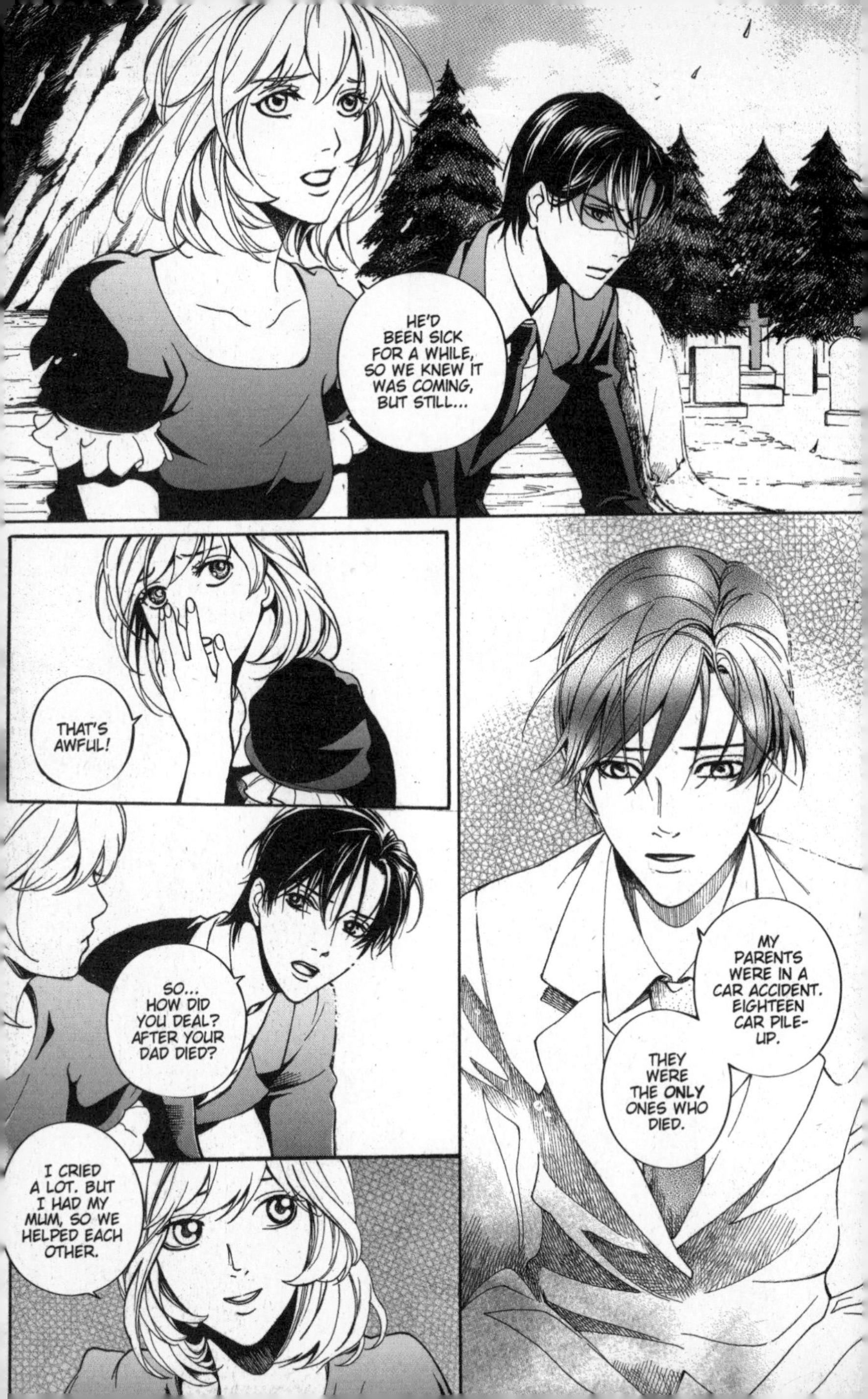
HE'D BEEN SICK FOR A WHILE, SO WE KNEW IT WAS COMING, BUT STILL...
MY PARENTS WERE IN A CAR ACCIDENT. EIGHTEEN CAR PILE-UP.
THEY WERE THE ONLY ONES WHO DIED.
THAT'S AWFUL!
SO... HOW DID YOU DEAL? AFTER YOUR DAD DIED?
I CRIED A LOT. BUT I HAD MY MUM, SO WE HELPED EACH OTHER.

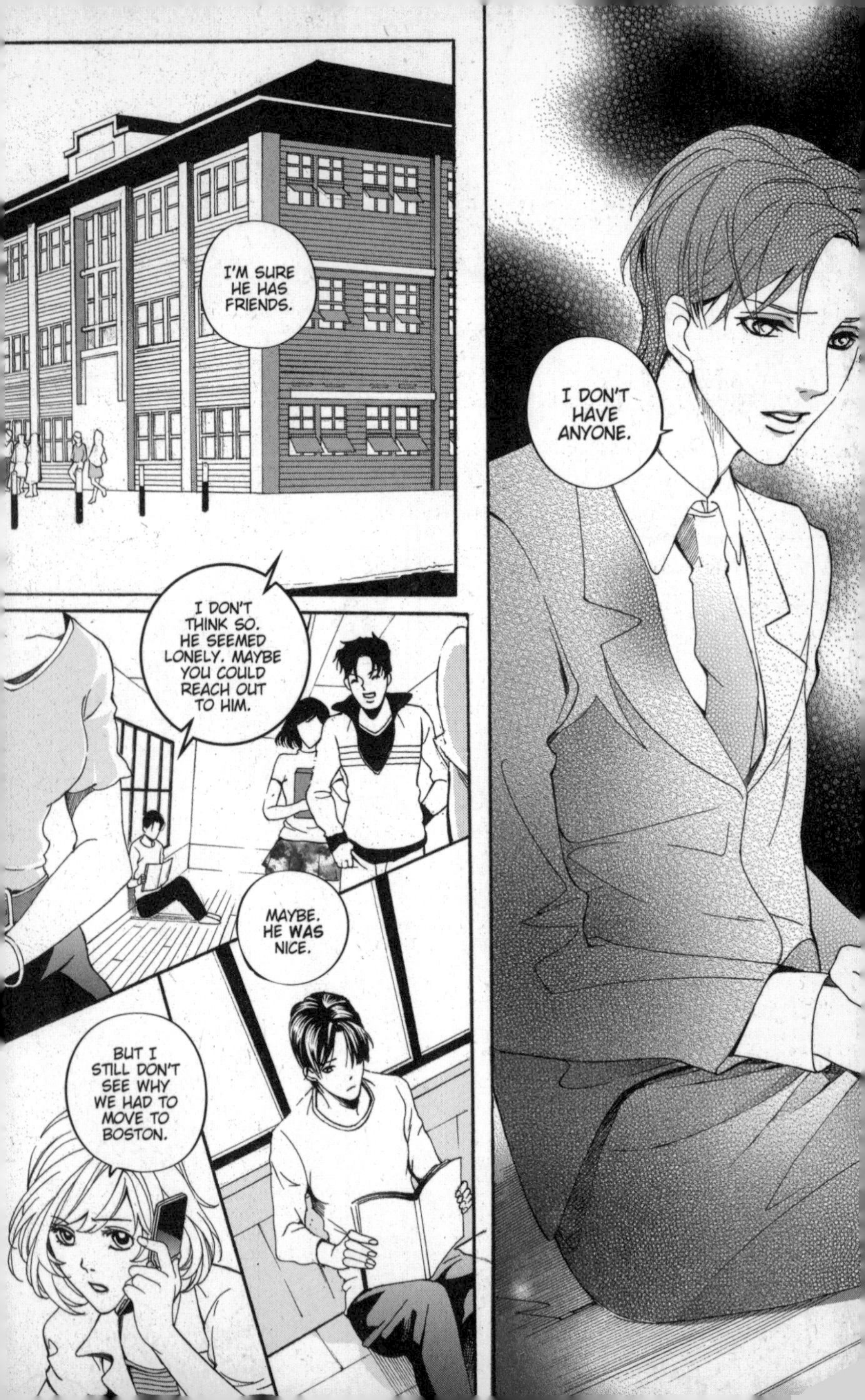
I DON'T HAVE ANYONE.
I'M SURE HE HAS FRIENDS.
I DON'T THINK SO. HE SEEMED LONELY. MAYBE YOU COULD REACH OUT TO HIM.
MAYBE. HE WAS NICE.
BUT I STILL DON'T SEE WHY WE HAD TO MOVE TO BOSTON.

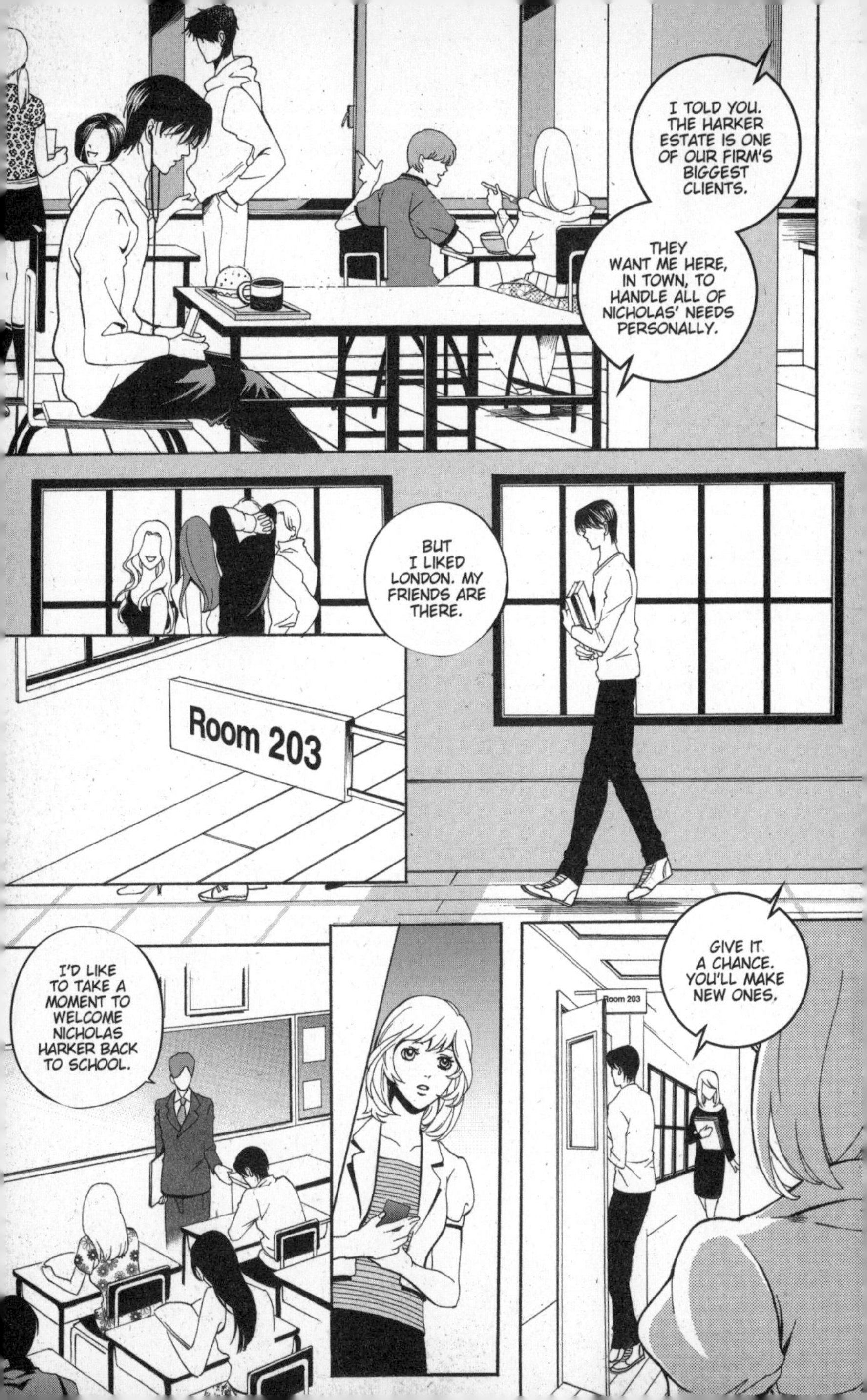
I TOLD YOU. THE HARKER ESTATE IS ONE OF OUR FIRM'S BIGGEST CLIENTS.
THEY WANT ME HERE, IN TOWN, TO HANDLE ALL OF NICHOLAS' NEEDS PERSONALLY.
BUT I LIKED LONDON. MY FRIENDS ARE THERE.
Room 203
GIVE IT A CHANCE. YOU'LL MAKE NEW ONES.
Room 203
I'D LIKE TO TAKE A MOMENT TO WELCOME NICHOLAS HARKER BACK TO SCHOOL.

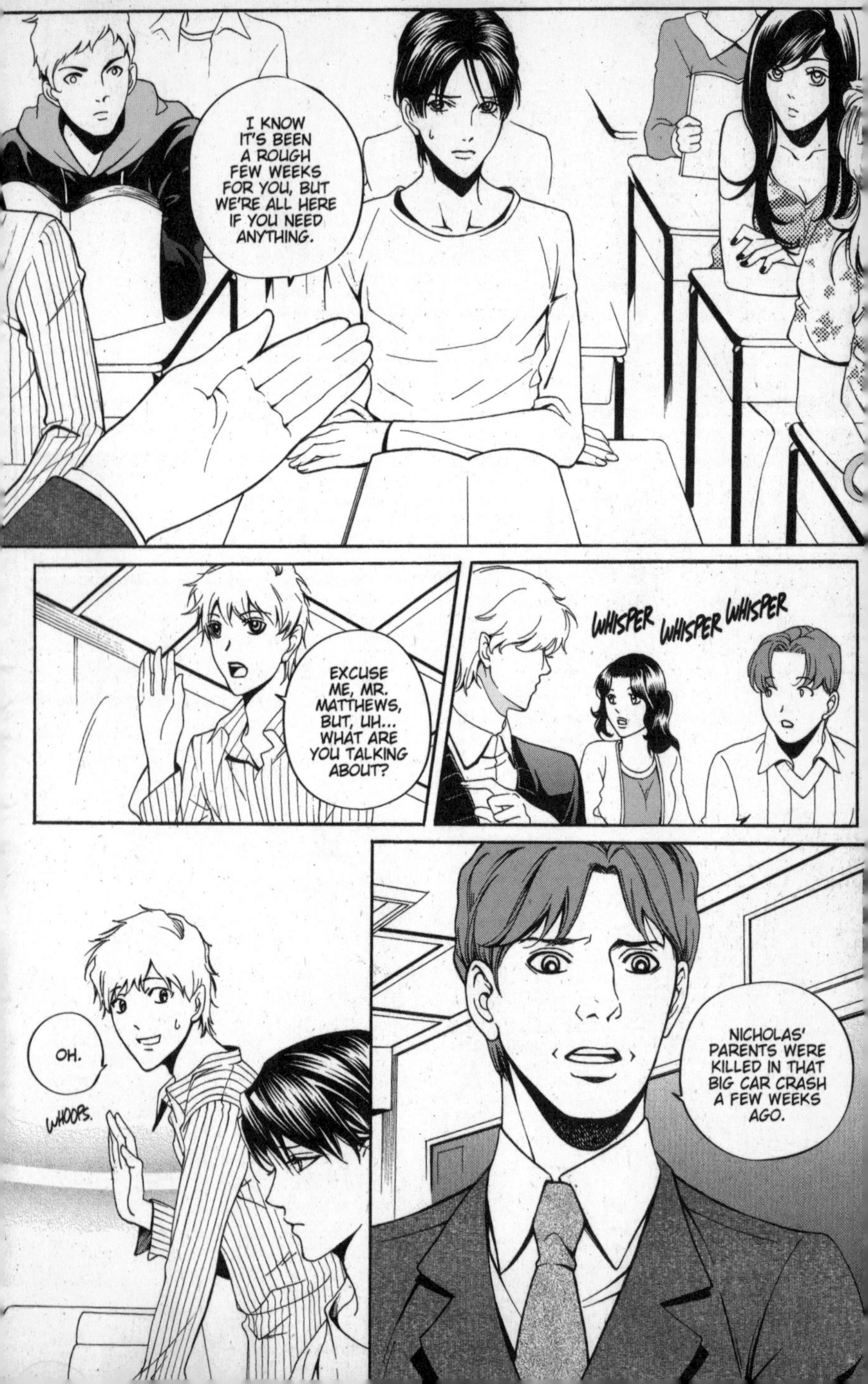
I KNOW IT'S BEEN A ROUGH FEW WEEKS FOR YOU, BUT WE'RE ALL HERE IF YOU NEED ANYTHING.
WHISPER WHISPER WHISPER
EXCUSE ME, MR. MATTHEWS, BUT, UH... WHAT ARE YOU TALKING ABOUT?
NICHOLAS' PARENTS WERE KILLED IN THAT BIG CAR CRASH A FEW WEEKS AGO.
OH.
WHOOPS.

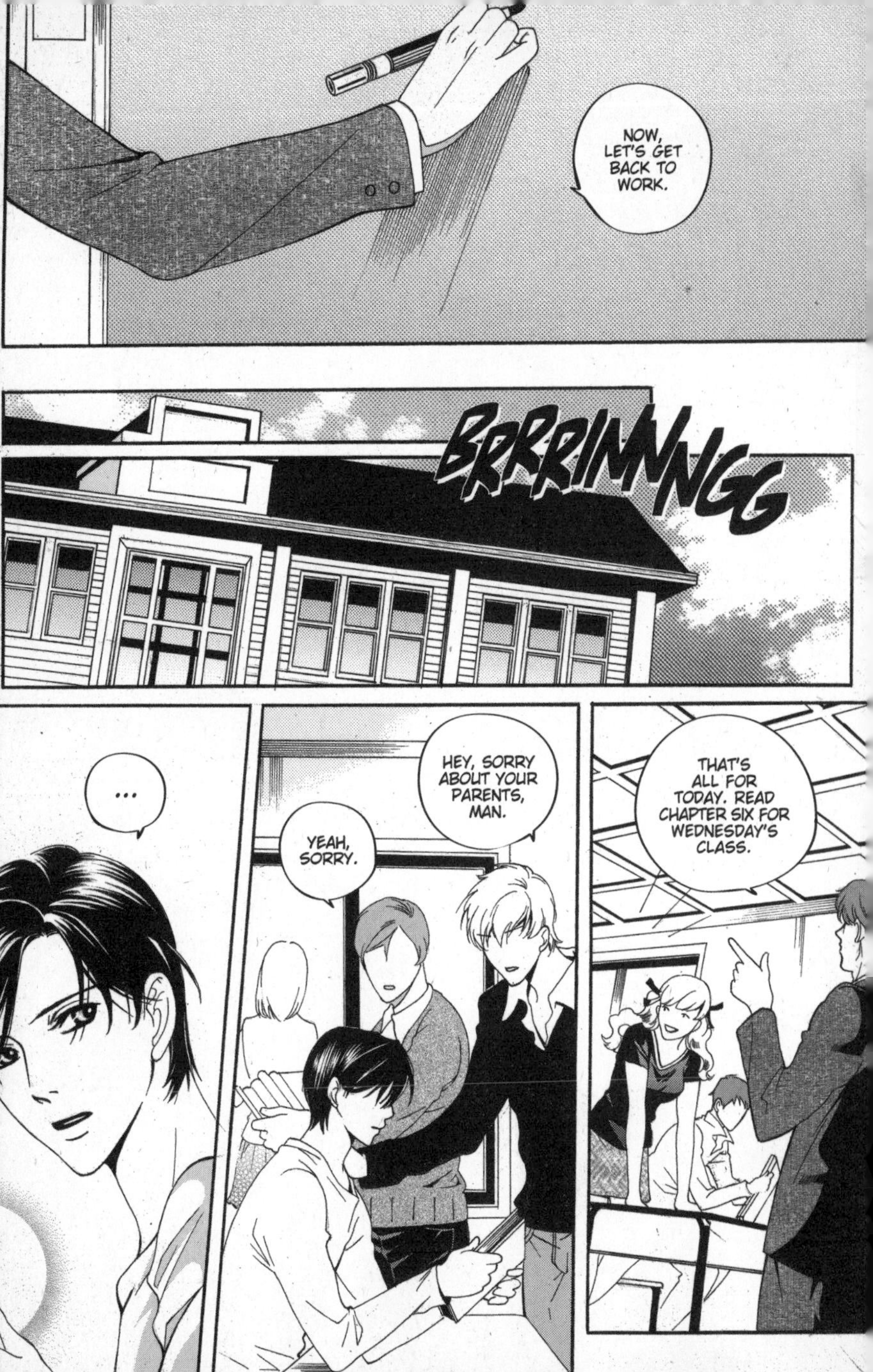
NOW, LET'S GET BACK TO WORK.
BRRRINNNGG
THAT'S ALL FOR TODAY. READ CHAPTER SIX FOR WEDNESDAY'S CLASS.
HEY, SORRY ABOUT YOUR PARENTS, MAN.
YEAH, SORRY.
...

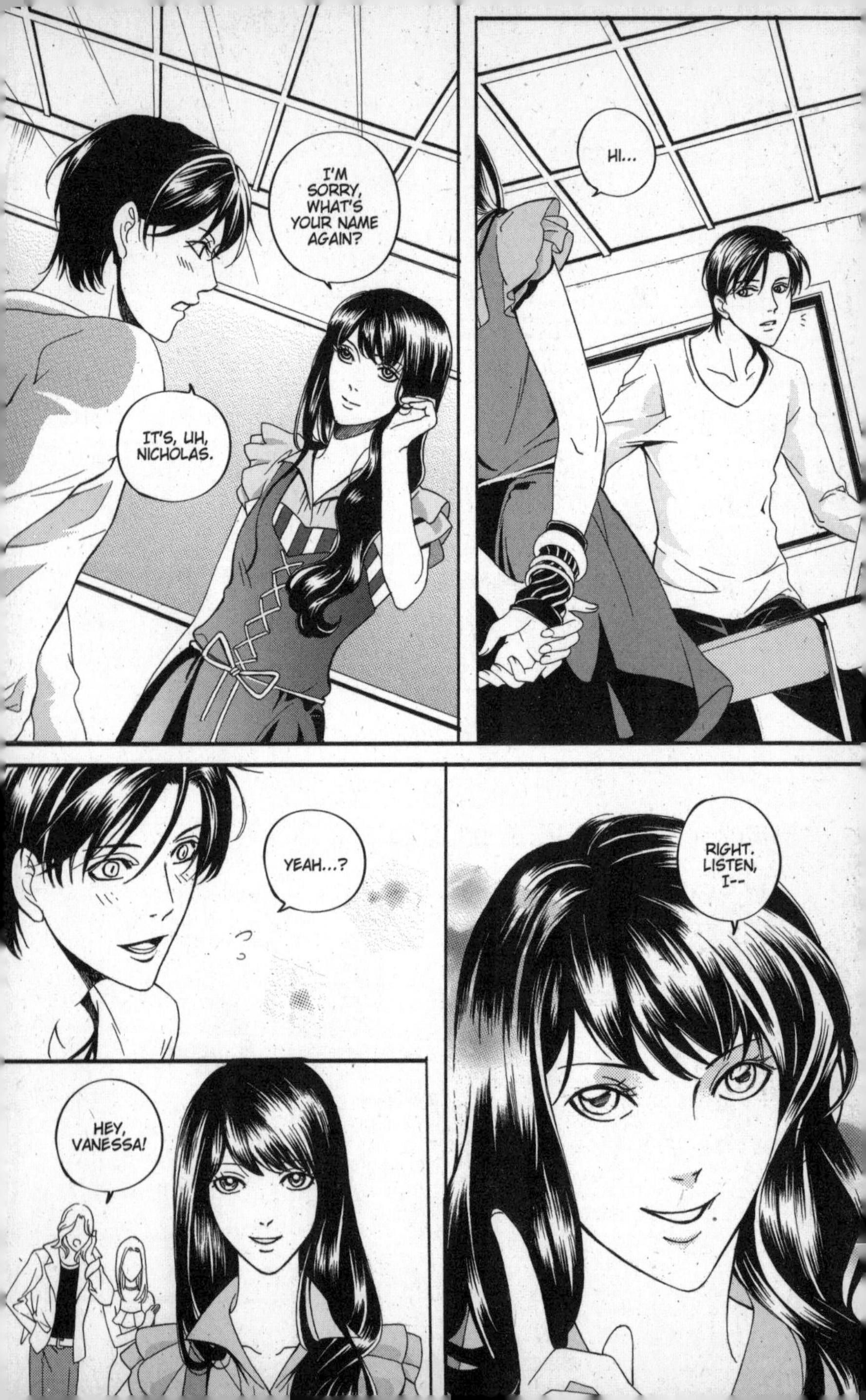
HI...
I'M SORRY, WHAT'S YOUR NAME AGAIN?
IT'S, UH, NICHOLAS.
RIGHT. LISTEN, I--
YEAH...?
HEY, VANESSA!

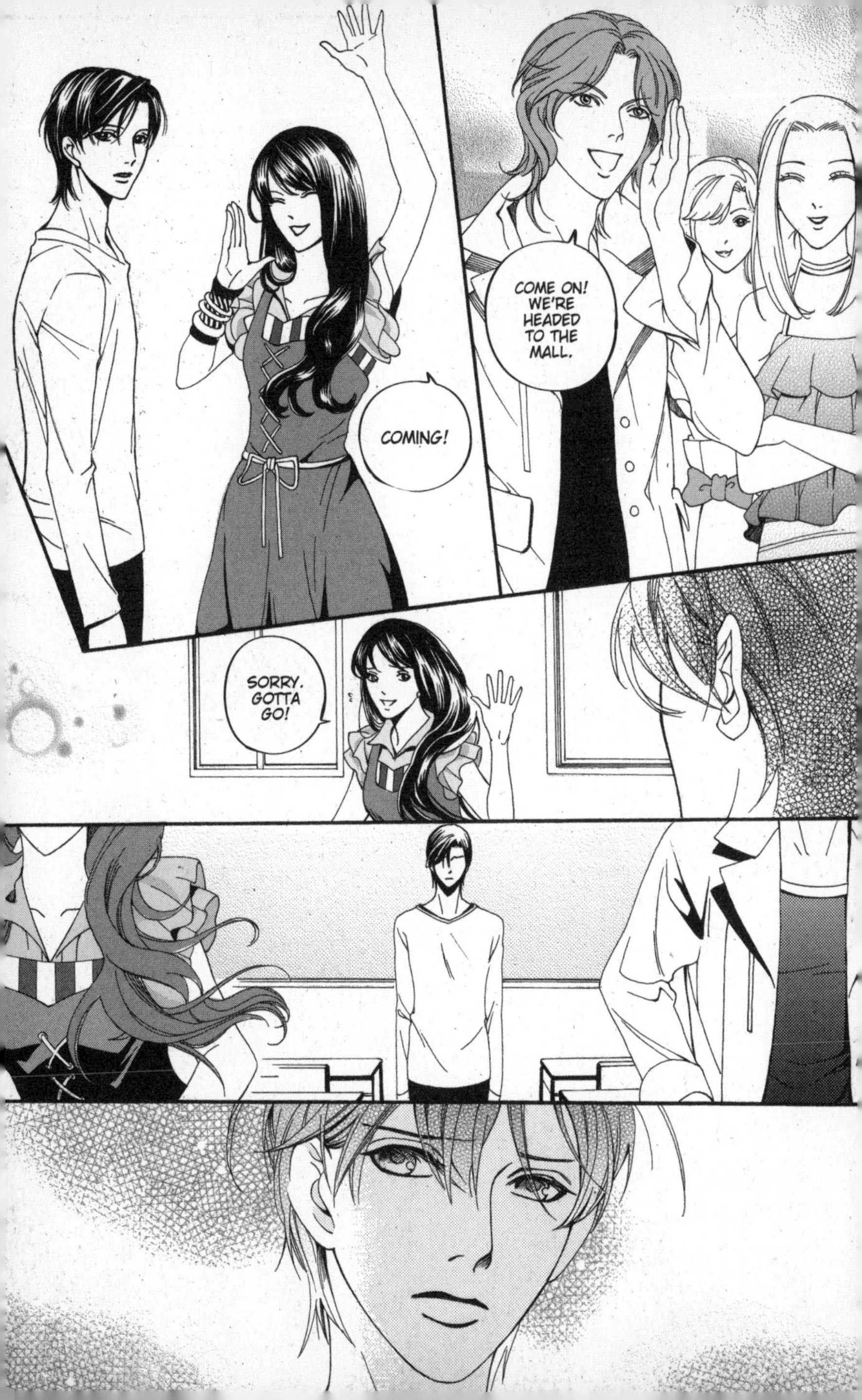
COME ON! WE'RE HEADED TO THE MALL.
COMING!
SORRY. GOTTA GO!

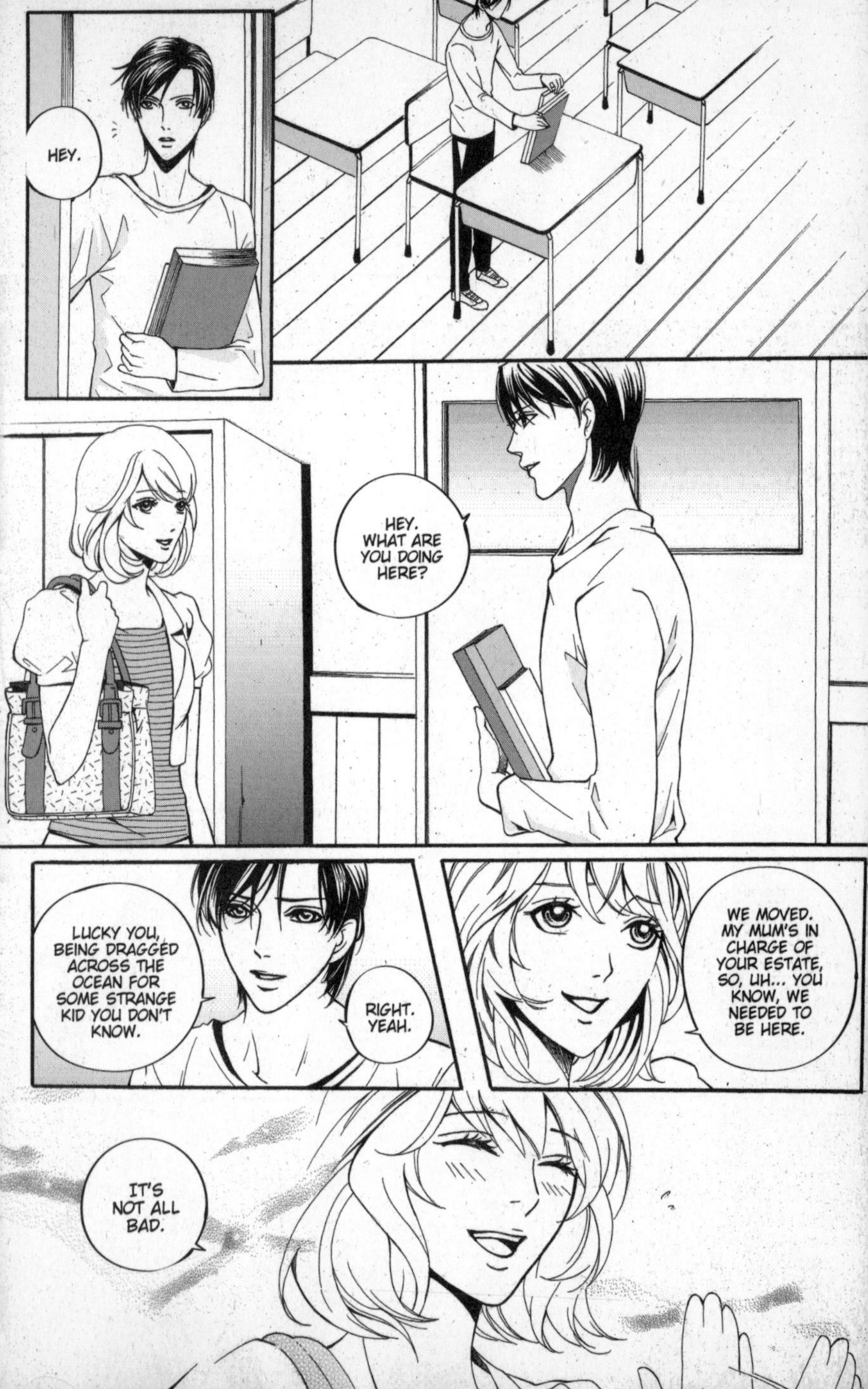
HEY.
HEY. WHAT ARE YOU DOING HERE?
WE MOVED. MY MUM'S IN CHARGE OF YOUR ESTATE, SO, UH... YOU KNOW, WE NEEDED TO BE HERE.
LUCKY YOU, BEING DRAGGED ACROSS THE OCEAN FOR SOME STRANGE KID YOU DON'T KNOW.
RIGHT. YEAH.
IT'S NOT ALL BAD.

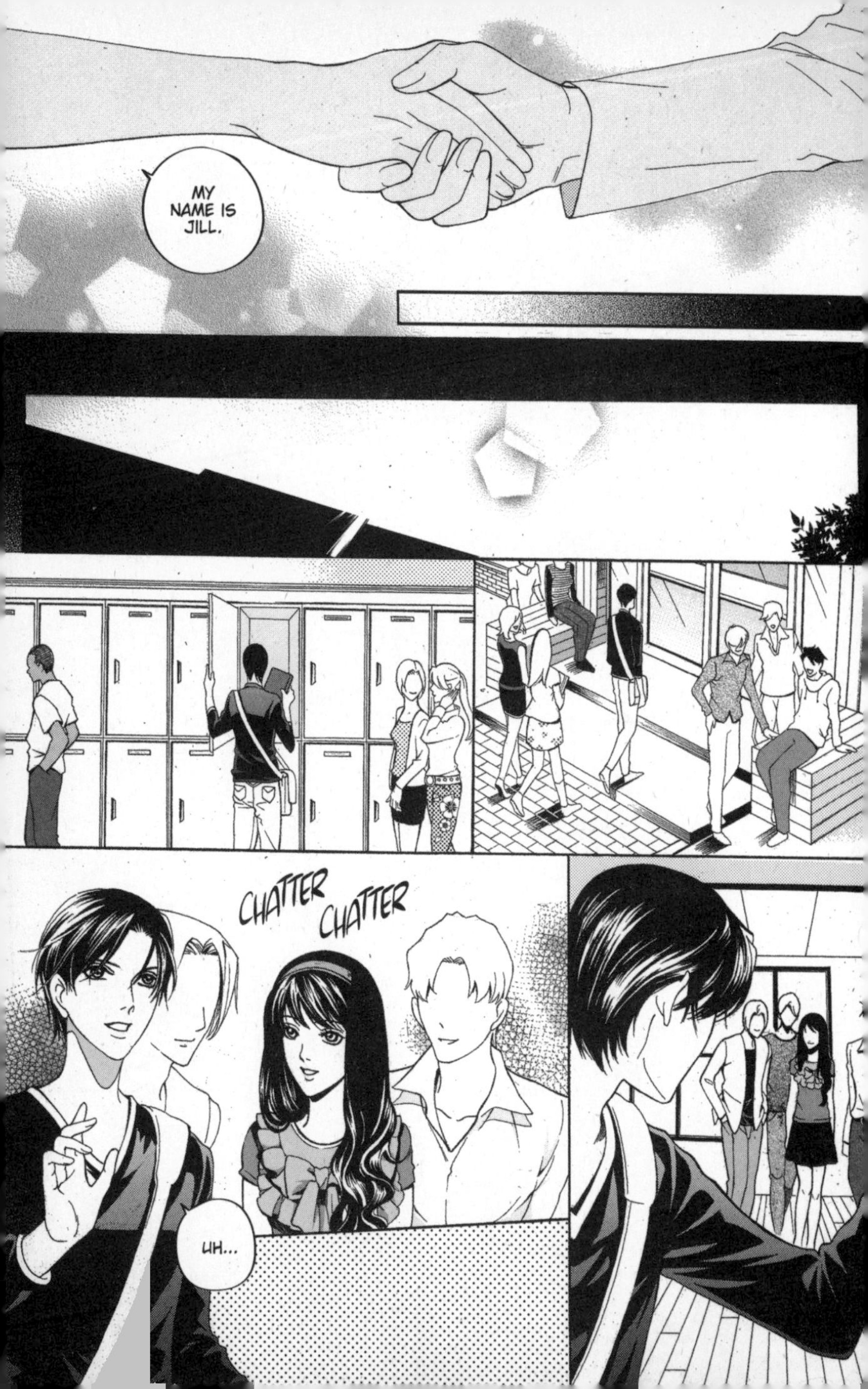
MY NAME IS JILL.
CHATTER CHATTER
UH...

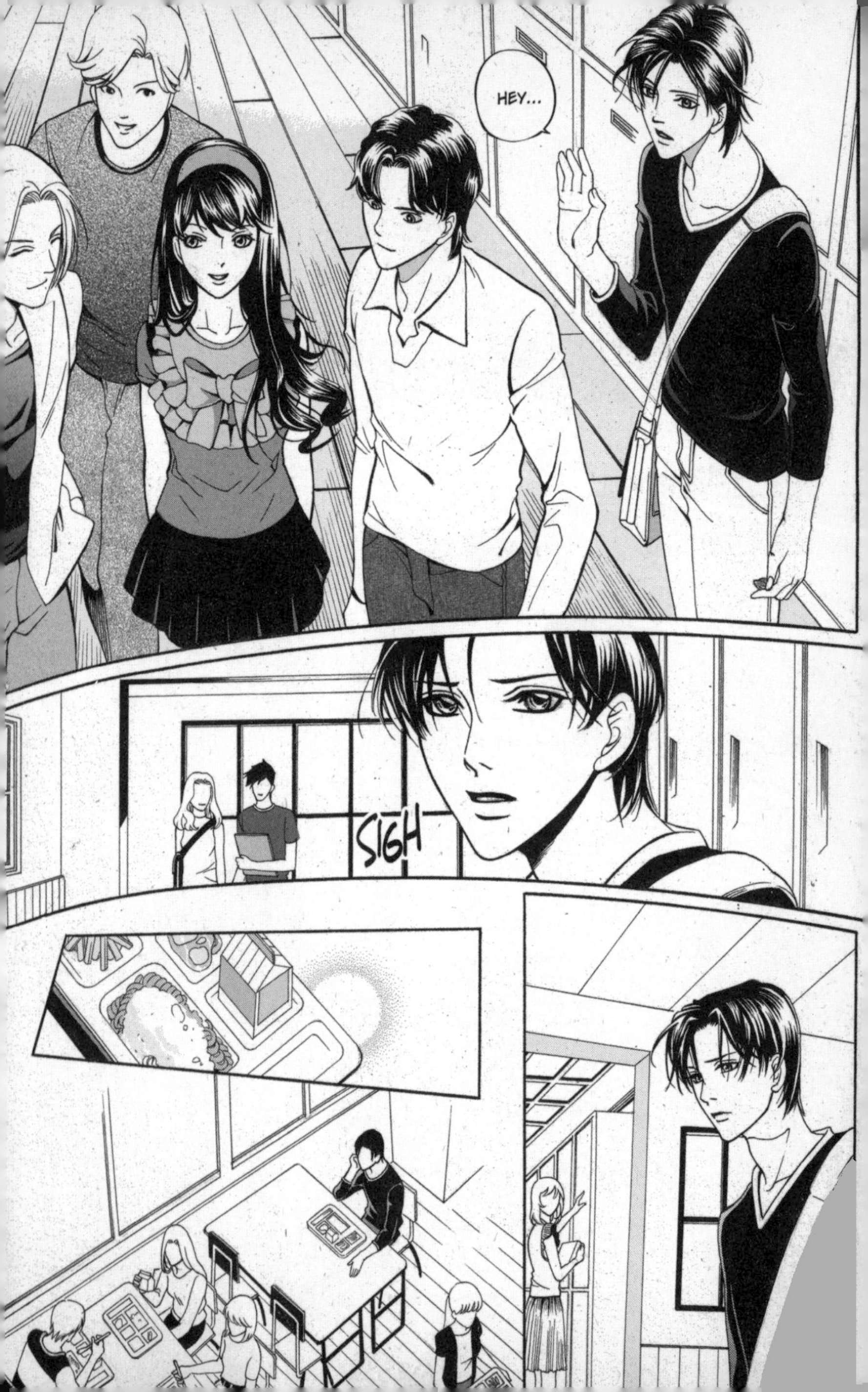
HEY...
SIGH

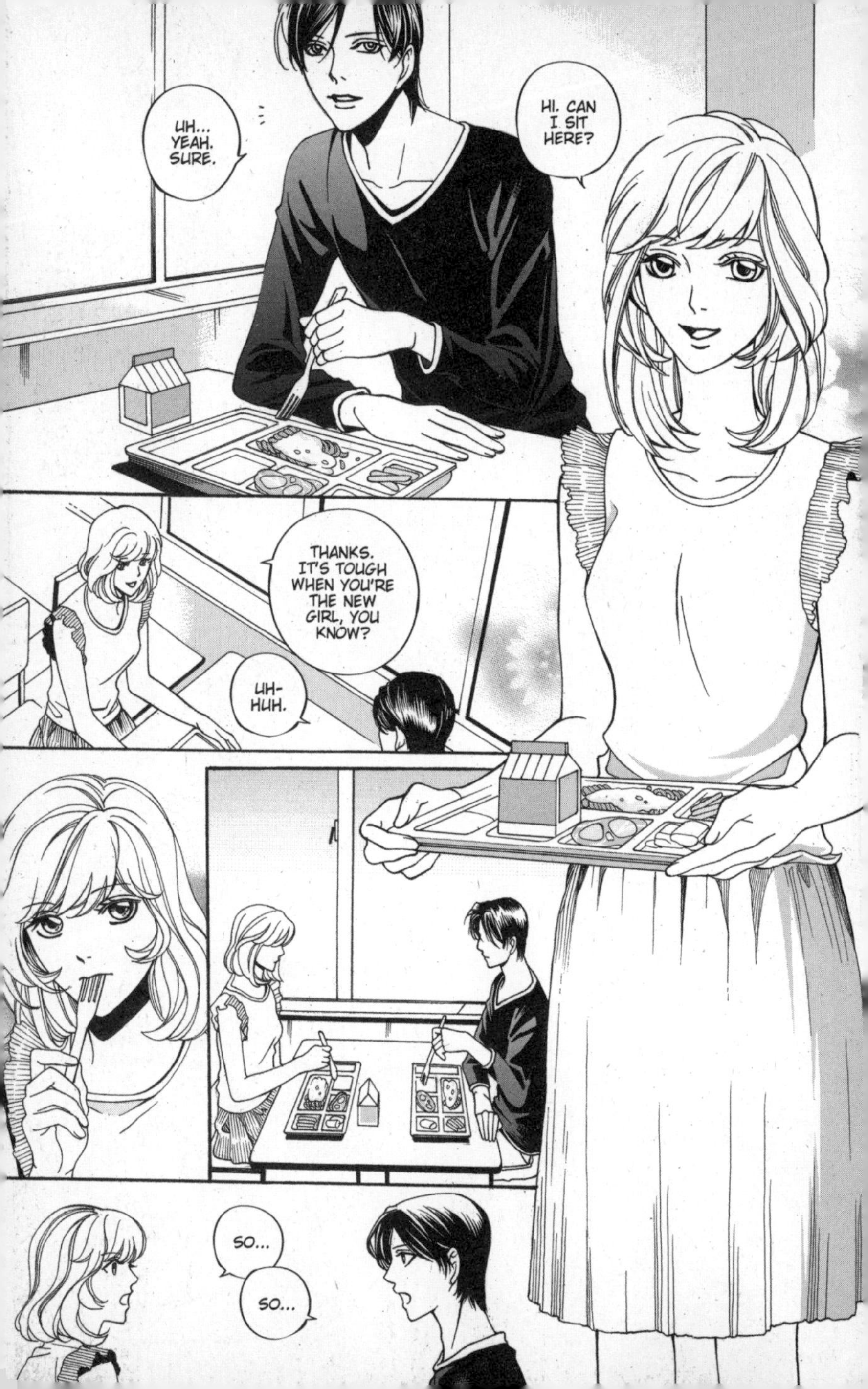
HI. CAN I SIT HERE?
UH... YEAH. SURE.
THANKS. IT'S TOUGH WHEN YOU'RE THE NEW GIRL, YOU KNOW?
UH-HUH.
SO...
SO...

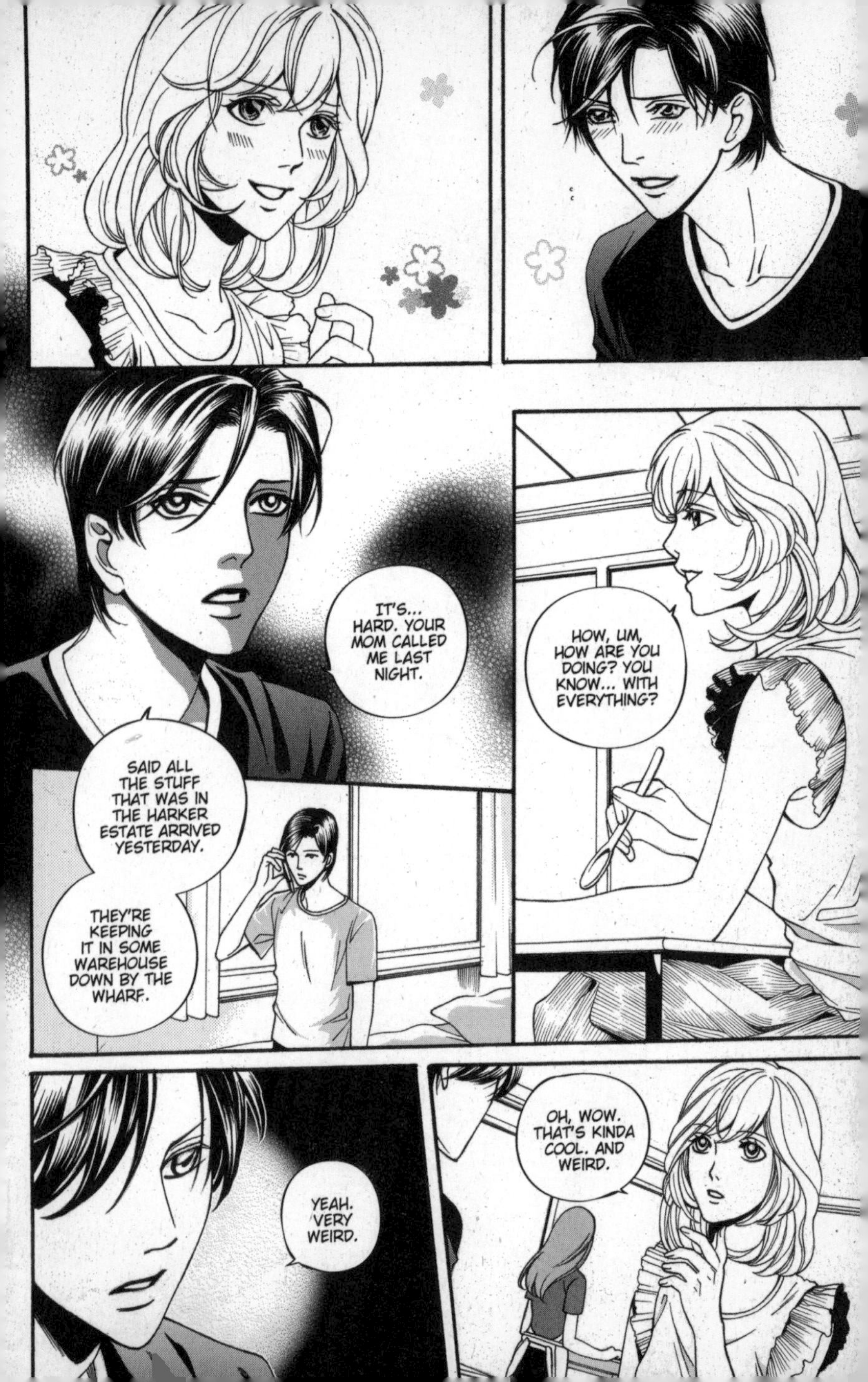
HOW, UM, HOW ARE YOU DOING? YOU KNOW... WITH EVERYTHING?
IT'S... HARD. YOUR MOM CALLED ME LAST NIGHT.
SAID ALL THE STUFF THAT WAS IN THE HARKER ESTATE ARRIVED YESTERDAY.
THEY'RE KEEPING IT IN SOME WAREHOUSE DOWN BY THE WHARF.
OH, WOW. THAT'S KINDA COOL. AND WEIRD.
YEAH. VERY WEIRD.

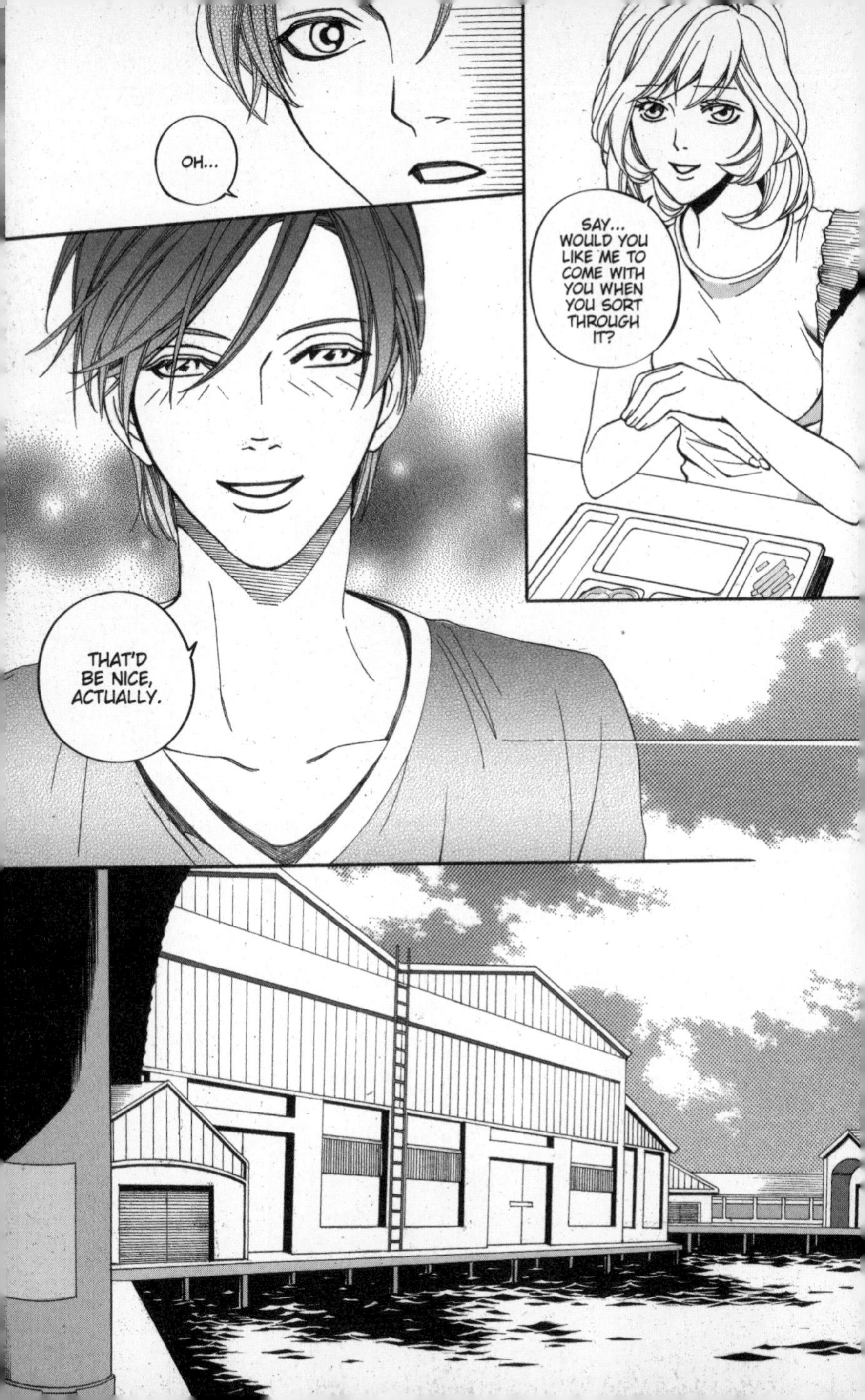
SAY... WOULD YOU LIKE ME TO COME WITH YOU WHEN YOU SORT THROUGH IT?
OH...
THAT'D BE NICE, ACTUALLY.

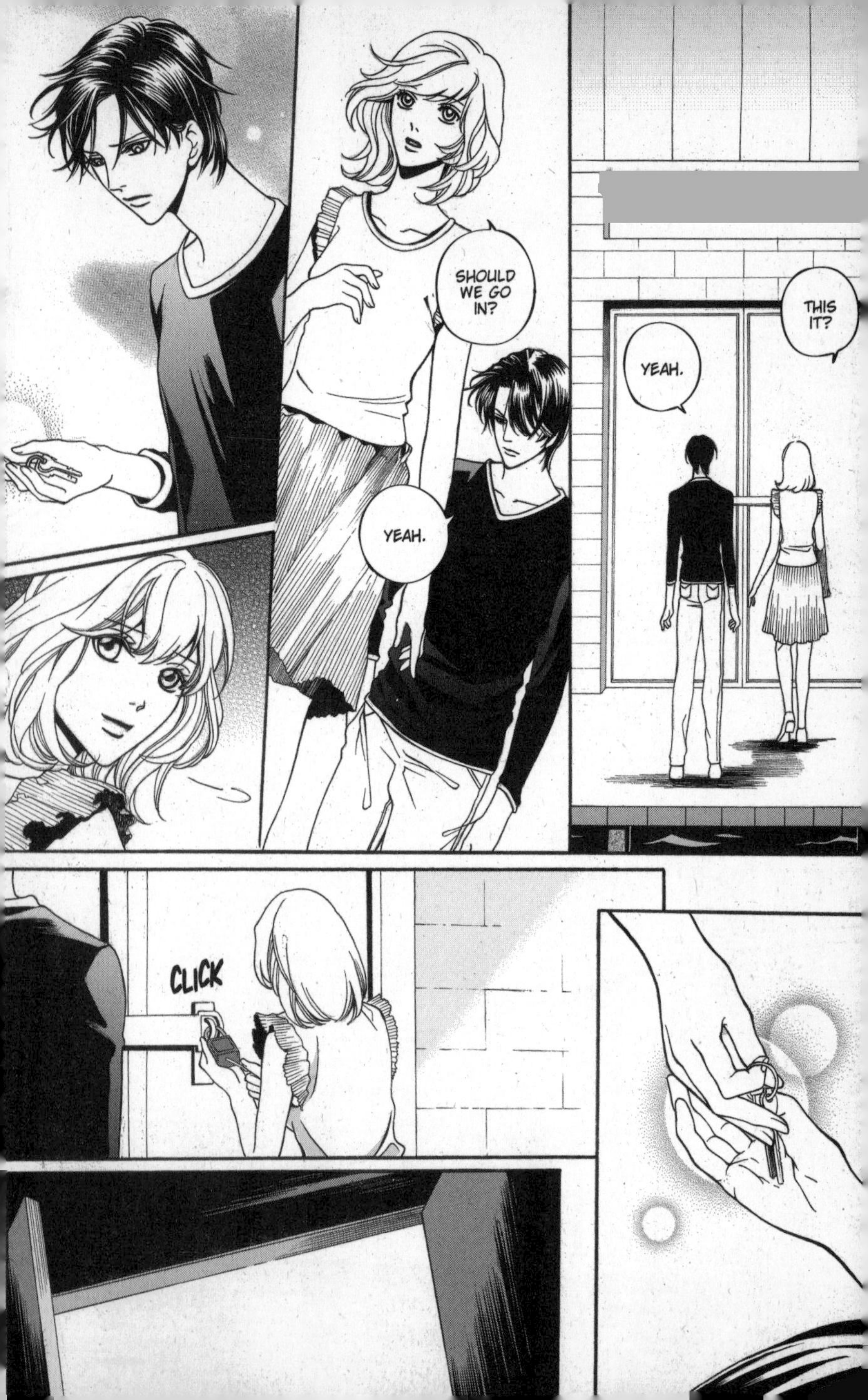
THIS IT?
YEAH.
SHOULD WE GO IN?
YEAH.
CLICK

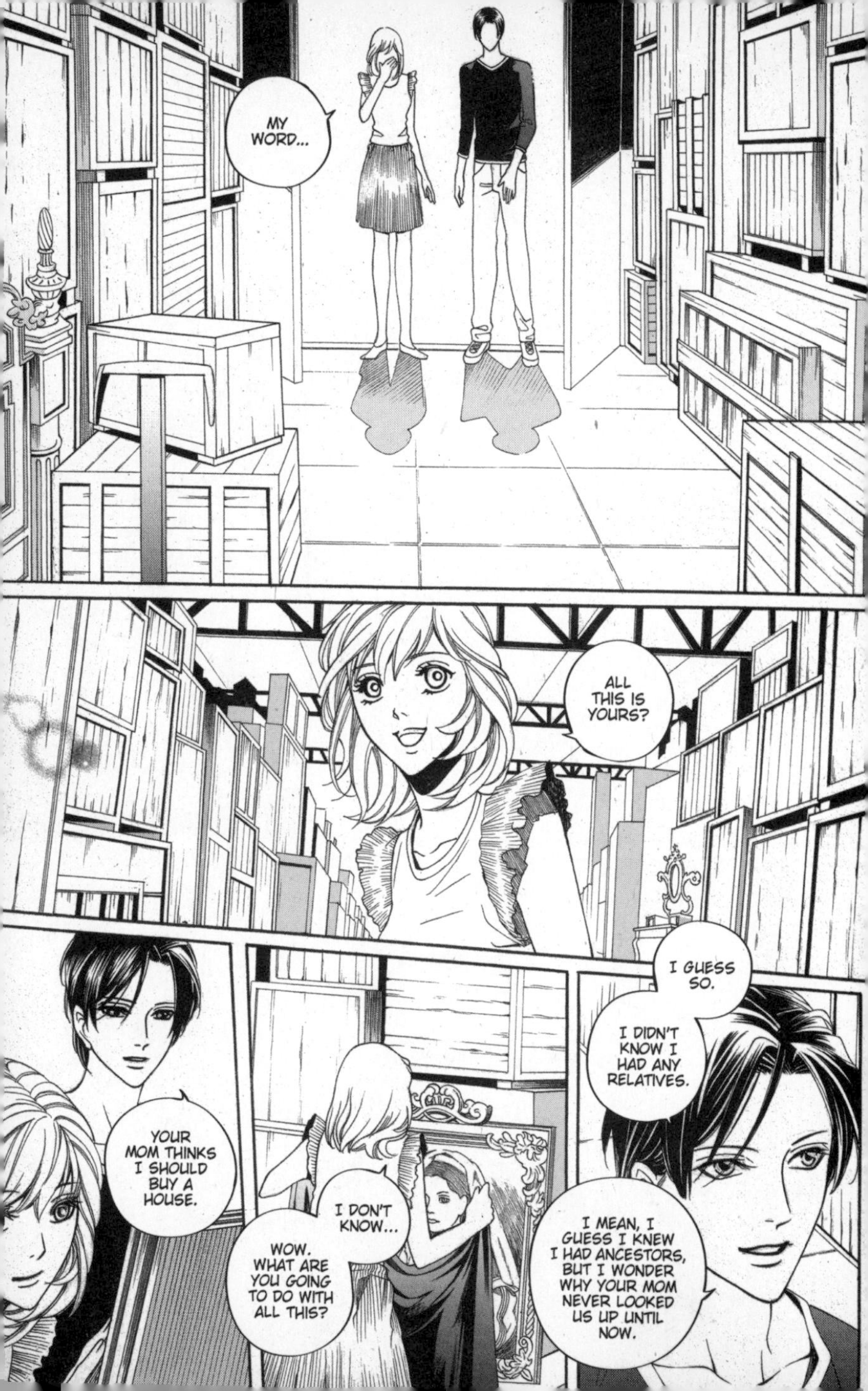
MY WORD...
ALL THIS IS YOURS?
I GUESS SO.
I DIDN'T KNOW I HAD ANY RELATIVES.
I MEAN, I GUESS I KNEW I HAD ANCESTORS, BUT I WONDER WHY YOUR MOM NEVER LOOKED US UP UNTIL NOW.
I DON'T KNOW...
WOW. WHAT ARE YOU GOING TO DO WITH ALL THIS?
YOUR MOM THINKS I SHOULD BUY A HOUSE.

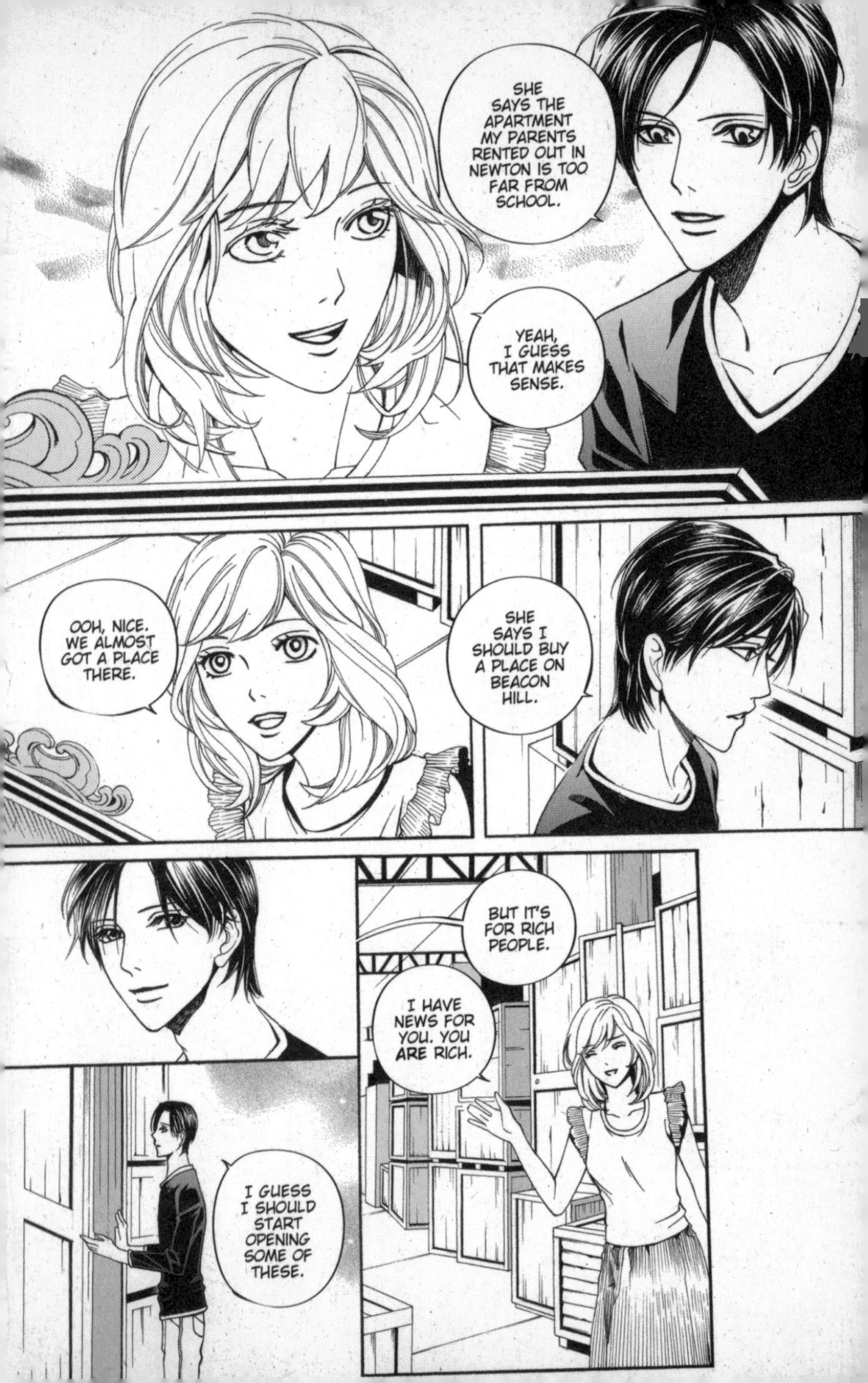
SHE SAYS THE APARTMENT MY PARENTS RENTED OUT IN NEWTON IS TOO FAR FROM SCHOOL.
YEAH, I GUESS THAT MAKES SENSE.
SHE SAYS I SHOULD BUY A PLACE ON BEACON HILL.
OOH, NICE. WE ALMOST GOT A PLACE THERE.
BUT IT'S FOR RICH PEOPLE.
I HAVE NEWS FOR YOU. YOU ARE RICH.
I GUESS I SHOULD START OPENING SOME OF THESE.

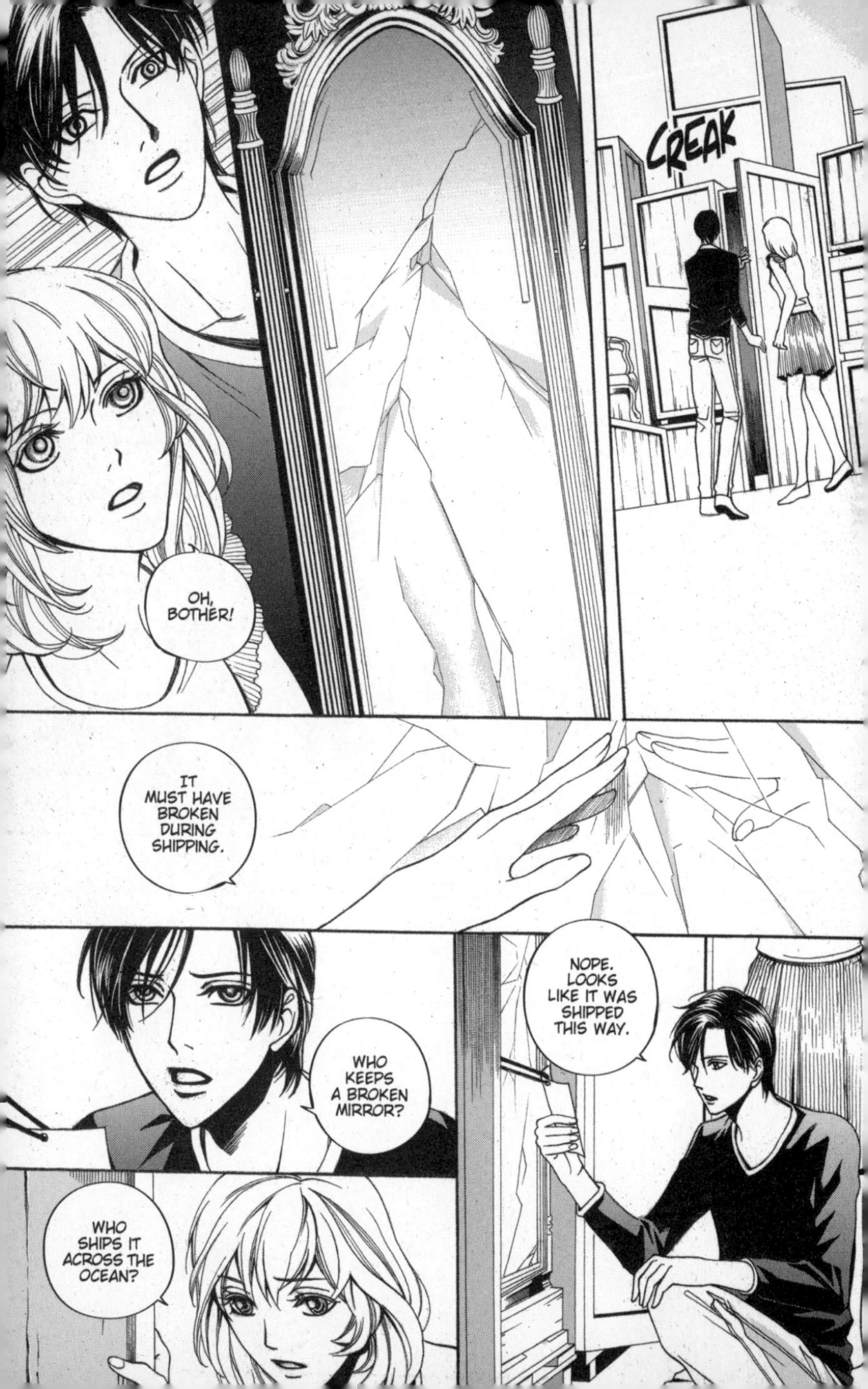
CREAK
OH, BOTHER!
IT MUST HAVE BROKEN DURING SHIPPING.
NOPE. LOOKS LIKE IT WAS SHIPPED THIS WAY.
WHO KEEPS A BROKEN MIRROR?
WHO SHIPS IT ACROSS THE OCEAN?

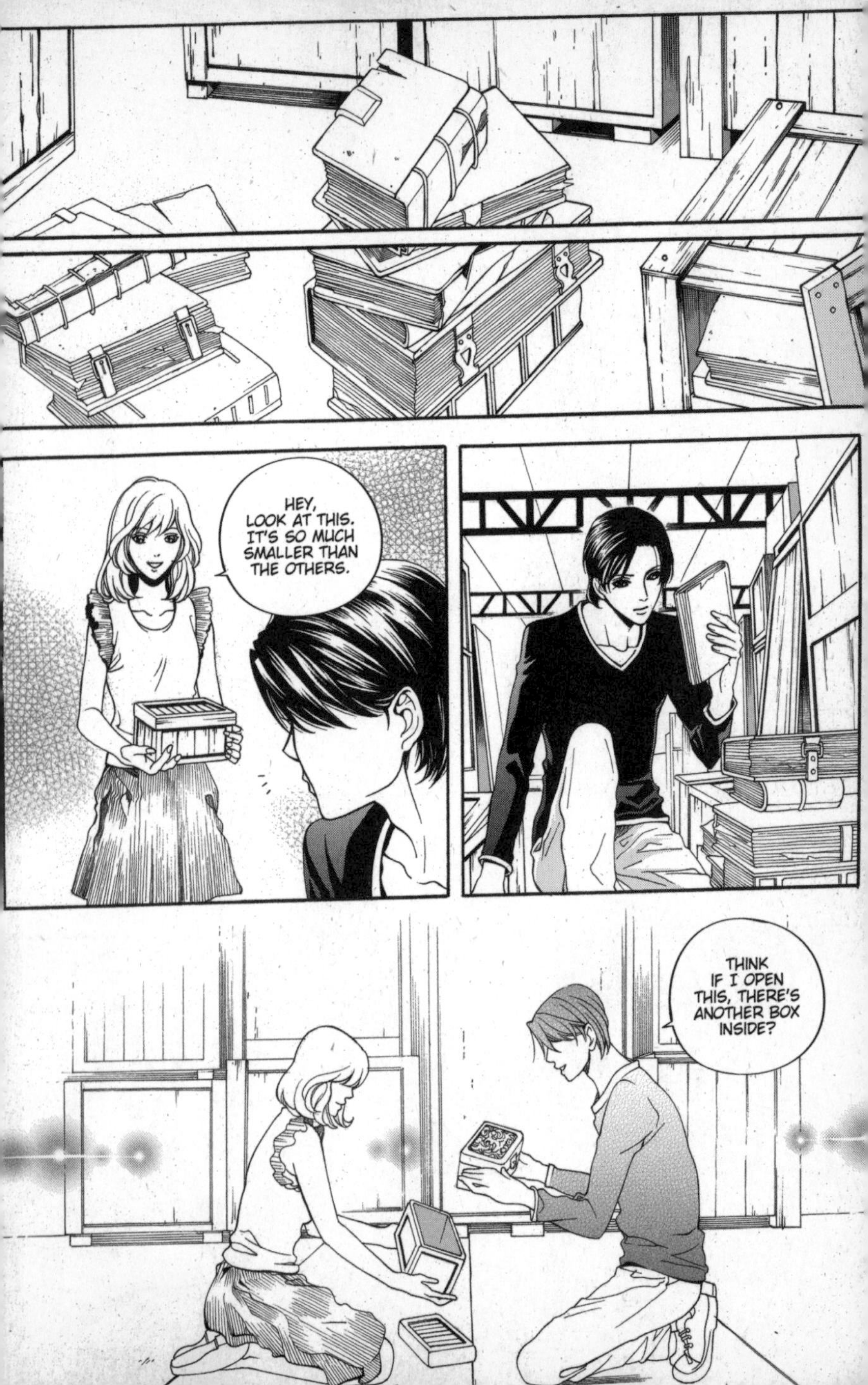
HEY, LOOK AT THIS. IT'S SO MUCH SMALLER THAN THE OTHERS.
THINK IF I OPEN THIS, THERE'S ANOTHER BOX INSIDE?

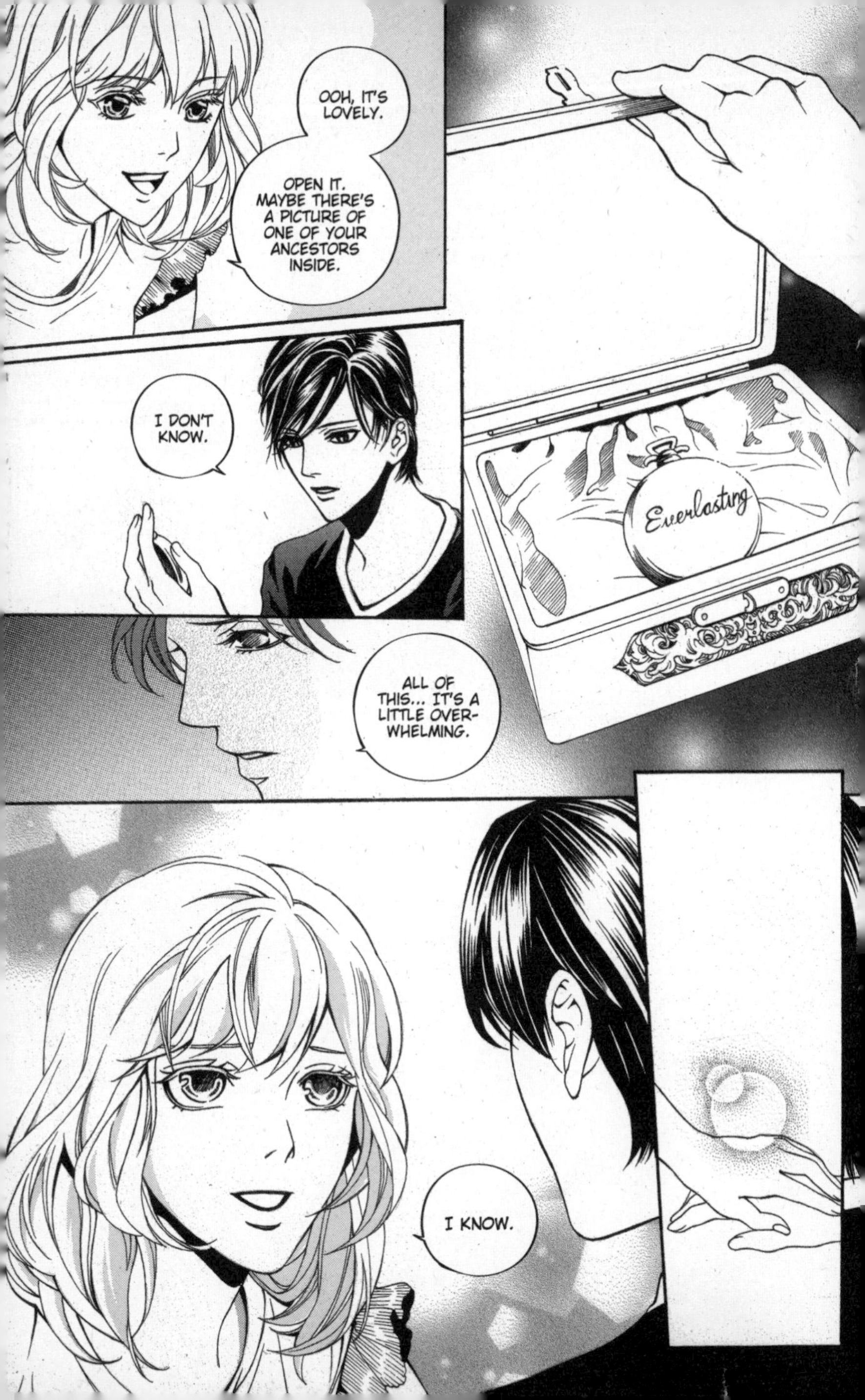
Everlasting
OOH, IT'S LOVELY.
OPEN IT. MAYBE THERE'S A PICTURE OF ONE OF YOUR ANCESTORS INSIDE.
I DON'T KNOW.
ALL OF THIS... IT'S A LITTLE OVER-WHELMING.
I KNOW.

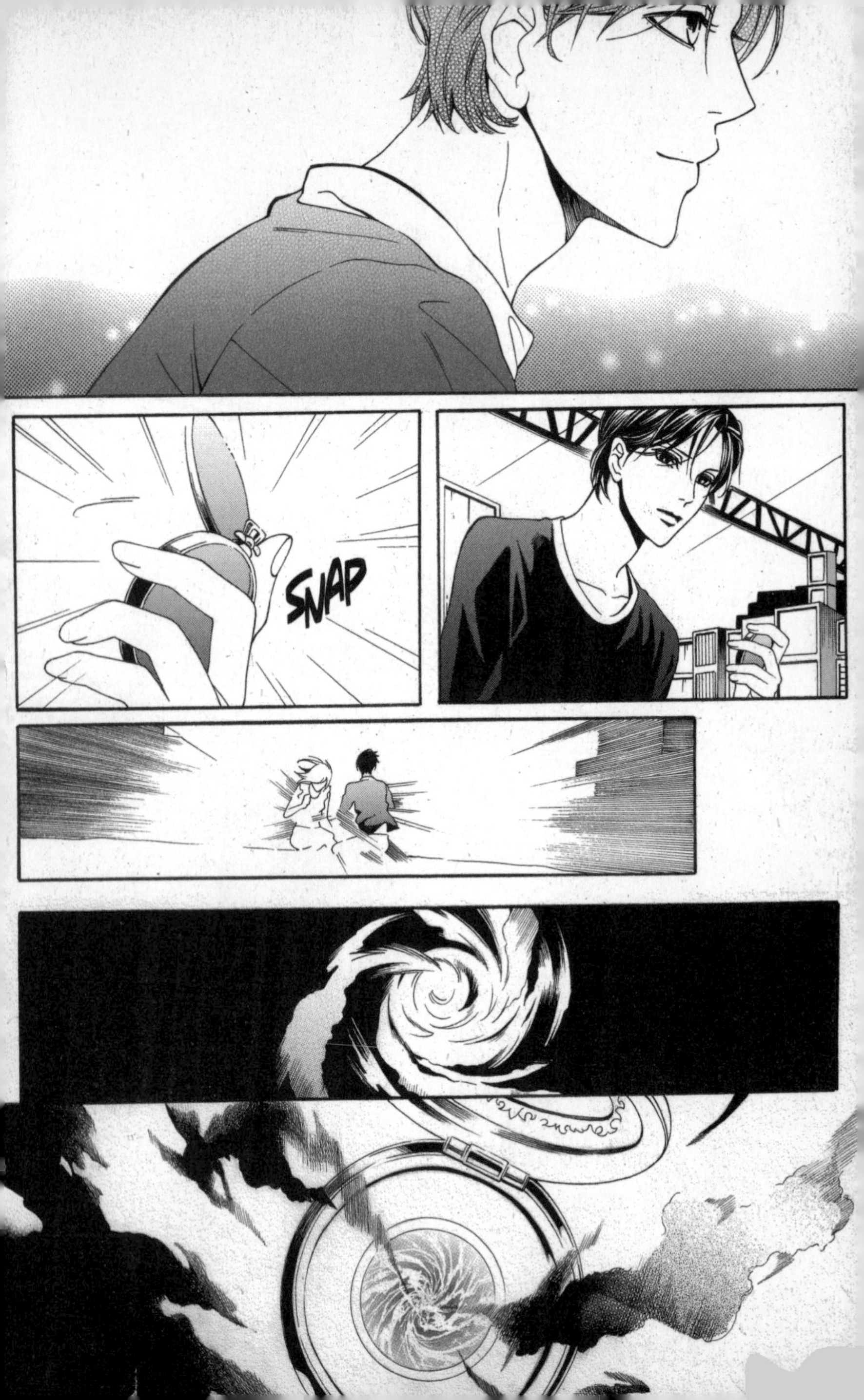
SNAP

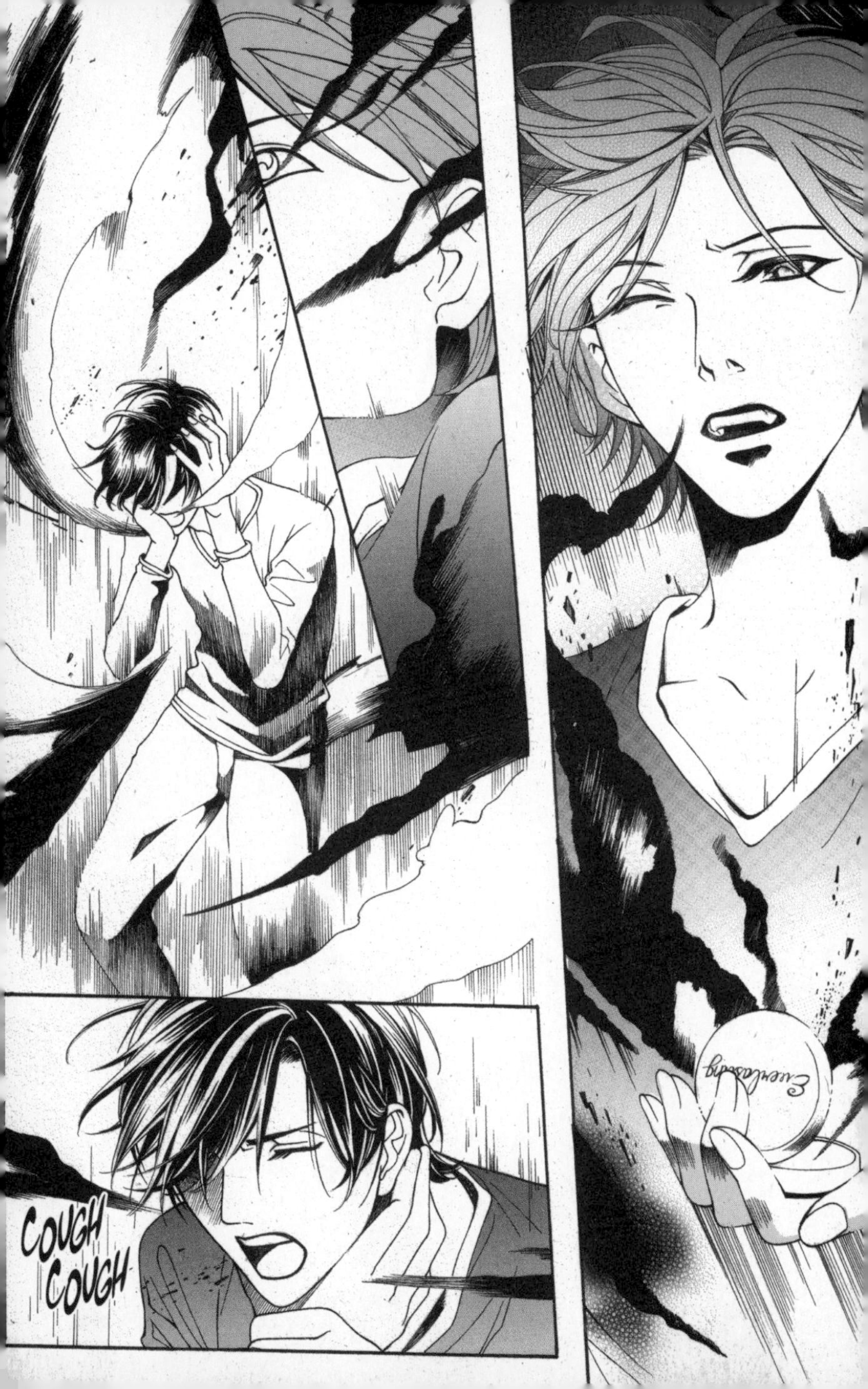
Everlasting
COUGH COUGH

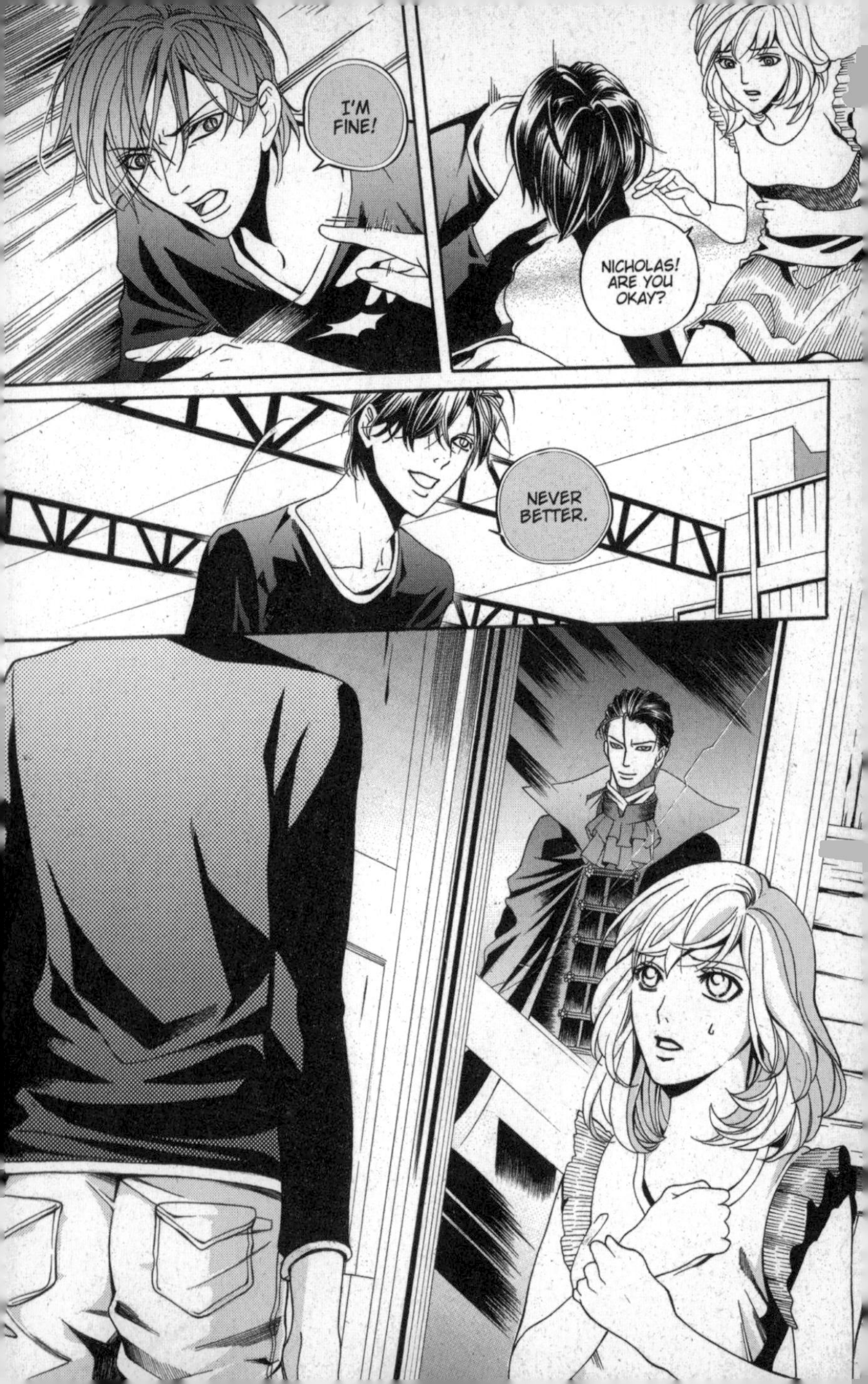
NICHOLAS! ARE YOU OKAY?
I'M FINE!
NEVER BETTER.

CHAPTER
2

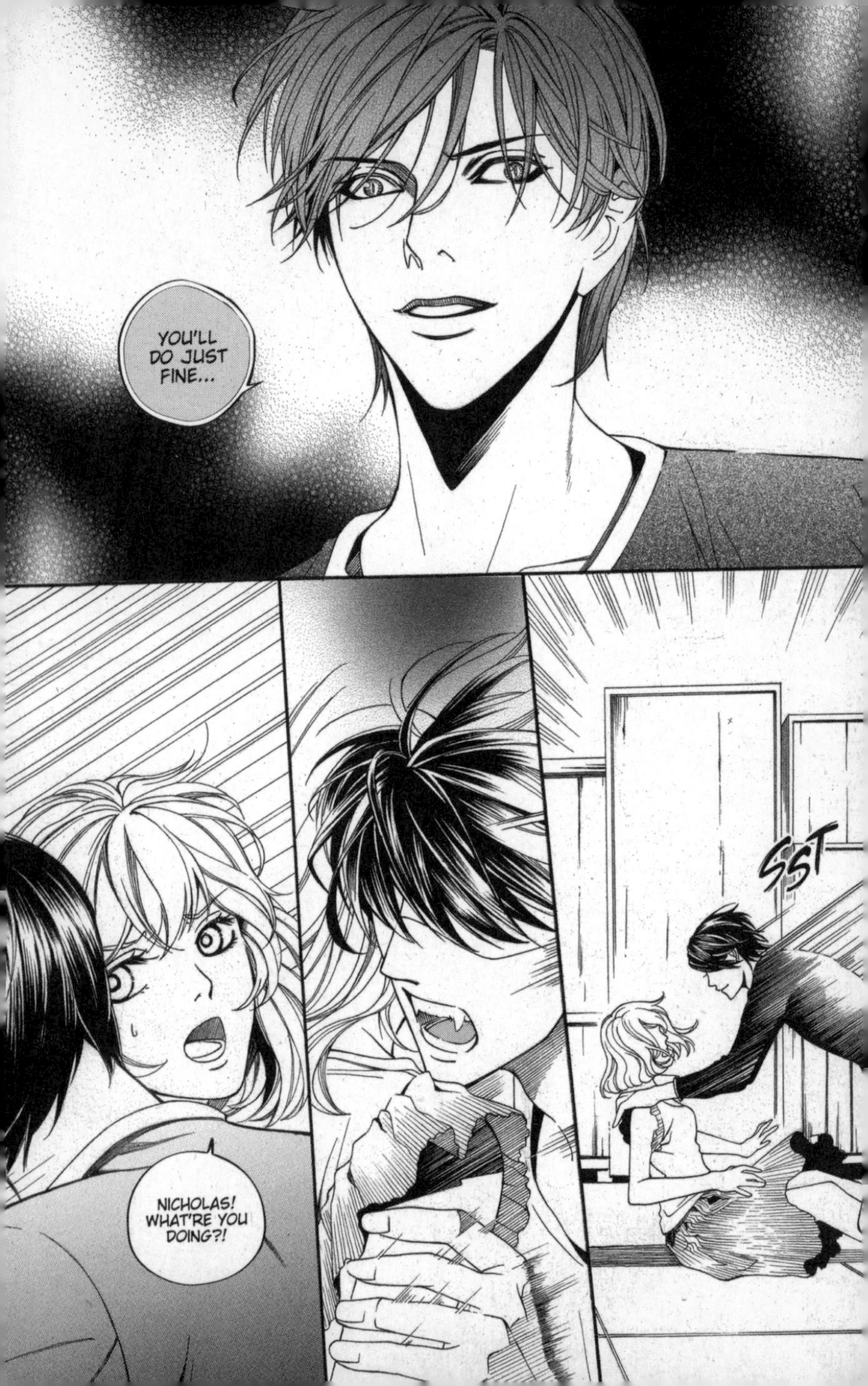
YOU'LL DO JUST FINE...
SST
NICHOLAS! WHAT'RE YOU DOING?!

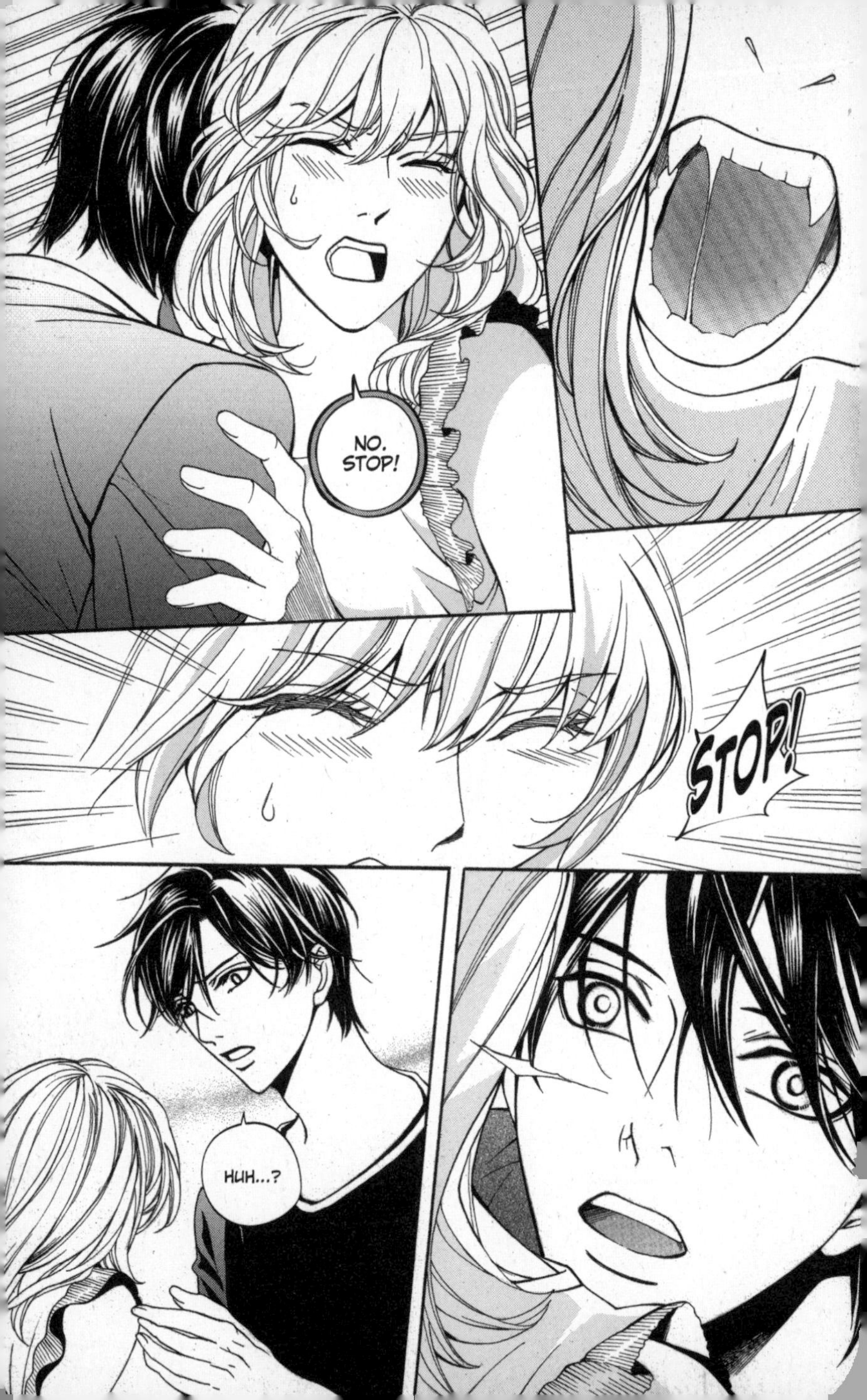
NO. STOP!
STOP!
HUH...?

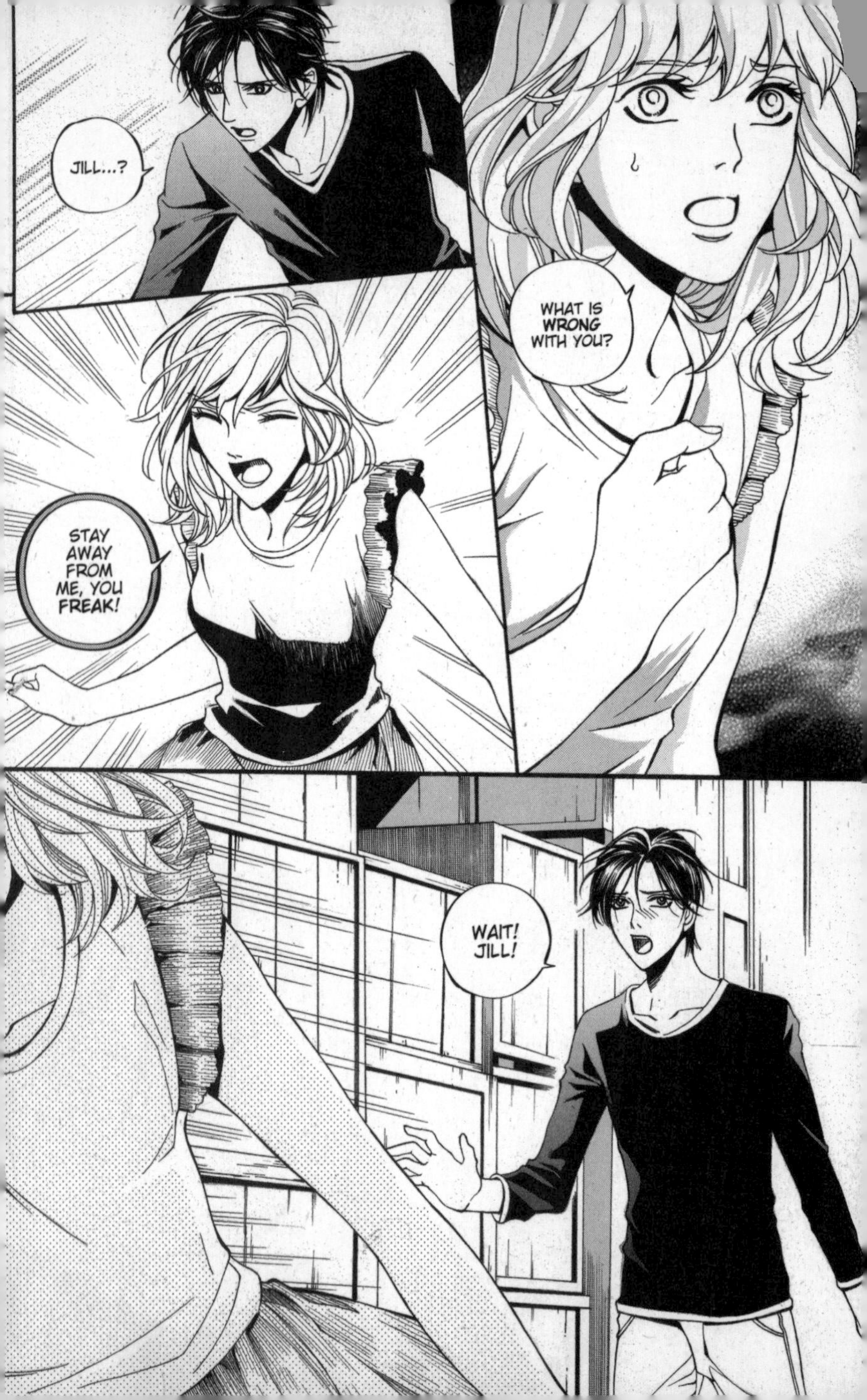
WHAT IS WRONG WITH YOU?
JILL...?
STAY AWAY FROM ME, YOU FREAK!
WAIT! JILL!

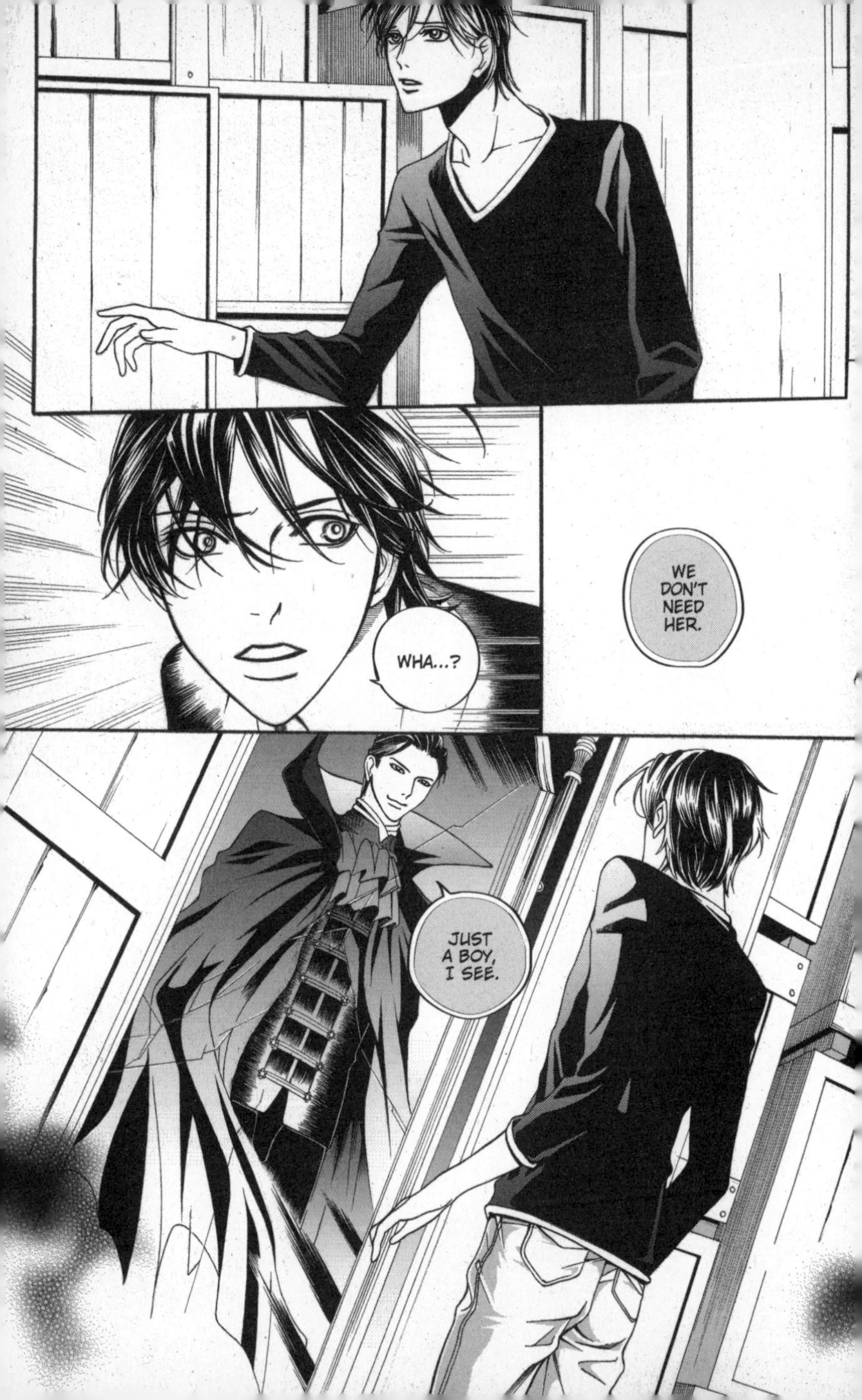
WE DON'T NEED HER.
WHA...?
JUST A BOY, I SEE.

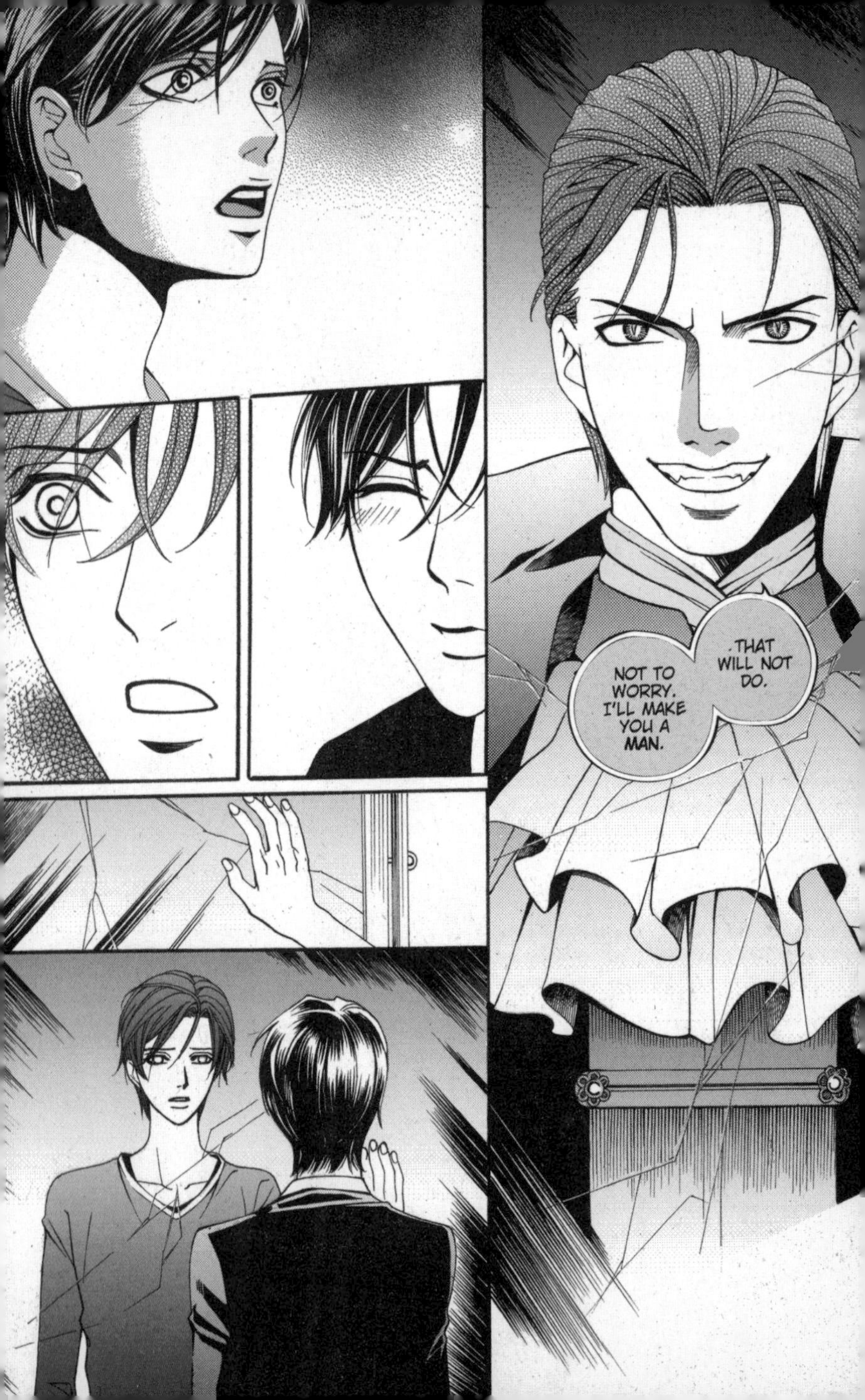
...THAT WILL NOT DO.
NOT TO WORRY. I'LL MAKE YOU A MAN.

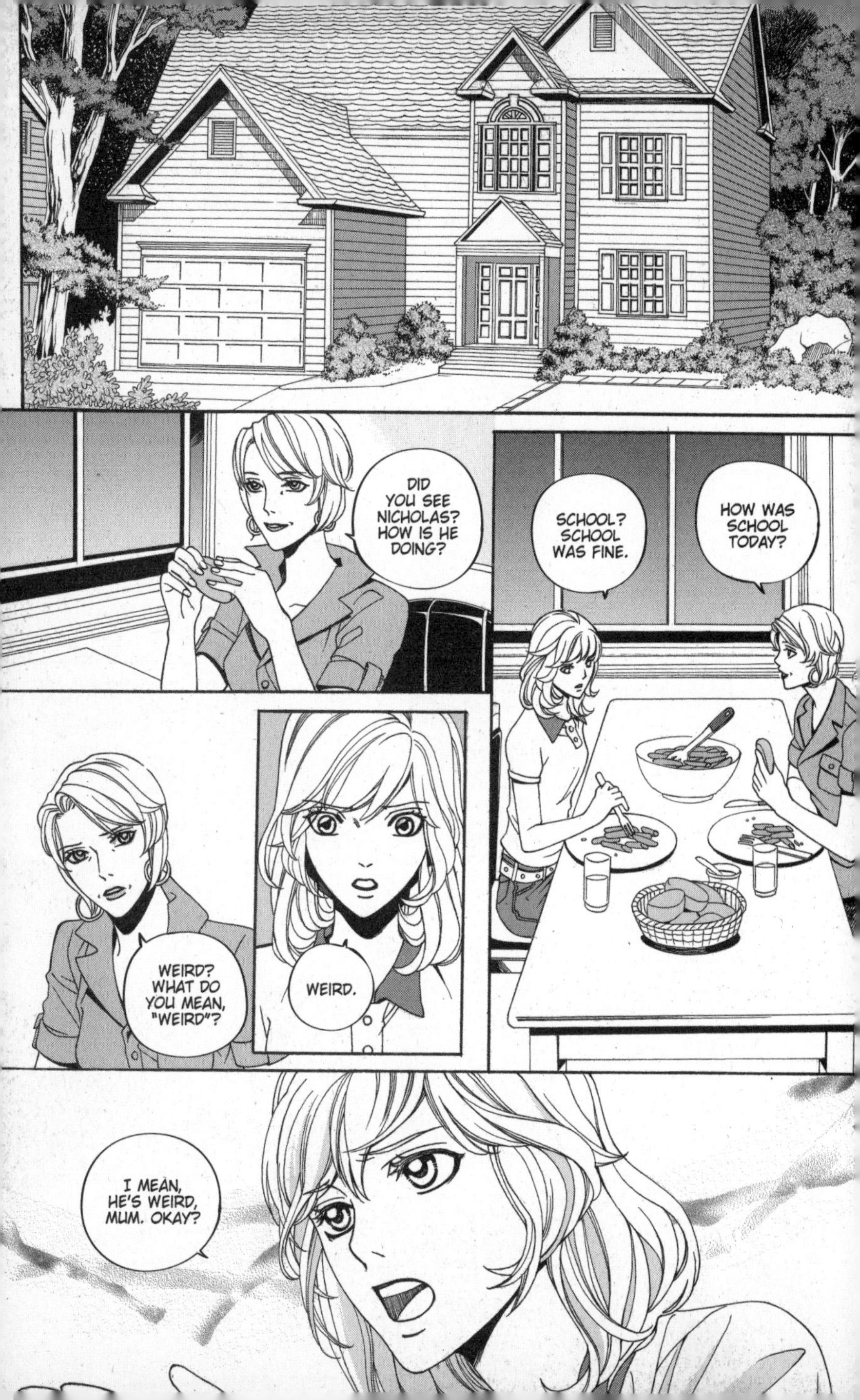
HOW WAS SCHOOL TODAY?
SCHOOL? SCHOOL WAS FINE.
DID YOU SEE NICHOLAS? HOW IS HE DOING?
WEIRD.
WEIRD? WHAT DO YOU MEAN, "WEIRD"?
I MEAN, HE'S WEIRD, MUM. OKAY?

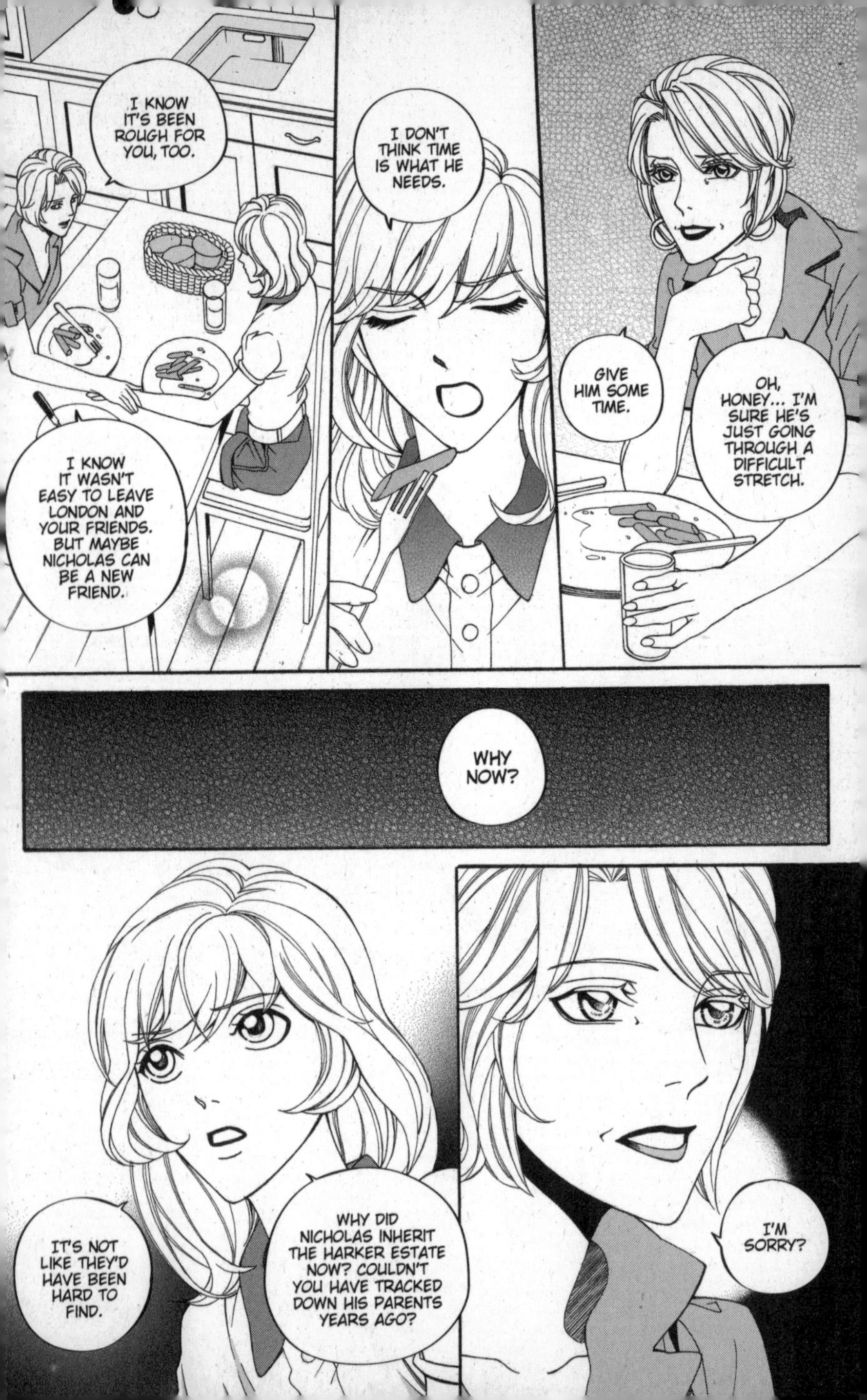
OH, HONEY... I'M SURE HE'S JUST GOING THROUGH A DIFFICULT STRETCH.
GIVE HIM SOME TIME.
I DON'T THINK TIME IS WHAT HE NEEDS.
I KNOW IT'S BEEN ROUGH FOR YOU, TOO.
I KNOW IT WASN'T EASY TO LEAVE LONDON AND YOUR FRIENDS. BUT MAYBE NICHOLAS CAN BE A NEW FRIEND.
WHY NOW?
I'M SORRY?
WHY DID NICHOLAS INHERIT THE HARKER ESTATE NOW? COULDN'T YOU HAVE TRACKED DOWN HIS PARENTS YEARS AGO?
IT'S NOT LIKE THEY'D HAVE BEEN HARD TO FIND.

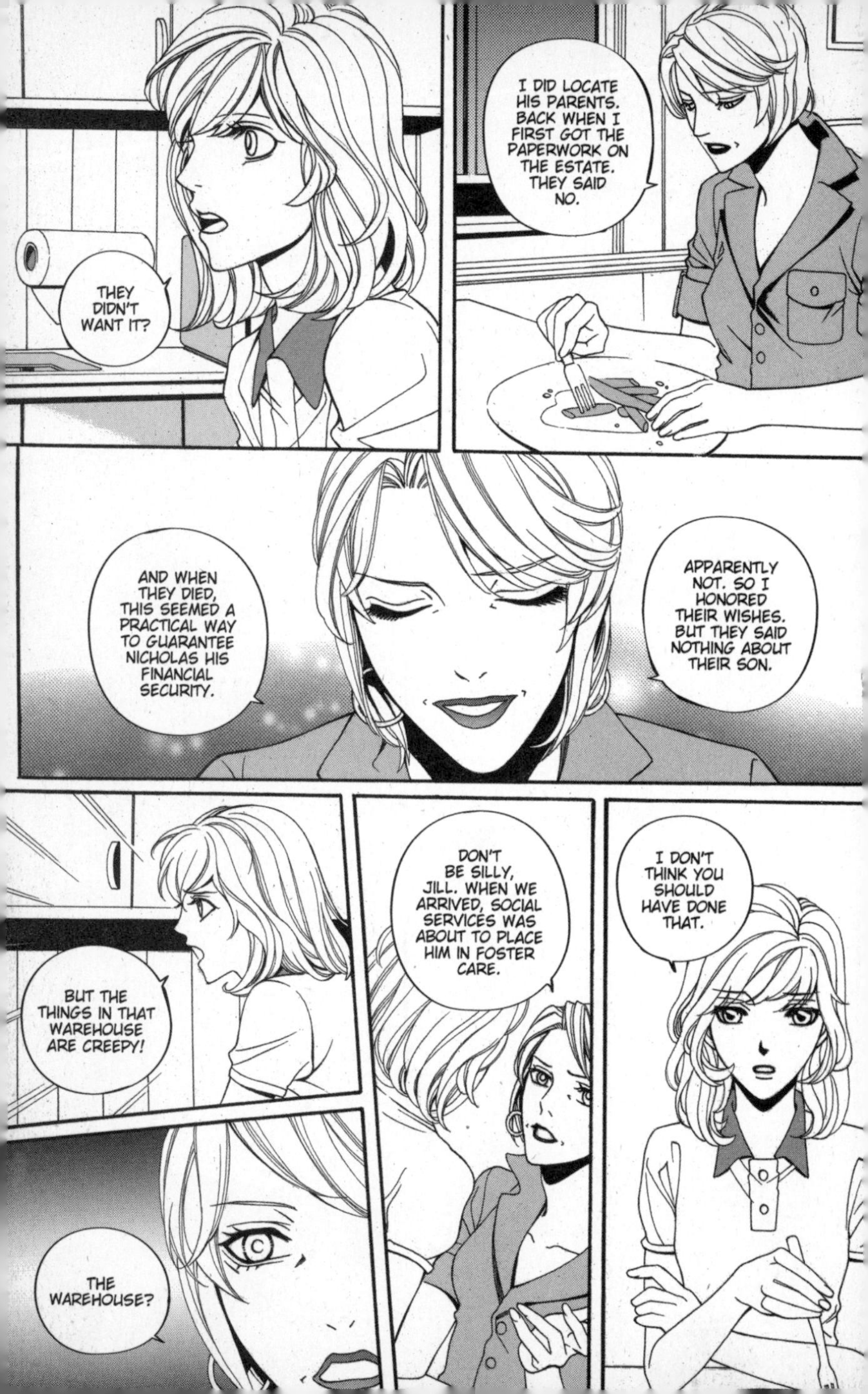
I DID LOCATE HIS PARENTS. BACK WHEN I FIRST GOT THE PAPERWORK ON THE ESTATE. THEY SAID NO.
THEY DIDN'T WANT IT?
APPARENTLY NOT. SO I HONORED THEIR WISHES. BUT THEY SAID NOTHING ABOUT THEIR SON.
AND WHEN THEY DIED, THIS SEEMED A PRACTICAL WAY TO GUARANTEE NICHOLAS HIS FINANCIAL SECURITY.
I DON'T THINK YOU SHOULD HAVE DONE THAT.
DON'T BE SILLY, JILL. WHEN WE ARRIVED, SOCIAL SERVICES WAS ABOUT TO PLACE HIM IN FOSTER CARE.
BUT THE THINGS IN THAT WAREHOUSE ARE CREEPY!
THE WAREHOUSE?

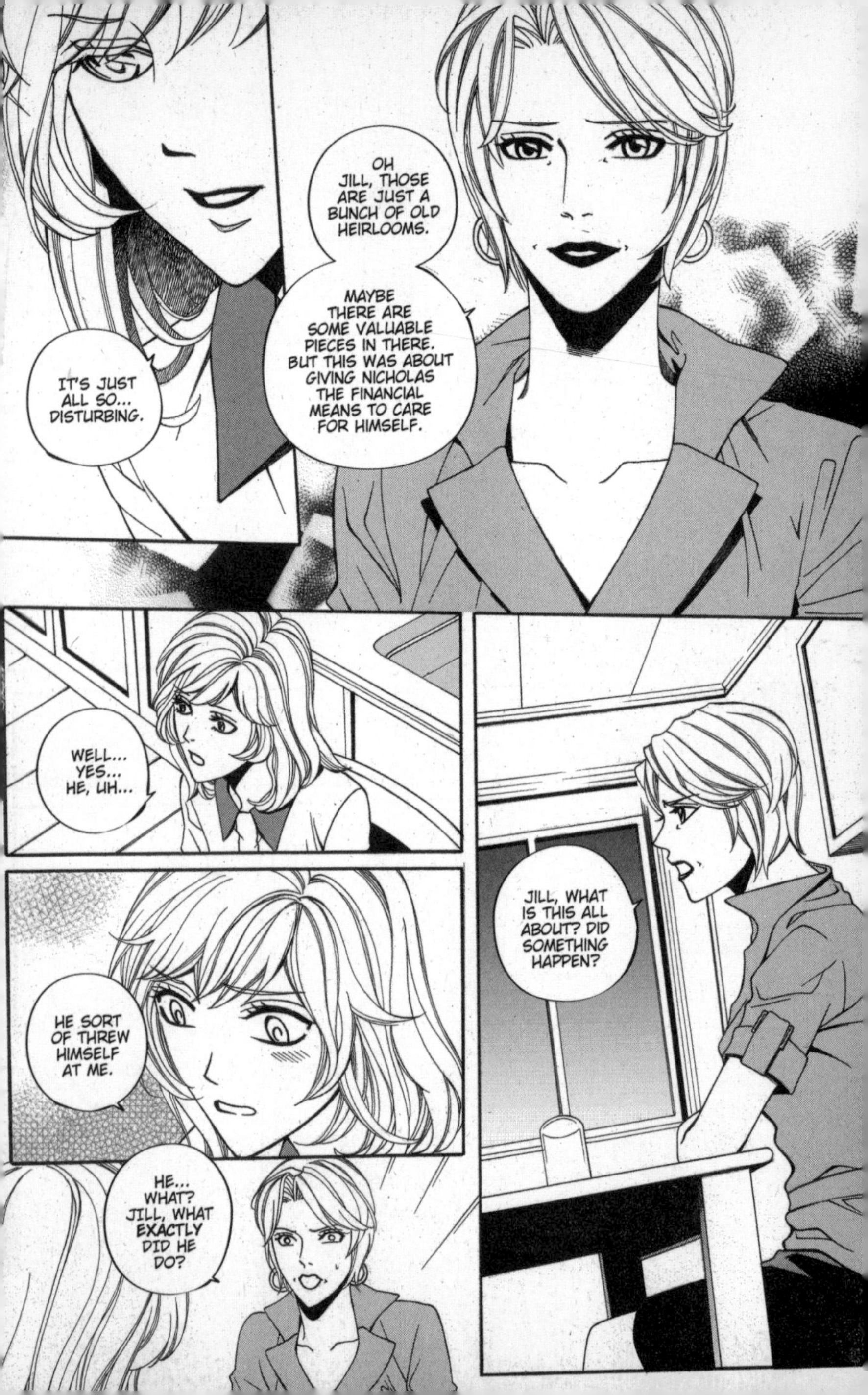
OH JILL, THOSE ARE JUST A BUNCH OF OLD HEIRLOOMS.
MAYBE THERE ARE SOME VALUABLE PIECES IN THERE. BUT THIS WAS ABOUT GIVING NICHOLAS THE FINANCIAL MEANS TO CARE FOR HIMSELF.
IT'S JUST ALL SO... DISTURBING.
JILL, WHAT IS THIS ALL ABOUT? DID SOMETHING HAPPEN?
WELL... YES... HE, UH...
HE SORT OF THREW HIMSELF AT ME.
HE... WHAT? JILL, WHAT EXACTLY DID HE DO?

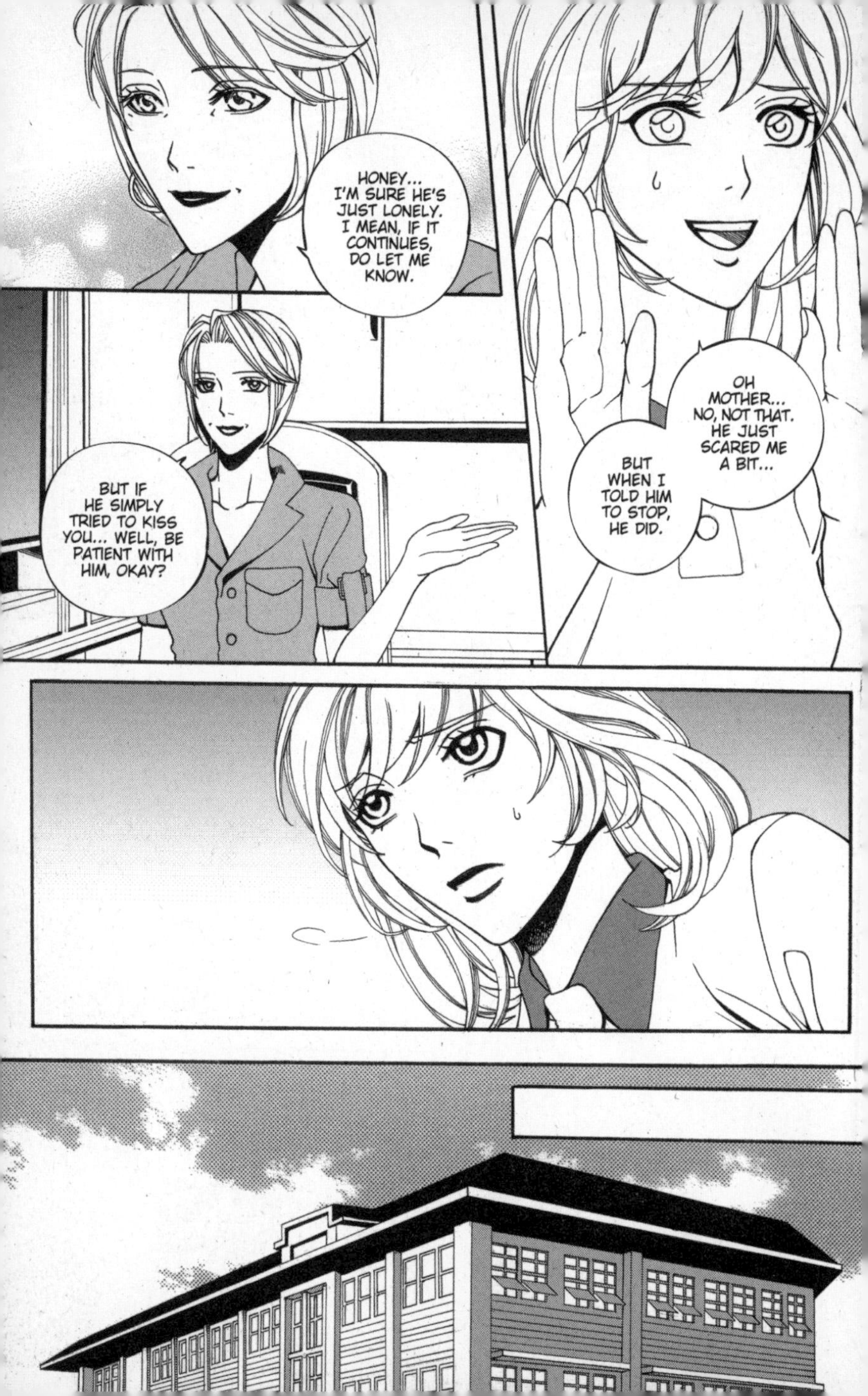
OH MOTHER... NO, NOT THAT. HE JUST SCARED ME A BIT...
BUT WHEN I TOLD HIM TO STOP, HE DID.
HONEY... I'M SURE HE'S JUST LONELY. I MEAN, IF IT CONTINUES, DO LET ME KNOW.
BUT IF HE SIMPLY TRIED TO KISS YOU... WELL, BE PATIENT WITH HIM, OKAY?

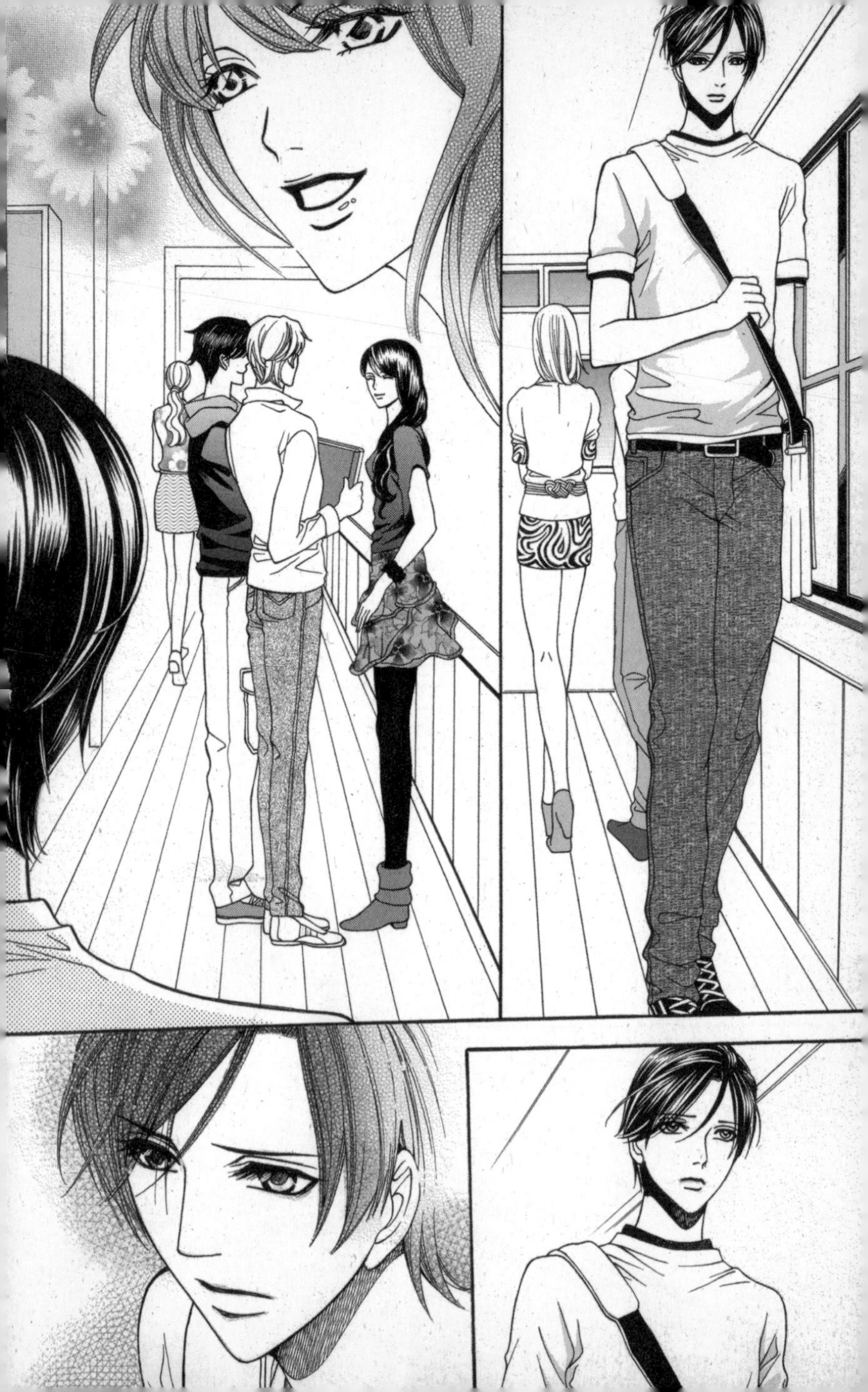

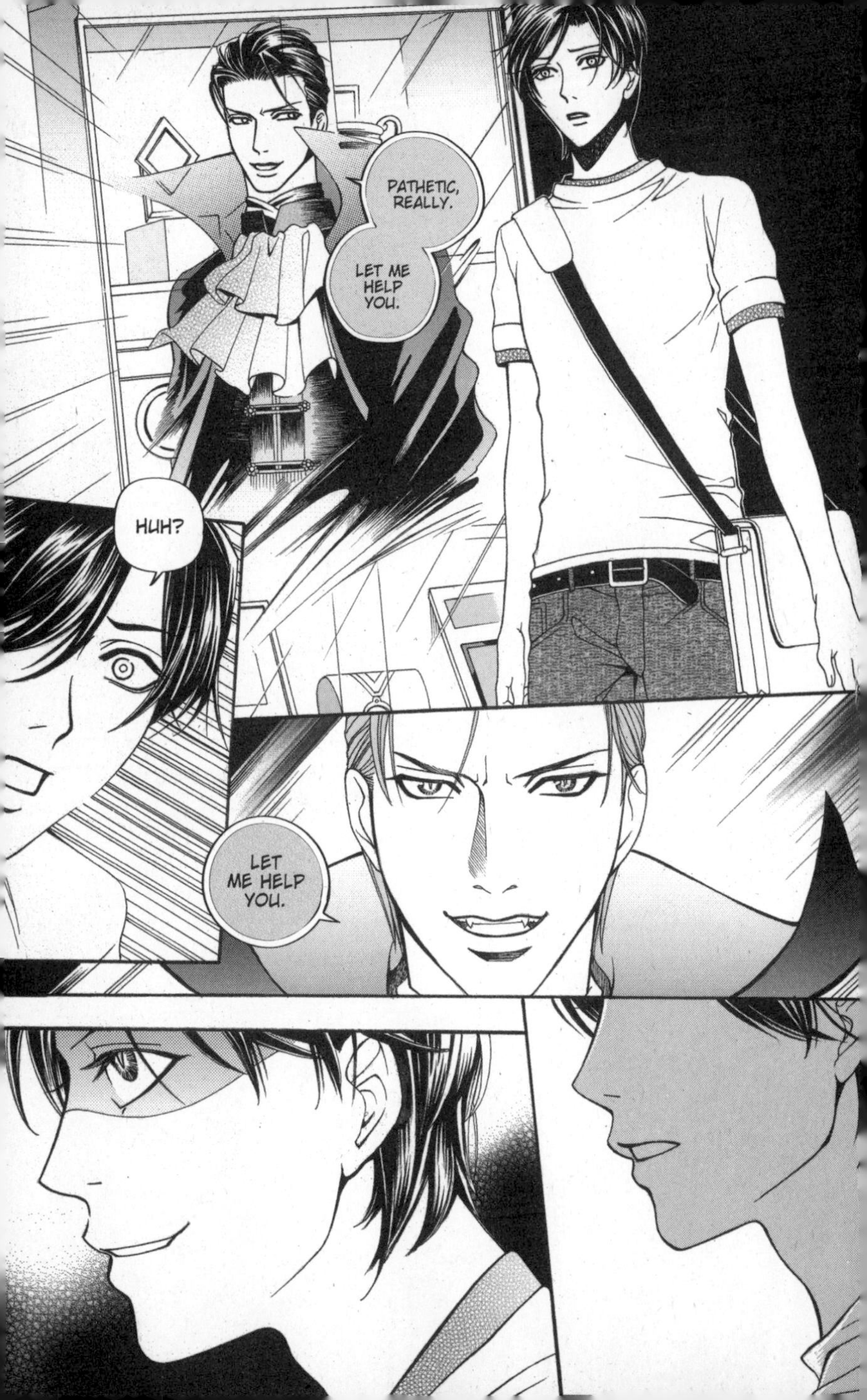
PATHETIC, REALLY.
LET ME HELP YOU.
HUH?
LET ME HELP YOU.

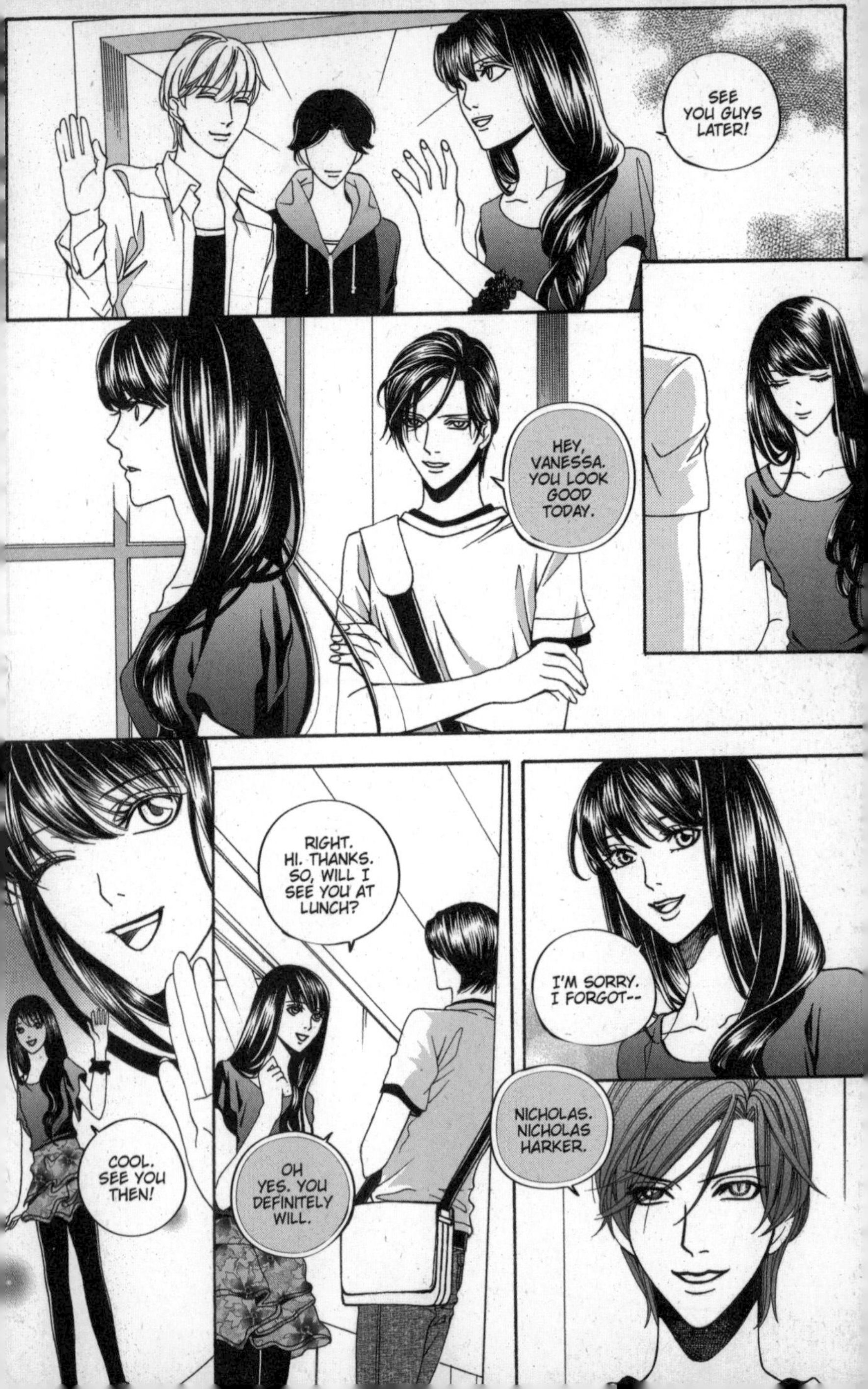
SEE YOU GUYS LATER!
HEY, VANESSA. YOU LOOK GOOD TODAY.
I'M SORRY. I FORGOT--
NICHOLAS. NICHOLAS HARKER.
RIGHT. HI. THANKS. SO, WILL I SEE YOU AT LUNCH?
OH YES. YOU DEFINITELY WILL.
COOL. SEE YOU THEN!

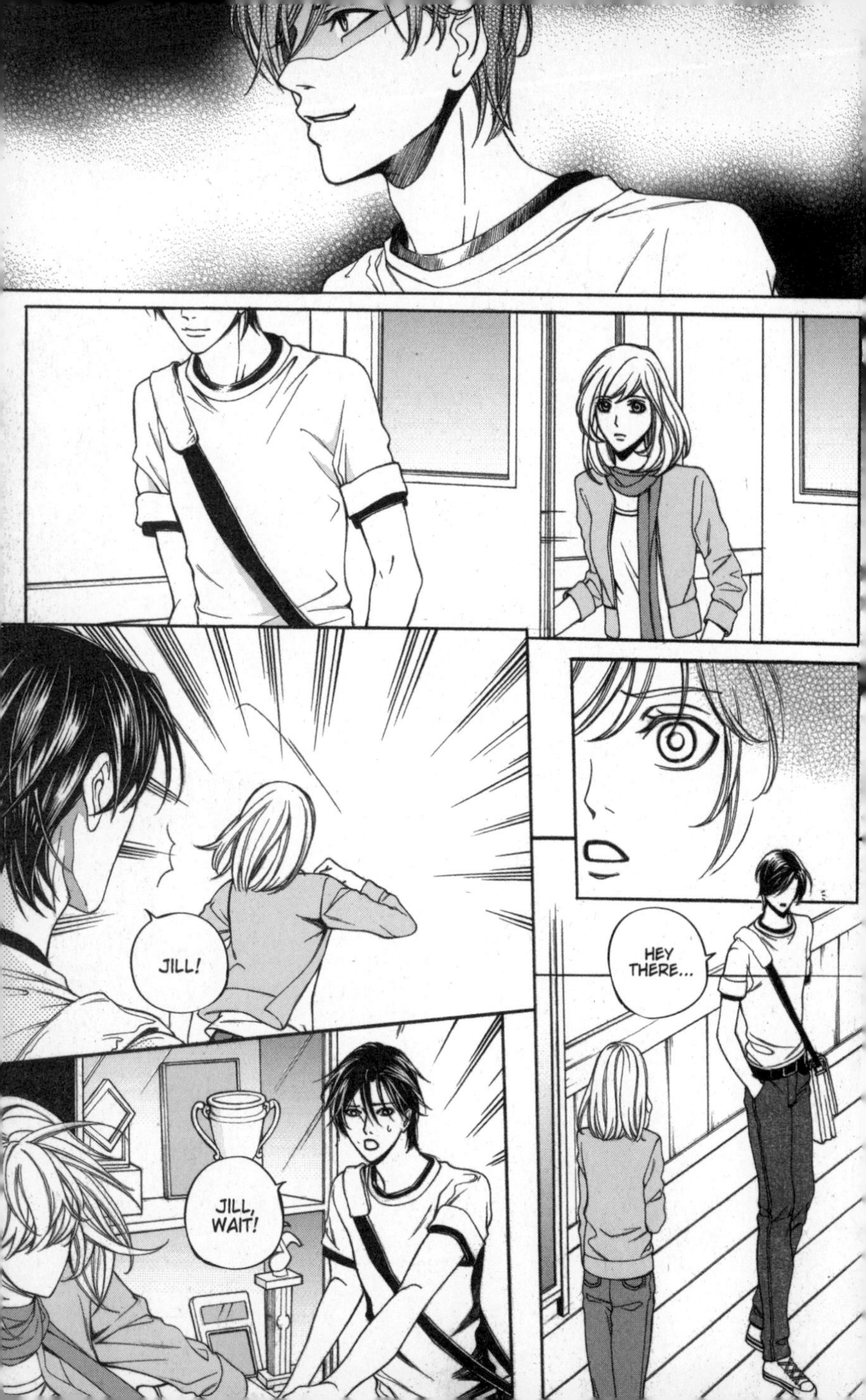
HEY THERE...
JILL!
JILL, WAIT!

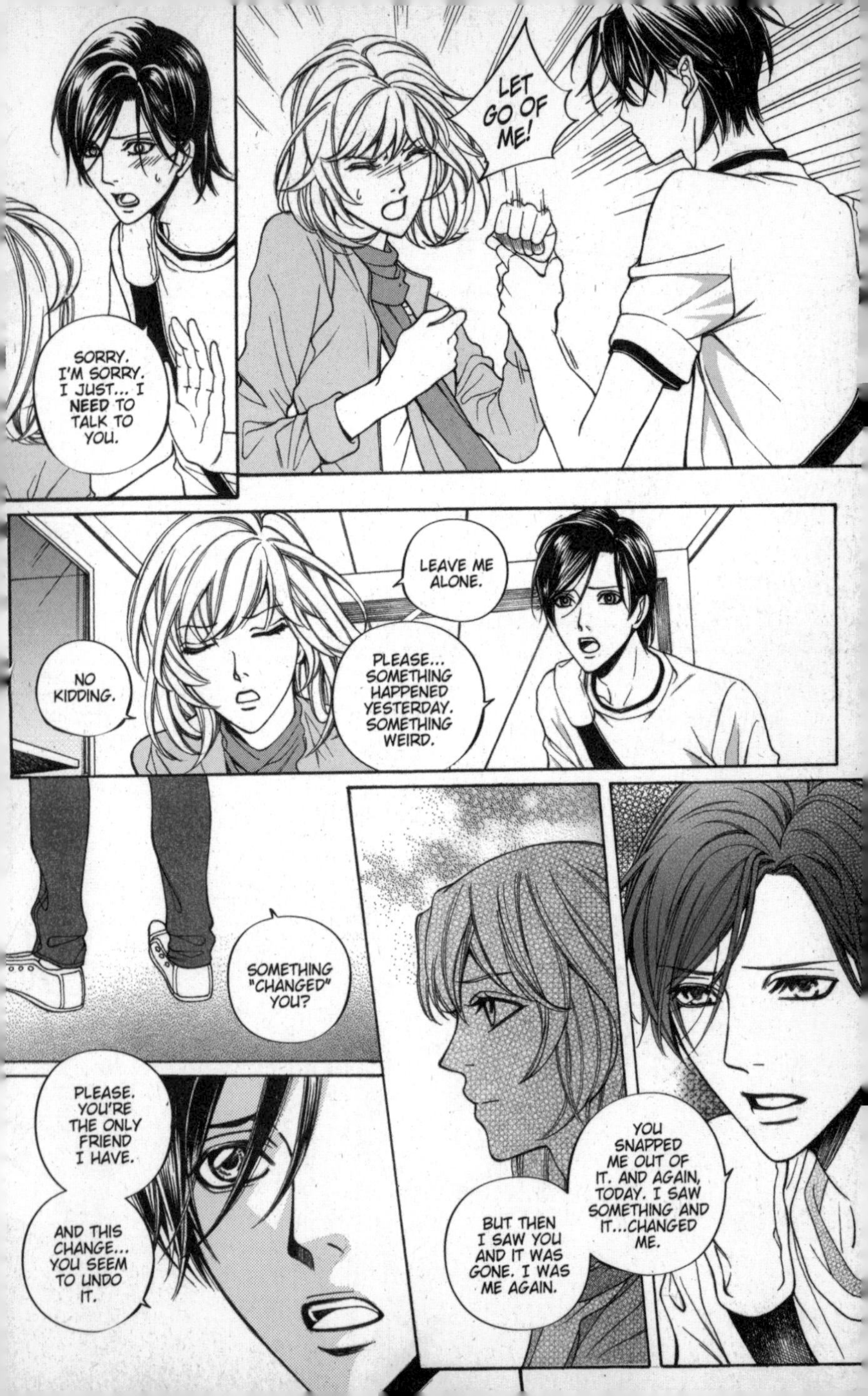
LET GO OF ME!
SORRY. I'M SORRY. I JUST... I NEED TO TALK TO YOU.
LEAVE ME ALONE.
PLEASE... SOMETHING HAPPENED YESTERDAY. SOMETHING WEIRD.
NO KIDDING.
YOU SNAPPED ME OUT OF IT. AND AGAIN, TODAY. I SAW SOMETHING AND IT...CHANGED ME.
BUT THEN I SAW YOU AND IT WAS GONE. I WAS ME AGAIN.
SOMETHING "CHANGED" YOU?
PLEASE. YOU'RE THE ONLY FRIEND I HAVE.
AND THIS CHANGE... YOU SEEM TO UNDO IT.

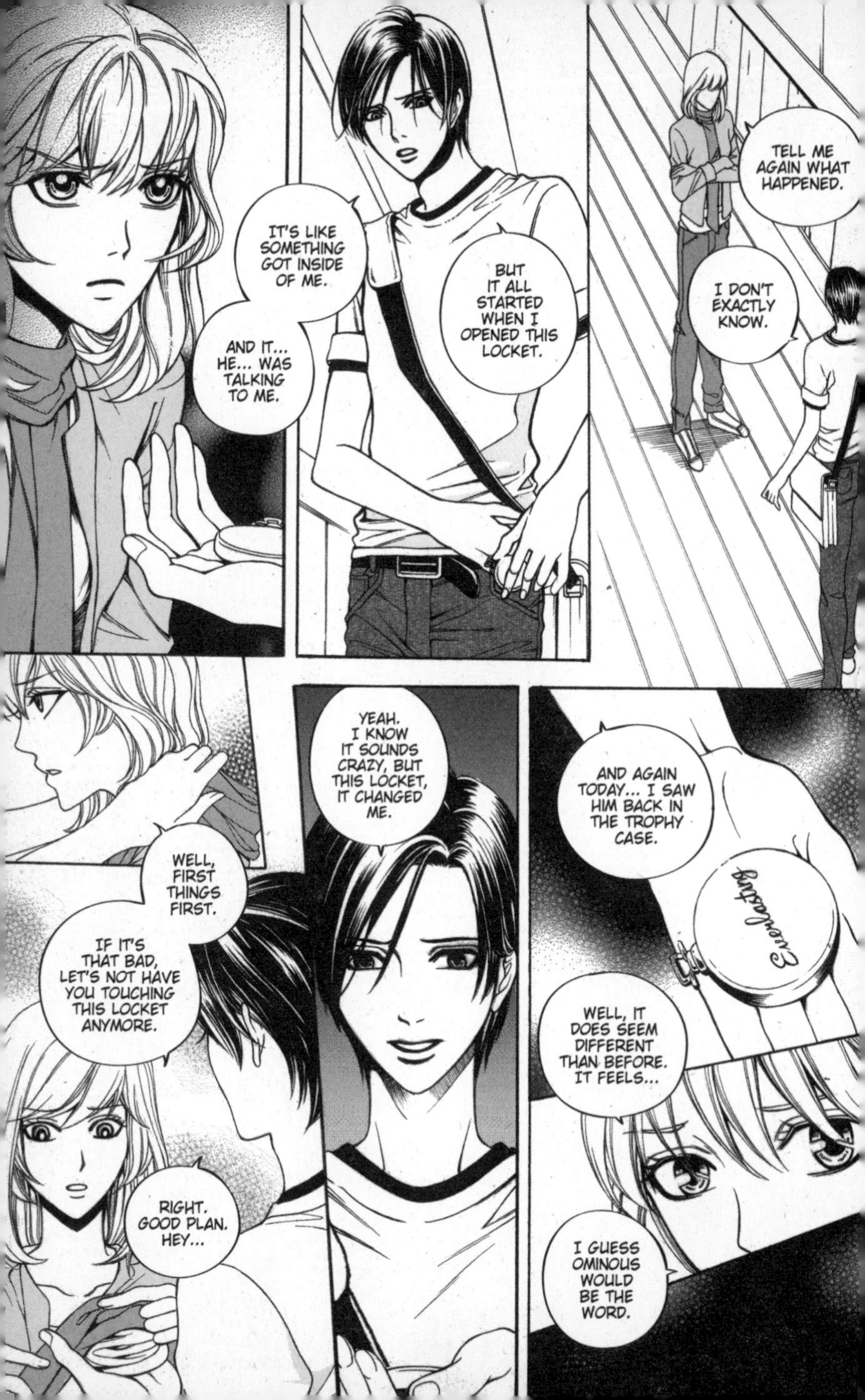
TELL ME AGAIN WHAT HAPPENED.
I DON'T EXACTLY KNOW.
BUT IT ALL STARTED WHEN I OPENED THIS LOCKET.
IT'S LIKE SOMETHING GOT INSIDE OF ME.
AND IT... HE... WAS TALKING TO ME.
AND AGAIN TODAY... I SAW HIM BACK IN THE TROPHY CASE.
Everlasting
WELL, IT DOES SEEM DIFFERENT THAN BEFORE. IT FEELS...
I GUESS OMINOUS WOULD BE THE WORD.
YEAH. I KNOW IT SOUNDS CRAZY, BUT THIS LOCKET, IT CHANGED ME.
WELL, FIRST THINGS FIRST.
IF IT'S THAT BAD, LET'S NOT HAVE YOU TOUCHING THIS LOCKET ANYMORE.
RIGHT. GOOD PLAN. HEY...

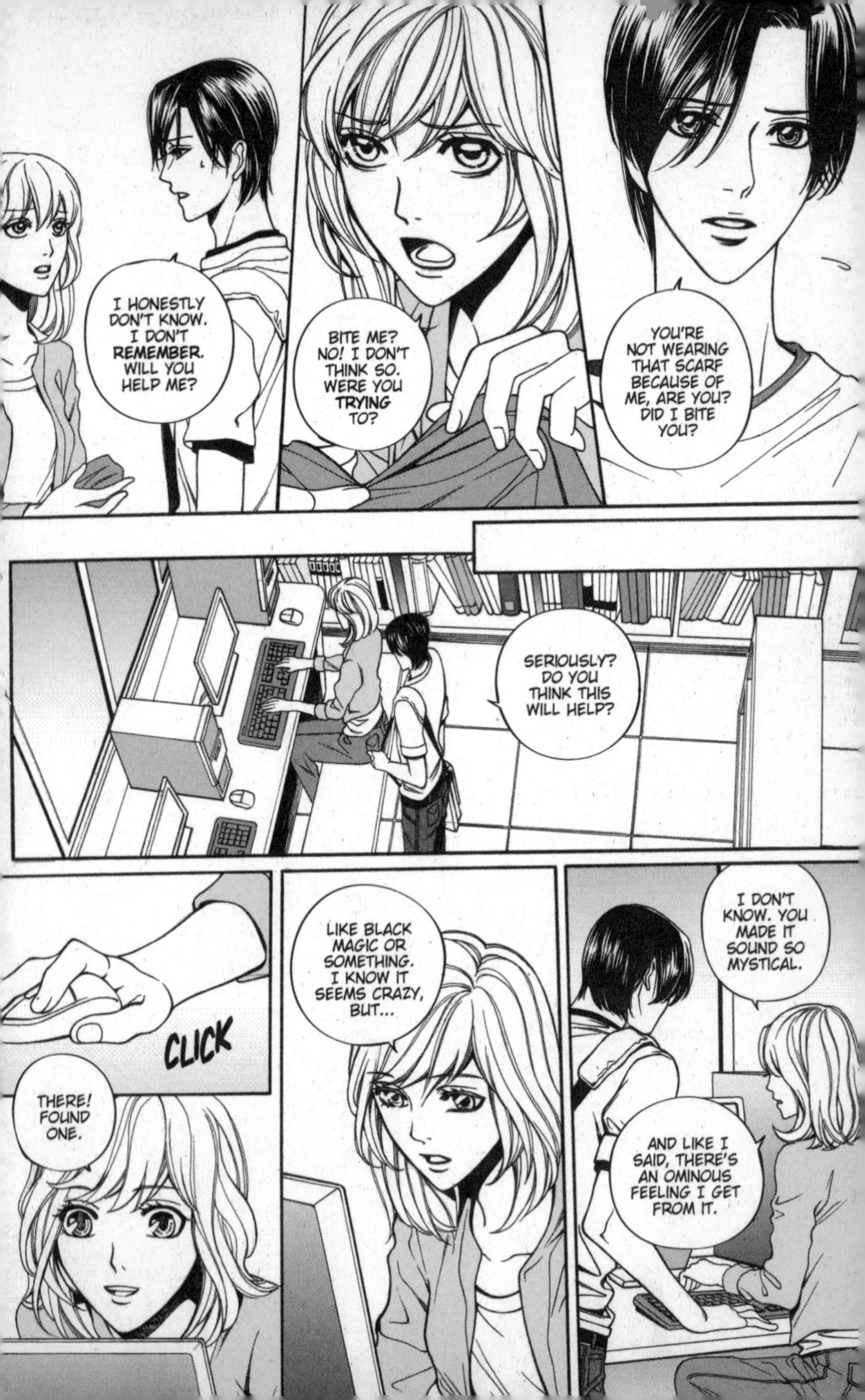
YOU'RE NOT WEARING THAT SCARF BECAUSE OF ME, ARE YOU? DID I BITE YOU?
BITE ME? NO! I DON'T THINK SO. WERE YOU **TRYING** TO?
I HONESTLY DON'T KNOW. I DON'T **REMEMBER.** WILL YOU HELP ME?
SERIOUSLY? DO YOU THINK THIS WILL HELP?
I DON'T KNOW. YOU MADE IT SOUND SO MYSTICAL.
AND LIKE I SAID, THERE'S AN OMINOUS FEELING I GET FROM IT.
LIKE BLACK MAGIC OR SOMETHING. I KNOW IT SEEMS CRAZY, BUT...
CLICK
THERE! FOUND ONE.

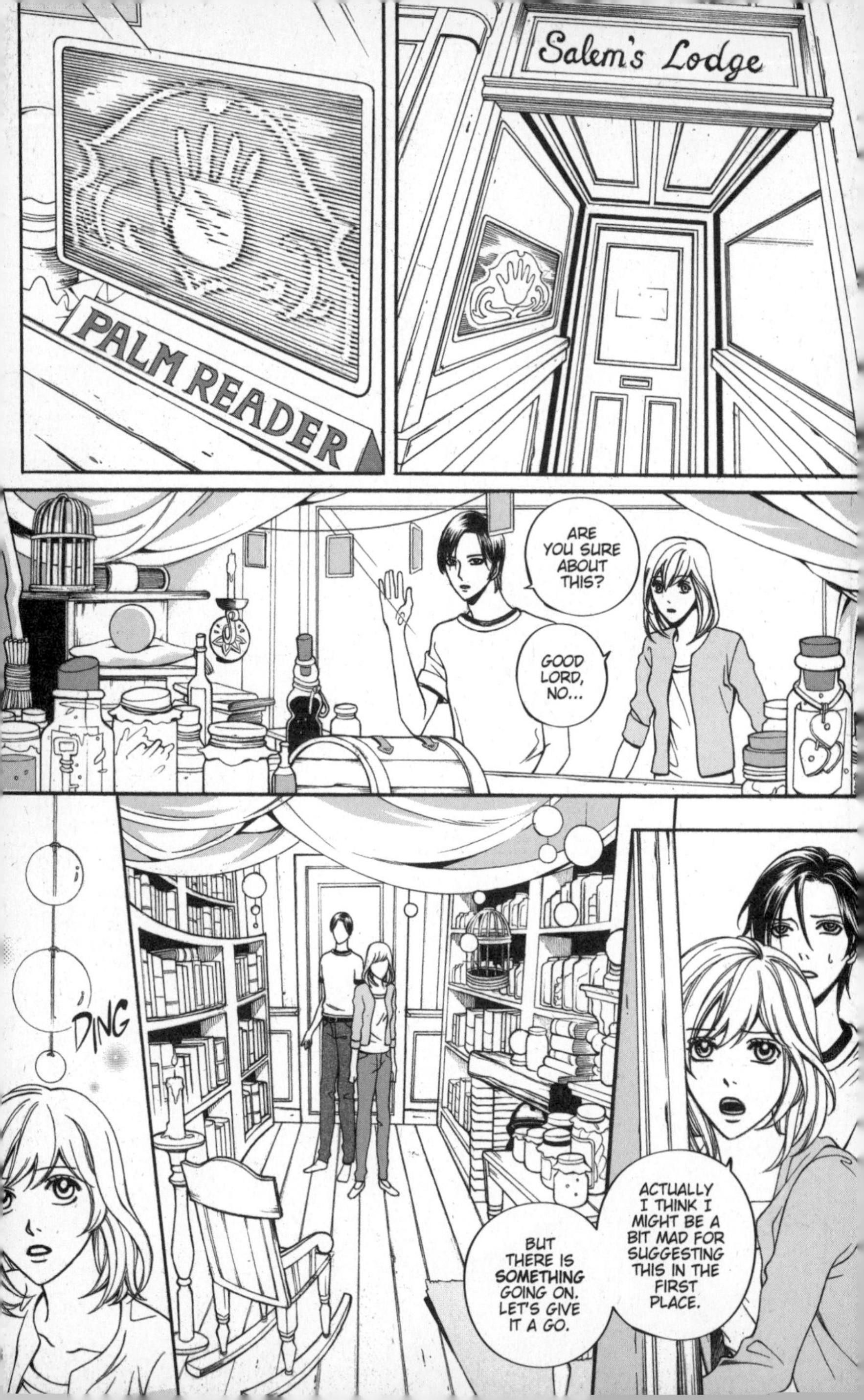
Salem's Lodge
PALM READER
ARE YOU SURE ABOUT THIS?
GOOD LORD, NO...
ACTUALLY I THINK I MIGHT BE A BIT MAD FOR SUGGESTING THIS IN THE FIRST PLACE.
BUT THERE IS SOMETHING GOING ON. LET'S GIVE IT A GO.
DING

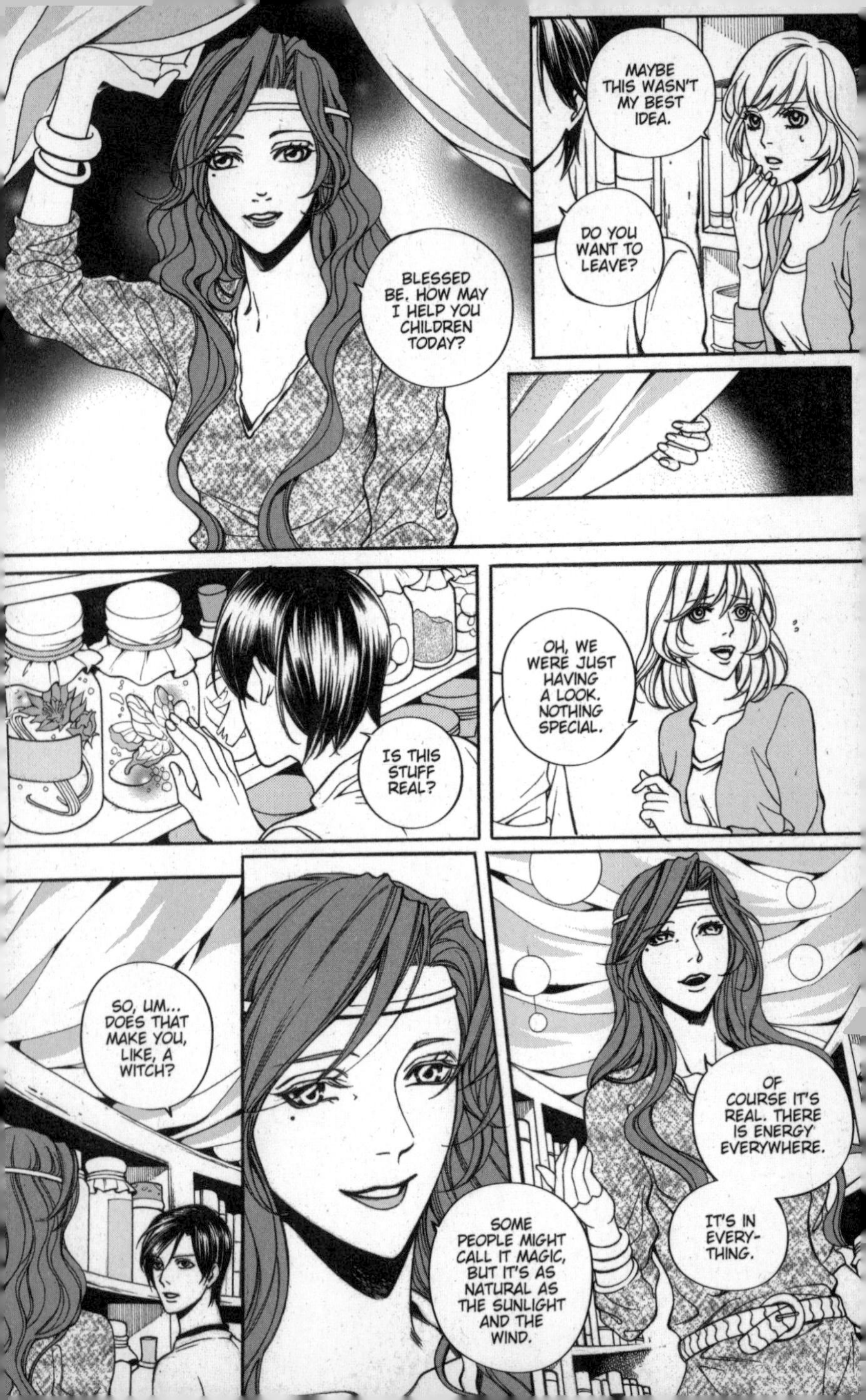
MAYBE THIS WASN'T MY BEST IDEA.
DO YOU WANT TO LEAVE?
BLESSED BE. HOW MAY I HELP YOU CHILDREN TODAY?
OH, WE WERE JUST HAVING A LOOK. NOTHING SPECIAL.
IS THIS STUFF REAL?
OF COURSE IT'S REAL. THERE IS ENERGY EVERYWHERE.
IT'S IN EVERY-THING.
SOME PEOPLE MIGHT CALL IT MAGIC, BUT IT'S AS NATURAL AS THE SUNLIGHT AND THE WIND.
SO, UM... DOES THAT MAKE YOU, LIKE, A WITCH?

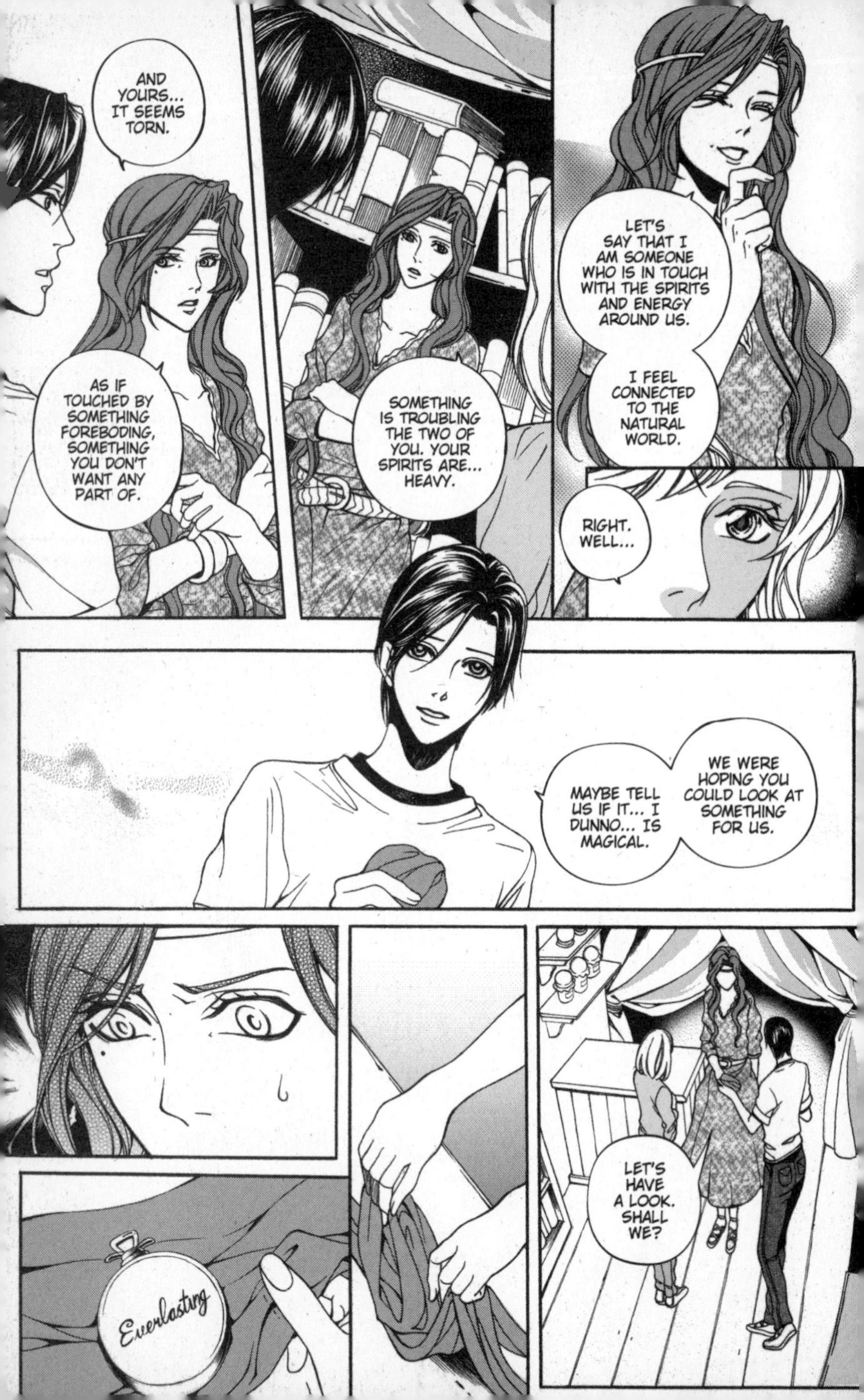
LET'S SAY THAT I AM SOMEONE WHO IS IN TOUCH WITH THE SPIRITS AND ENERGY AROUND US.
I FEEL CONNECTED TO THE NATURAL WORLD.
RIGHT. WELL...
SOMETHING IS TROUBLING THE TWO OF YOU. YOUR SPIRITS ARE... HEAVY.
AND YOURS... IT SEEMS TORN.
AS IF TOUCHED BY SOMETHING FOREBODING, SOMETHING YOU DON'T WANT ANY PART OF.
WE WERE HOPING YOU COULD LOOK AT SOMETHING FOR US.
MAYBE TELL US IF IT... I DUNNO... IS MAGICAL.
LET'S HAVE A LOOK. SHALL WE?
Everlasting

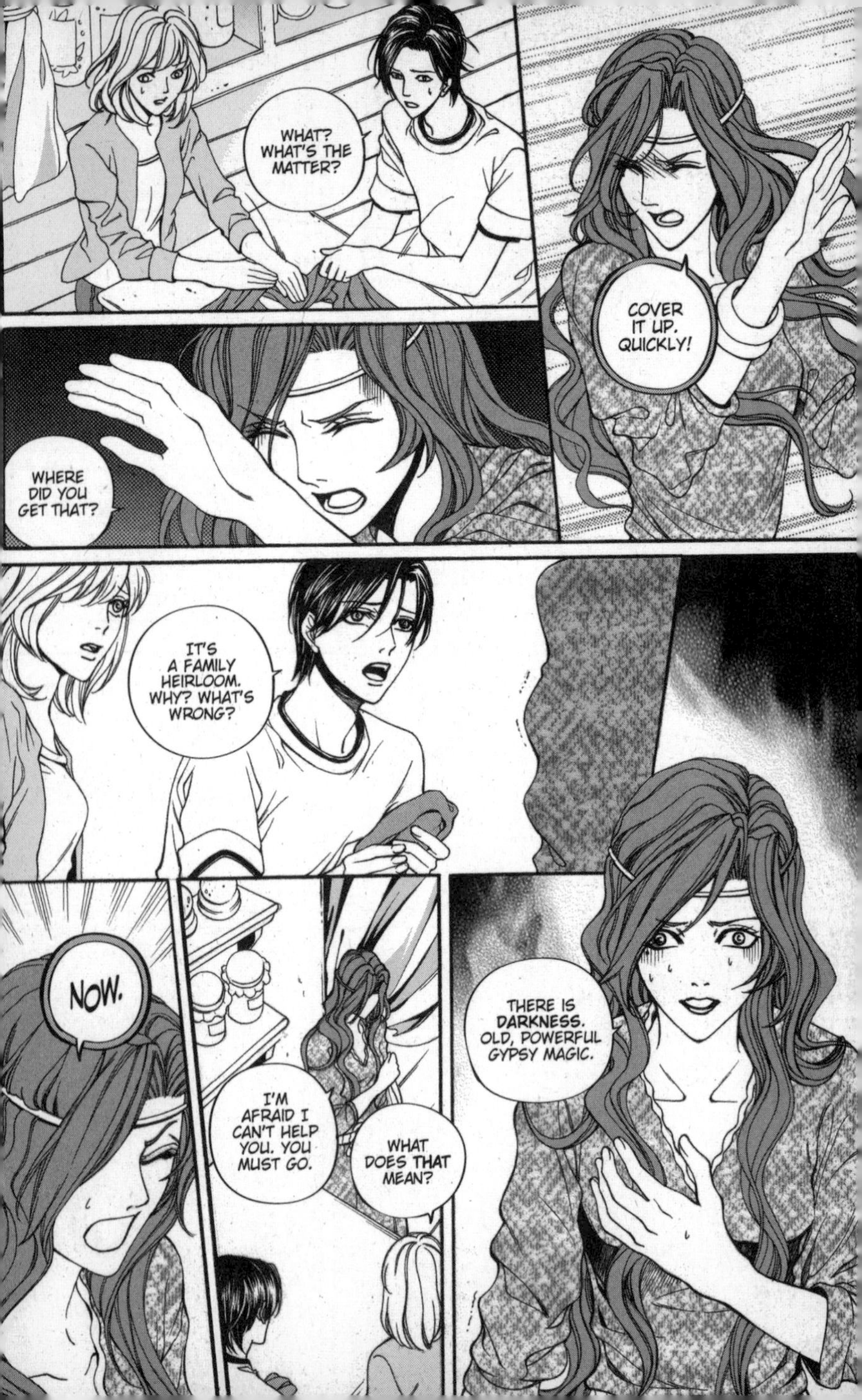
COVER IT UP. QUICKLY!
WHAT? WHAT'S THE MATTER?
WHERE DID YOU GET THAT?
THERE IS DARKNESS. OLD, POWERFUL GYPSY MAGIC.
IT'S A FAMILY HEIRLOOM. WHY? WHAT'S WRONG?
I'M AFRAID I CAN'T HELP YOU. YOU MUST GO.
WHAT DOES THAT MEAN?
NOW.

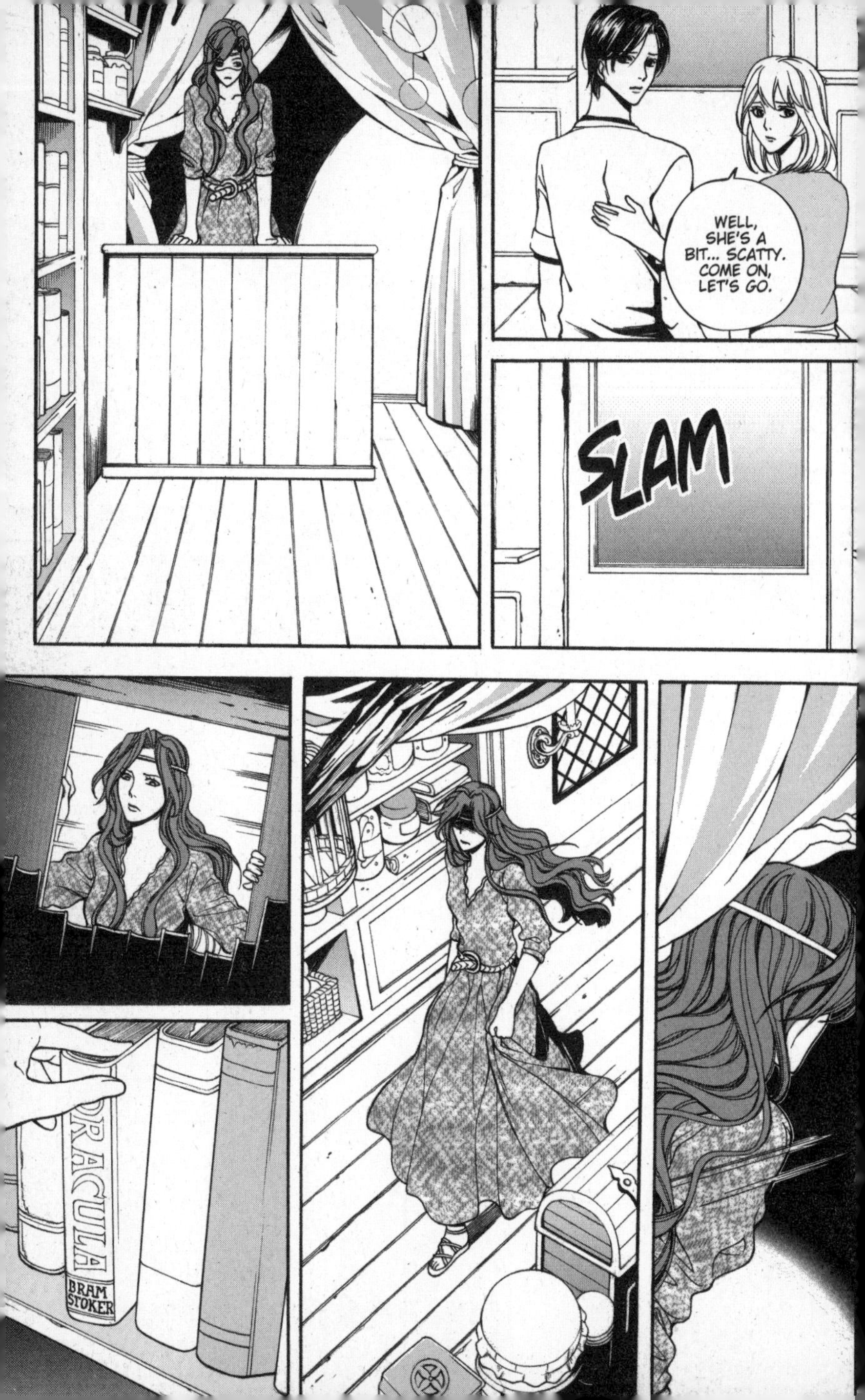
WELL, SHE'S A BIT... SCATTY. COME ON, LET'S GO.
SLAM
DRACULA
BRAM STOKER

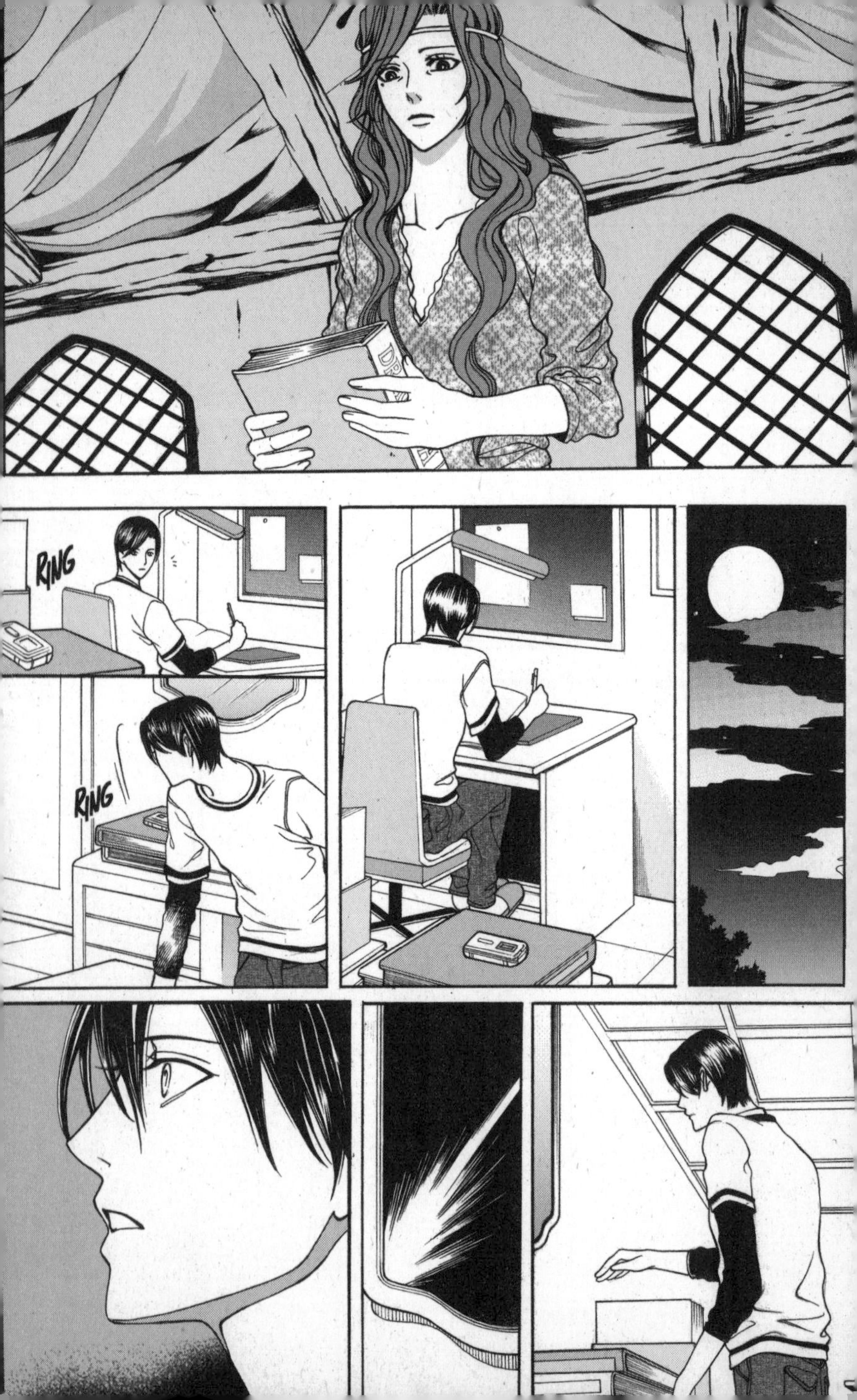
RING
RING

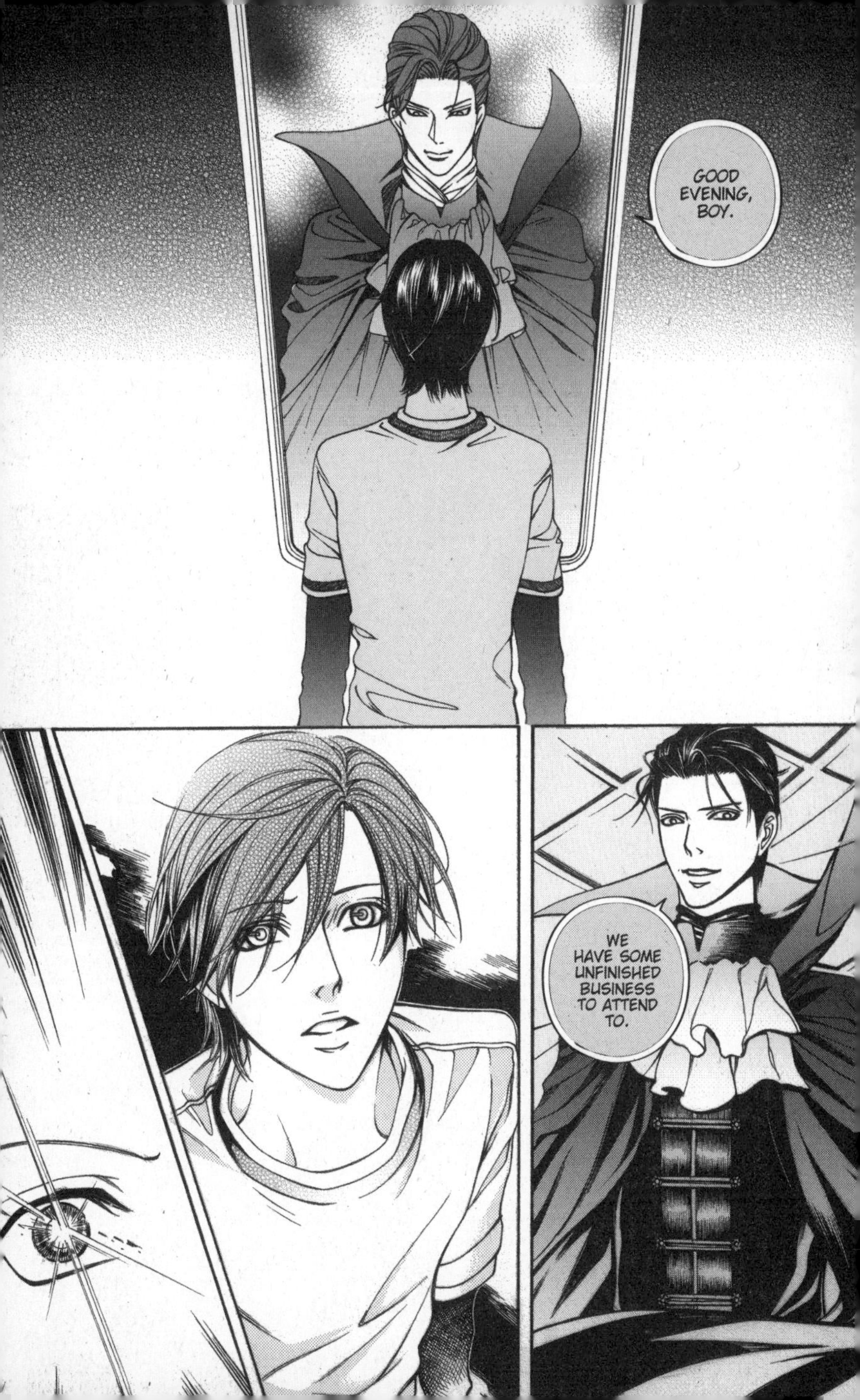
GOOD EVENING, BOY.
WE HAVE SOME UNFINISHED BUSINESS TO ATTEND TO.

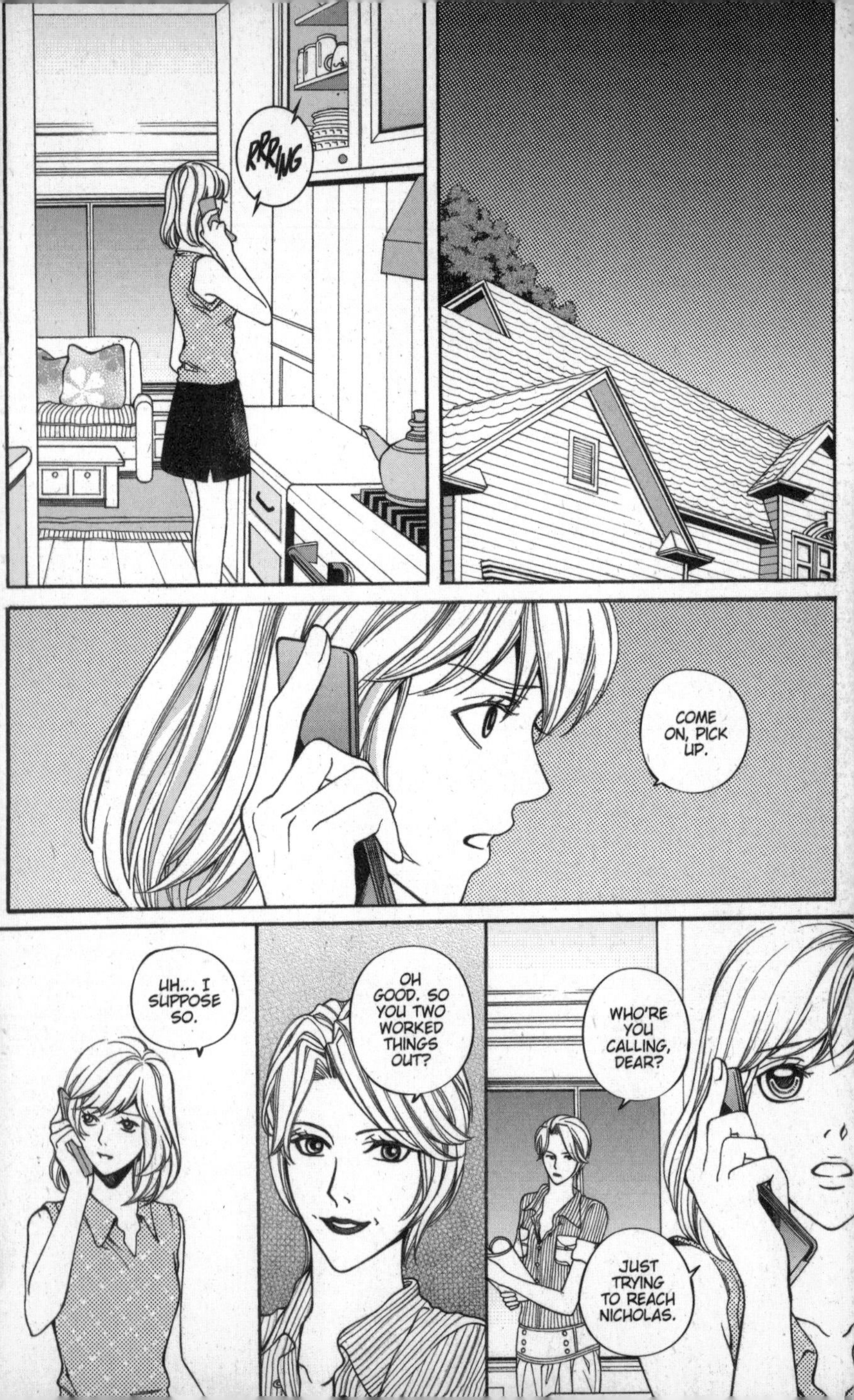
RRRING
COME ON, PICK UP.
WHO'RE YOU CALLING, DEAR?
JUST TRYING TO REACH NICHOLAS.
OH GOOD. SO YOU TWO WORKED THINGS OUT?
UH... I SUPPOSE SO.

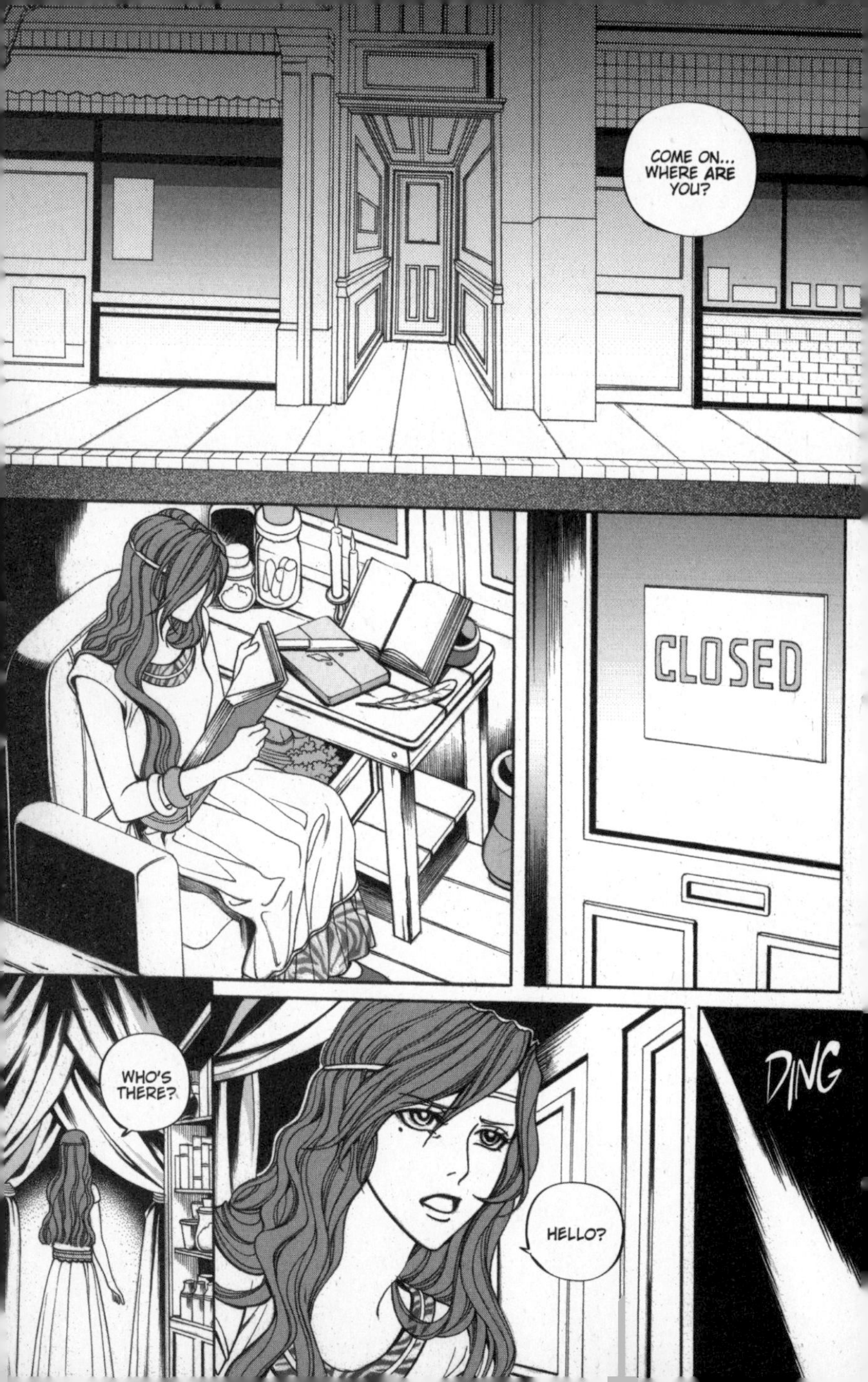
COME ON... WHERE ARE YOU?
CLOSED
DING
HELLO?
WHO'S THERE?

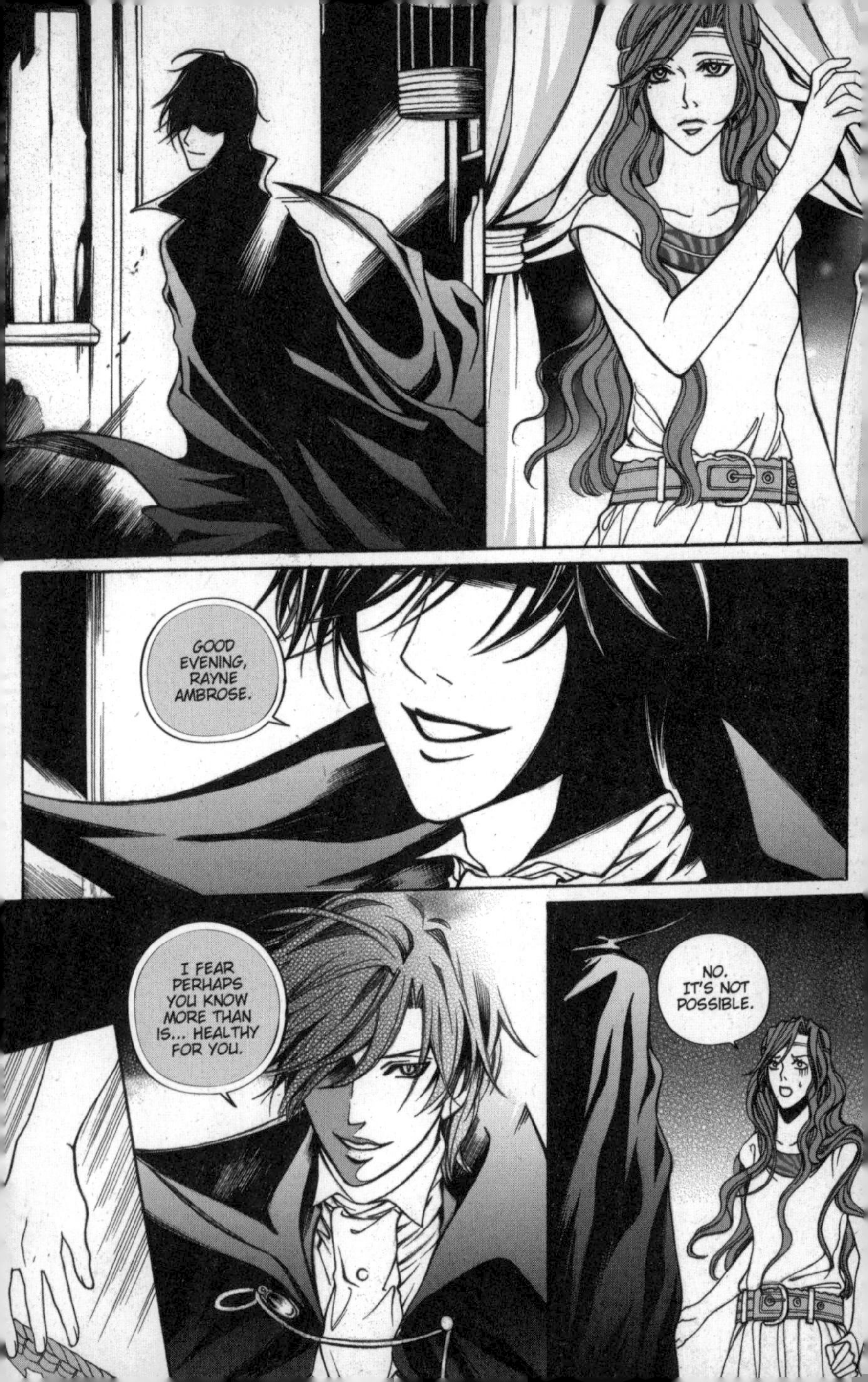
GOOD EVENING, RAYNE AMBROSE.
NO. IT'S NOT POSSIBLE.
I FEAR PERHAPS YOU KNOW MORE THAN IS... HEALTHY FOR YOU.

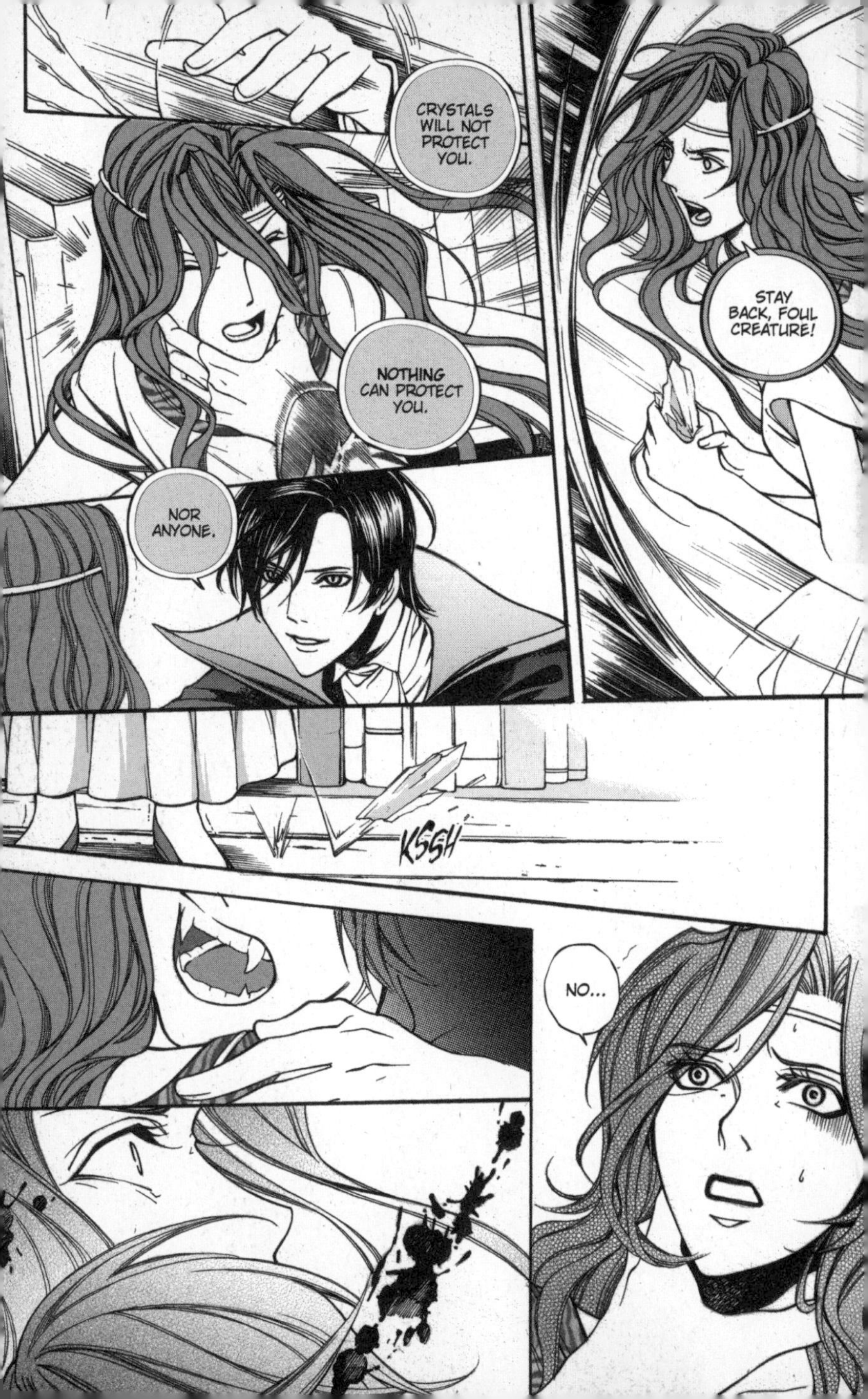
STAY BACK, FOUL CREATURE!
CRYSTALS WILL NOT PROTECT YOU.
NOTHING CAN PROTECT YOU.
NOR ANYONE.
KSSH
NO...

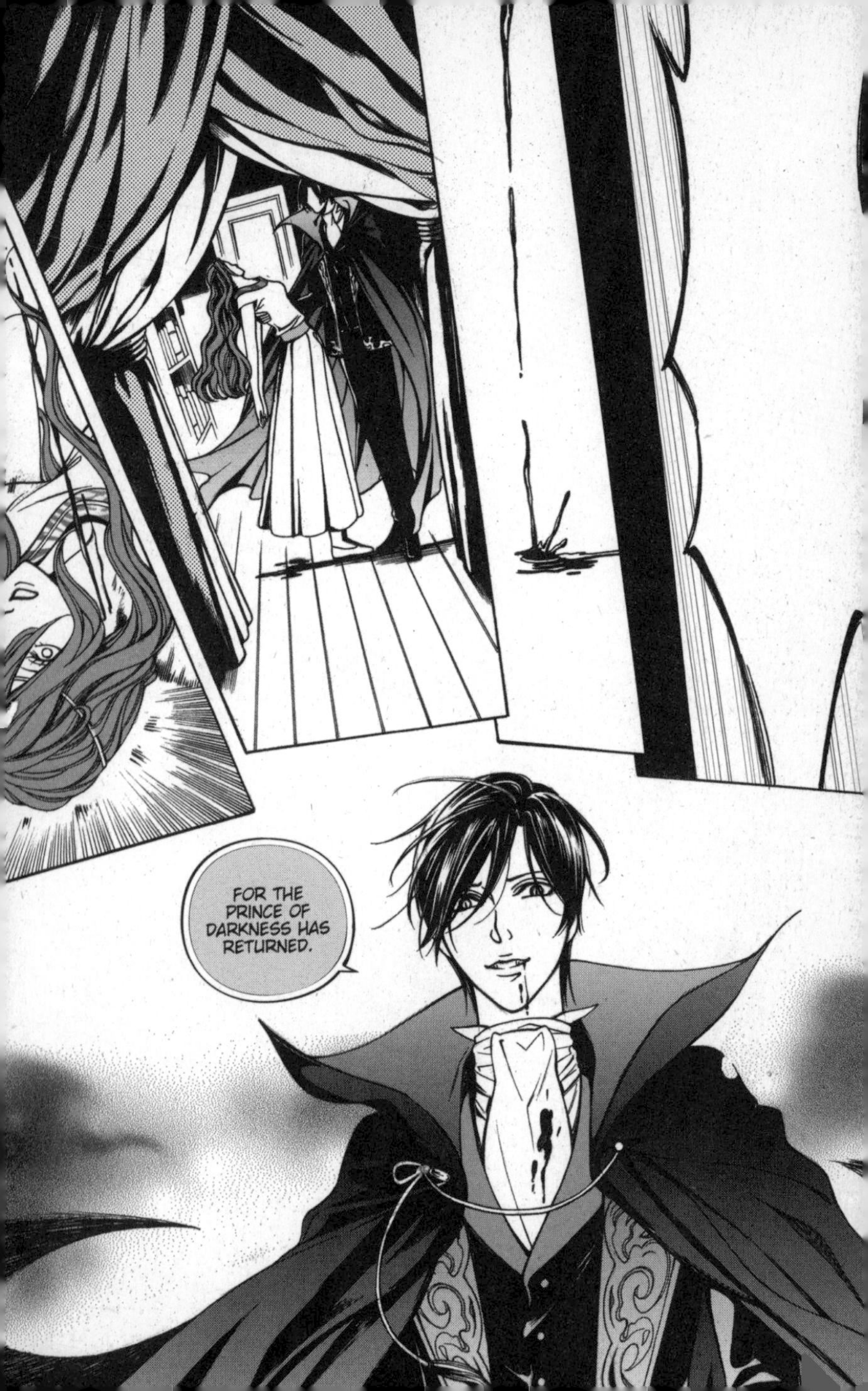
FOR THE PRINCE OF DARKNESS HAS RETURNED.

CHAPTER
3

Dracula

EVERLASTING

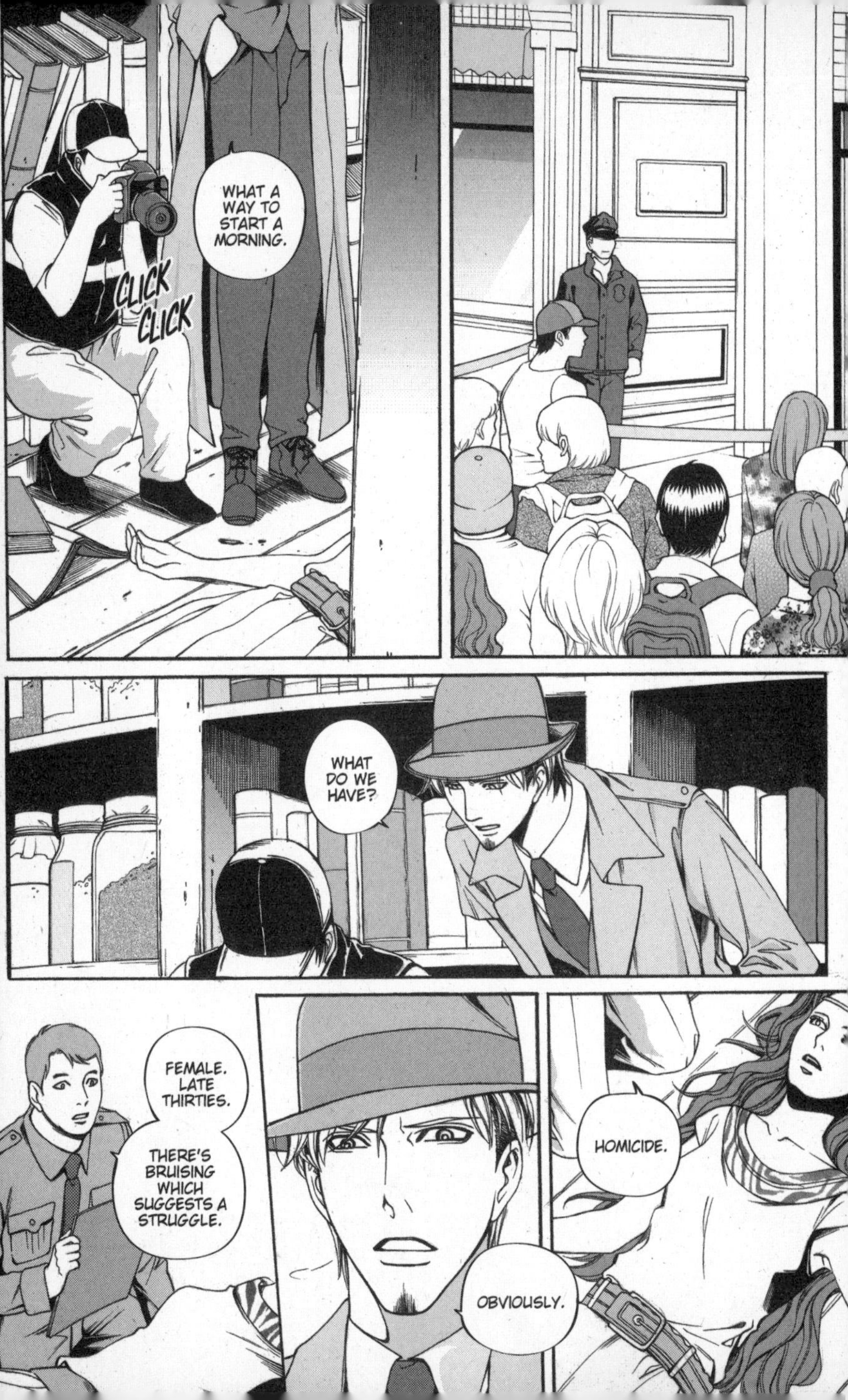
WHAT A WAY TO START A MORNING.
CLICK CLICK
WHAT DO WE HAVE?
HOMICIDE.
OBVIOUSLY.
FEMALE. LATE THIRTIES.
THERE'S BRUISING WHICH SUGGESTS A STRUGGLE.

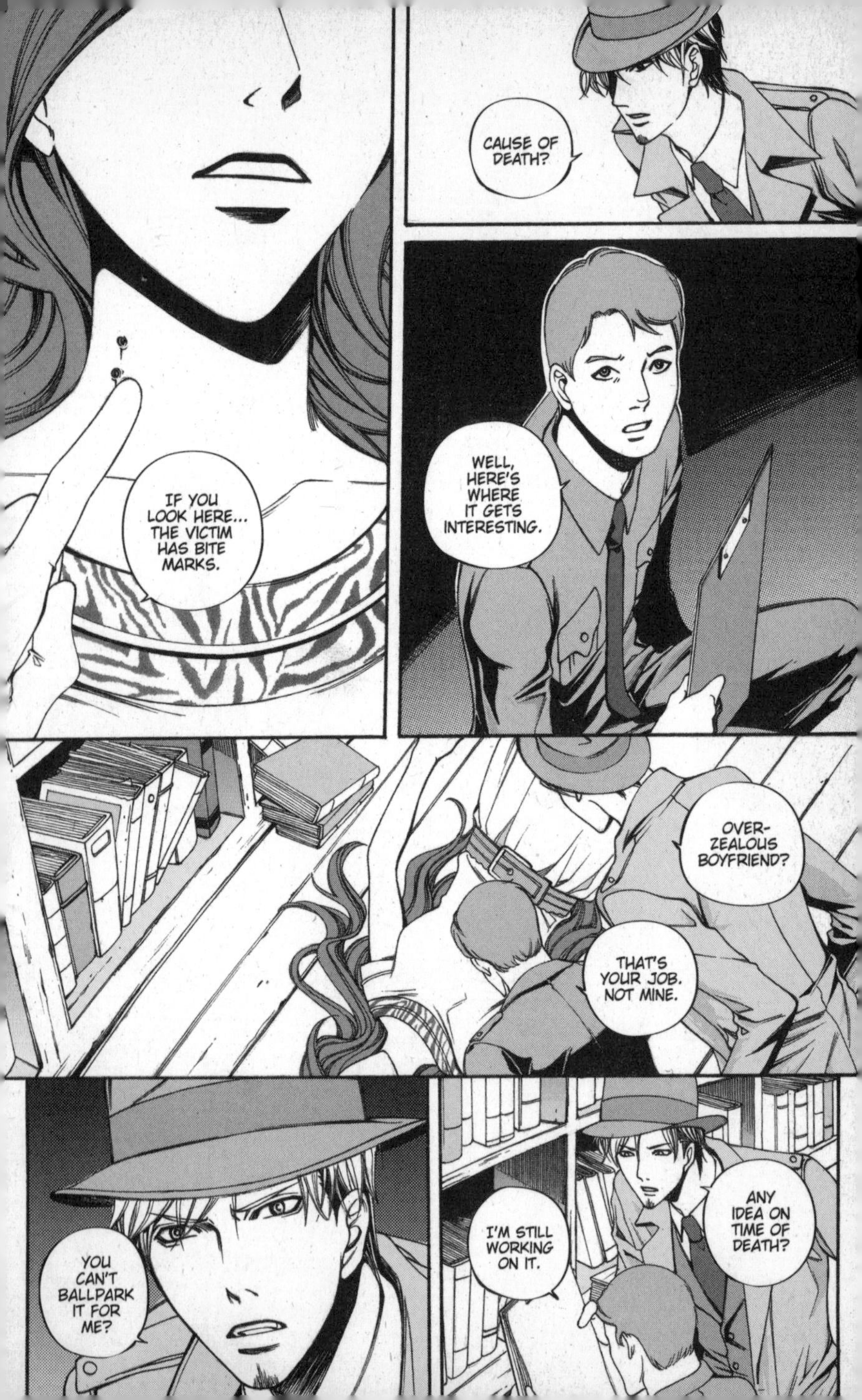
CAUSE OF DEATH?
WELL, HERE'S WHERE IT GETS INTERESTING.
IF YOU LOOK HERE... THE VICTIM HAS BITE MARKS.
OVER-ZEALOUS BOYFRIEND?
THAT'S YOUR JOB. NOT MINE.
ANY IDEA ON TIME OF DEATH?
I'M STILL WORKING ON IT.
YOU CAN'T BALLPARK IT FOR ME?

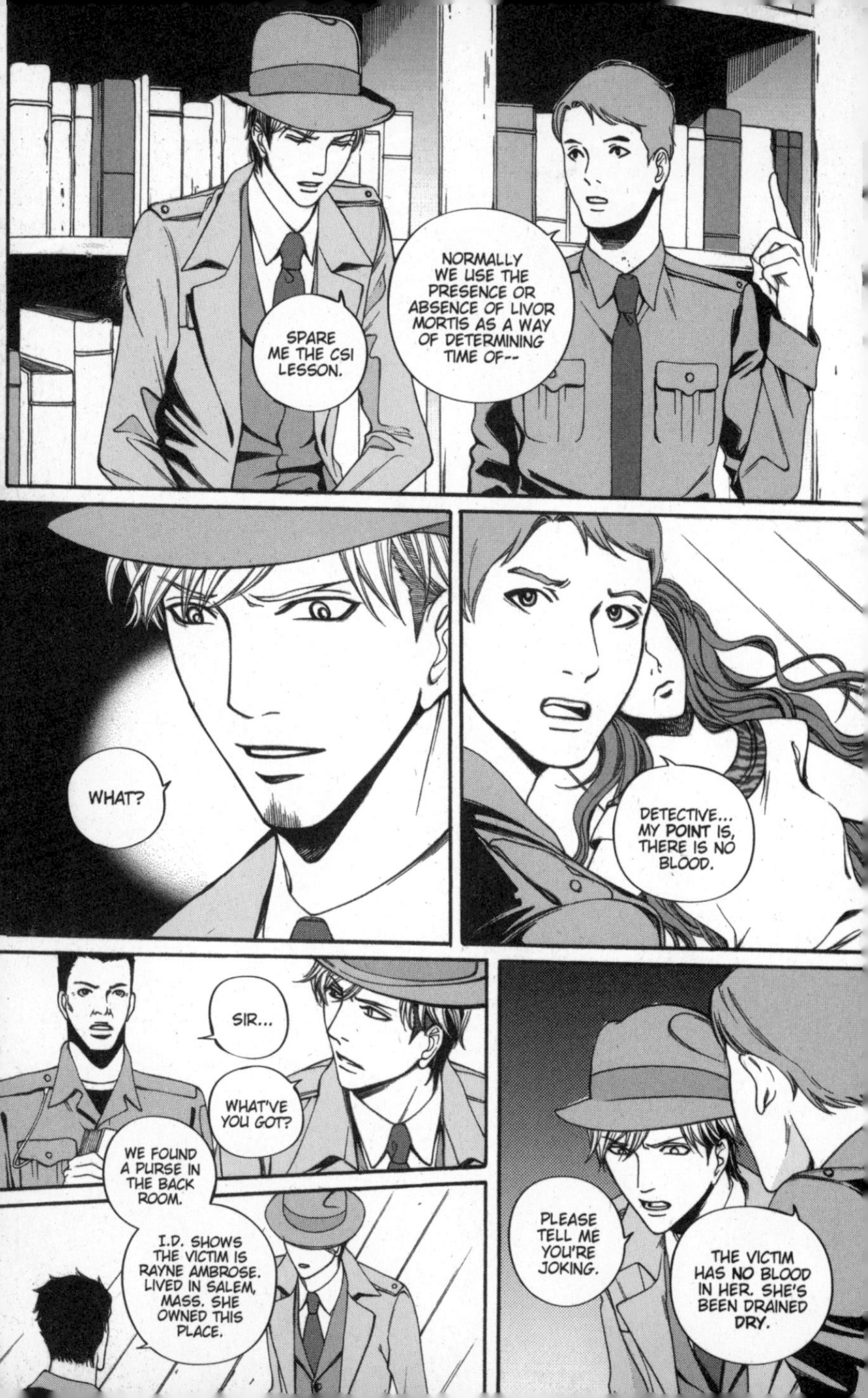
NORMALLY WE USE THE PRESENCE OR ABSENCE OF LIVOR MORTIS AS A WAY OF DETERMINING TIME OF--
SPARE ME THE CSI LESSON.
DETECTIVE... MY POINT IS, THERE IS NO BLOOD.
WHAT?
PLEASE TELL ME YOU'RE JOKING.
THE VICTIM HAS NO BLOOD IN HER. SHE'S BEEN DRAINED DRY.
SIR...
WHAT'VE YOU GOT?
WE FOUND A PURSE IN THE BACK ROOM.
I.D. SHOWS THE VICTIM IS RAYNE AMBROSE. LIVED IN SALEM, MASS. SHE OWNED THIS PLACE.

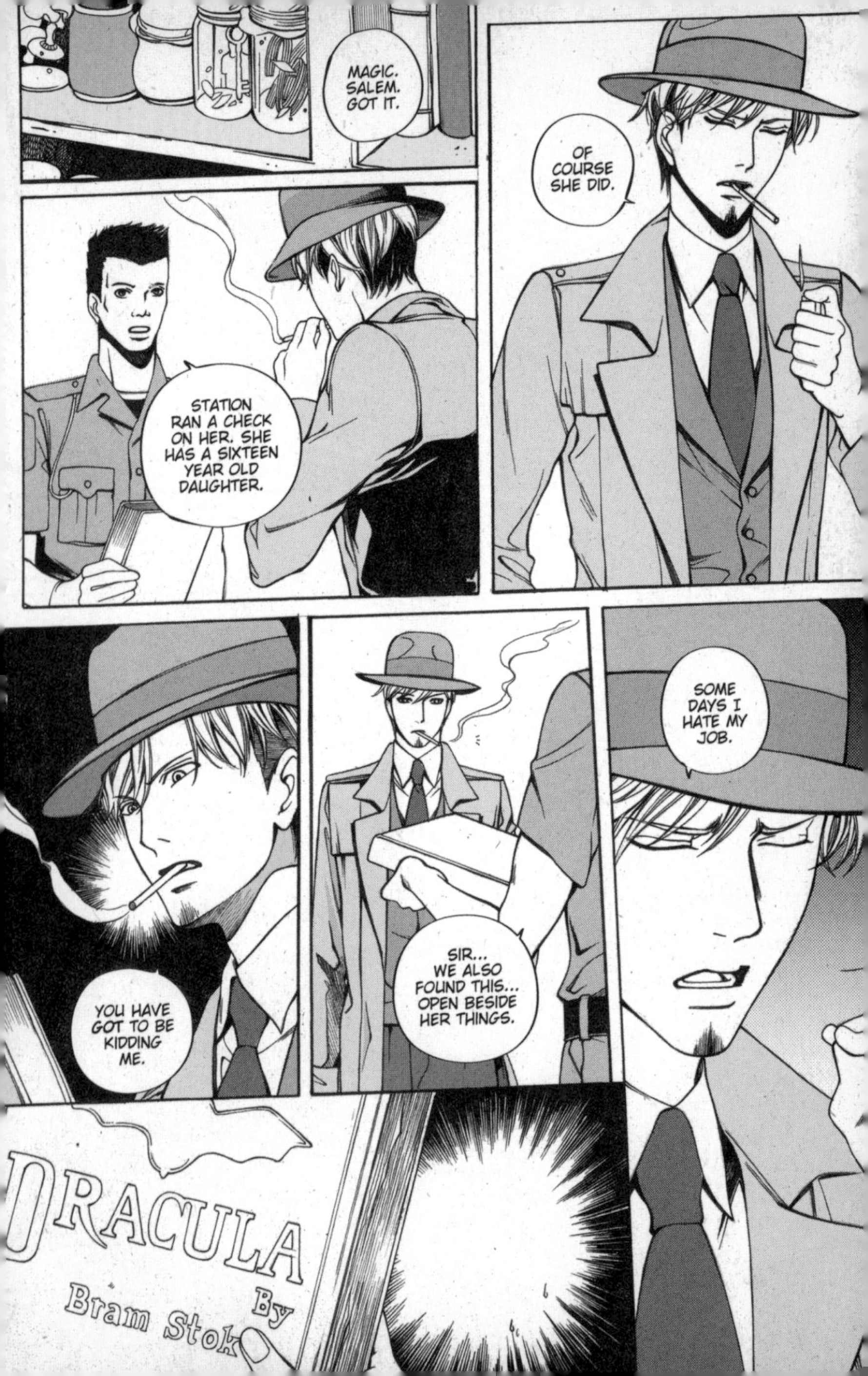
MAGIC. SALEM. GOT IT.
STATION RAN A CHECK ON HER. SHE HAS A SIXTEEN YEAR OLD DAUGHTER.
OF COURSE SHE DID.
YOU HAVE GOT TO BE KIDDING ME.
SIR... WE ALSO FOUND THIS... OPEN BESIDE HER THINGS.
SOME DAYS I HATE MY JOB.
DRACULA
By
Bram Stok

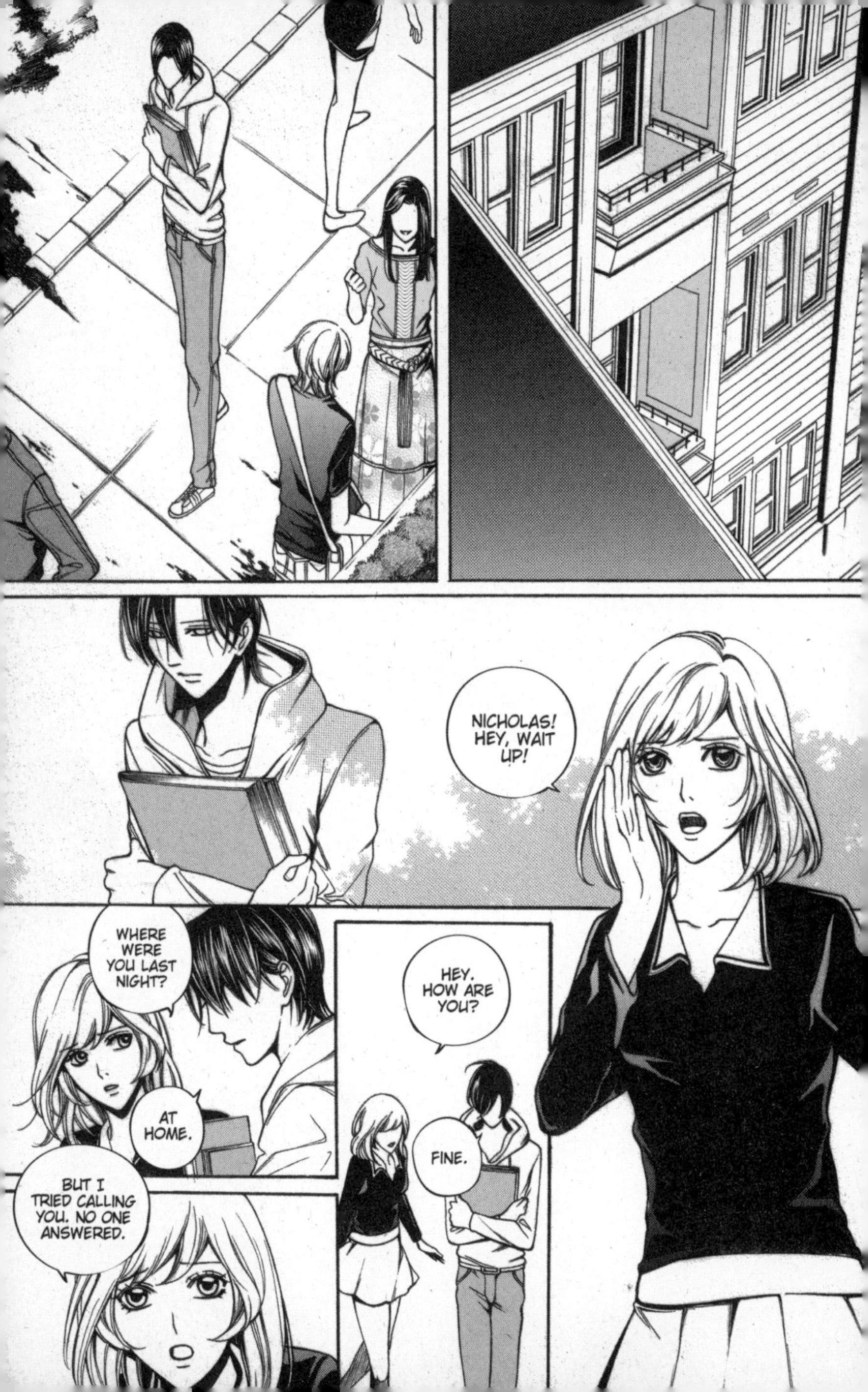
NICHOLAS! HEY, WAIT UP!
HEY. HOW ARE YOU?
FINE.
WHERE WERE YOU LAST NIGHT?
AT HOME.
BUT I TRIED CALLING YOU. NO ONE ANSWERED.

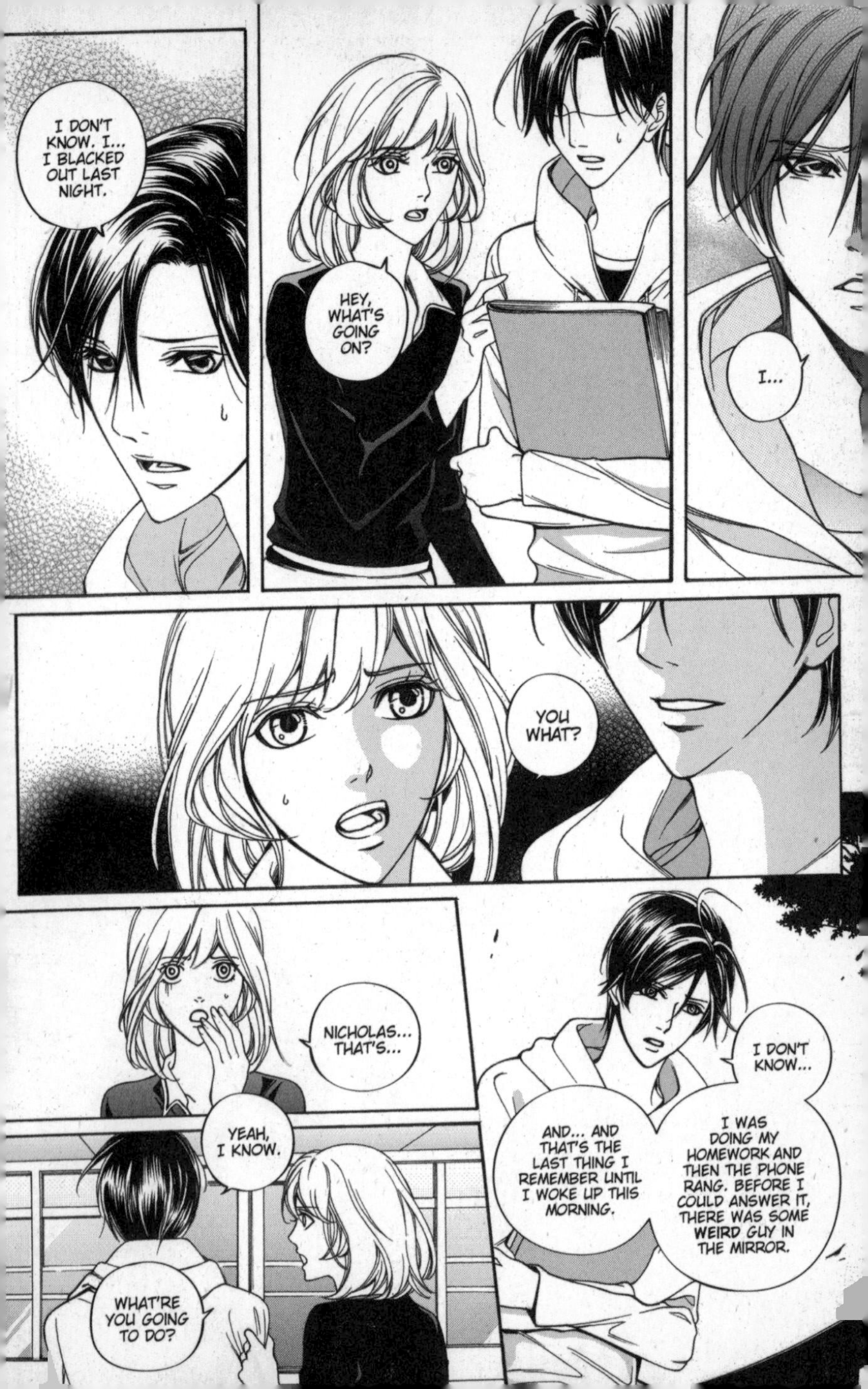
I...
HEY, WHAT'S GOING ON?
I DON'T KNOW. I... I BLACKED OUT LAST NIGHT.
YOU WHAT?
I DON'T KNOW...
I WAS DOING MY HOMEWORK AND THEN THE PHONE RANG. BEFORE I COULD ANSWER IT, THERE WAS SOME WEIRD GUY IN THE MIRROR.
AND... AND THAT'S THE LAST THING I REMEMBER UNTIL I WOKE UP THIS MORNING.
NICHOLAS... THAT'S...
YEAH, I KNOW.
WHAT'RE YOU GOING TO DO?

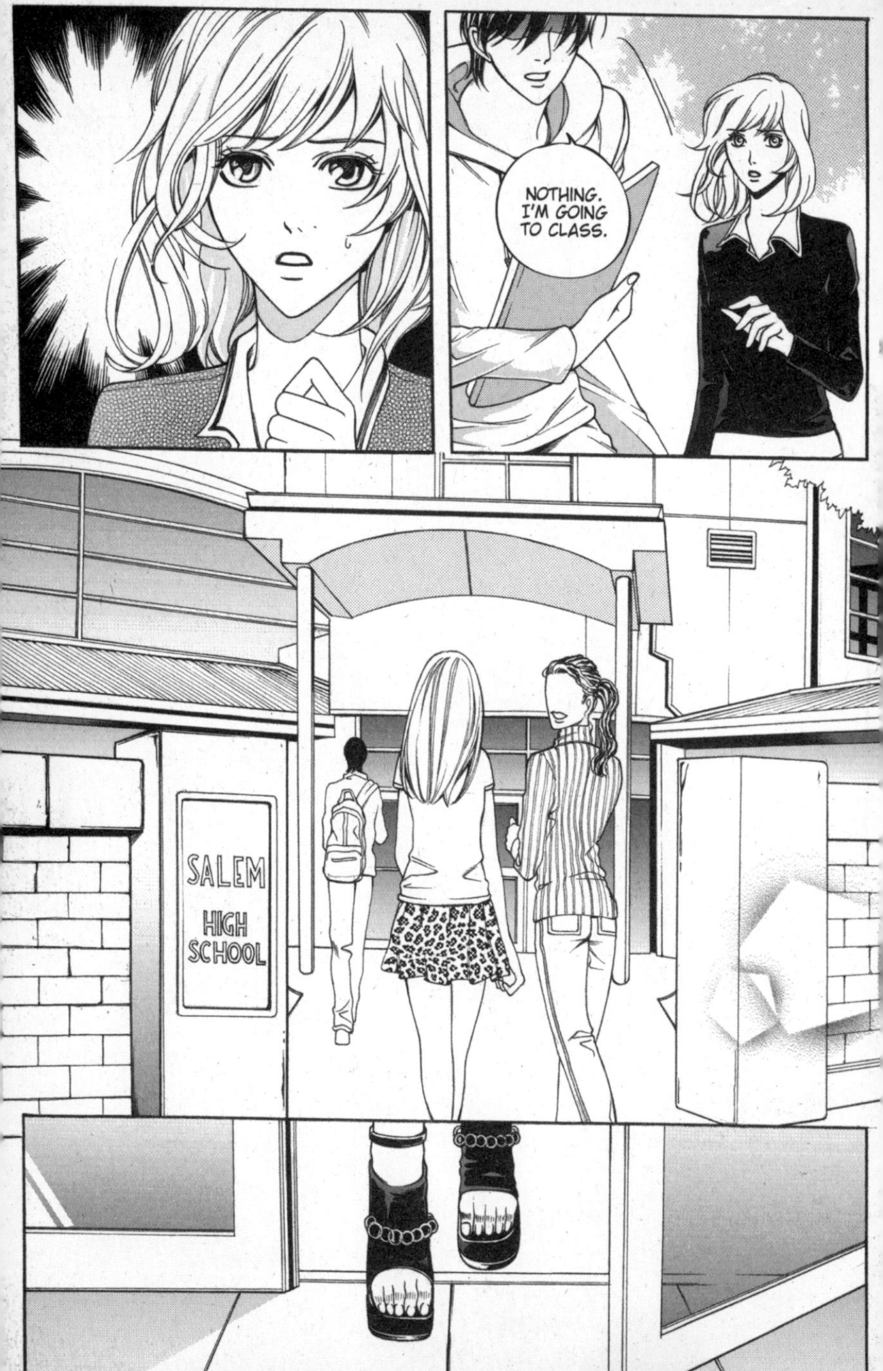
NOTHING. I'M GOING TO CLASS.
SALEM HIGH SCHOOL

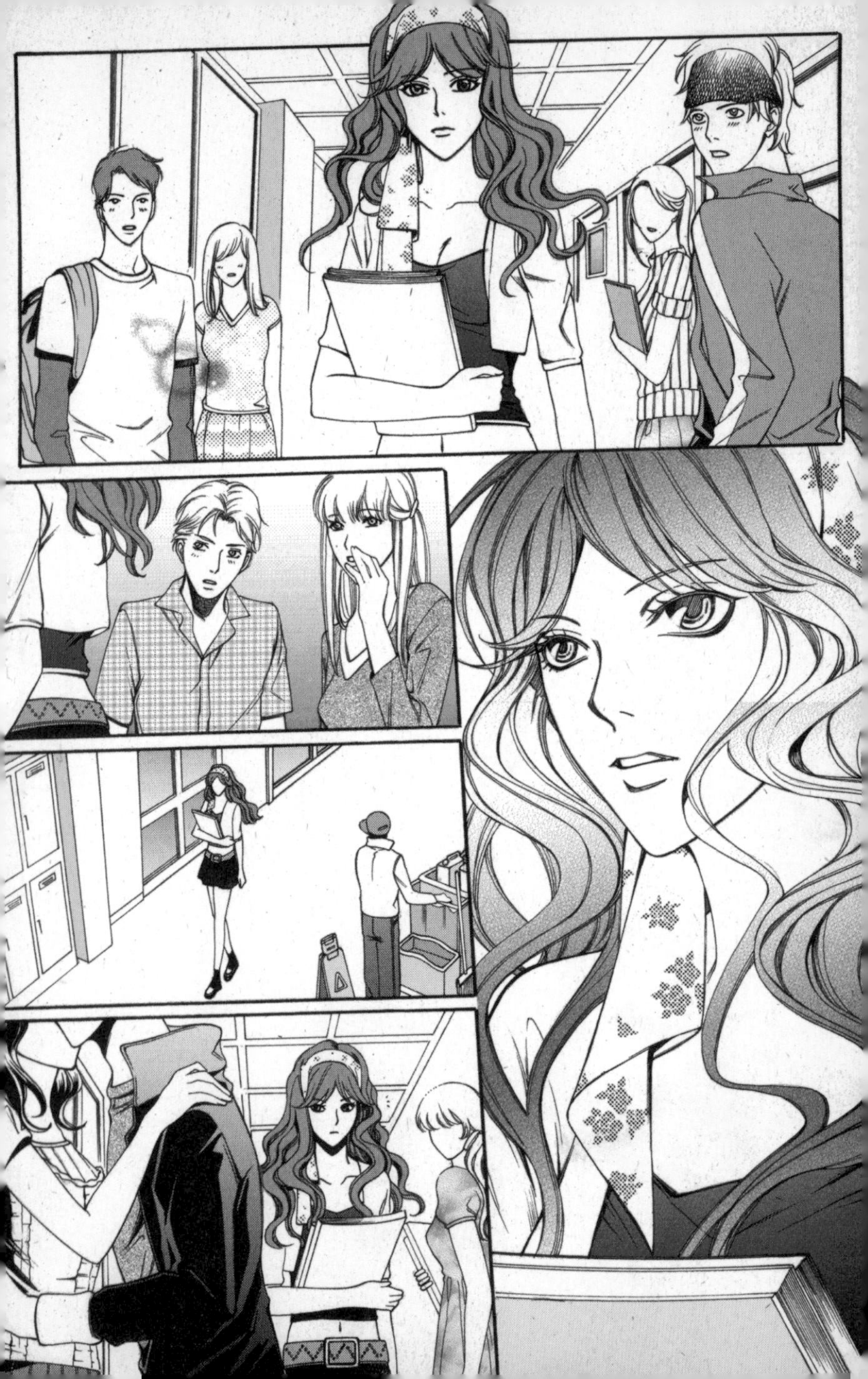

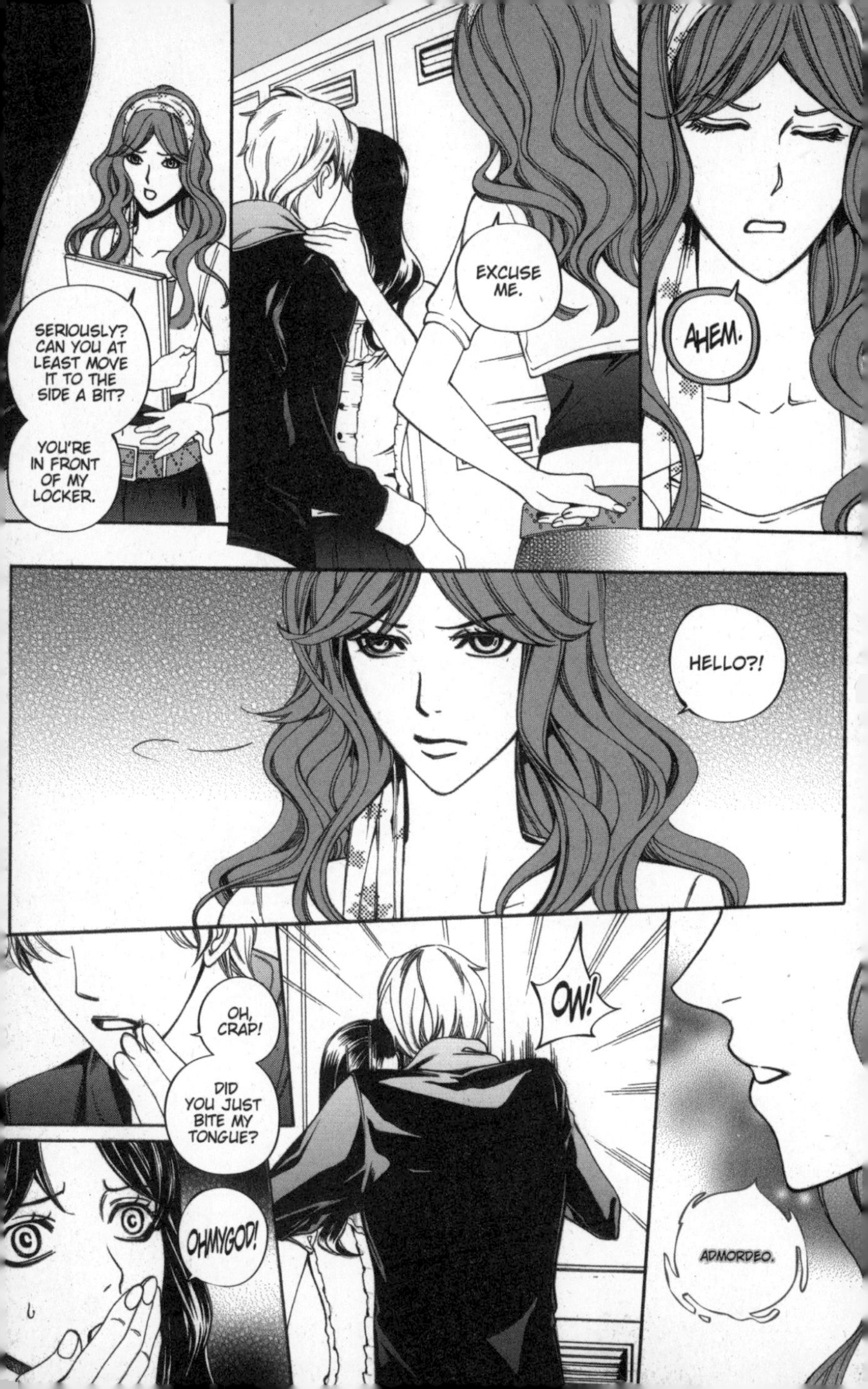
AHEM.
EXCUSE ME.
SERIOUSLY? CAN YOU AT LEAST MOVE IT TO THE SIDE A BIT?
YOU'RE IN FRONT OF MY LOCKER.
HELLO?!
ADMORDEO.
OW!
OH, CRAP!
DID YOU JUST BITE MY TONGUE?
OHMYGOD!

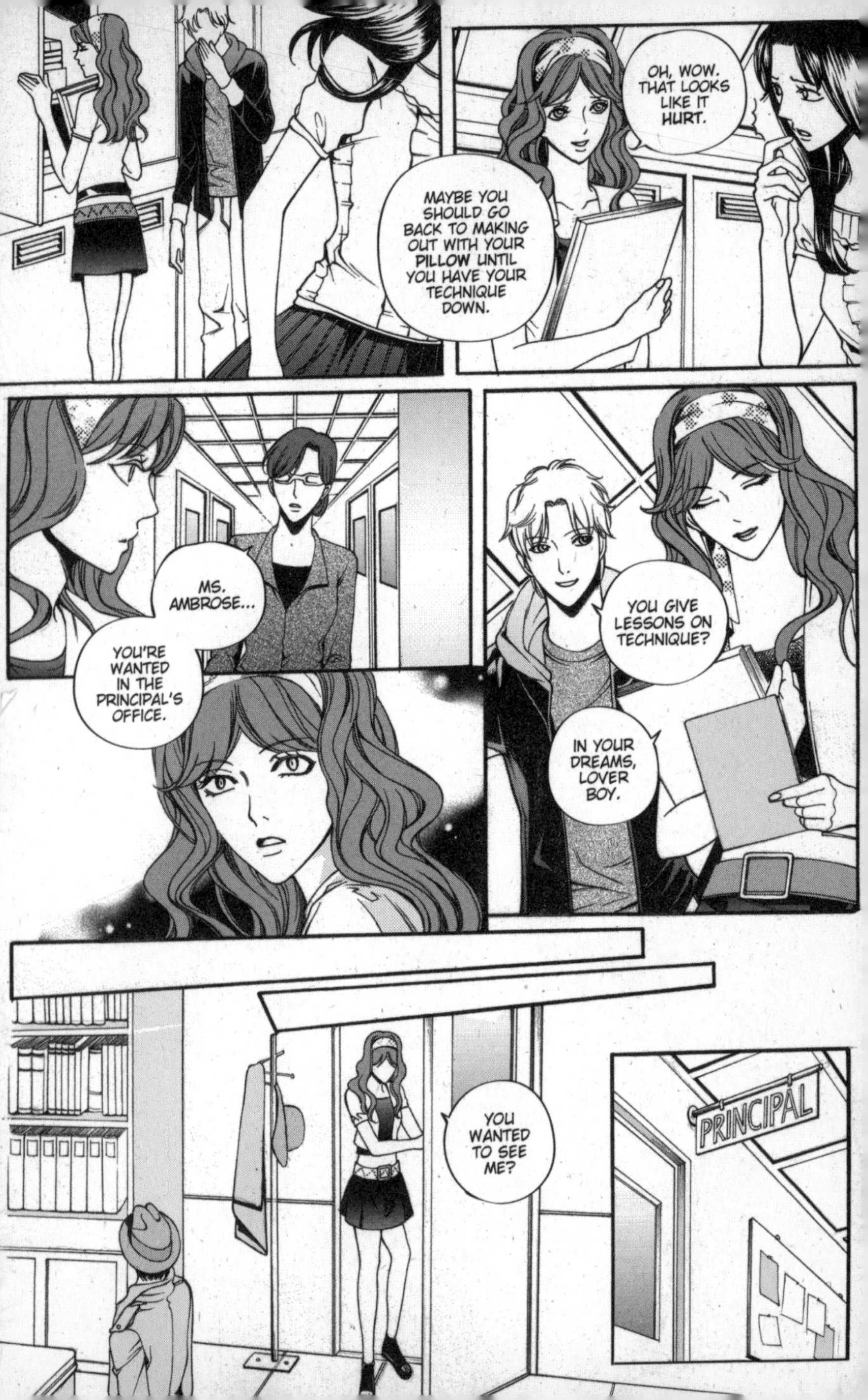
OH, WOW. THAT LOOKS LIKE IT HURT.
MAYBE YOU SHOULD GO BACK TO MAKING OUT WITH YOUR PILLOW UNTIL YOU HAVE YOUR TECHNIQUE DOWN.
YOU GIVE LESSONS ON TECHNIQUE?
IN YOUR DREAMS, LOVER BOY.
MS. AMBROSE...
YOU'RE WANTED IN THE PRINCIPAL'S OFFICE.
PRINCIPAL
YOU WANTED TO SEE ME?

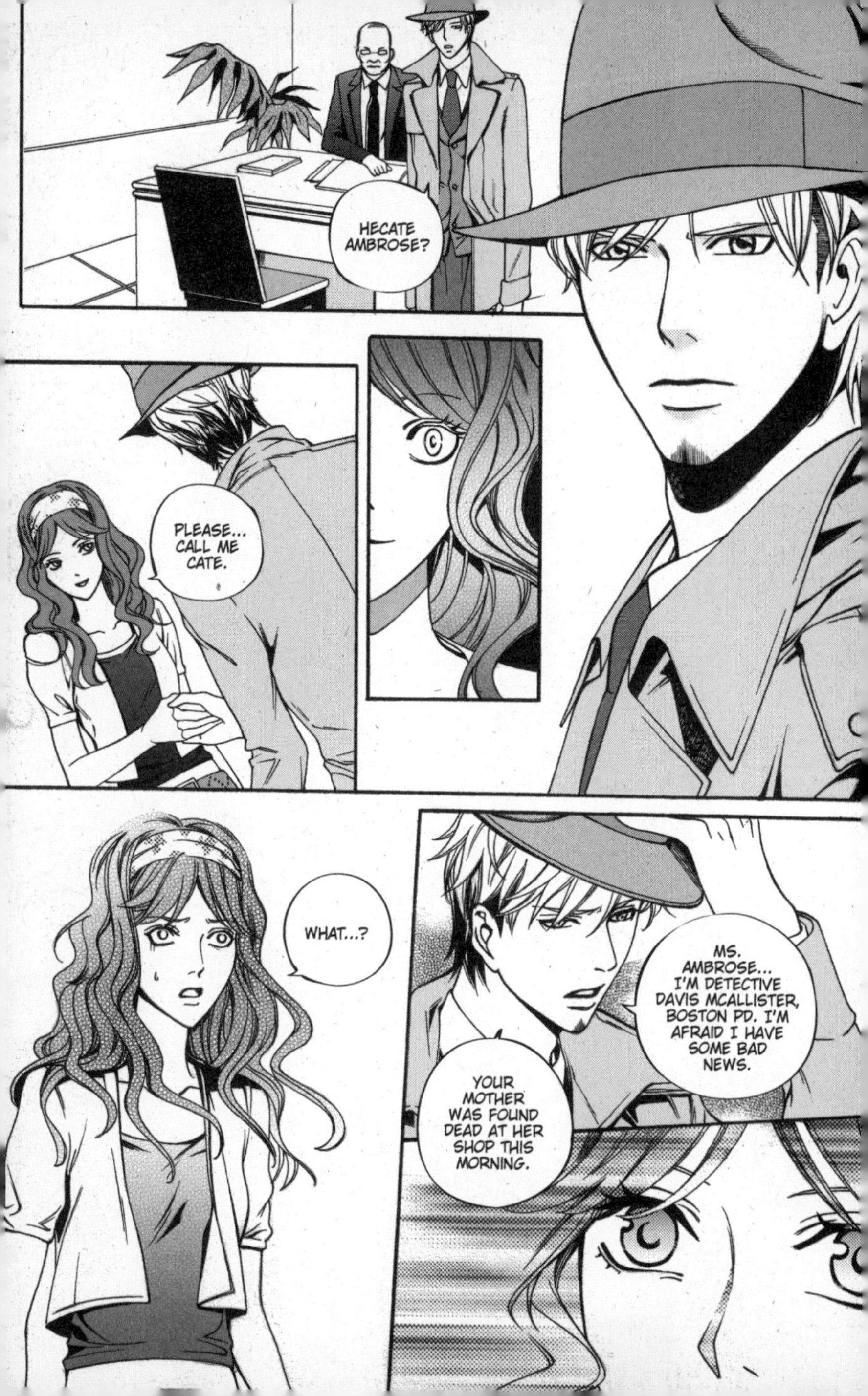

HECATE AMBROSE?
PLEASE... CALL ME CATE.
MS. AMBROSE... I'M DETECTIVE DAVIS MCALLISTER, BOSTON PD. I'M AFRAID I HAVE SOME BAD NEWS.
YOUR MOTHER WAS FOUND DEAD AT HER SHOP THIS MORNING.
WHAT...?

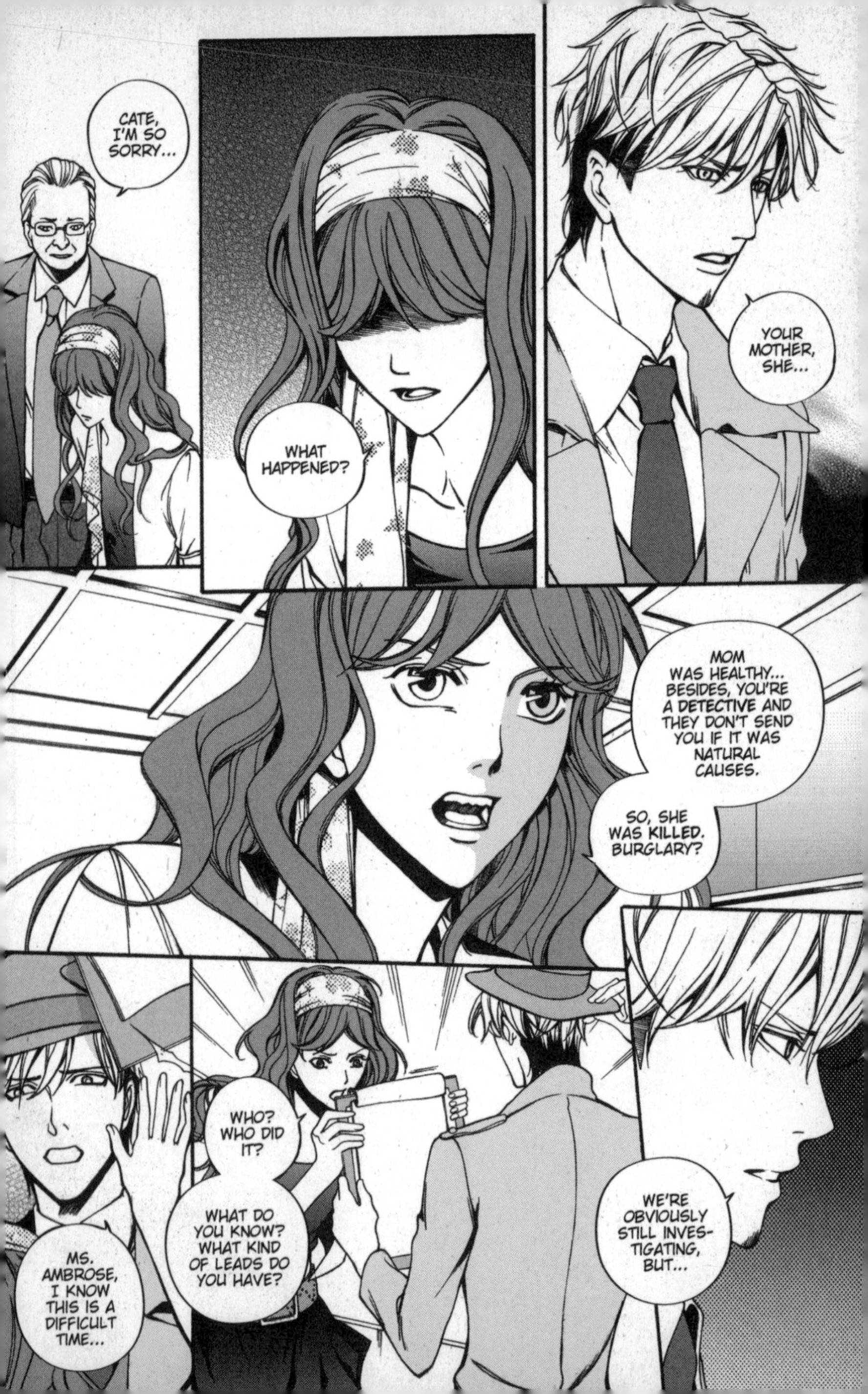
CATE, I'M SO SORRY...
WHAT HAPPENED?
YOUR MOTHER, SHE...
MOM WAS HEALTHY... BESIDES, YOU'RE A DETECTIVE AND THEY DON'T SEND YOU IF IT WAS NATURAL CAUSES.
SO, SHE WAS KILLED. BURGLARY?
MS. AMBROSE, I KNOW THIS IS A DIFFICULT TIME...
WHO? WHO DID IT?
WHAT DO YOU KNOW? WHAT KIND OF LEADS DO YOU HAVE?
WE'RE OBVIOUSLY STILL INVES-TIGATING, BUT...

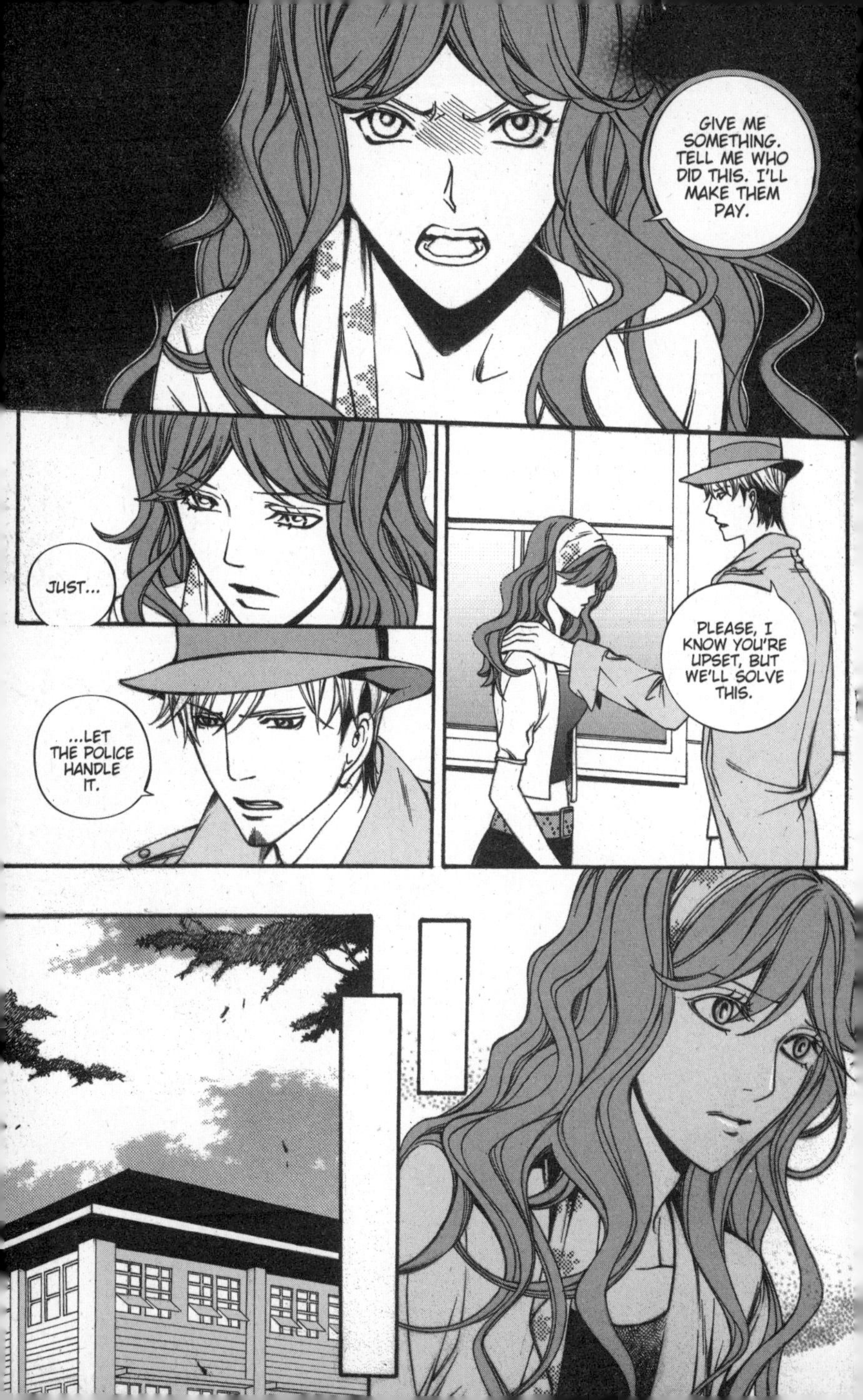

GIVE ME SOMETHING. TELL ME WHO DID THIS. I'LL MAKE THEM PAY.
PLEASE, I KNOW YOU'RE UPSET, BUT WE'LL SOLVE THIS.
JUST...
...LET THE POLICE HANDLE IT.

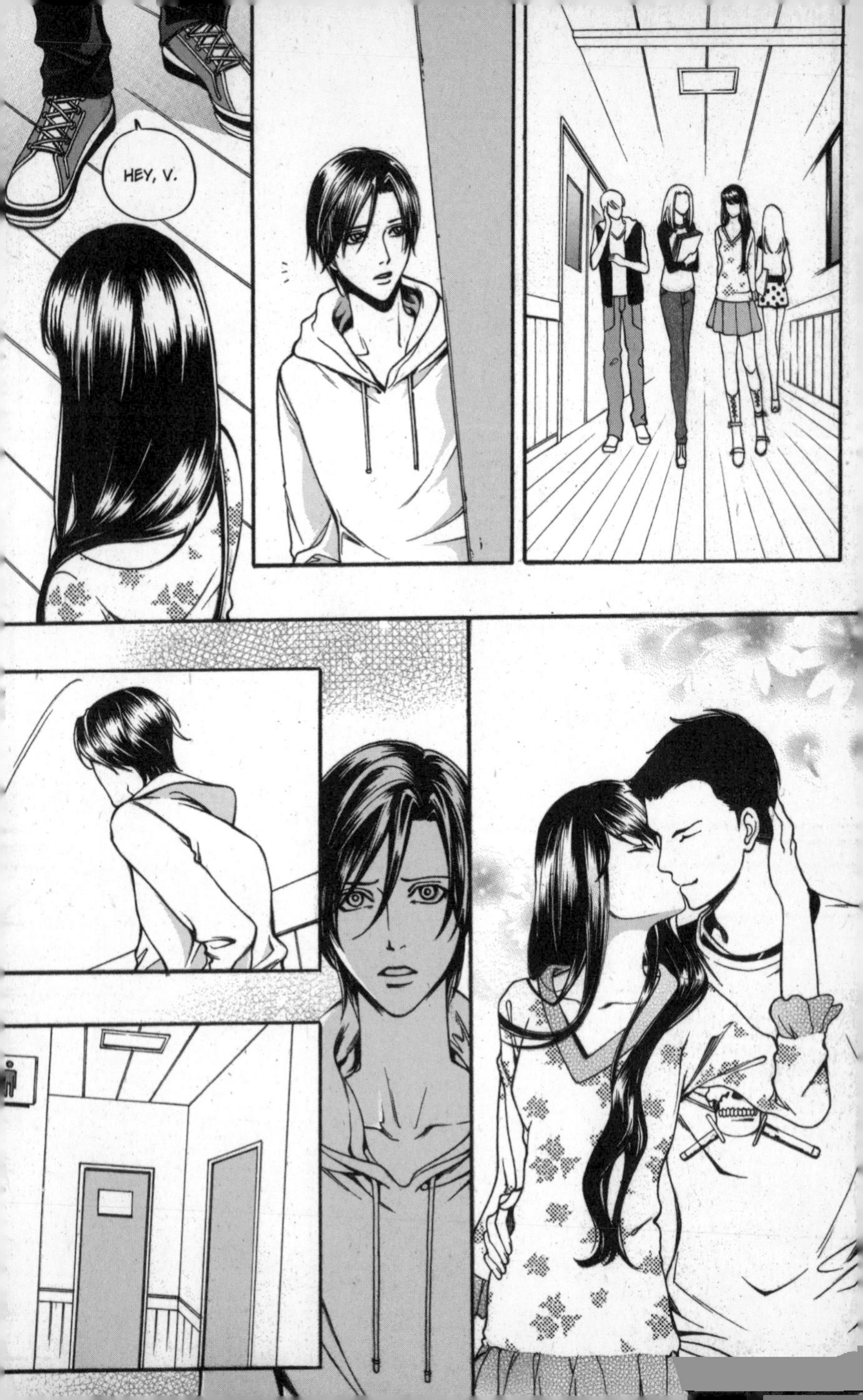
HEY, V.

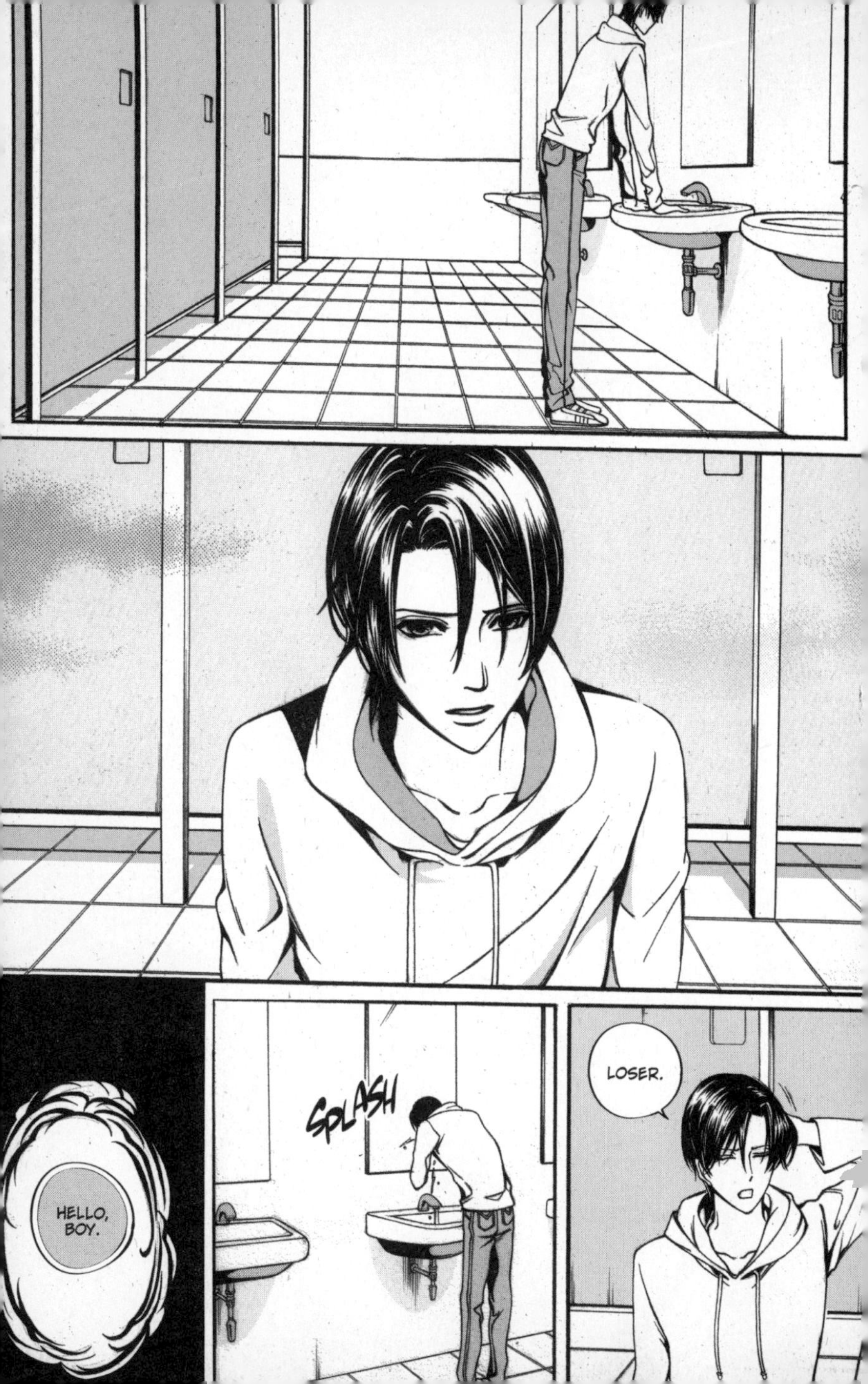
LOSER.
SPLASH
HELLO, BOY.

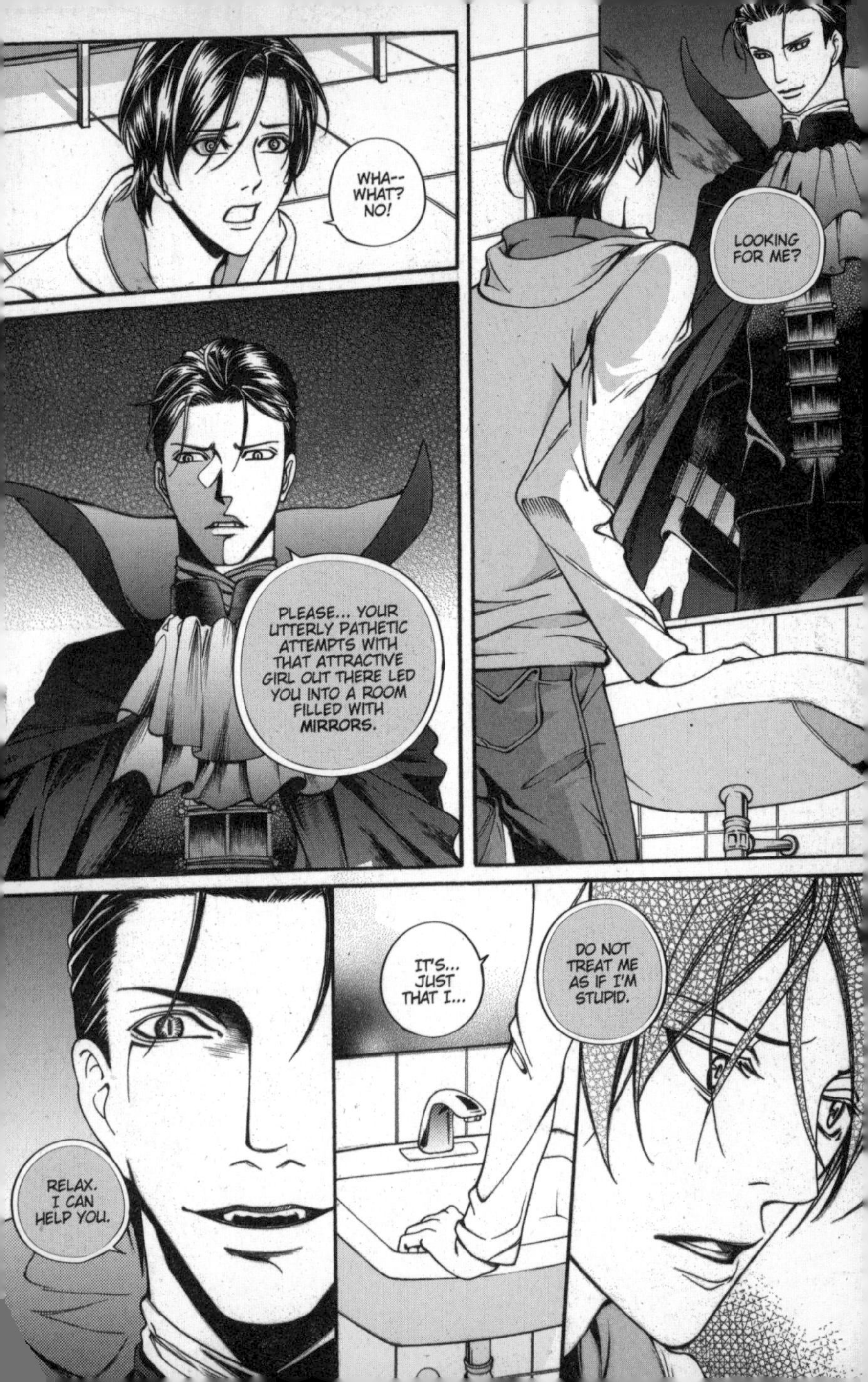
LOOKING FOR ME?
WHA-- WHAT? NO!
PLEASE... YOUR UTTERLY PATHETIC ATTEMPTS WITH THAT ATTRACTIVE GIRL OUT THERE LED YOU INTO A ROOM FILLED WITH **MIRRORS.**
DO NOT TREAT ME AS IF I'M STUPID.
IT'S... JUST THAT I...
RELAX. I CAN HELP YOU.

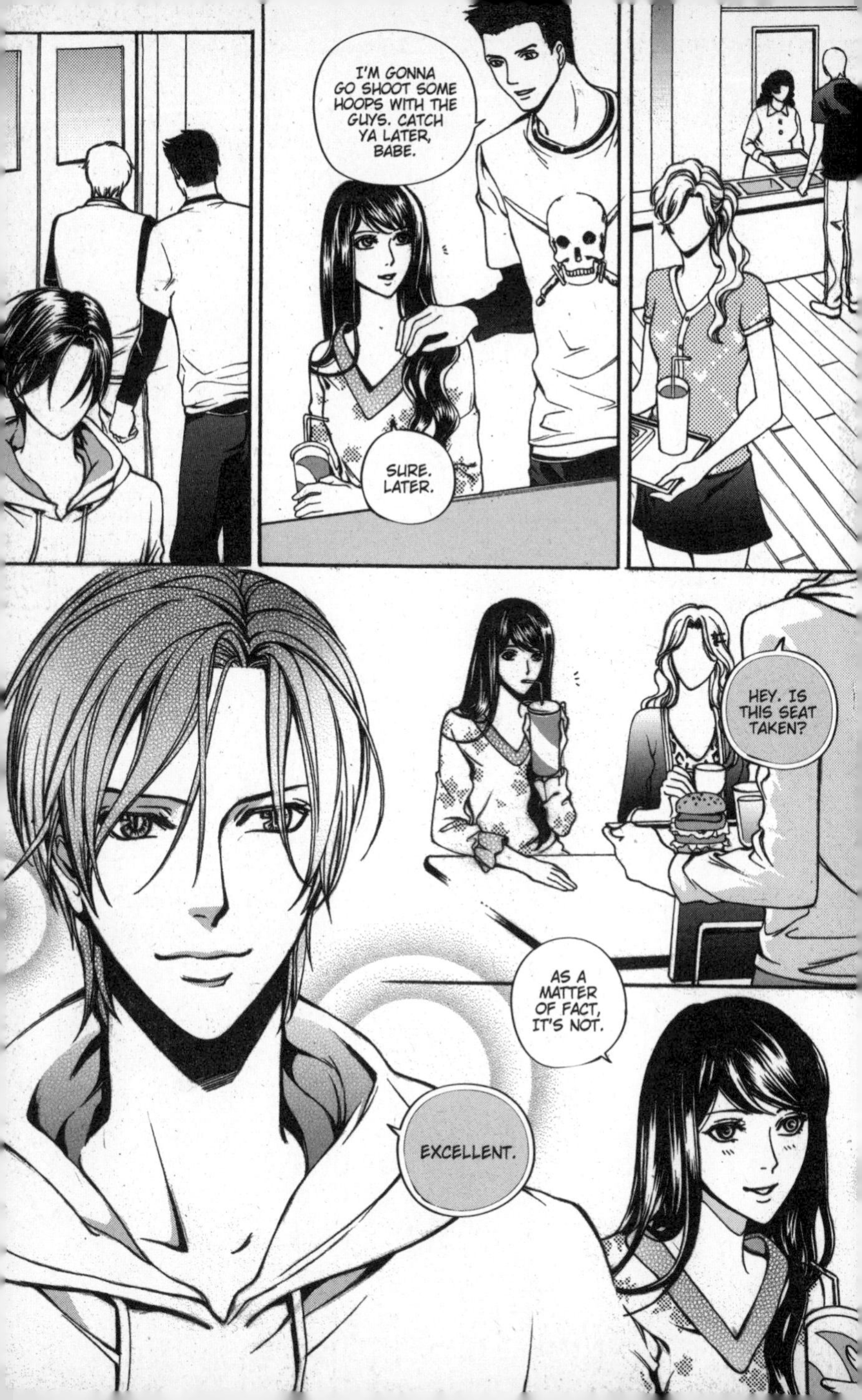
I'M GONNA GO SHOOT SOME HOOPS WITH THE GUYS. CATCH YA LATER, BABE.
SURE. LATER.
HEY. IS THIS SEAT TAKEN?
AS A MATTER OF FACT, IT'S NOT.
EXCELLENT.

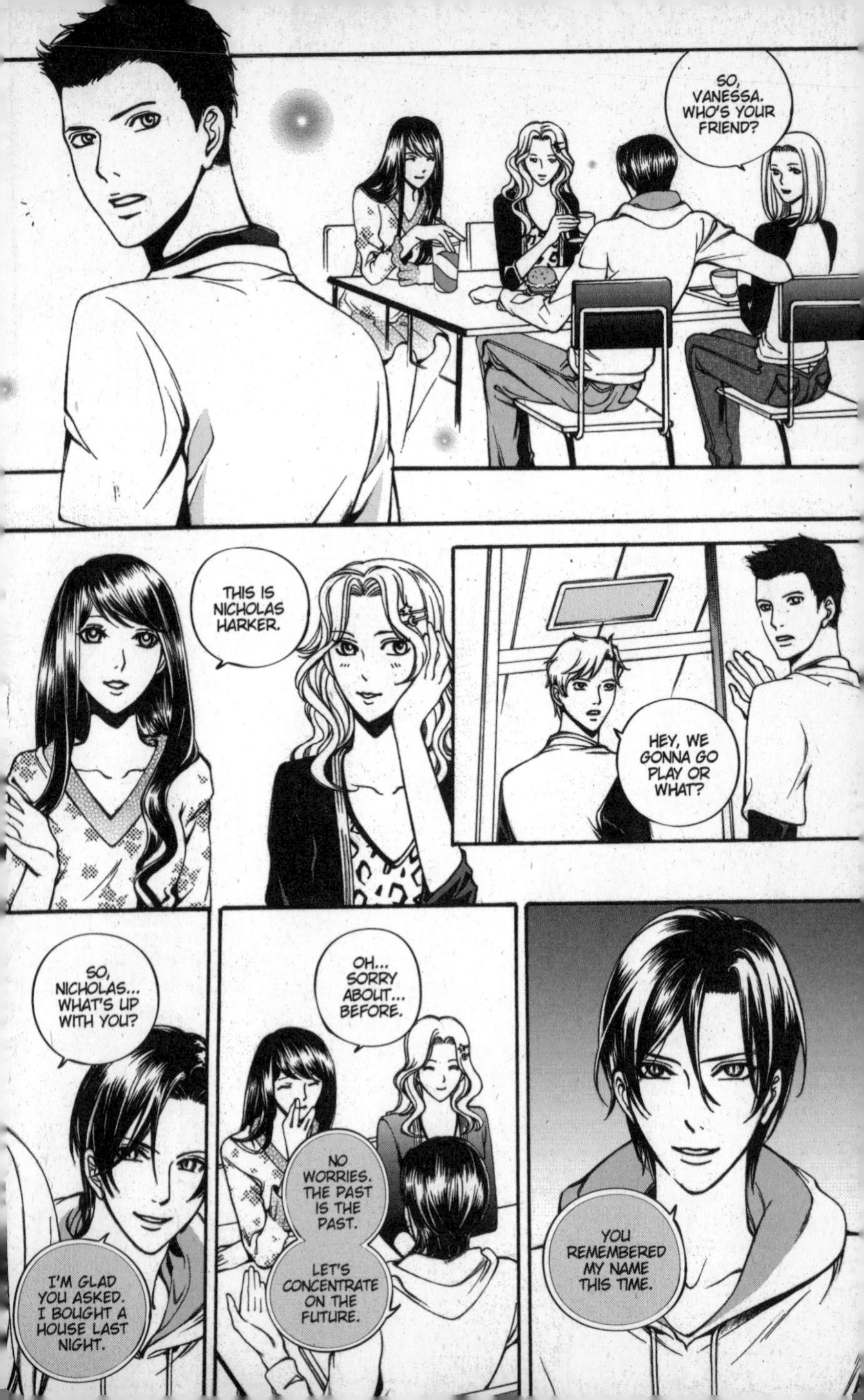
SO, VANESSA. WHO'S YOUR FRIEND?
HEY, WE GONNA GO PLAY OR WHAT?
THIS IS NICHOLAS HARKER.
YOU REMEMBERED MY NAME THIS TIME.
OH... SORRY ABOUT... BEFORE.
NO WORRIES. THE PAST IS THE PAST.
LET'S CONCENTRATE ON THE FUTURE.
SO, NICHOLAS... WHAT'S UP WITH YOU?
I'M GLAD YOU ASKED. I BOUGHT A HOUSE LAST NIGHT.

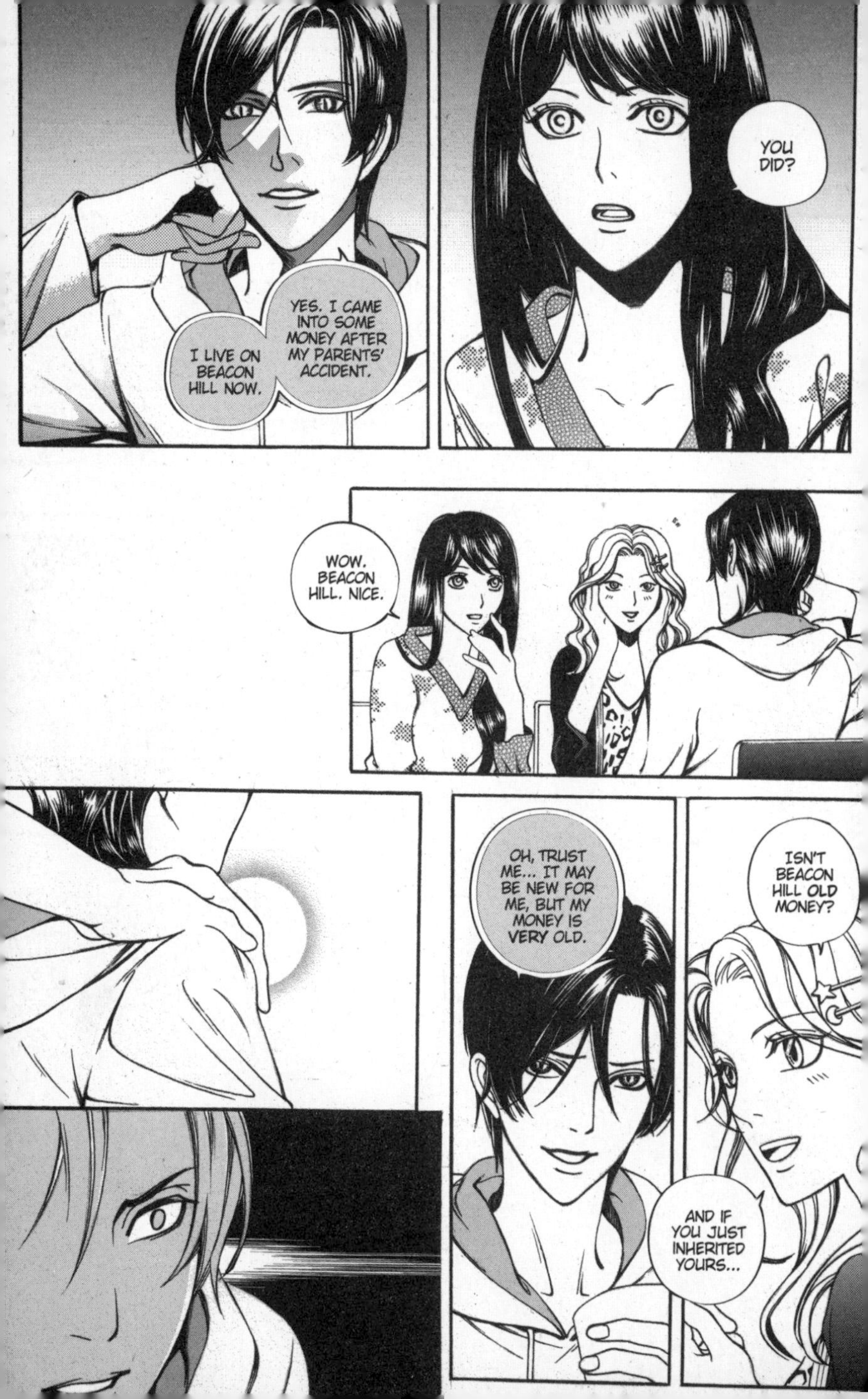
YOU DID?
YES. I CAME INTO SOME MONEY AFTER MY PARENTS' ACCIDENT.
I LIVE ON BEACON HILL NOW.
WOW. BEACON HILL. NICE.
ISN'T BEACON HILL OLD MONEY?
AND IF YOU JUST INHERITED YOURS...
OH, TRUST ME... IT MAY BE NEW FOR ME, BUT MY MONEY IS VERY OLD.

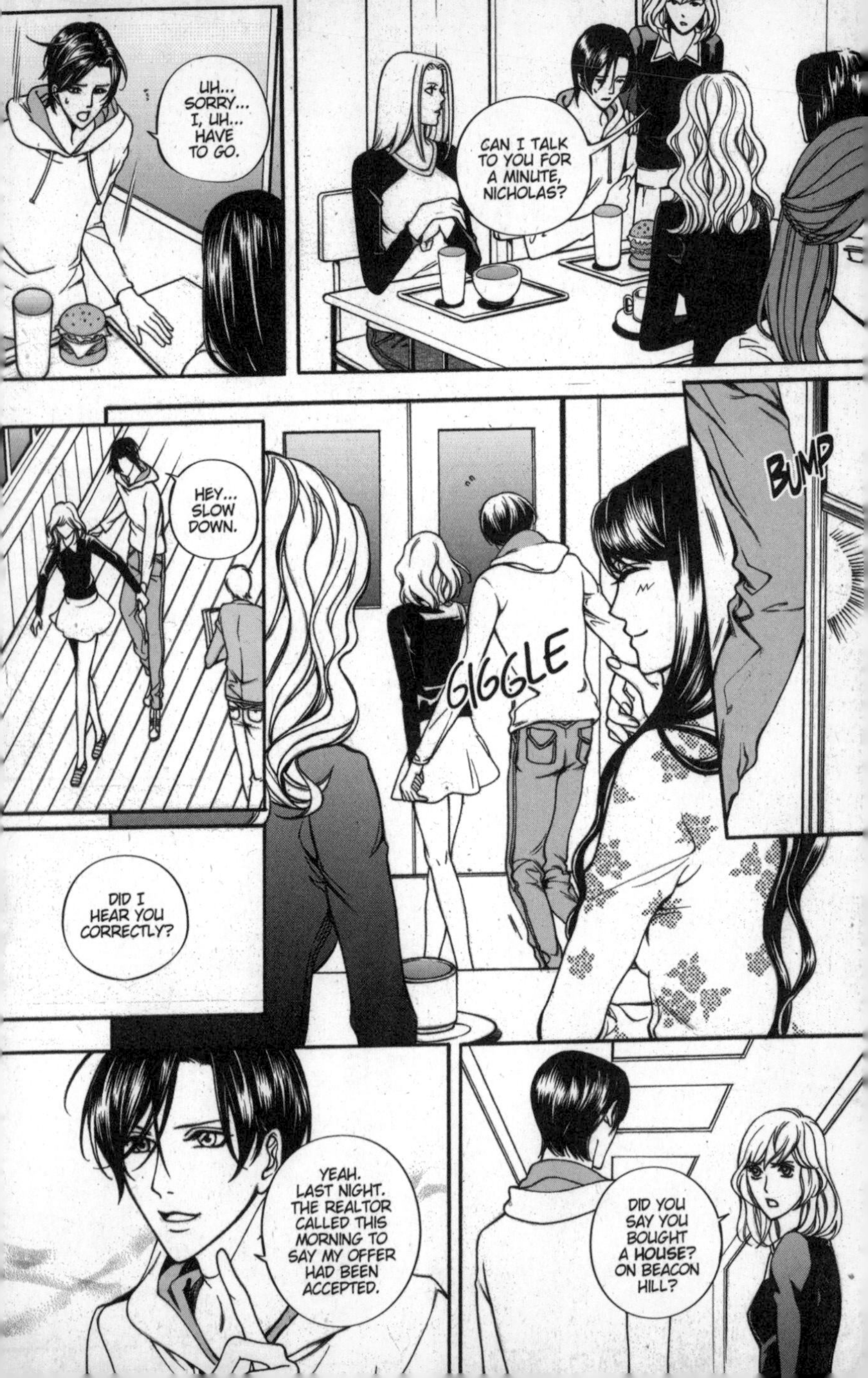
CAN I TALK TO YOU FOR A MINUTE, NICHOLAS?
UH... SORRY... I, UH... HAVE TO GO.
BUMP
GIGGLE
HEY... SLOW DOWN.
DID I HEAR YOU CORRECTLY?
DID YOU SAY YOU BOUGHT A HOUSE? ON BEACON HILL?
YEAH. LAST NIGHT. THE REALTOR CALLED THIS MORNING TO SAY MY OFFER HAD BEEN ACCEPTED.

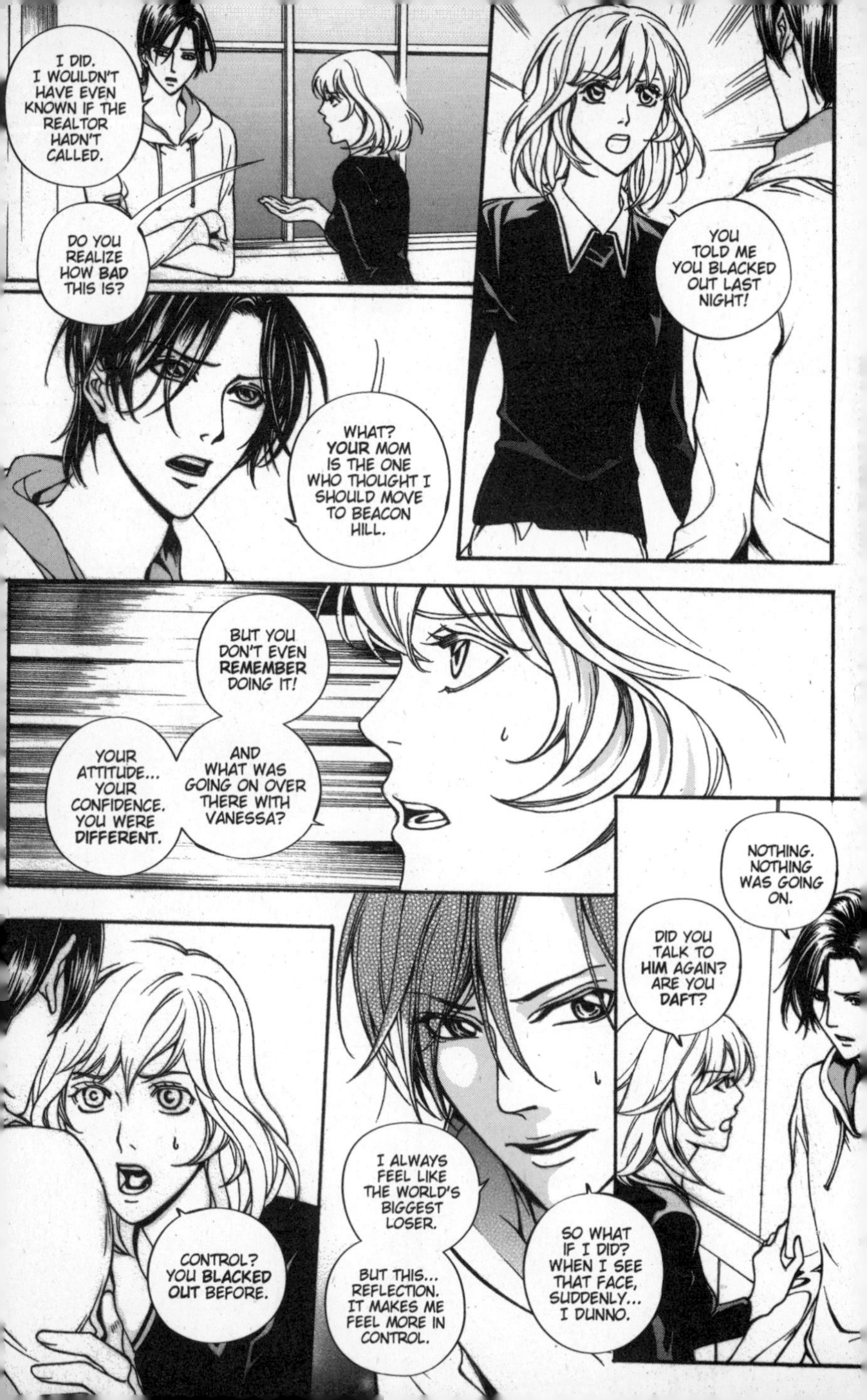
YOU TOLD ME YOU BLACKED OUT LAST NIGHT!
I DID. I WOULDN'T HAVE EVEN KNOWN IF THE REALTOR HADN'T CALLED.
DO YOU REALIZE HOW BAD THIS IS?
WHAT? YOUR MOM IS THE ONE WHO THOUGHT I SHOULD MOVE TO BEACON HILL.
BUT YOU DON'T EVEN REMEMBER DOING IT!
AND WHAT WAS GOING ON OVER THERE WITH VANESSA?
YOUR ATTITUDE... YOUR CONFIDENCE. YOU WERE DIFFERENT.
NOTHING. NOTHING WAS GOING ON.
DID YOU TALK TO HIM AGAIN? ARE YOU DAFT?
SO WHAT IF I DID? WHEN I SEE THAT FACE, SUDDENLY... I DUNNO.
I ALWAYS FEEL LIKE THE WORLD'S BIGGEST LOSER.
BUT THIS... REFLECTION. IT MAKES ME FEEL MORE IN CONTROL.
CONTROL? YOU BLACKED OUT BEFORE.

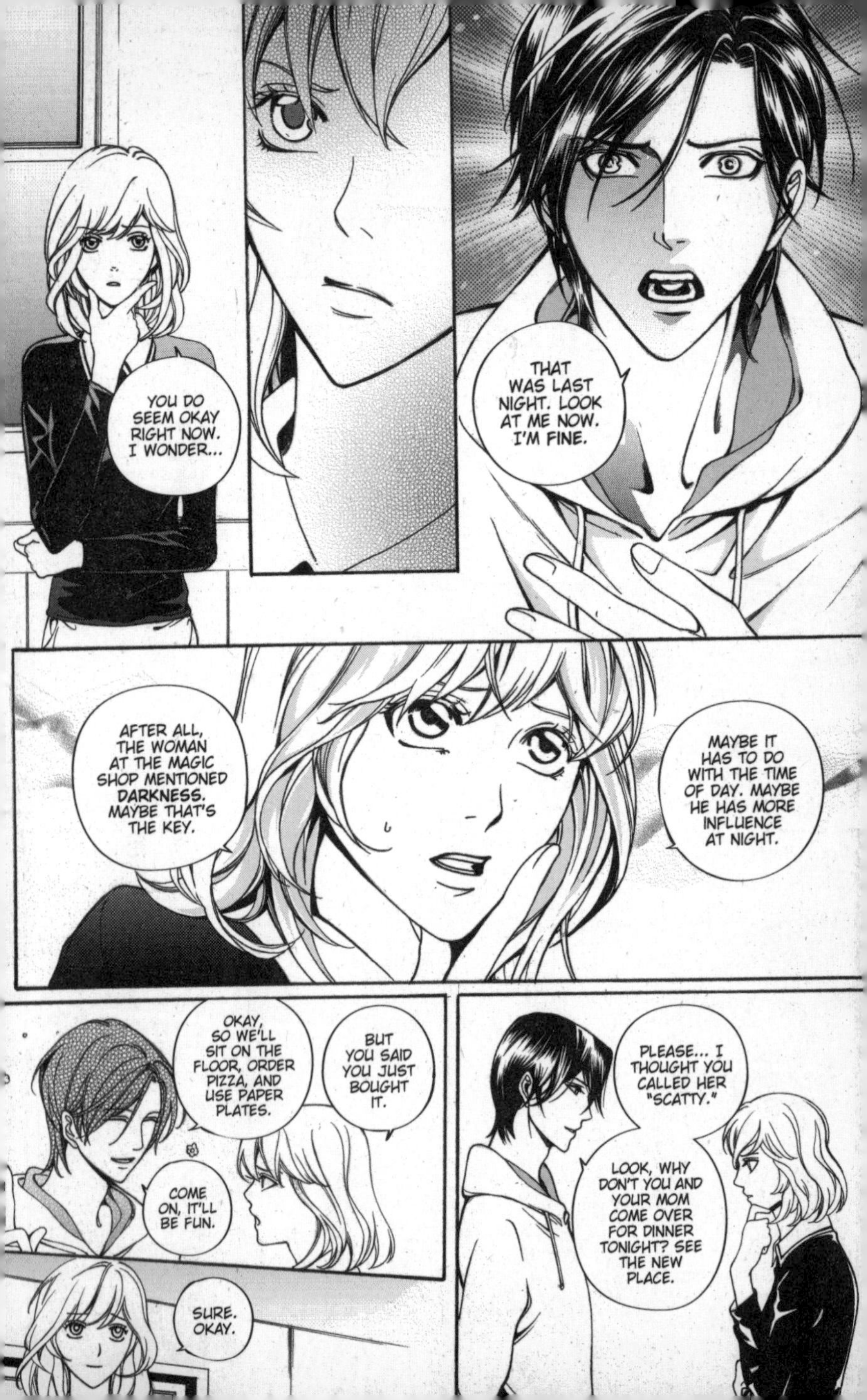
THAT WAS LAST NIGHT. LOOK AT ME NOW. I'M FINE.
YOU DO SEEM OKAY RIGHT NOW. I WONDER...
MAYBE IT HAS TO DO WITH THE TIME OF DAY. MAYBE HE HAS MORE INFLUENCE AT NIGHT.
AFTER ALL, THE WOMAN AT THE MAGIC SHOP MENTIONED **DARKNESS.** MAYBE THAT'S THE KEY.
PLEASE... I THOUGHT YOU CALLED HER "SCATTY."
LOOK, WHY DON'T YOU AND YOUR MOM COME OVER FOR DINNER TONIGHT? SEE THE NEW PLACE.
BUT YOU SAID YOU JUST BOUGHT IT.
OKAY, SO WE'LL SIT ON THE FLOOR, ORDER PIZZA, AND USE PAPER PLATES.
COME ON, IT'LL BE FUN.
SURE. OKAY.

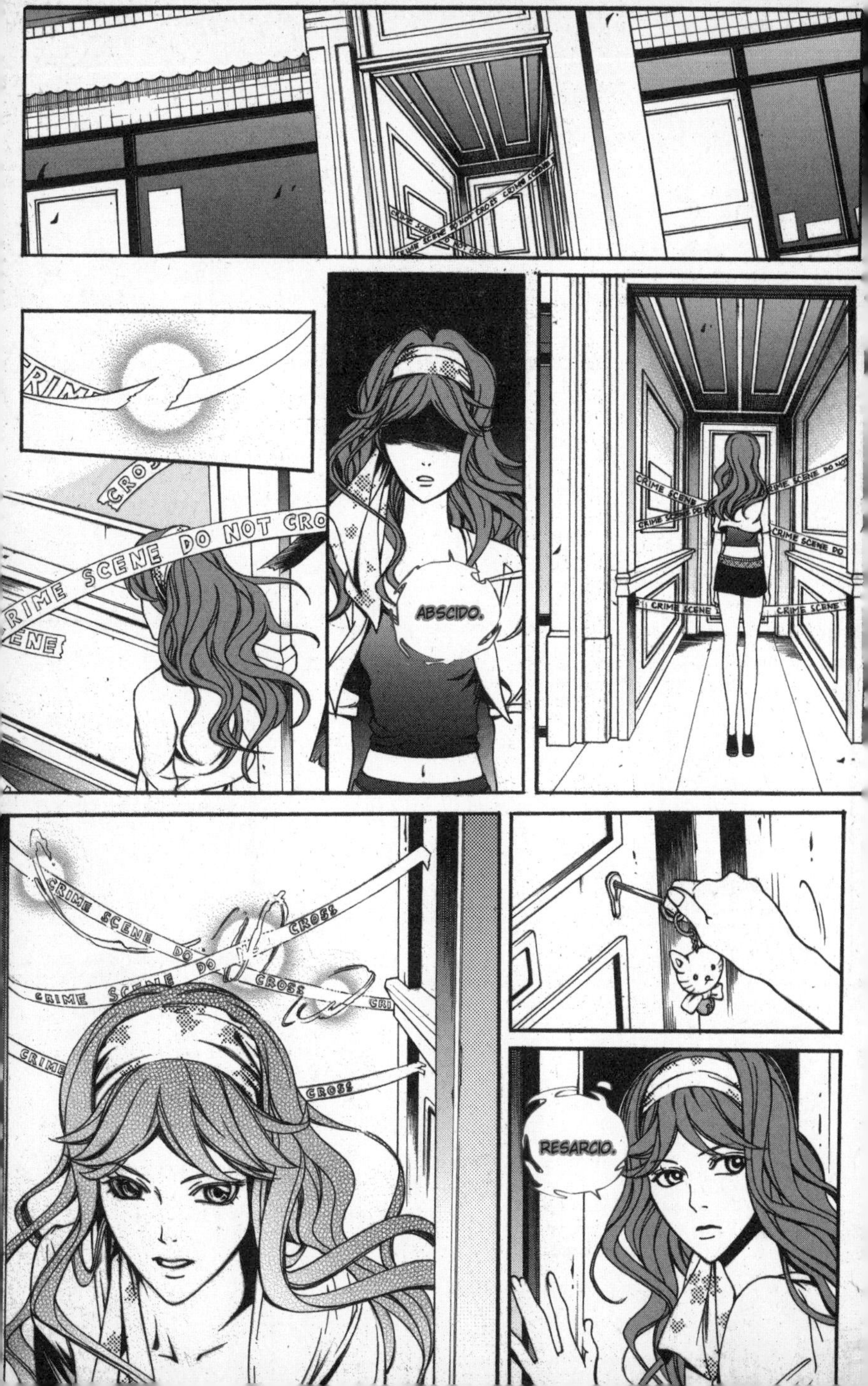
CRIME SCENE DO NOT
CRIME SCENE
ABSCIDO.
CRIME
CROSS
CRIME SCENE DO NOT CRO
ENE
RESARCIO.
CRIME SCENE DO
CROSS
CRIME SCENE
CROSS
CRIME
CROSS

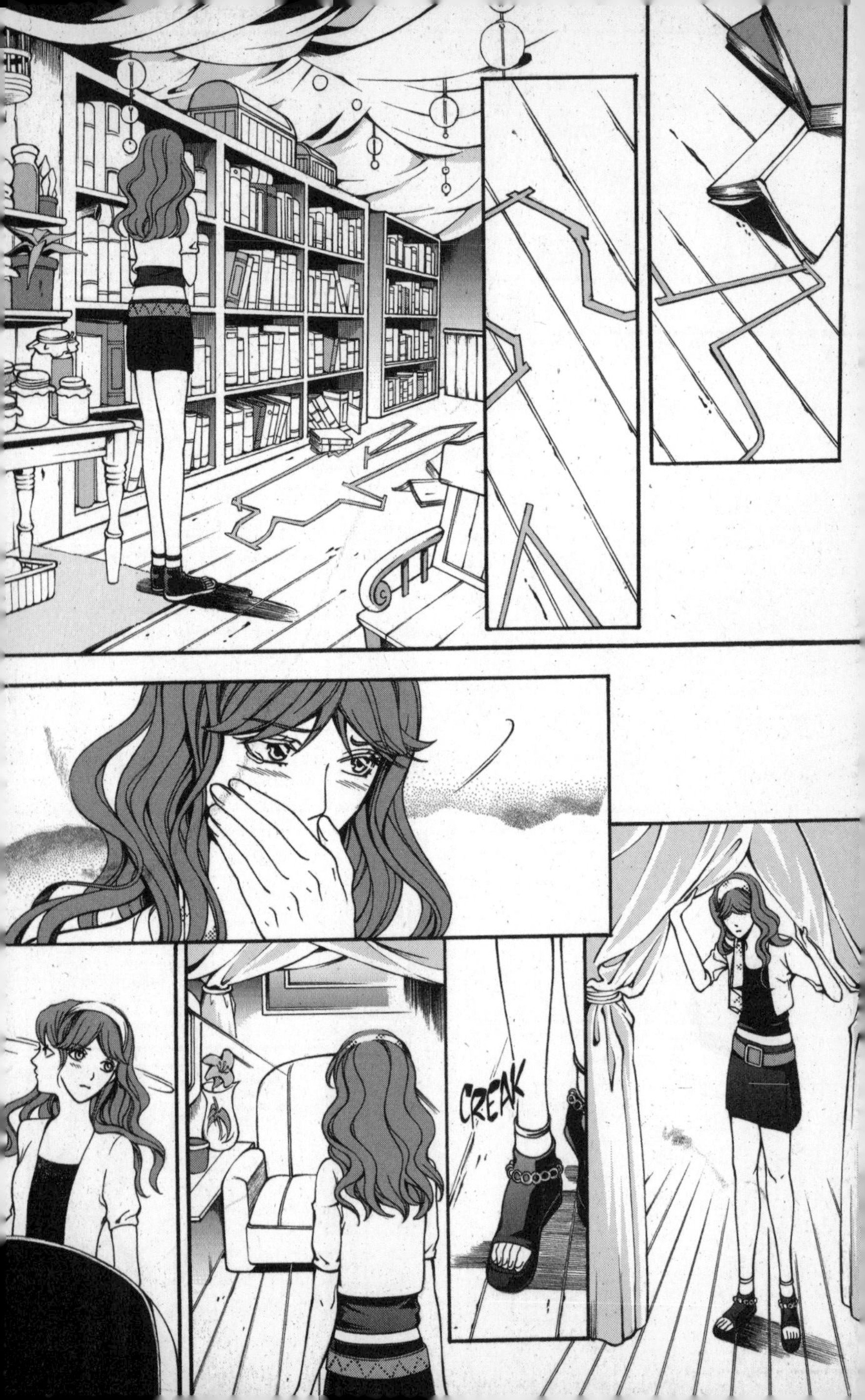
CREAK

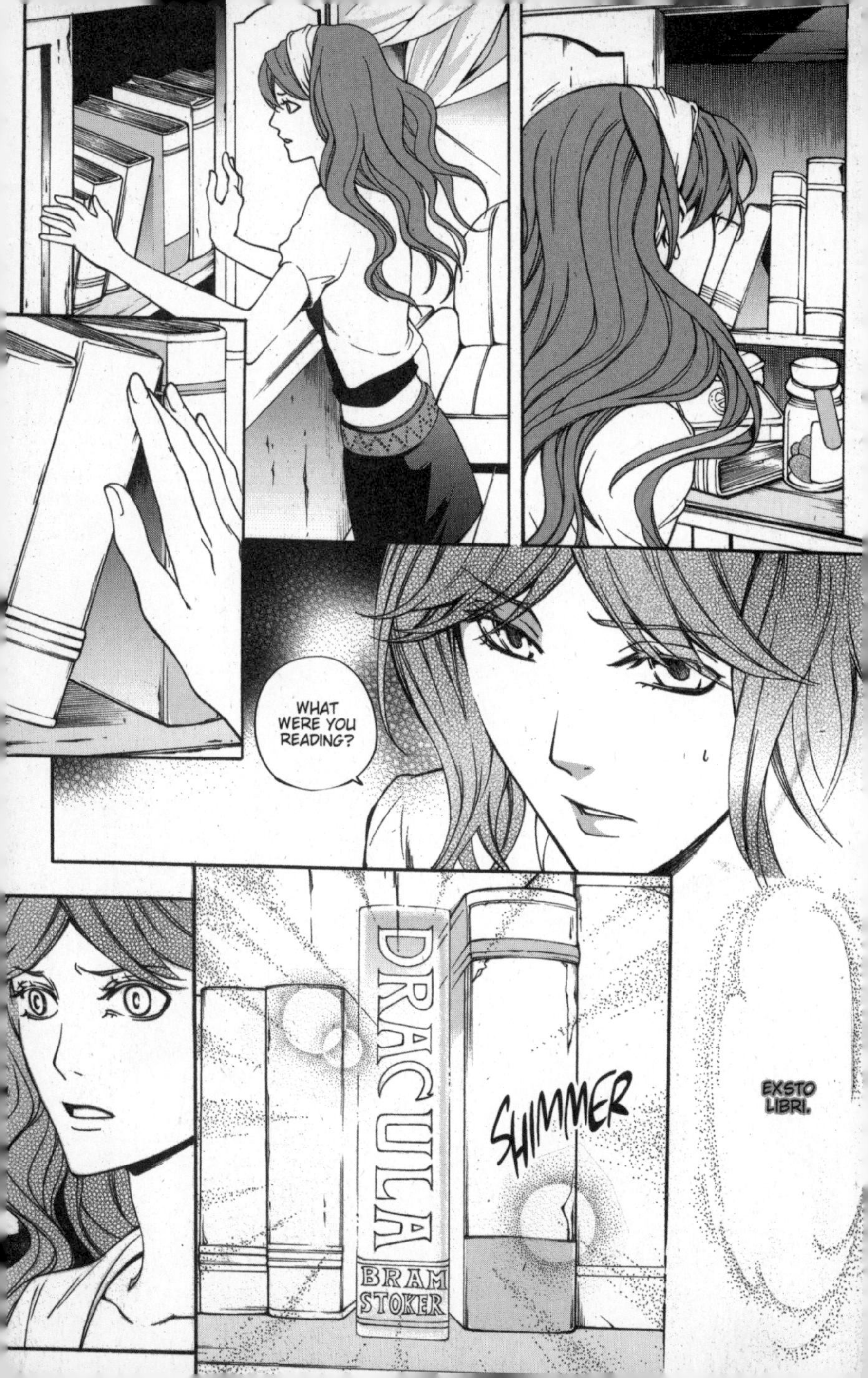
WHAT WERE YOU READING?
EXSTO LIBRI.
DRACULA
BRAM STOKER
SHIMMER

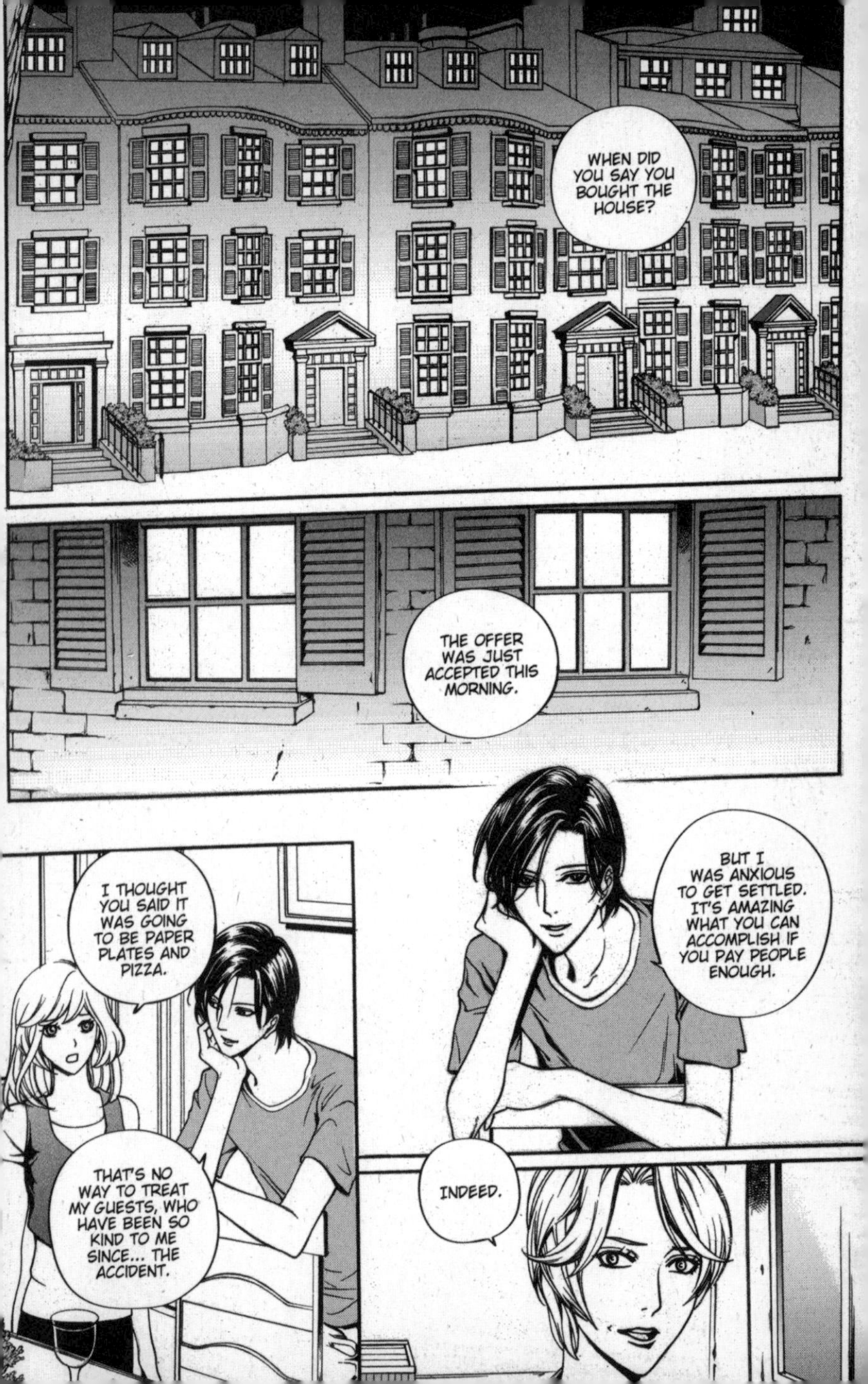
WHEN DID YOU SAY YOU BOUGHT THE HOUSE?
THE OFFER WAS JUST ACCEPTED THIS MORNING.
BUT I WAS ANXIOUS TO GET SETTLED. IT'S AMAZING WHAT YOU CAN ACCOMPLISH IF YOU PAY PEOPLE ENOUGH.
I THOUGHT YOU SAID IT WAS GOING TO BE PAPER PLATES AND PIZZA.
THAT'S NO WAY TO TREAT MY GUESTS, WHO HAVE BEEN SO KIND TO ME SINCE... THE ACCIDENT.
INDEED.

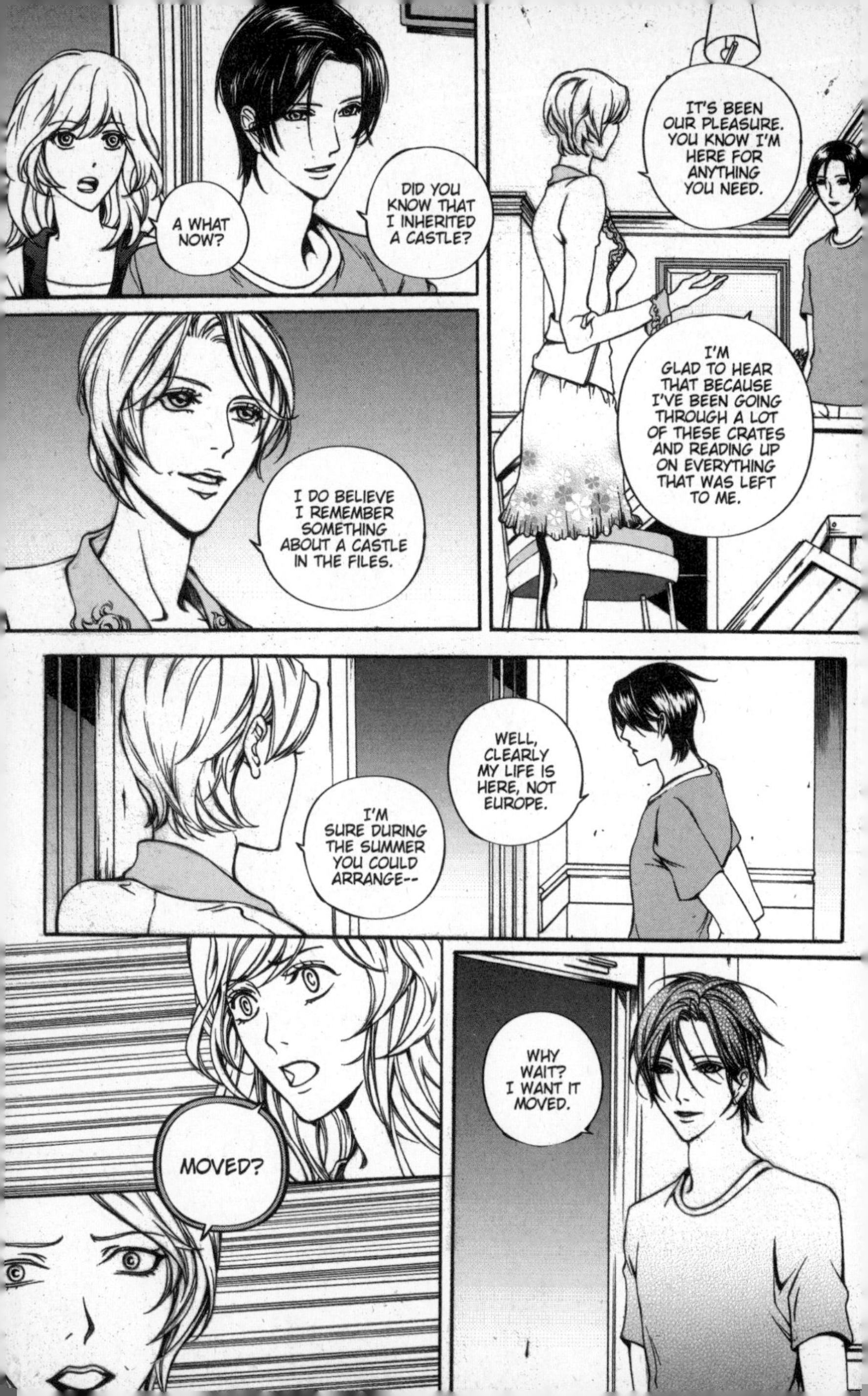
IT'S BEEN OUR PLEASURE. YOU KNOW I'M HERE FOR ANYTHING YOU NEED.
I'M GLAD TO HEAR THAT BECAUSE I'VE BEEN GOING THROUGH A LOT OF THESE CRATES AND READING UP ON EVERYTHING THAT WAS LEFT TO ME.
DID YOU KNOW THAT I INHERITED A CASTLE?
A WHAT NOW?
I DO BELIEVE I REMEMBER SOMETHING ABOUT A CASTLE IN THE FILES.
WELL, CLEARLY MY LIFE IS HERE, NOT EUROPE.
I'M SURE DURING THE SUMMER YOU COULD ARRANGE--
WHY WAIT? I WANT IT MOVED.
MOVED?

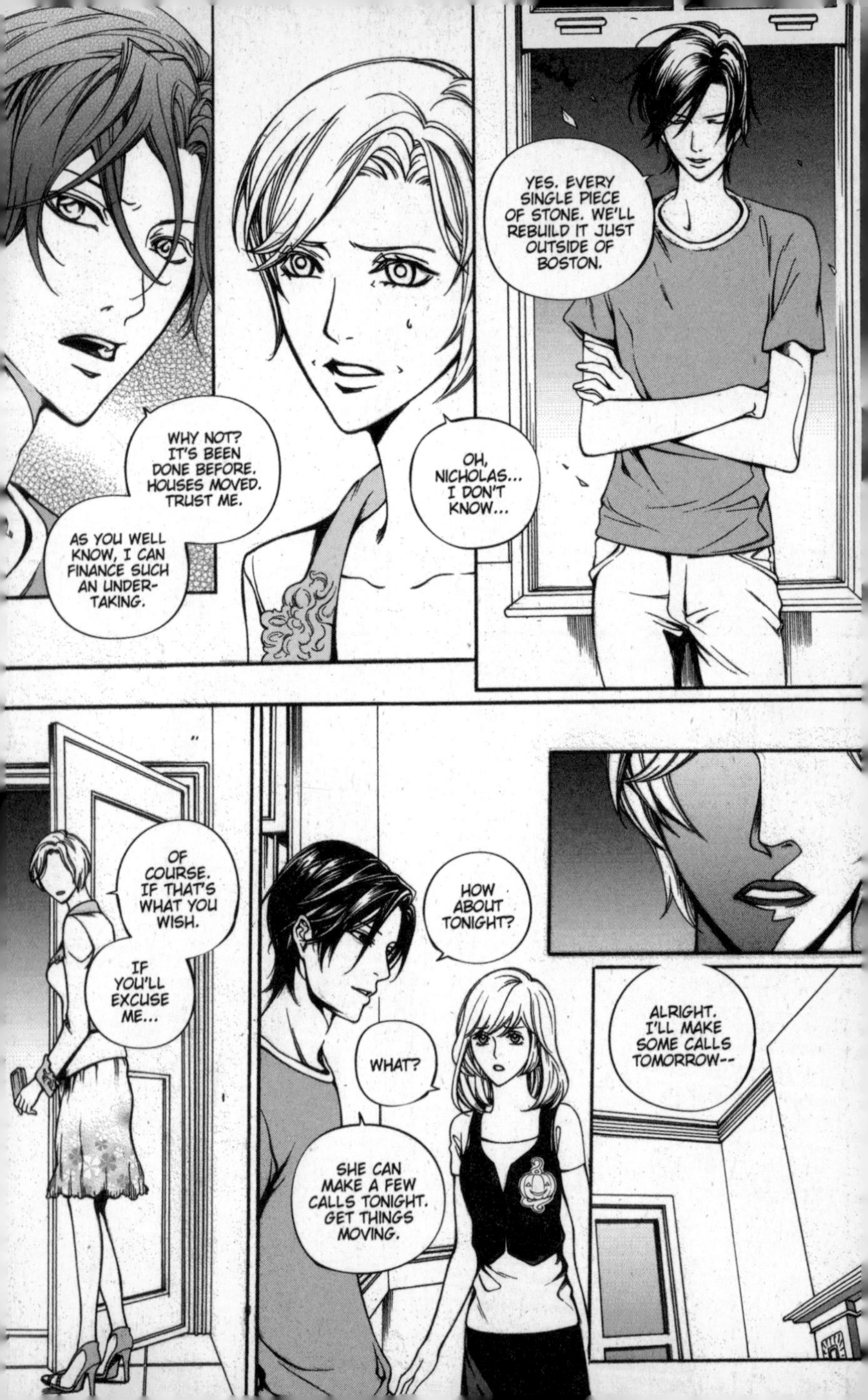
YES. EVERY SINGLE PIECE OF STONE. WE'LL REBUILD IT JUST OUTSIDE OF BOSTON.
OH, NICHOLAS... I DON'T KNOW...
WHY NOT? IT'S BEEN DONE BEFORE. HOUSES MOVED. TRUST ME.
AS YOU WELL KNOW, I CAN FINANCE SUCH AN UNDER-TAKING.
ALRIGHT. I'LL MAKE SOME CALLS TOMORROW--
HOW ABOUT TONIGHT?
WHAT?
SHE CAN MAKE A FEW CALLS TONIGHT. GET THINGS MOVING.
OF COURSE. IF THAT'S WHAT YOU WISH.
IF YOU'LL EXCUSE ME...

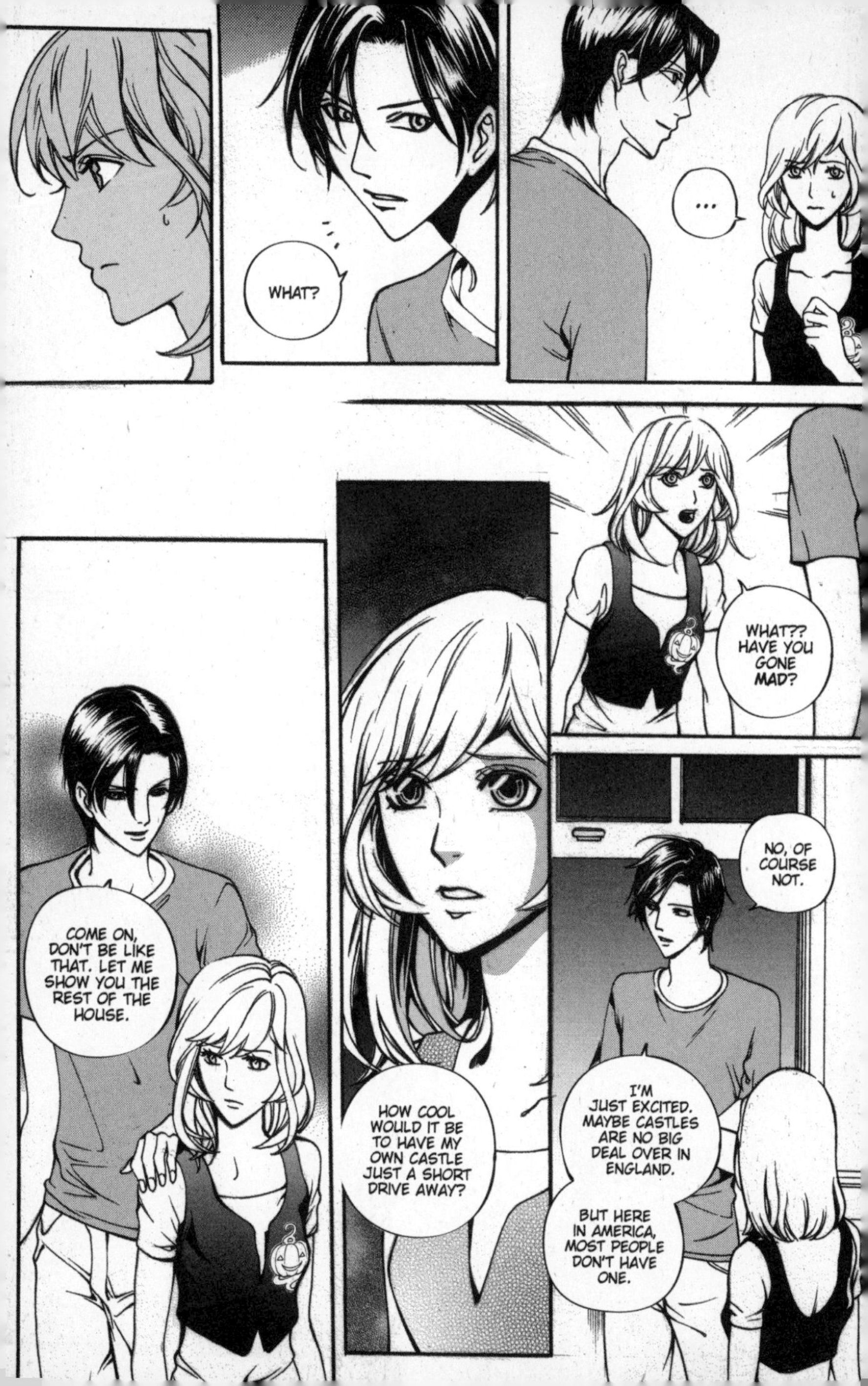
...
WHAT?
WHAT?? HAVE YOU GONE MAD?
NO, OF COURSE NOT.
I'M JUST EXCITED. MAYBE CASTLES ARE NO BIG DEAL OVER IN ENGLAND.
BUT HERE IN AMERICA, MOST PEOPLE DON'T HAVE ONE.
HOW COOL WOULD IT BE TO HAVE MY OWN CASTLE JUST A SHORT DRIVE AWAY?
COME ON, DON'T BE LIKE THAT. LET ME SHOW YOU THE REST OF THE HOUSE.

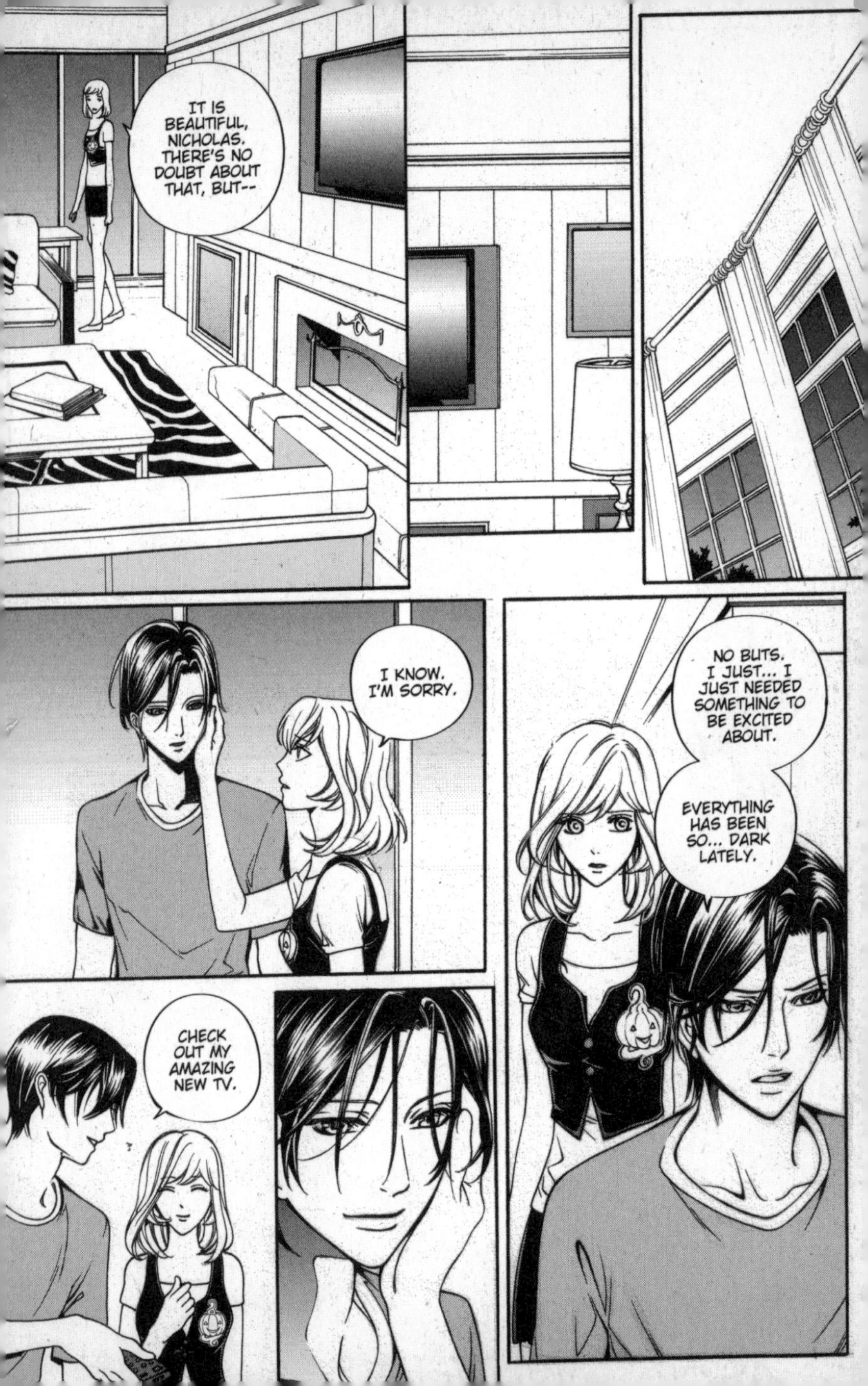
IT IS BEAUTIFUL, NICHOLAS. THERE'S NO DOUBT ABOUT THAT, BUT--
NO BUTS. I JUST... I JUST NEEDED SOMETHING TO BE EXCITED ABOUT.
EVERYTHING HAS BEEN SO... DARK LATELY.
I KNOW. I'M SORRY.
CHECK OUT MY AMAZING NEW TV.

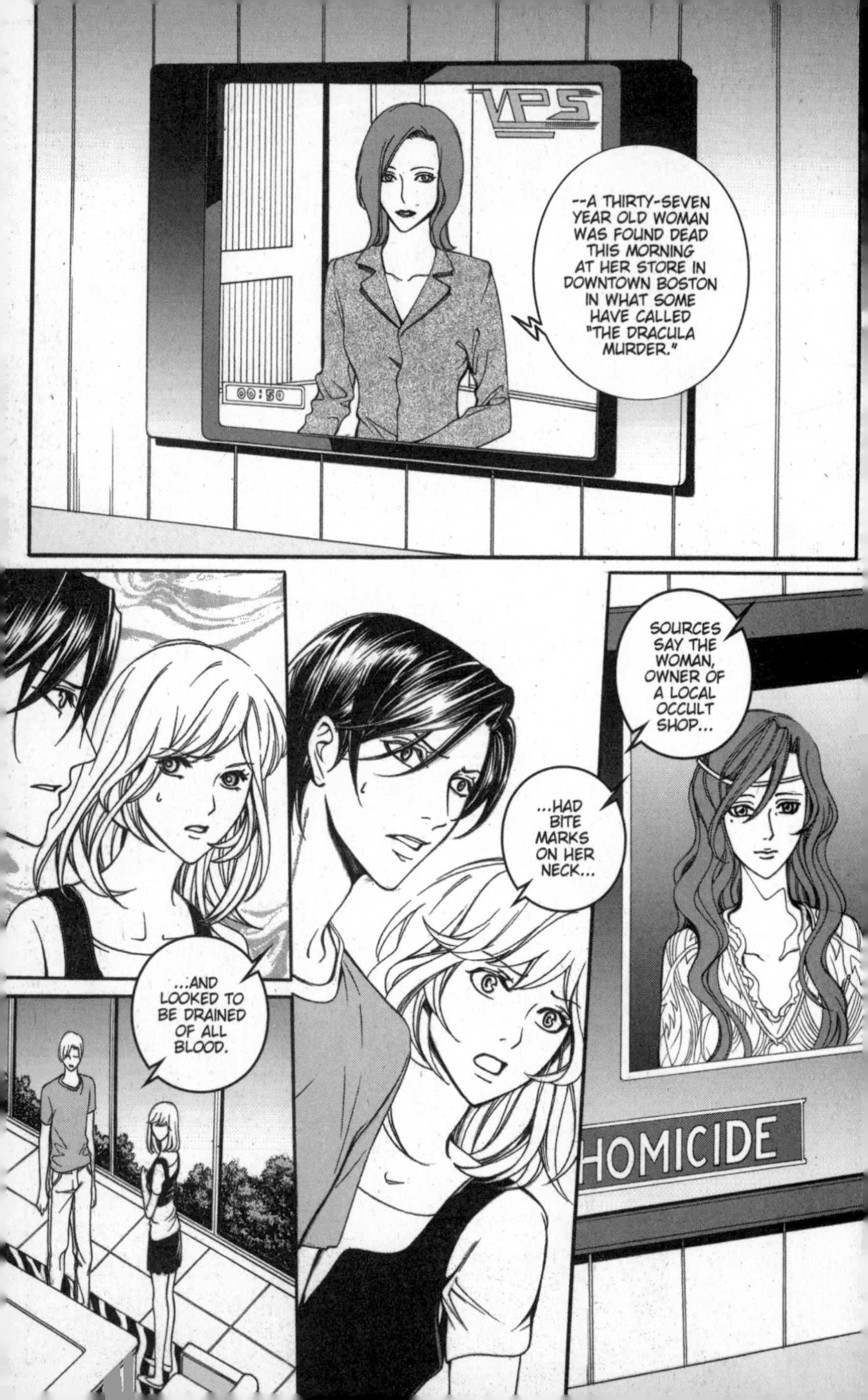
VPS
00:50
--A THIRTY-SEVEN YEAR OLD WOMAN WAS FOUND DEAD THIS MORNING AT HER STORE IN DOWNTOWN BOSTON IN WHAT SOME HAVE CALLED "THE DRACULA MURDER."
SOURCES SAY THE WOMAN, OWNER OF A LOCAL OCCULT SHOP...
HOMICIDE
...HAD BITE MARKS ON HER NECK...
...AND LOOKED TO BE DRAINED OF ALL BLOOD.

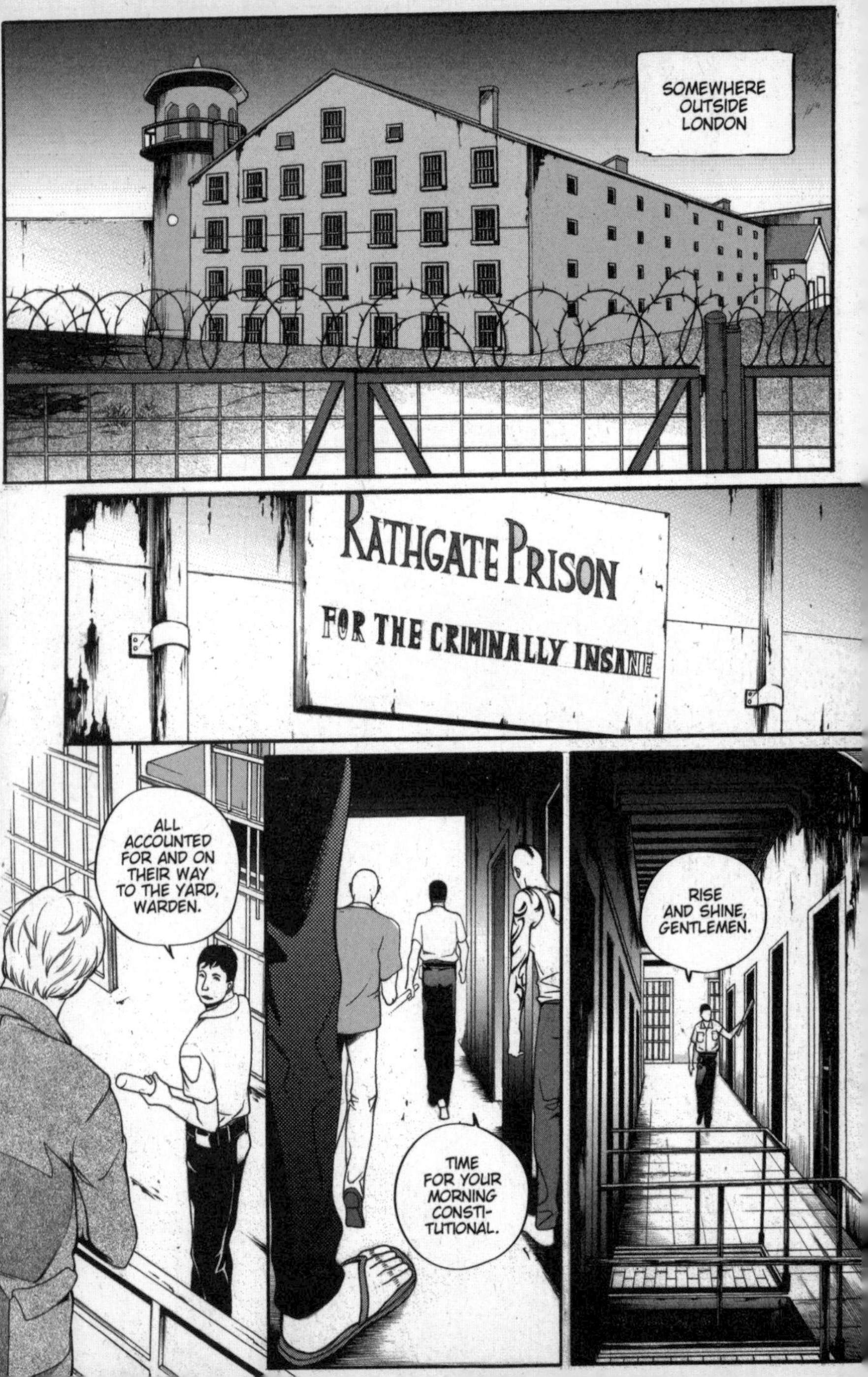
SOMEWHERE OUTSIDE LONDON
RATHGATE PRISON
FOR THE CRIMINALLY INSANE
RISE AND SHINE, GENTLEMEN.
TIME FOR YOUR MORNING CONSTI-TUTIONAL.
ALL ACCOUNTED FOR AND ON THEIR WAY TO THE YARD, WARDEN.

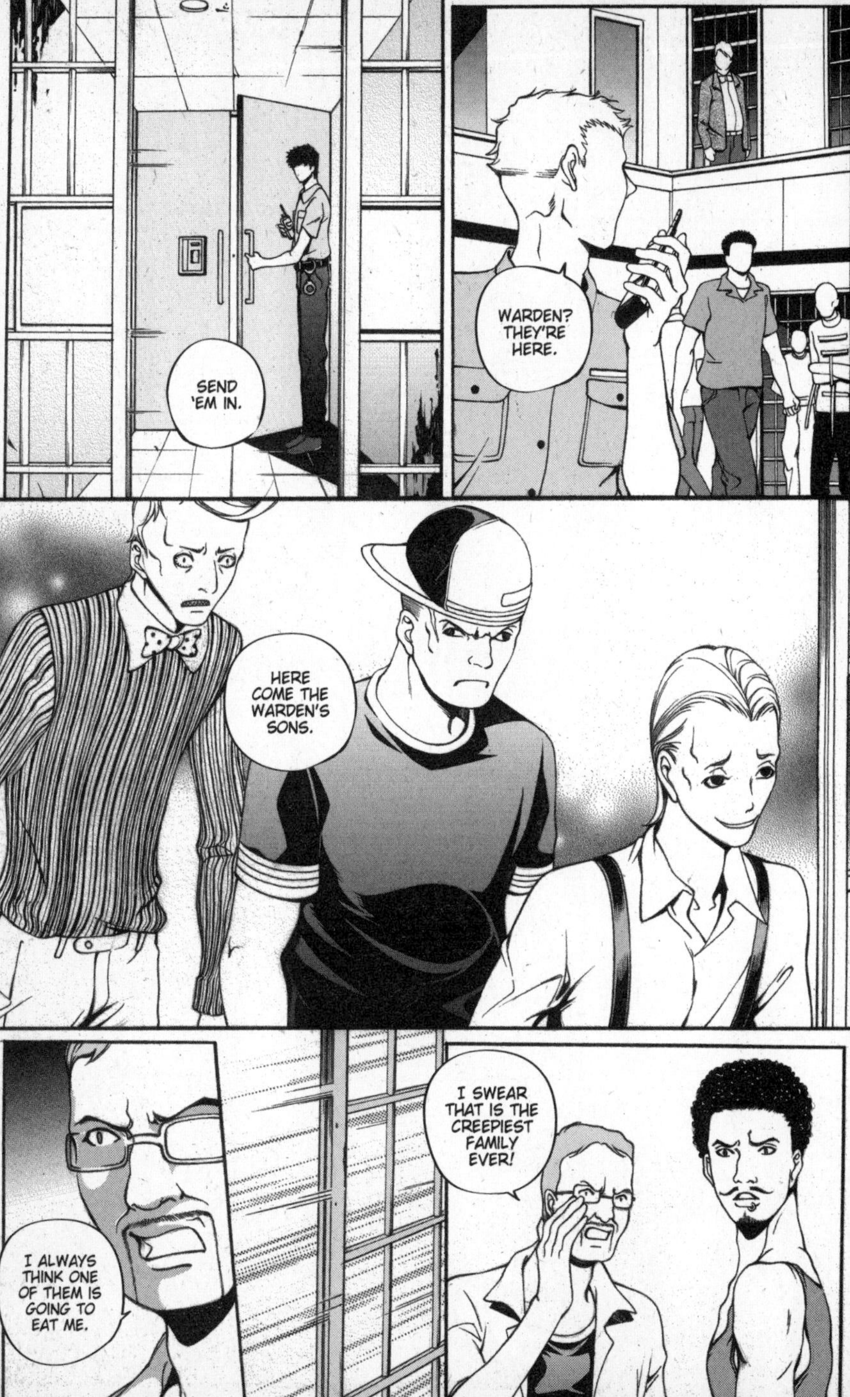
WARDEN? THEY'RE HERE.
SEND 'EM IN.
HERE COME THE WARDEN'S SONS.
I SWEAR THAT IS THE CREEPIEST FAMILY EVER!
I ALWAYS THINK ONE OF THEM IS GOING TO EAT ME.

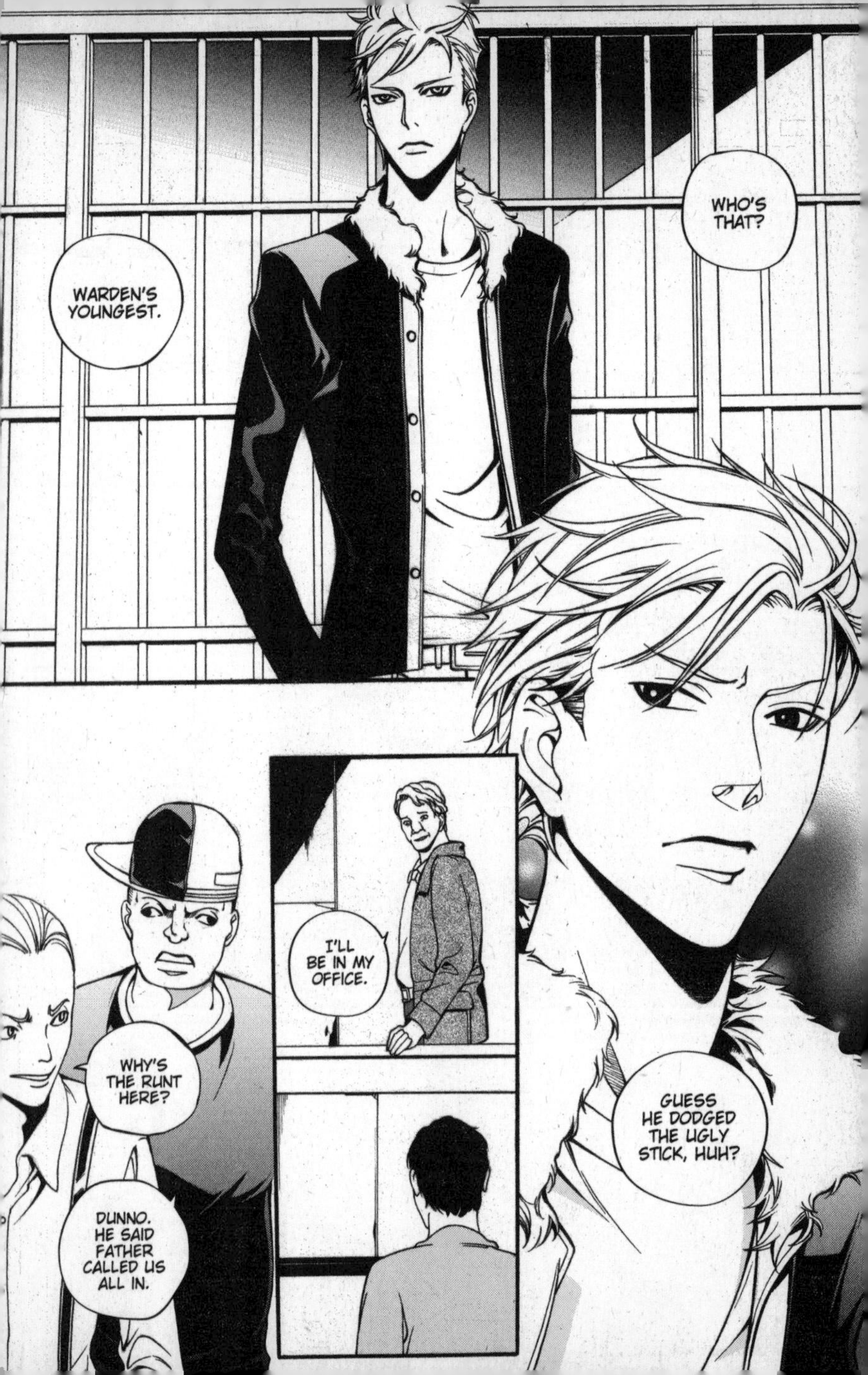
WHO'S THAT?
WARDEN'S YOUNGEST.
GUESS HE DODGED THE UGLY STICK, HUH?
I'LL BE IN MY OFFICE.
WHY'S THE RUNT HERE?
DUNNO. HE SAID FATHER CALLED US ALL IN.

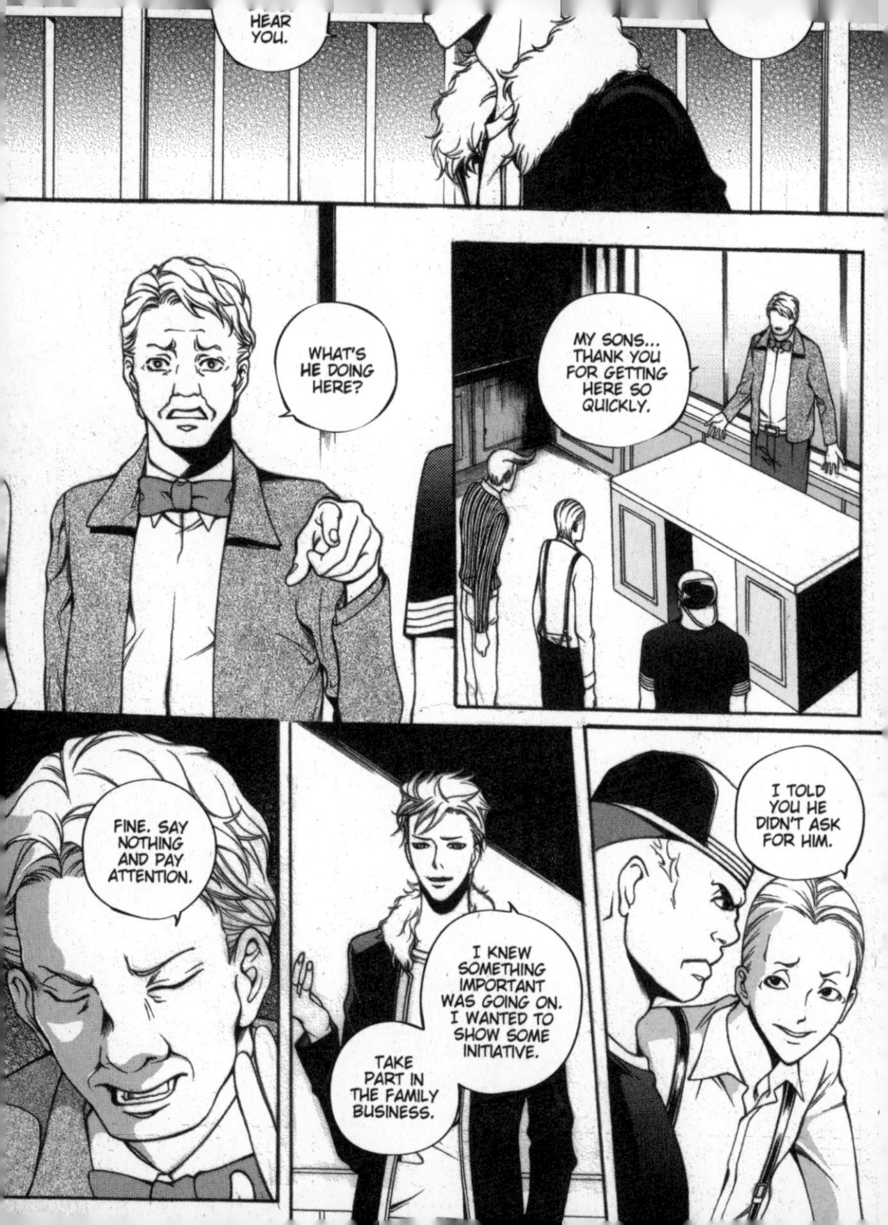
HEAR YOU.
MY SONS... THANK YOU FOR GETTING HERE SO QUICKLY.
WHAT'S HE DOING HERE?
I TOLD YOU HE DIDN'T ASK FOR HIM.
I KNEW SOMETHING IMPORTANT WAS GOING ON. I WANTED TO SHOW SOME INITIATIVE.
TAKE PART IN THE FAMILY BUSINESS.
FINE. SAY NOTHING AND PAY ATTENTION.

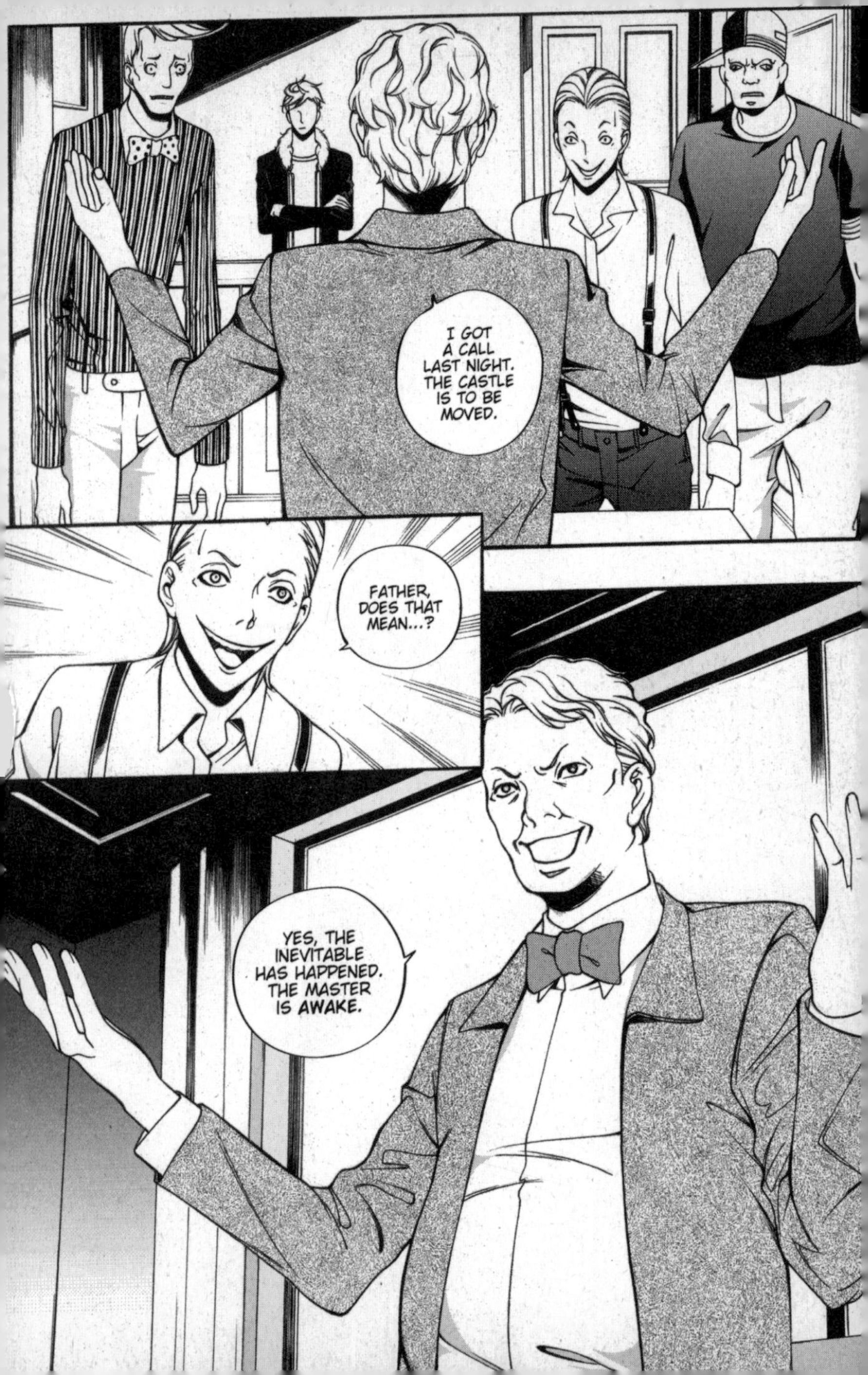
I GOT A CALL LAST NIGHT. THE CASTLE IS TO BE MOVED.
FATHER, DOES THAT MEAN...?
YES, THE INEVITABLE HAS HAPPENED. THE MASTER IS AWAKE.

CHAPTER
4

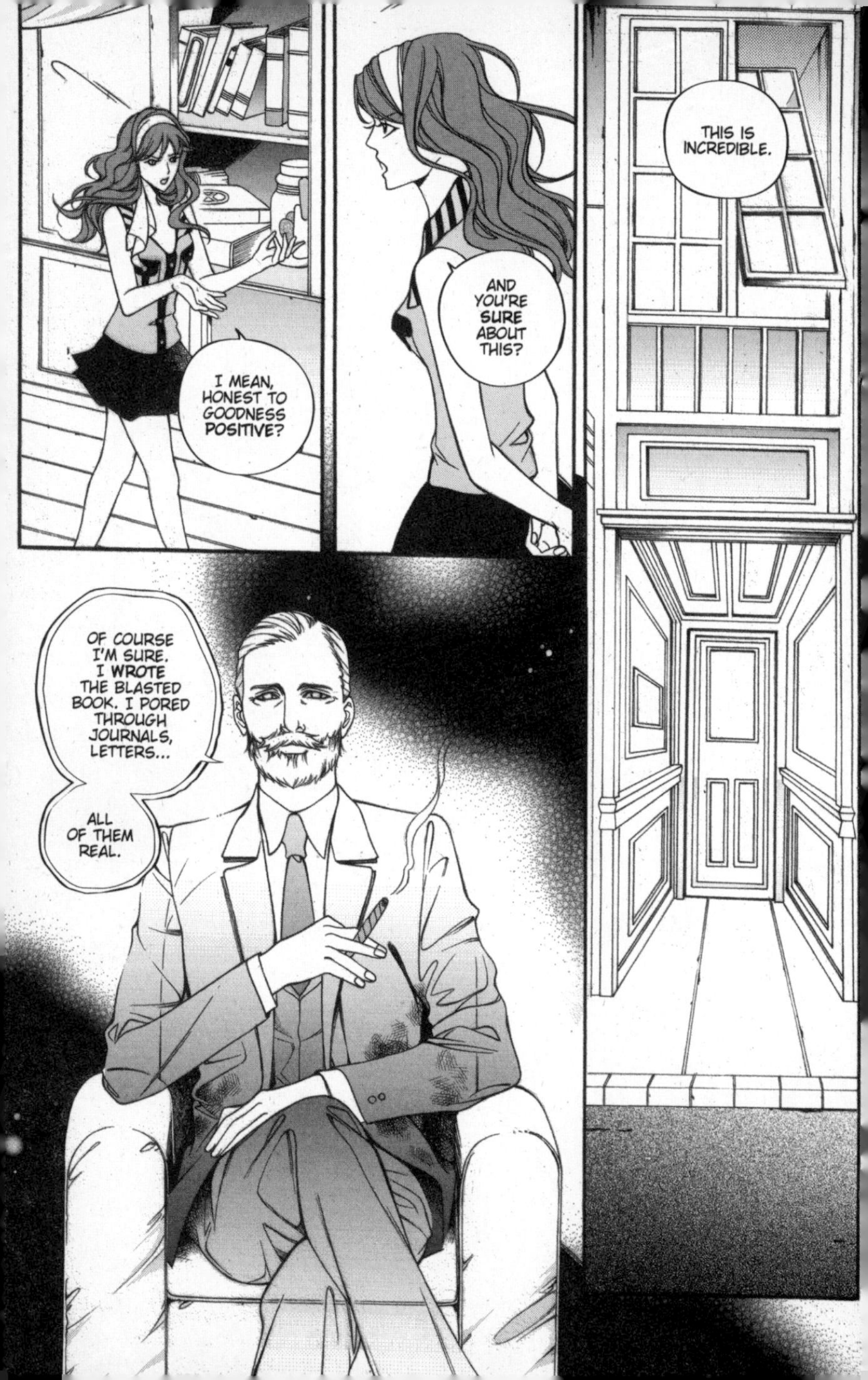
THIS IS INCREDIBLE.
AND YOU'RE SURE ABOUT THIS?
I MEAN, HONEST TO GOODNESS POSITIVE?
OF COURSE I'M SURE. I WROTE THE BLASTED BOOK. I PORED THROUGH JOURNALS, LETTERS...
ALL OF THEM REAL.

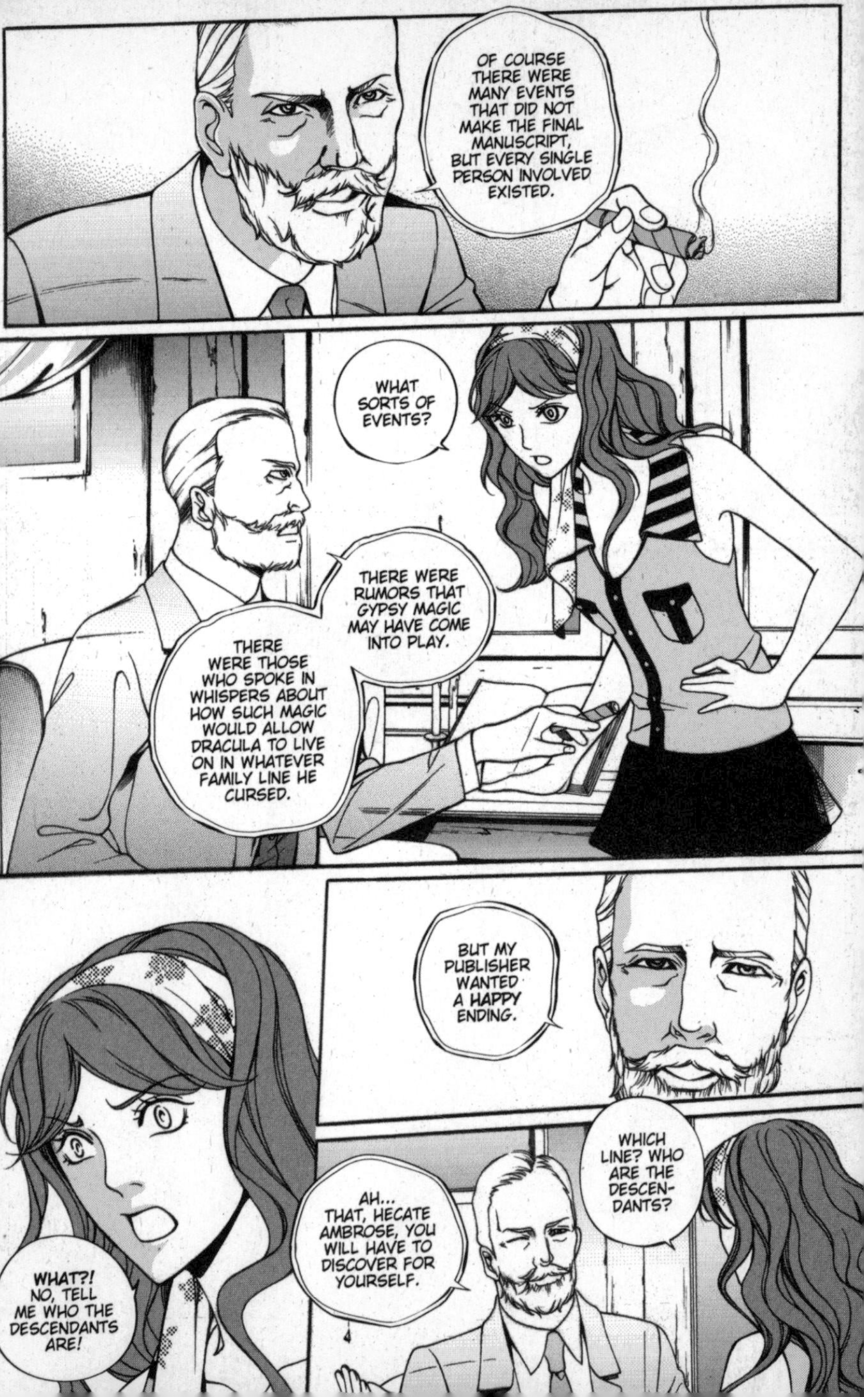
OF COURSE THERE WERE MANY EVENTS THAT DID NOT MAKE THE FINAL MANUSCRIPT, BUT EVERY SINGLE PERSON INVOLVED EXISTED.
WHAT SORTS OF EVENTS?
THERE WERE RUMORS THAT GYPSY MAGIC MAY HAVE COME INTO PLAY.
THERE WERE THOSE WHO SPOKE IN WHISPERS ABOUT HOW SUCH MAGIC WOULD ALLOW DRACULA TO LIVE ON IN WHATEVER FAMILY LINE HE CURSED.
BUT MY PUBLISHER WANTED A HAPPY ENDING.
WHICH LINE? WHO ARE THE DESCEN-DANTS?
AH... THAT, HECATE AMBROSE, YOU WILL HAVE TO DISCOVER FOR YOURSELF.
WHAT?! NO, TELL ME WHO THE DESCENDANTS ARE!

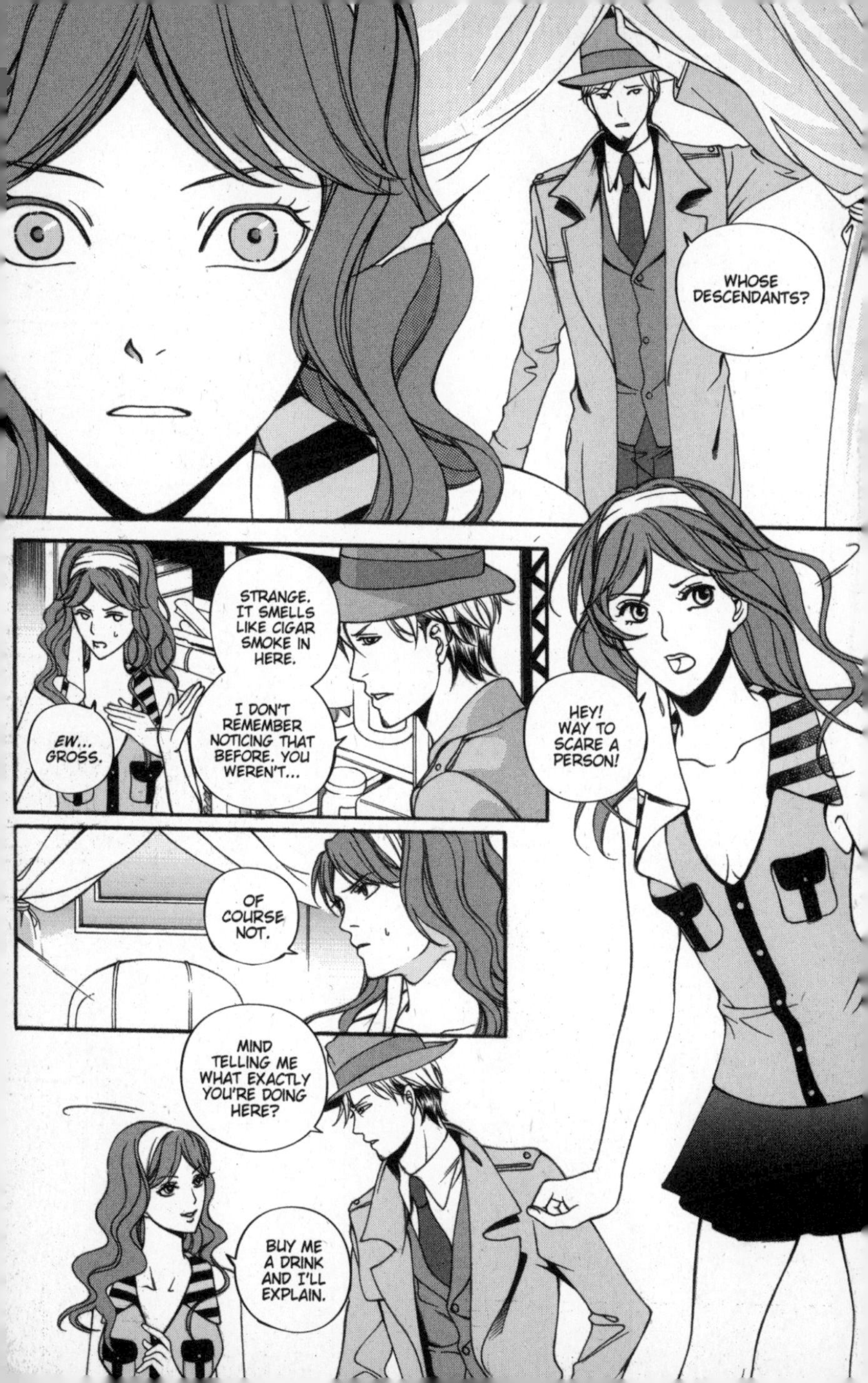
WHOSE DESCENDANTS?
HEY! WAY TO SCARE A PERSON!
STRANGE. IT SMELLS LIKE CIGAR SMOKE IN HERE.
I DON'T REMEMBER NOTICING THAT BEFORE. YOU WEREN'T...
EW... GROSS.
OF COURSE NOT.
MIND TELLING ME WHAT EXACTLY YOU'RE DOING HERE?
BUY ME A DRINK AND I'LL EXPLAIN.

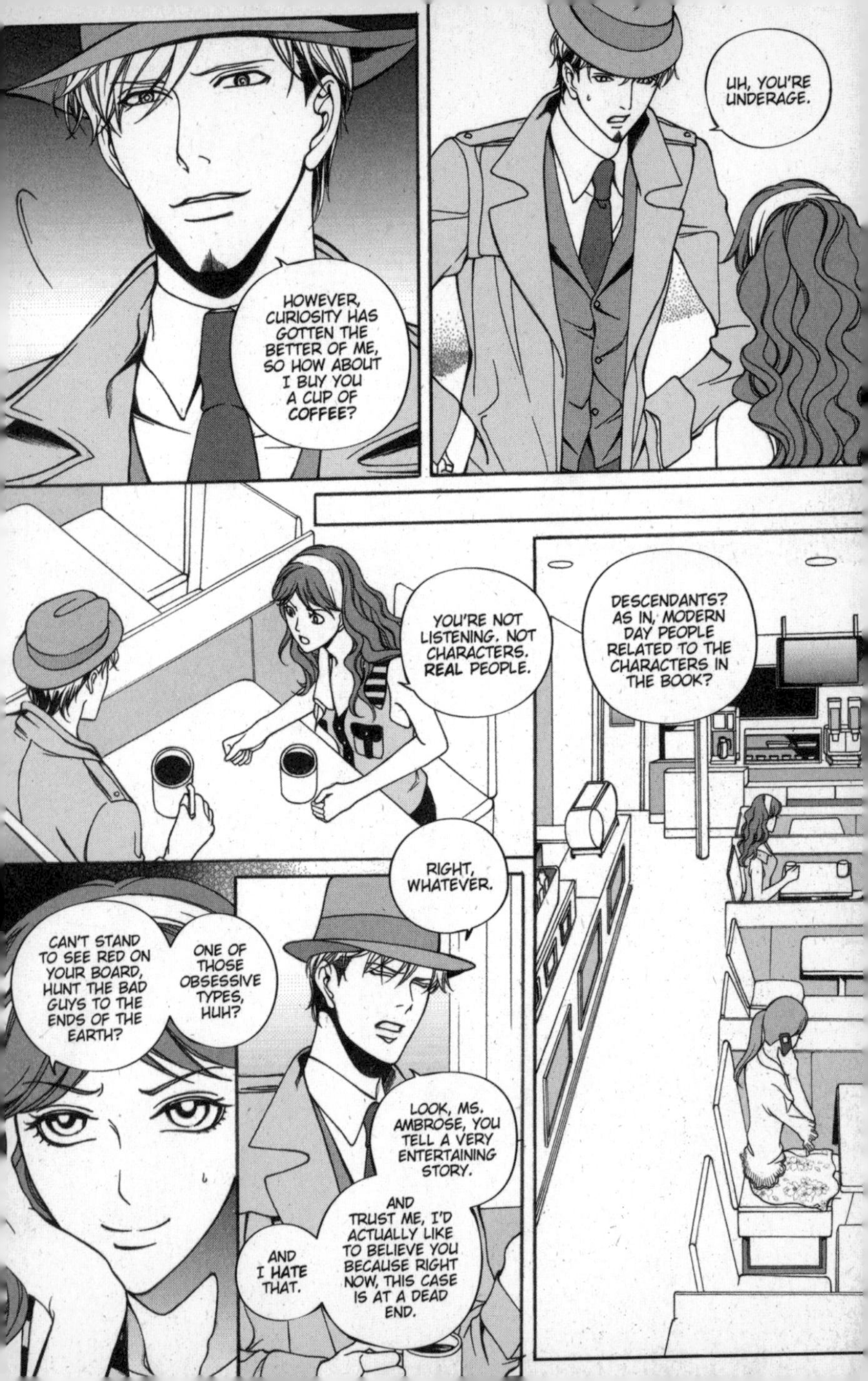
UH, YOU'RE UNDERAGE.
HOWEVER, CURIOSITY HAS GOTTEN THE BETTER OF ME, SO HOW ABOUT I BUY YOU A CUP OF COFFEE?
DESCENDANTS? AS IN, MODERN DAY PEOPLE RELATED TO THE CHARACTERS IN THE BOOK?
YOU'RE NOT LISTENING. NOT CHARACTERS. REAL PEOPLE.
RIGHT, WHATEVER.
ONE OF THOSE OBSESSIVE TYPES, HUH?
CAN'T STAND TO SEE RED ON YOUR BOARD, HUNT THE BAD GUYS TO THE ENDS OF THE EARTH?
LOOK, MS. AMBROSE, YOU TELL A VERY ENTERTAINING STORY.
AND TRUST ME, I'D ACTUALLY LIKE TO BELIEVE YOU BECAUSE RIGHT NOW, THIS CASE IS AT A DEAD END.
AND I HATE THAT.

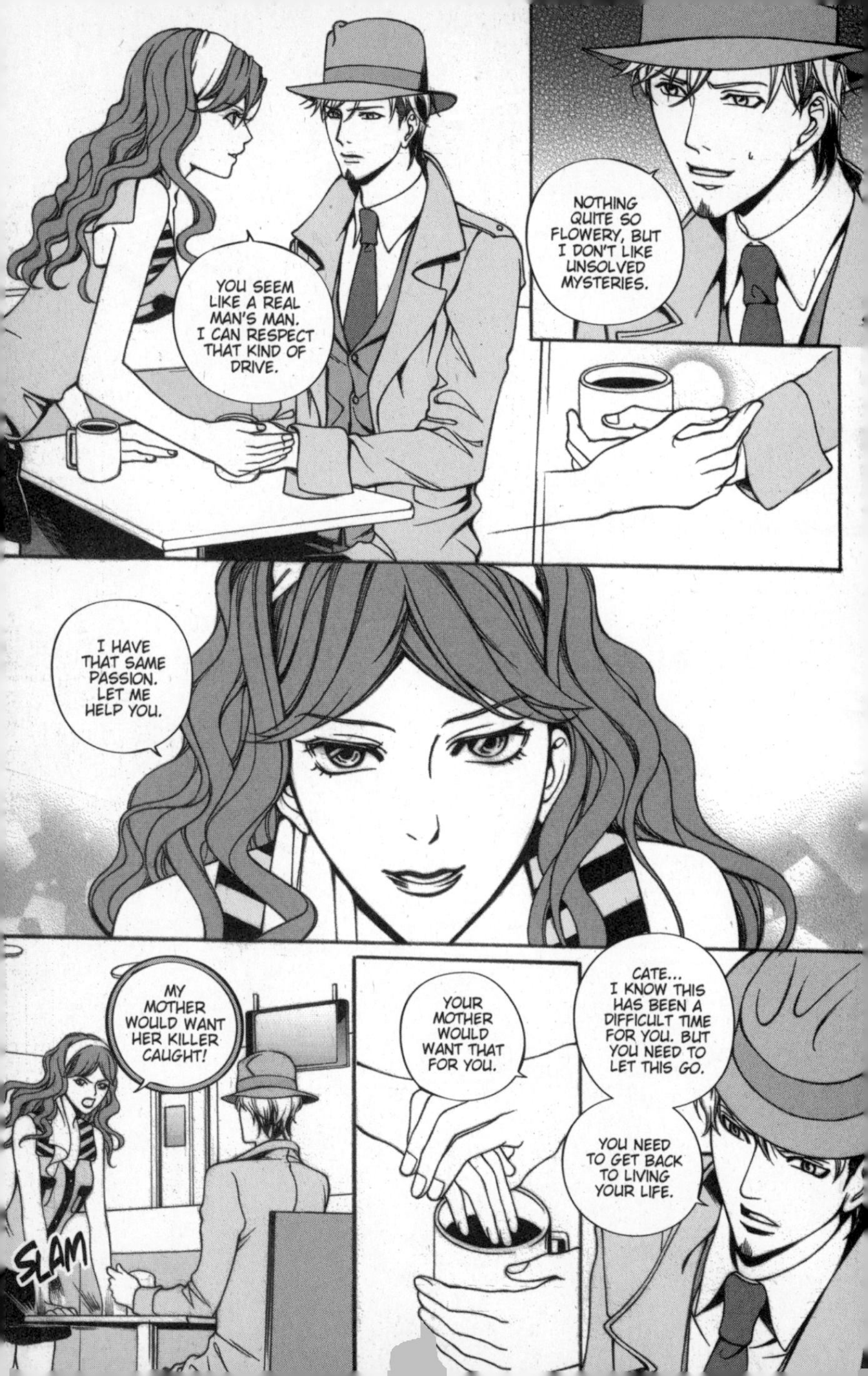
NOTHING QUITE SO FLOWERY, BUT I DON'T LIKE UNSOLVED MYSTERIES.
YOU SEEM LIKE A REAL MAN'S MAN. I CAN RESPECT THAT KIND OF DRIVE.
I HAVE THAT SAME PASSION. LET ME HELP YOU.
CATE... I KNOW THIS HAS BEEN A DIFFICULT TIME FOR YOU. BUT YOU NEED TO LET THIS GO.
YOU NEED TO GET BACK TO LIVING YOUR LIFE.
YOUR MOTHER WOULD WANT THAT FOR YOU.
MY MOTHER WOULD WANT HER KILLER CAUGHT!
SLAM

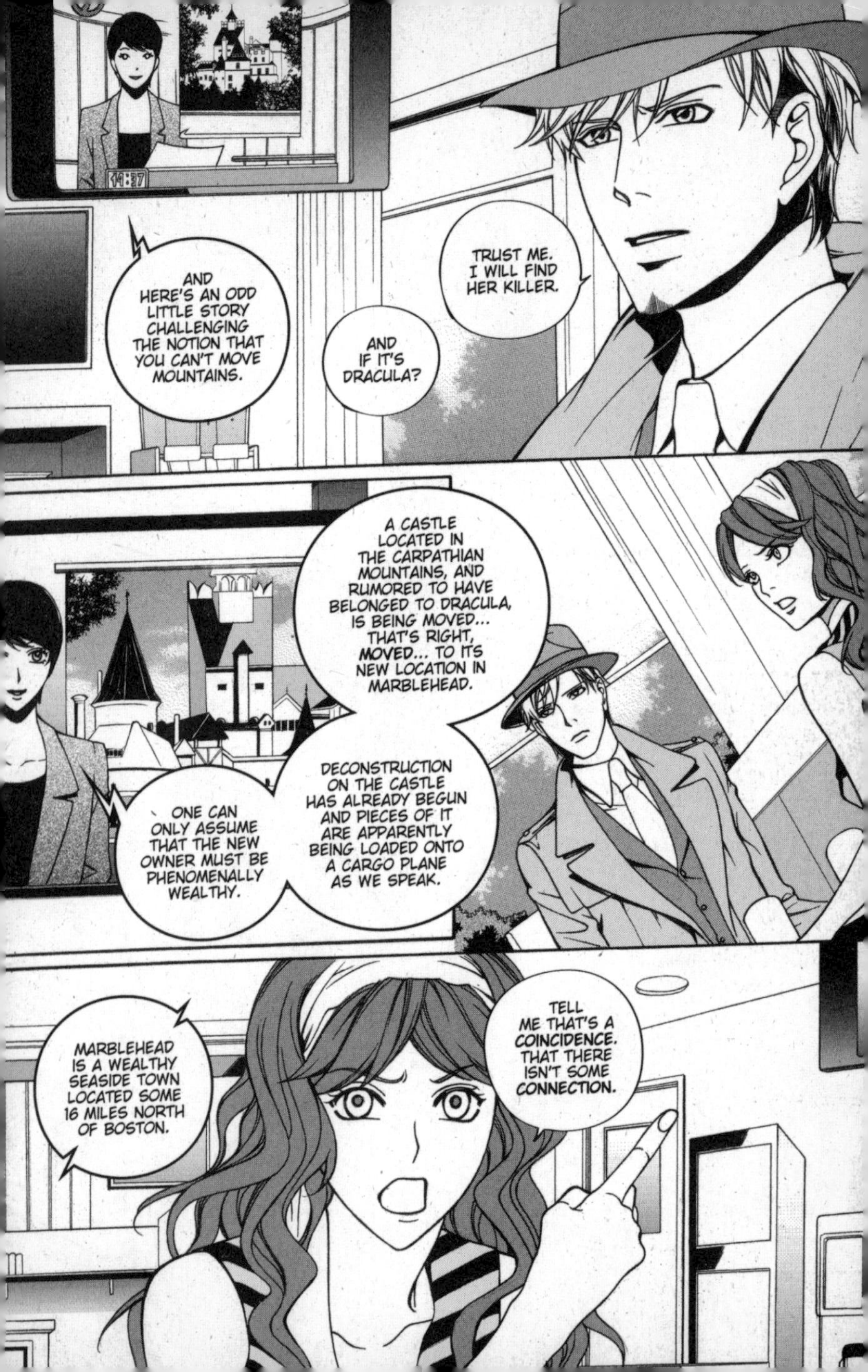
TRUST ME. I WILL FIND HER KILLER.
AND IF IT'S DRACULA?
AND HERE'S AN ODD LITTLE STORY CHALLENGING THE NOTION THAT YOU CAN'T MOVE MOUNTAINS.
A CASTLE LOCATED IN THE CARPATHIAN MOUNTAINS, AND RUMORED TO HAVE BELONGED TO DRACULA, IS BEING MOVED... THAT'S RIGHT, MOVED... TO ITS NEW LOCATION IN MARBLEHEAD.
DECONSTRUCTION ON THE CASTLE HAS ALREADY BEGUN AND PIECES OF IT ARE APPARENTLY BEING LOADED ONTO A CARGO PLANE AS WE SPEAK.
ONE CAN ONLY ASSUME THAT THE NEW OWNER MUST BE PHENOMENALLY WEALTHY.
TELL ME THAT'S A COINCIDENCE. THAT THERE ISN'T SOME CONNECTION.
MARBLEHEAD IS A WEALTHY SEASIDE TOWN LOCATED SOME 16 MILES NORTH OF BOSTON.

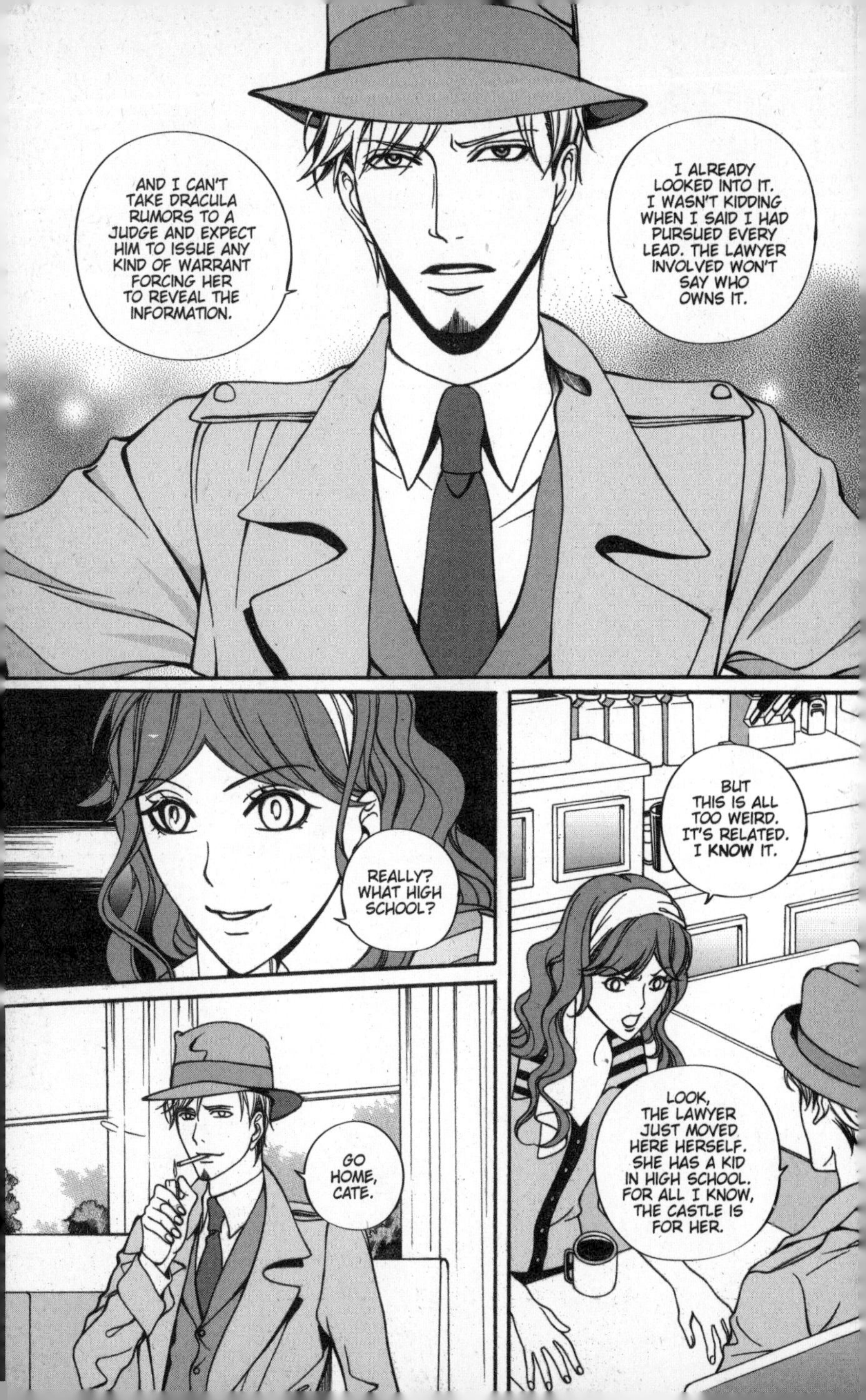
I ALREADY LOOKED INTO IT. I WASN'T KIDDING WHEN I SAID I HAD PURSUED EVERY LEAD. THE LAWYER INVOLVED WON'T SAY WHO OWNS IT.
AND I CAN'T TAKE DRACULA RUMORS TO A JUDGE AND EXPECT HIM TO ISSUE ANY KIND OF WARRANT FORCING HER TO REVEAL THE INFORMATION.
BUT THIS IS ALL TOO WEIRD. IT'S RELATED. I KNOW IT.
LOOK, THE LAWYER JUST MOVED HERE HERSELF. SHE HAS A KID IN HIGH SCHOOL. FOR ALL I KNOW, THE CASTLE IS FOR HER.
REALLY? WHAT HIGH SCHOOL?
GO HOME, CATE.

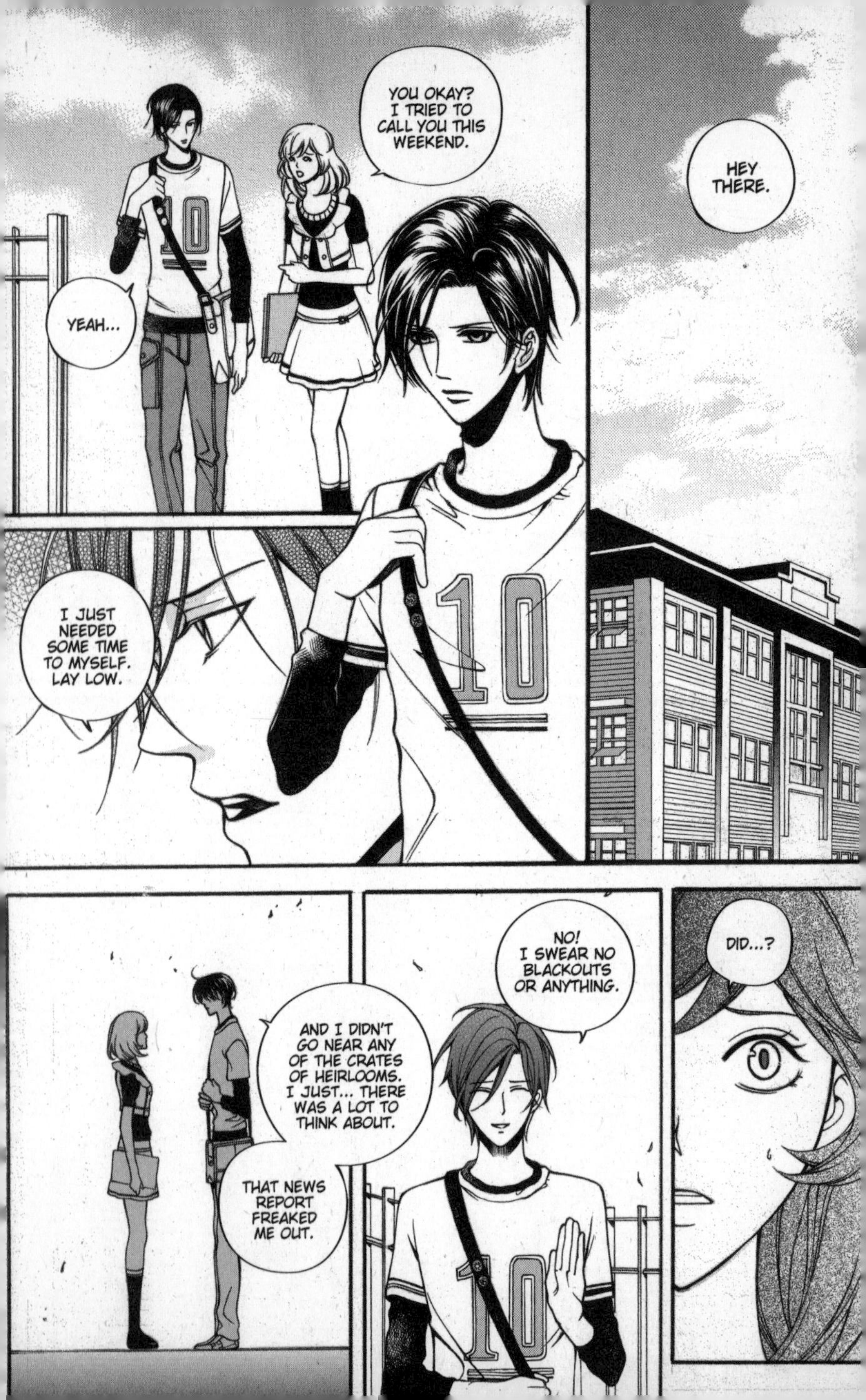
HEY THERE.
YOU OKAY? I TRIED TO CALL YOU THIS WEEKEND.
YEAH...
I JUST NEEDED SOME TIME TO MYSELF. LAY LOW.
DID...?
NO! I SWEAR NO BLACKOUTS OR ANYTHING.
AND I DIDN'T GO NEAR ANY OF THE CRATES OF HEIRLOOMS. I JUST... THERE WAS A LOT TO THINK ABOUT.
THAT NEWS REPORT FREAKED ME OUT.

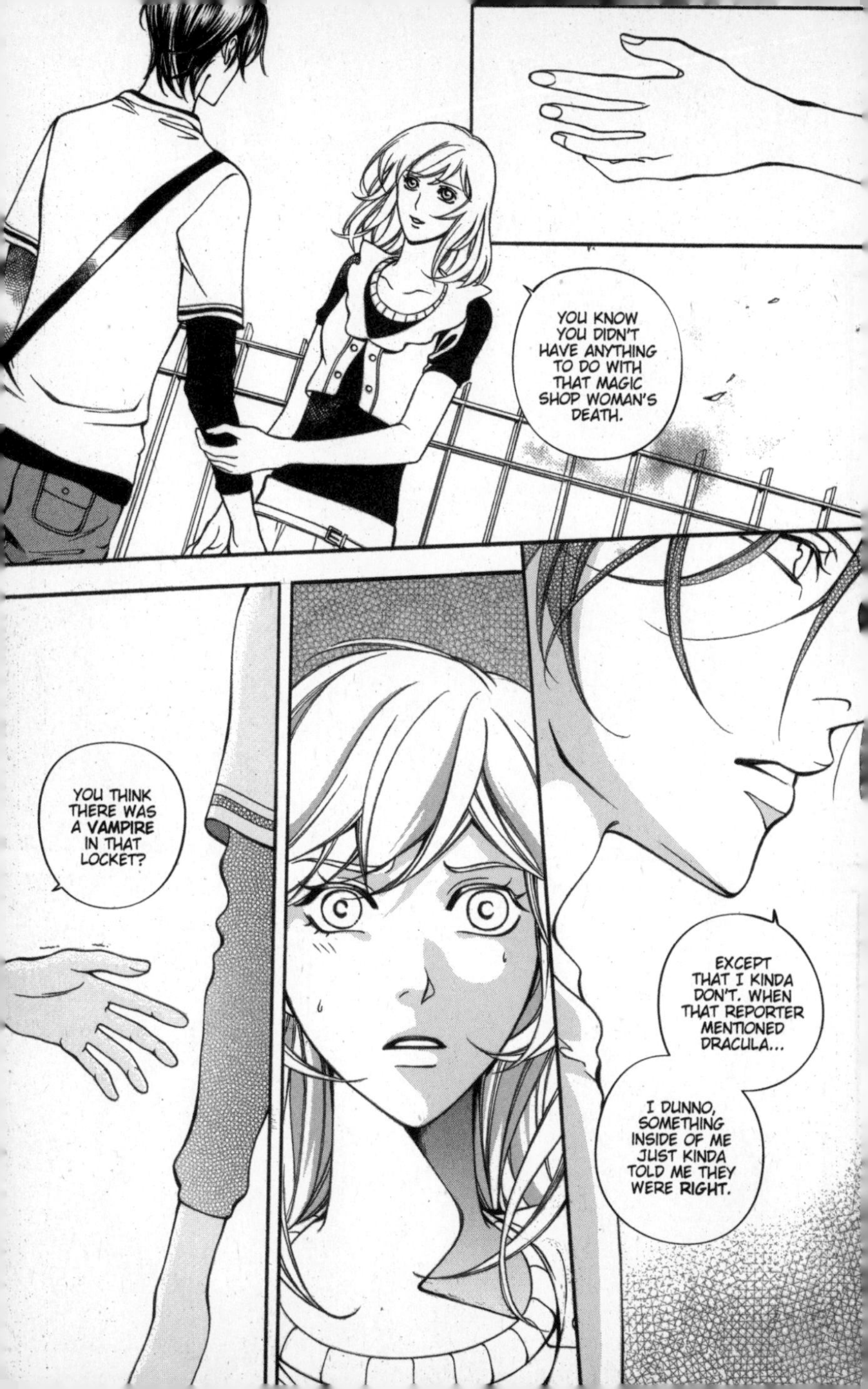
YOU KNOW YOU DIDN'T HAVE ANYTHING TO DO WITH THAT MAGIC SHOP WOMAN'S DEATH.
EXCEPT THAT I KINDA DON'T. WHEN THAT REPORTER MENTIONED DRACULA...
I DUNNO, SOMETHING INSIDE OF ME JUST KINDA TOLD ME THEY WERE RIGHT.
YOU THINK THERE WAS A VAMPIRE IN THAT LOCKET?

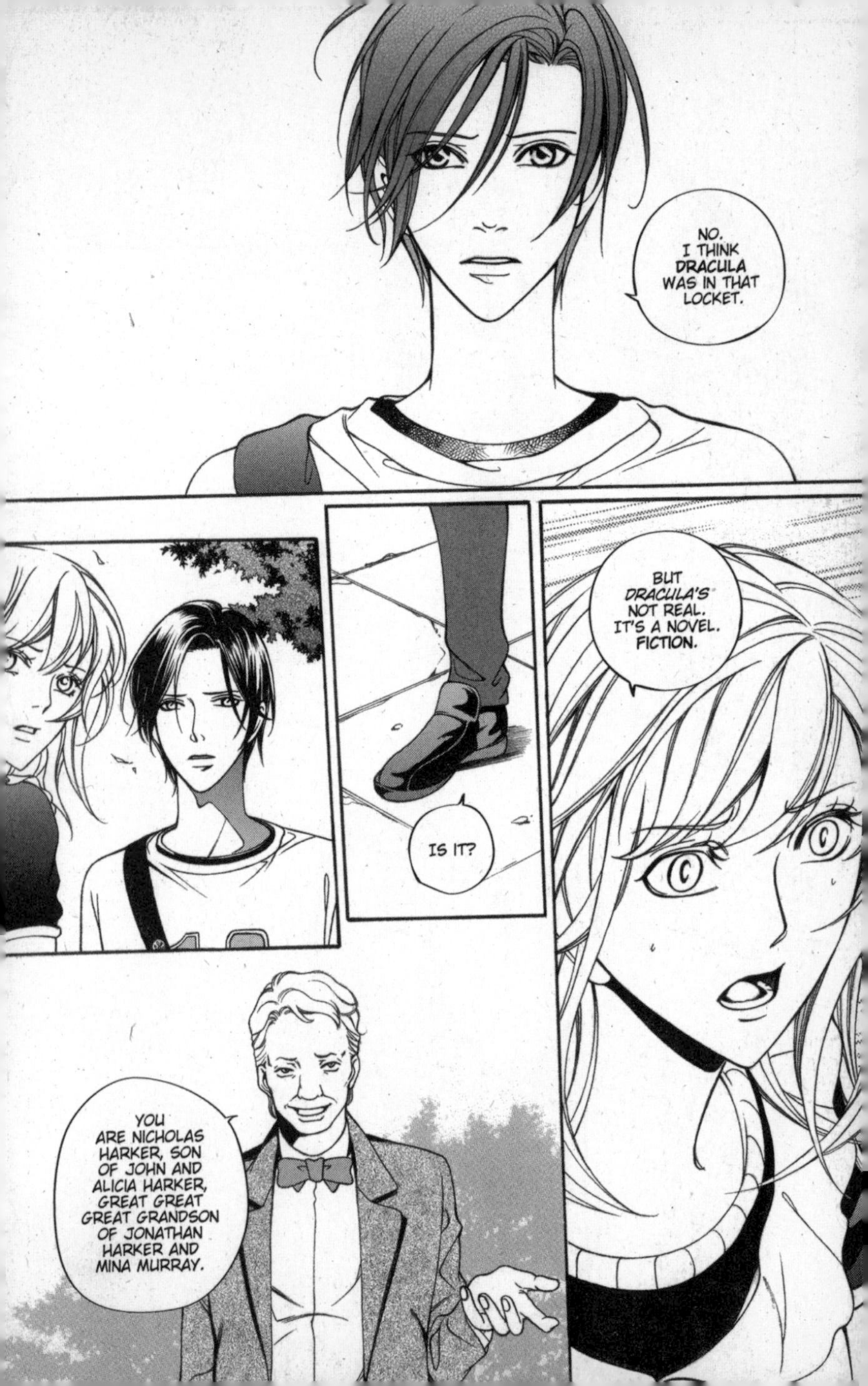
NO. I THINK *DRACULA* WAS IN THAT LOCKET.
BUT *DRACULA'S* NOT REAL. IT'S A NOVEL. FICTION.
IS IT?
YOU ARE NICHOLAS HARKER, SON OF JOHN AND ALICIA HARKER, GREAT GREAT GREAT GRANDSON OF JONATHAN HARKER AND MINA MURRAY.

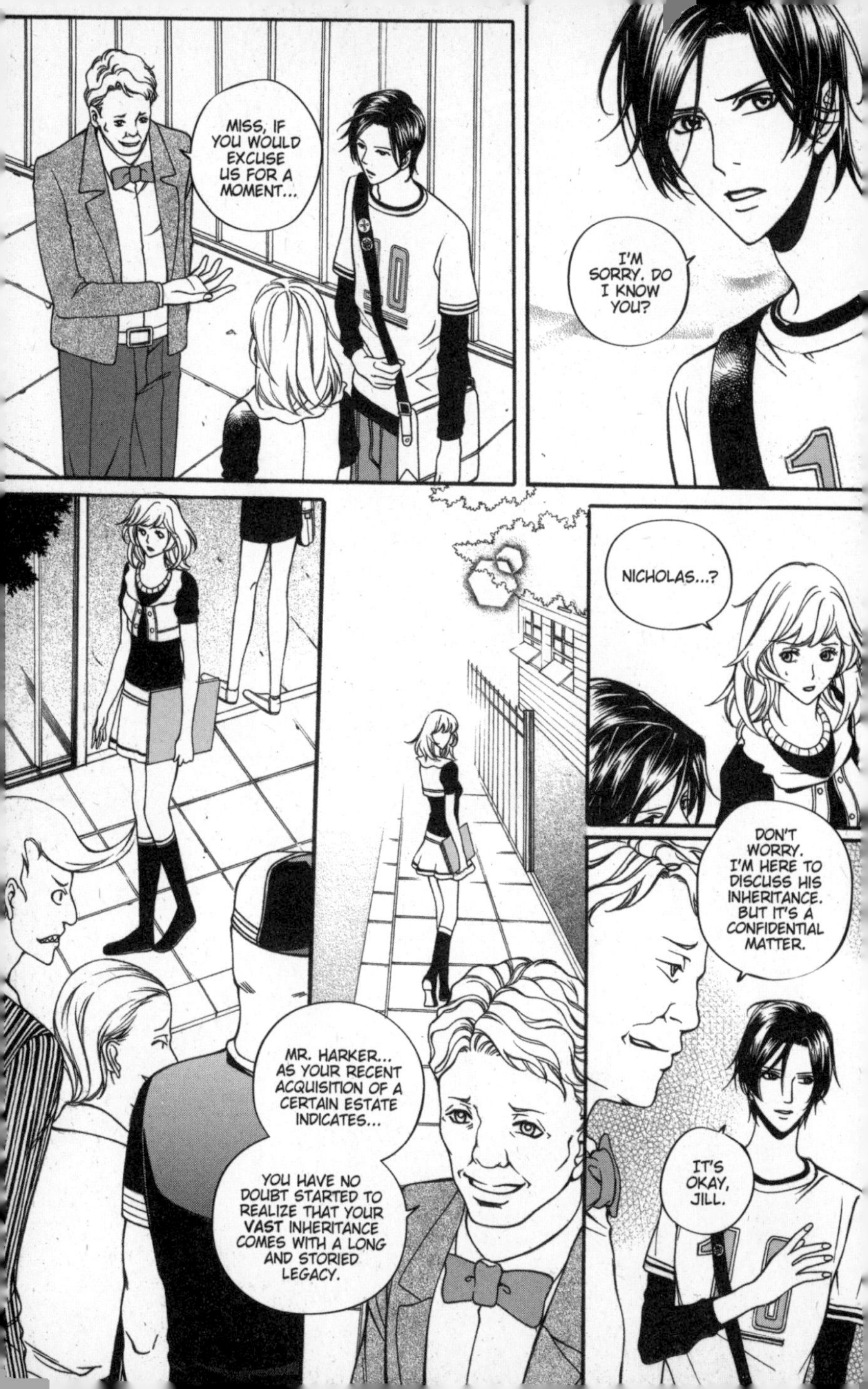
I'M SORRY. DO I KNOW YOU?
MISS, IF YOU WOULD EXCUSE US FOR A MOMENT...
NICHOLAS...?
DON'T WORRY. I'M HERE TO DISCUSS HIS INHERITANCE. BUT IT'S A CONFIDENTIAL MATTER.
IT'S OKAY, JILL.
MR. HARKER... AS YOUR RECENT ACQUISITION OF A CERTAIN ESTATE INDICATES...
YOU HAVE NO DOUBT STARTED TO REALIZE THAT YOUR VAST INHERITANCE COMES WITH A LONG AND STORIED LEGACY.

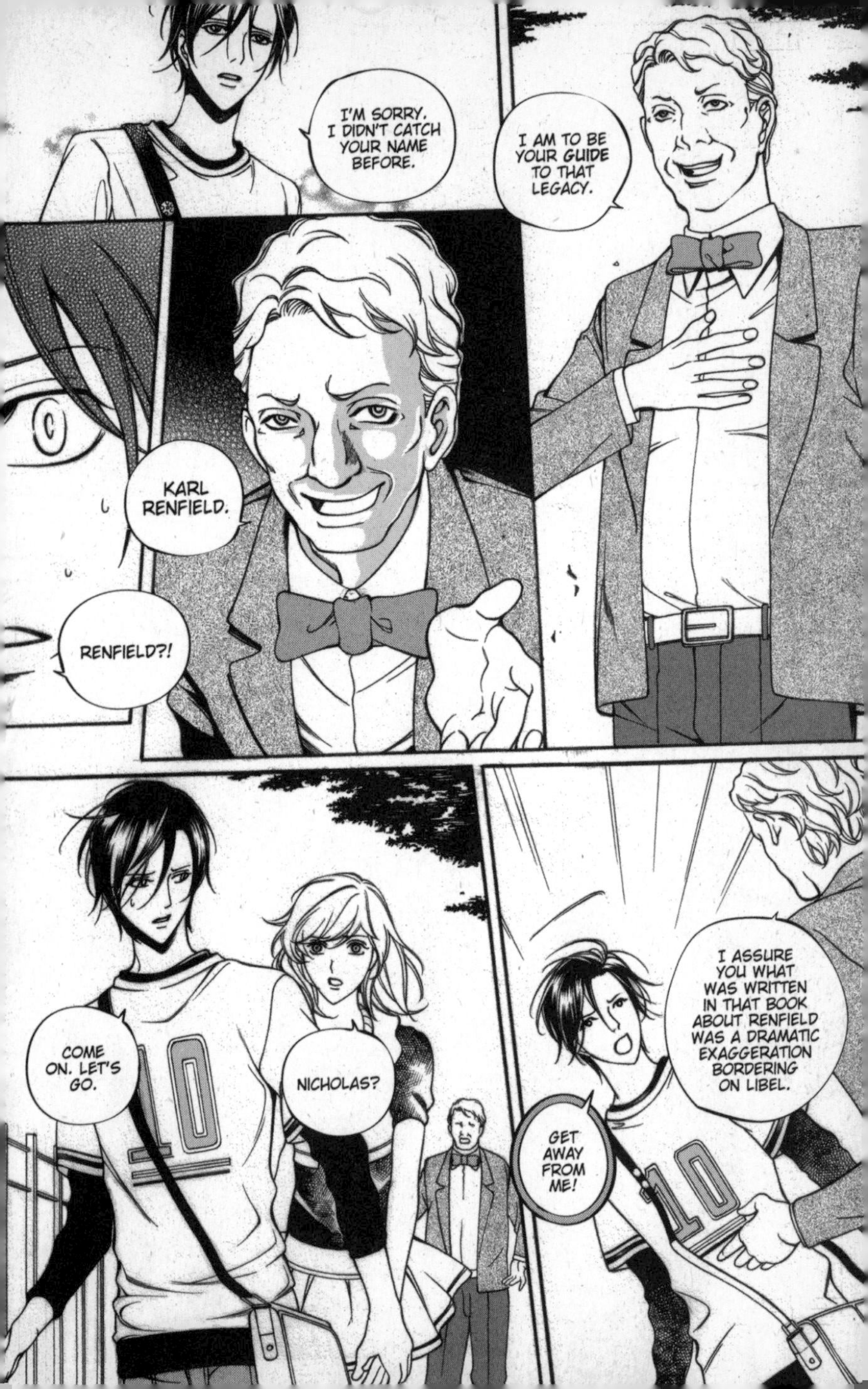
I AM TO BE YOUR GUIDE TO THAT LEGACY.
I'M SORRY. I DIDN'T CATCH YOUR NAME BEFORE.
KARL RENFIELD.
RENFIELD?!
I ASSURE YOU WHAT WAS WRITTEN IN THAT BOOK ABOUT RENFIELD WAS A DRAMATIC EXAGGERATION BORDERING ON LIBEL.
GET AWAY FROM ME!
NICHOLAS?
COME ON. LET'S GO.

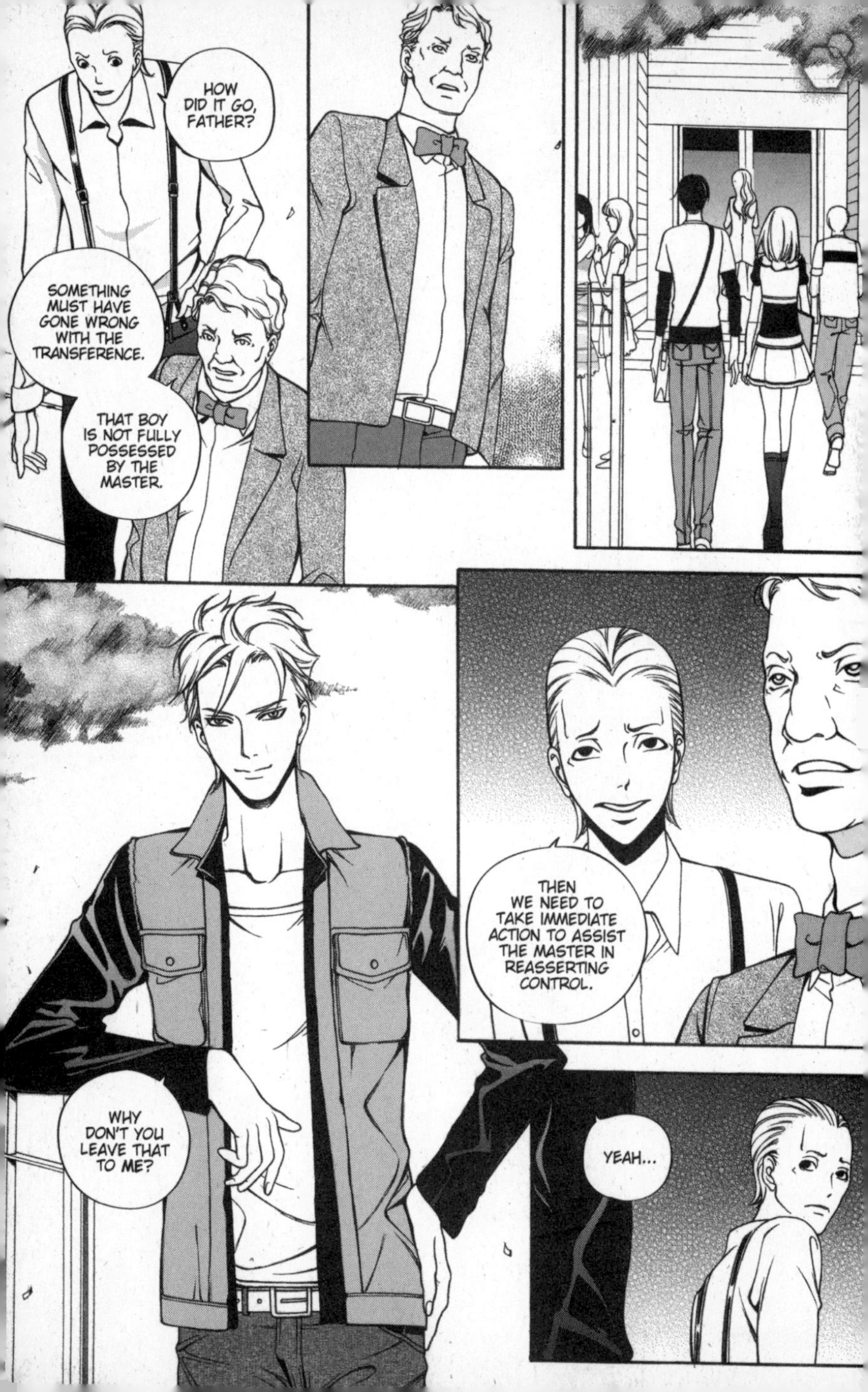
HOW DID IT GO, FATHER?
SOMETHING MUST HAVE GONE WRONG WITH THE TRANSFERENCE.
THAT BOY IS NOT FULLY POSSESSED BY THE MASTER.
THEN WE NEED TO TAKE IMMEDIATE ACTION TO ASSIST THE MASTER IN REASSERTING CONTROL.
YEAH...
WHY DON'T YOU LEAVE THAT TO ME?

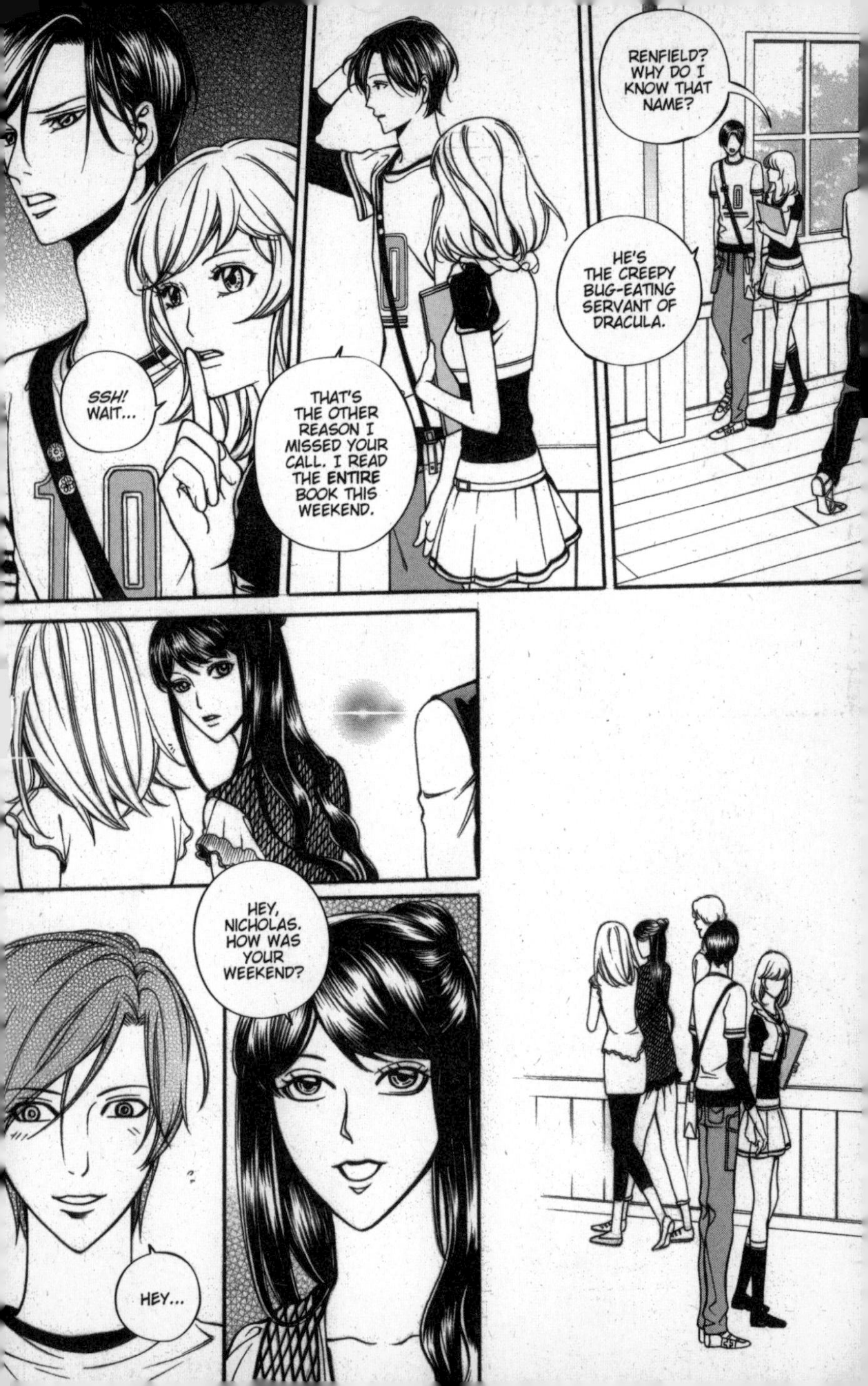
RENFIELD? WHY DO I KNOW THAT NAME?
HE'S THE CREEPY BUG-EATING SERVANT OF DRACULA.
THAT'S THE OTHER REASON I MISSED YOUR CALL. I READ THE ENTIRE BOOK THIS WEEKEND.
SSH! WAIT...
HEY, NICHOLAS. HOW WAS YOUR WEEKEND?
HEY...

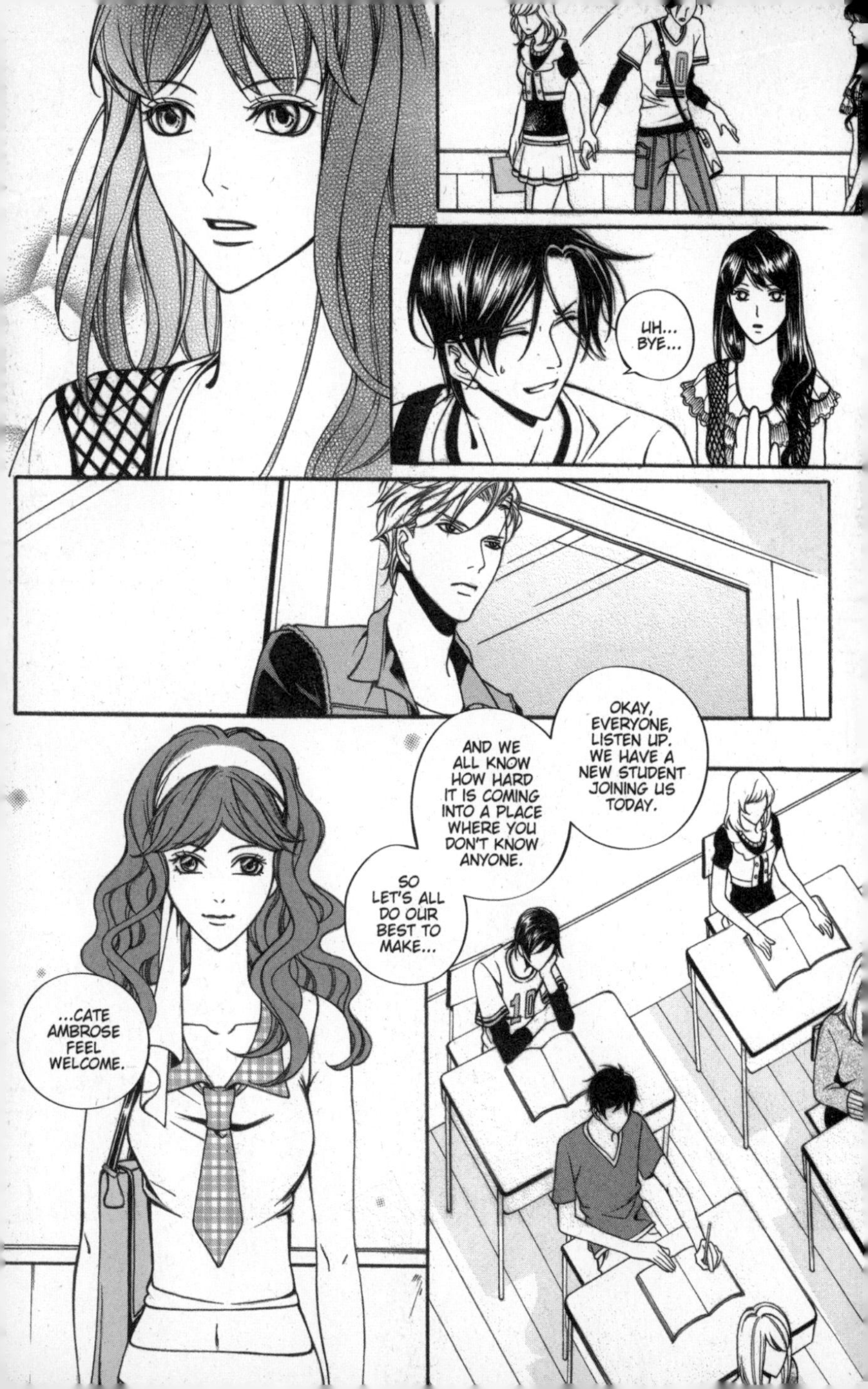
UH... BYE...
OKAY, EVERYONE, LISTEN UP. WE HAVE A NEW STUDENT JOINING US TODAY.
AND WE ALL KNOW HOW HARD IT IS COMING INTO A PLACE WHERE YOU DON'T KNOW ANYONE.
SO LET'S ALL DO OUR BEST TO MAKE...
...CATE AMBROSE FEEL WELCOME.

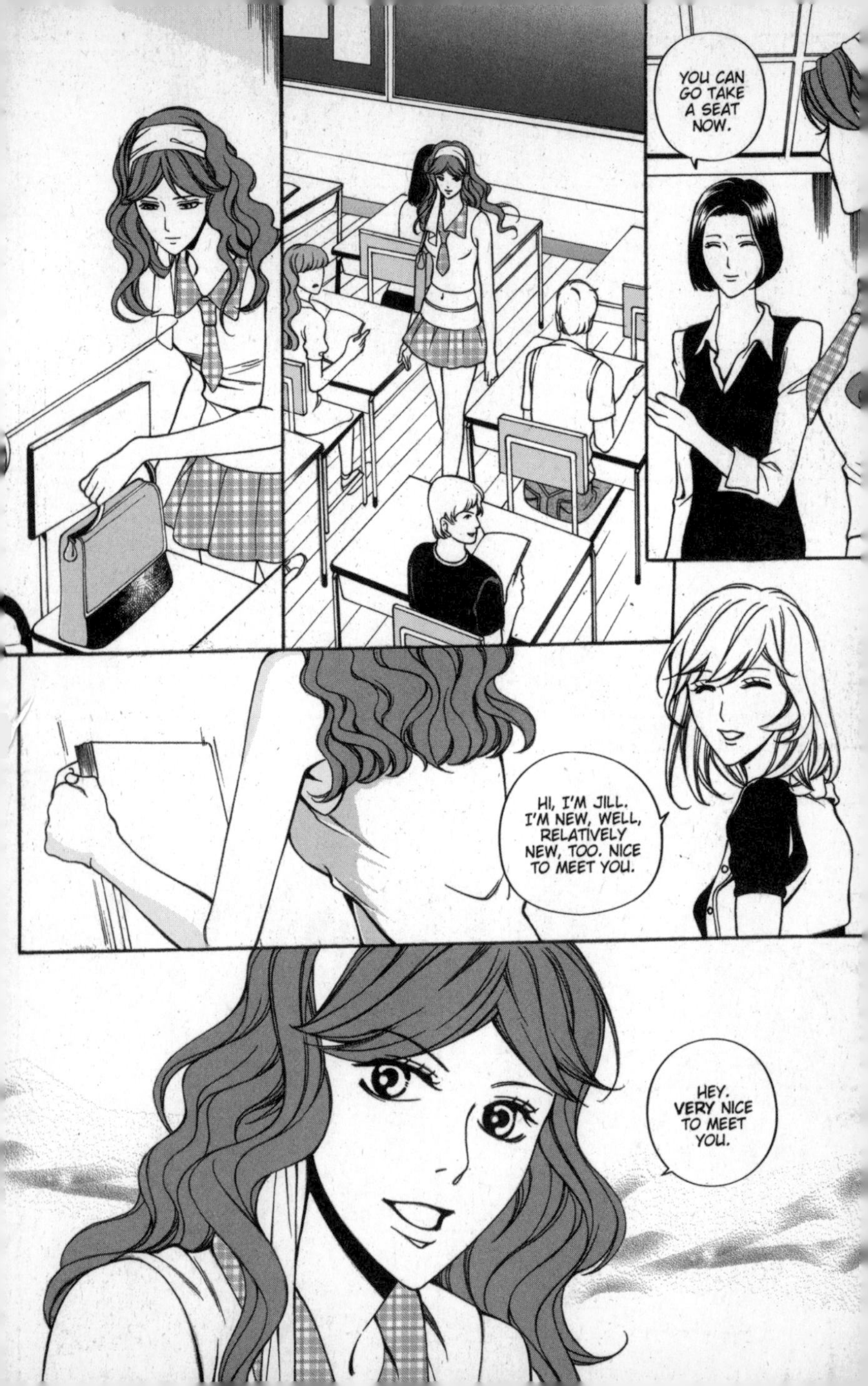
YOU CAN GO TAKE A SEAT NOW.
HI, I'M JILL. I'M NEW, WELL, RELATIVELY NEW, TOO. NICE TO MEET YOU.
HEY. VERY NICE TO MEET YOU.

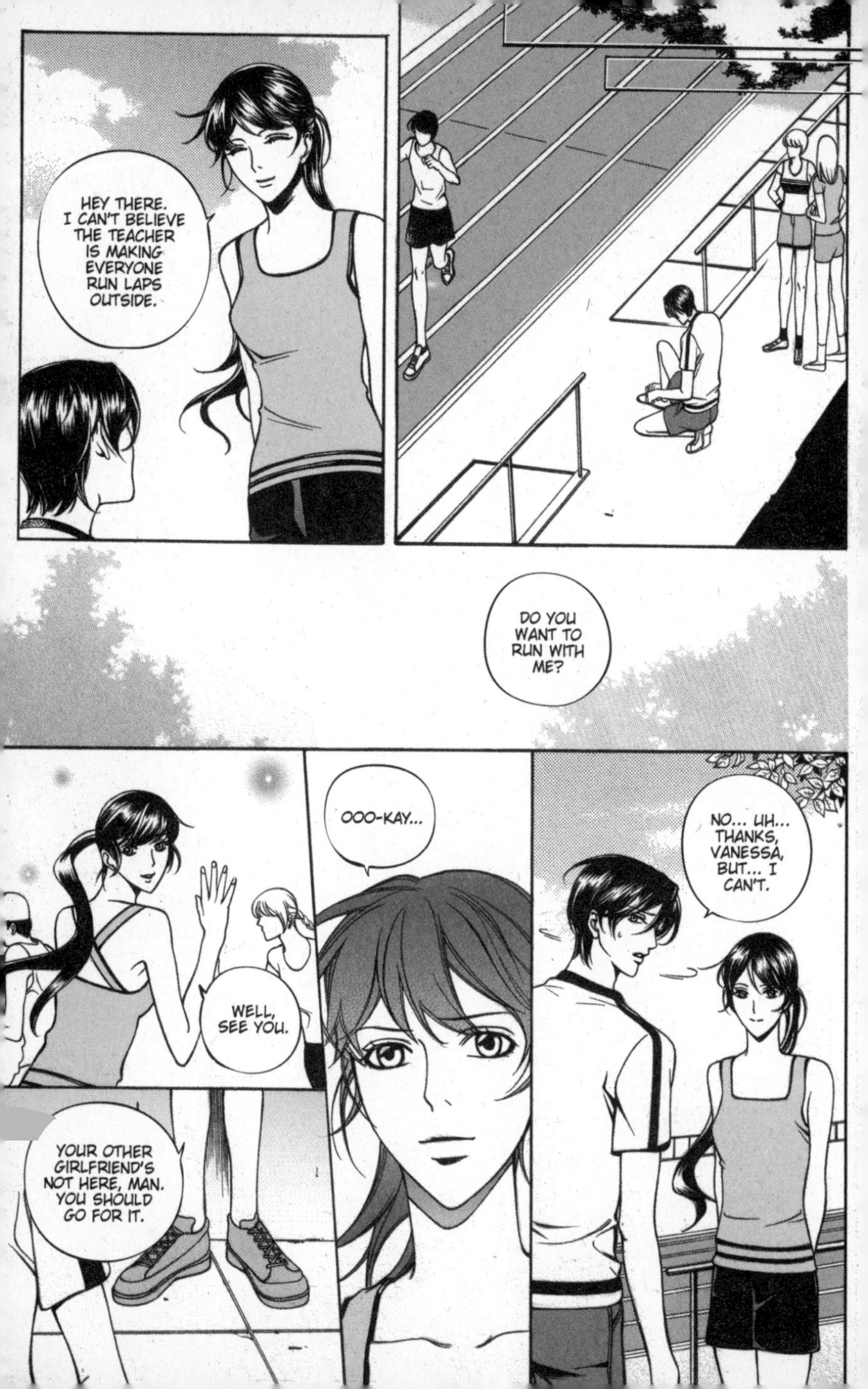
HEY THERE. I CAN'T BELIEVE THE TEACHER IS MAKING EVERYONE RUN LAPS OUTSIDE.
DO YOU WANT TO RUN WITH ME?
NO... UH... THANKS, VANESSA, BUT... I CAN'T.
OOO-KAY...
WELL, SEE YOU.
YOUR OTHER GIRLFRIEND'S NOT HERE, MAN. YOU SHOULD GO FOR IT.

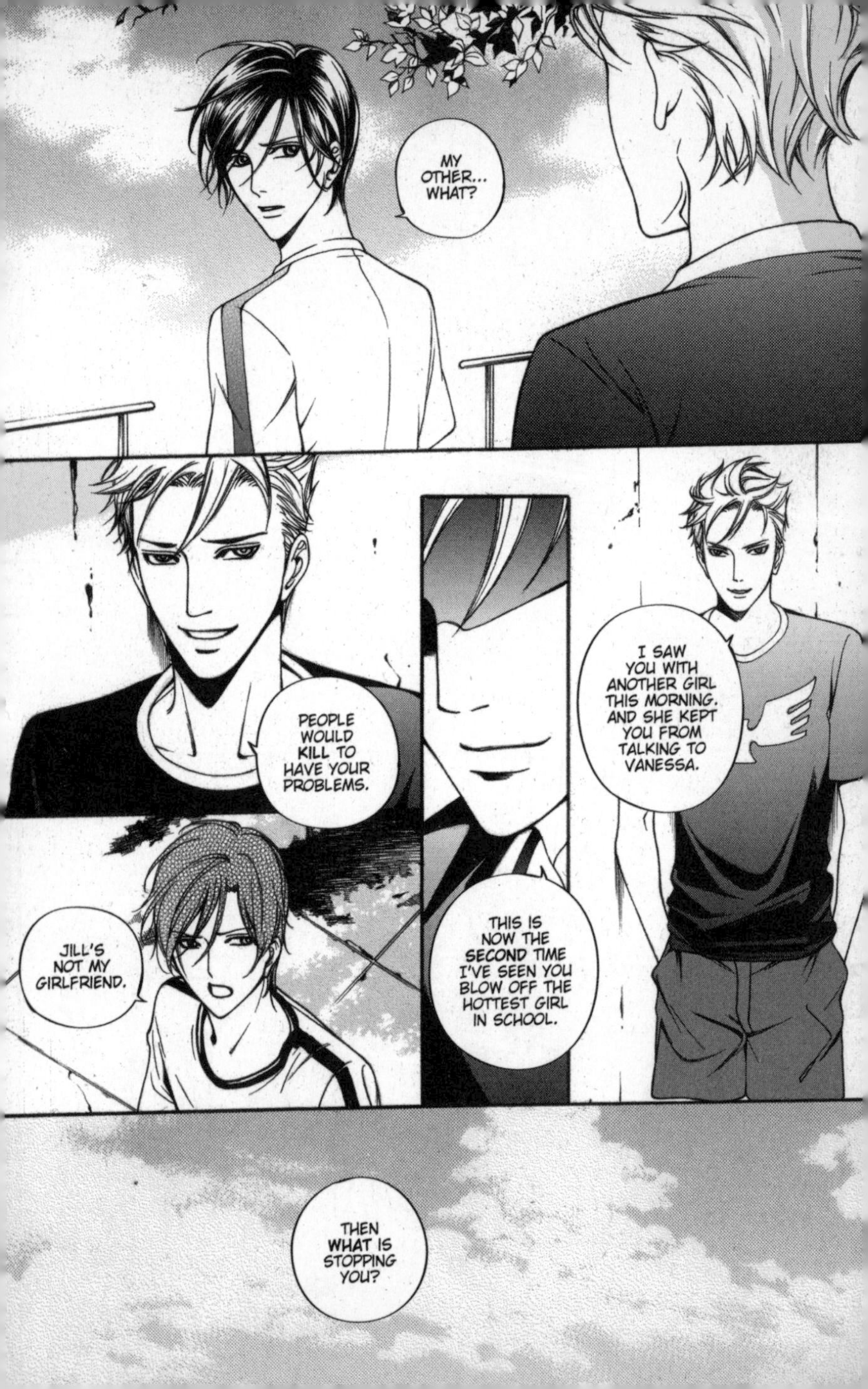
MY OTHER... WHAT?
I SAW YOU WITH ANOTHER GIRL THIS MORNING. AND SHE KEPT YOU FROM TALKING TO VANESSA.
THIS IS NOW THE SECOND TIME I'VE SEEN YOU BLOW OFF THE HOTTEST GIRL IN SCHOOL.
PEOPLE WOULD KILL TO HAVE YOUR PROBLEMS.
JILL'S NOT MY GIRLFRIEND.
THEN WHAT IS STOPPING YOU?

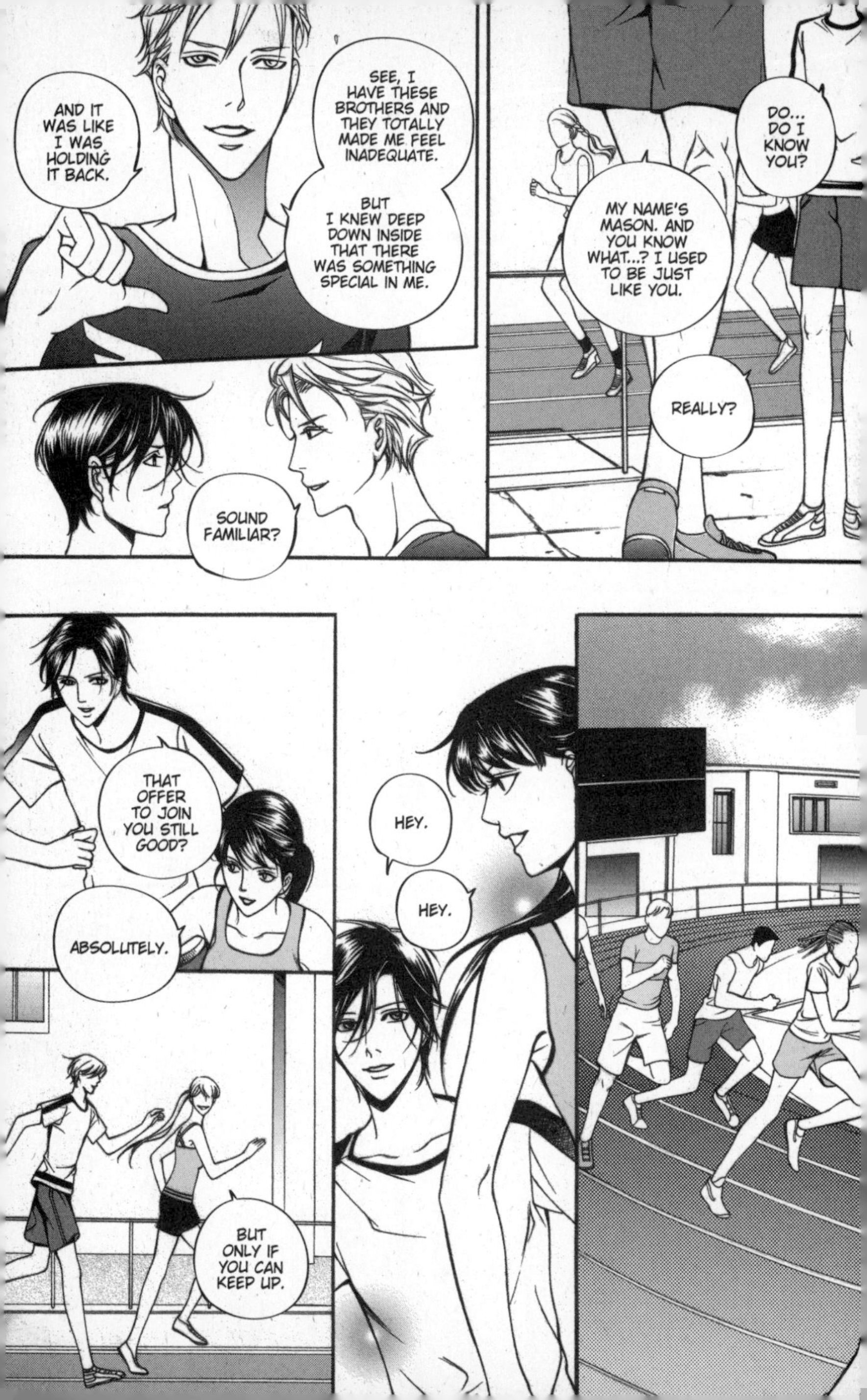
DO... DO I KNOW YOU?
MY NAME'S MASON. AND YOU KNOW WHAT...? I USED TO BE JUST LIKE YOU.
REALLY?
SEE, I HAVE THESE BROTHERS AND THEY TOTALLY MADE ME FEEL INADEQUATE.
BUT I KNEW DEEP DOWN INSIDE THAT THERE WAS SOMETHING SPECIAL IN ME.
AND IT WAS LIKE I WAS HOLDING IT BACK.
SOUND FAMILIAR?
HEY.
HEY.
THAT OFFER TO JOIN YOU STILL GOOD?
ABSOLUTELY.
BUT ONLY IF YOU CAN KEEP UP.

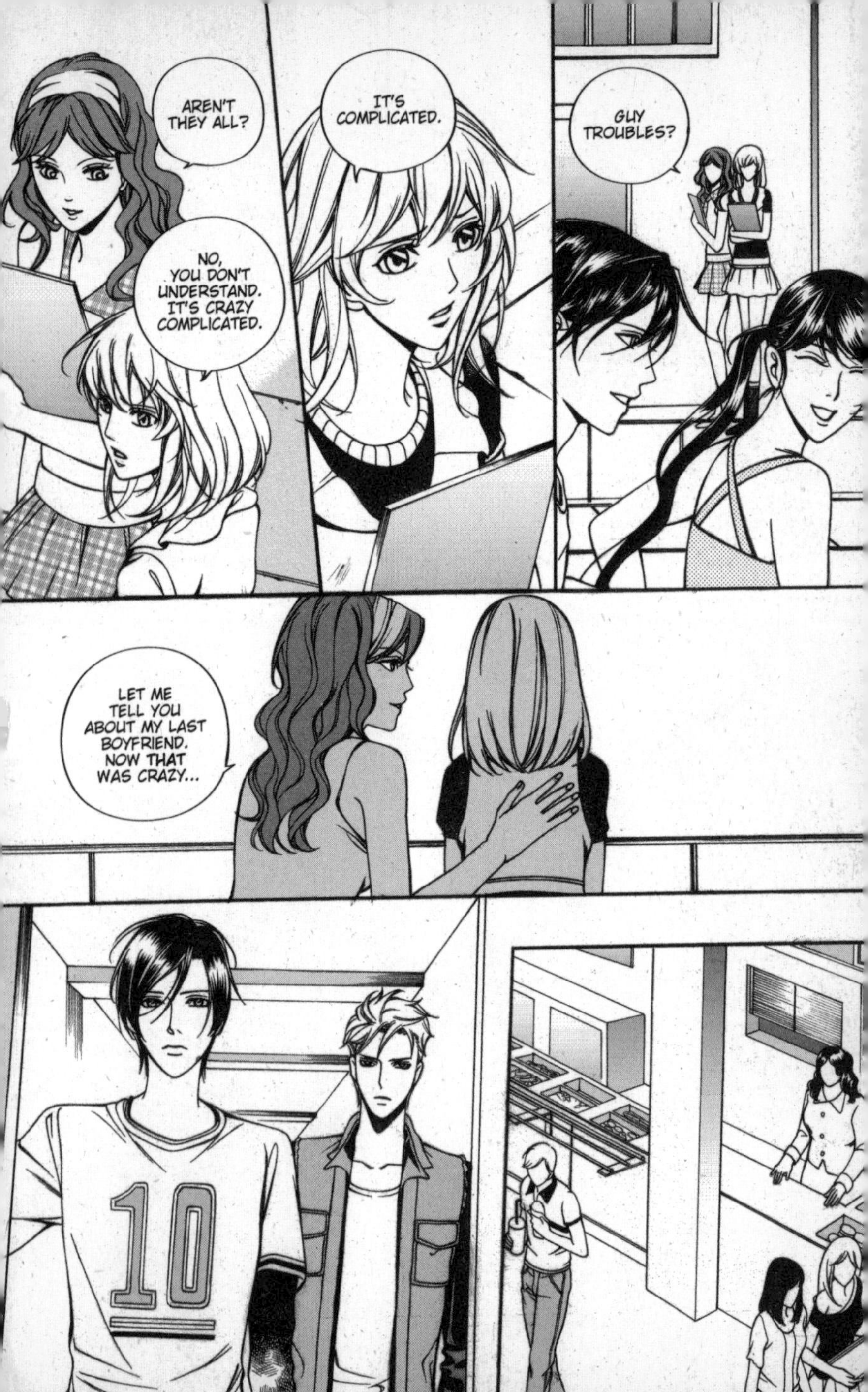
GUY TROUBLES?
IT'S COMPLICATED.
AREN'T THEY ALL?
NO, YOU DON'T UNDERSTAND. IT'S CRAZY COMPLICATED.
LET ME TELL YOU ABOUT MY LAST BOYFRIEND. NOW THAT WAS CRAZY...

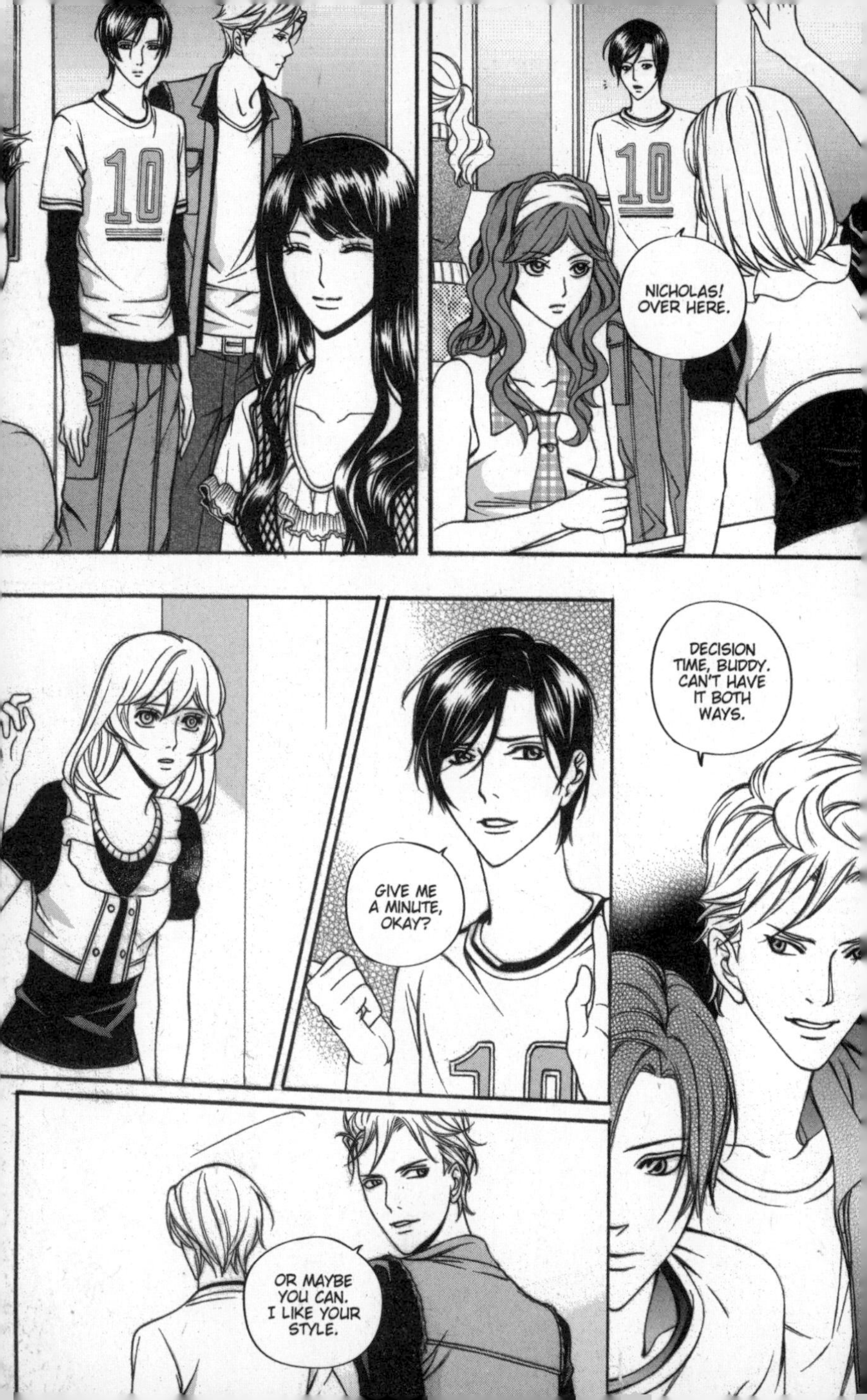
NICHOLAS! OVER HERE.
DECISION TIME, BUDDY. CAN'T HAVE IT BOTH WAYS.
GIVE ME A MINUTE, OKAY?
OR MAYBE YOU CAN. I LIKE YOUR STYLE.

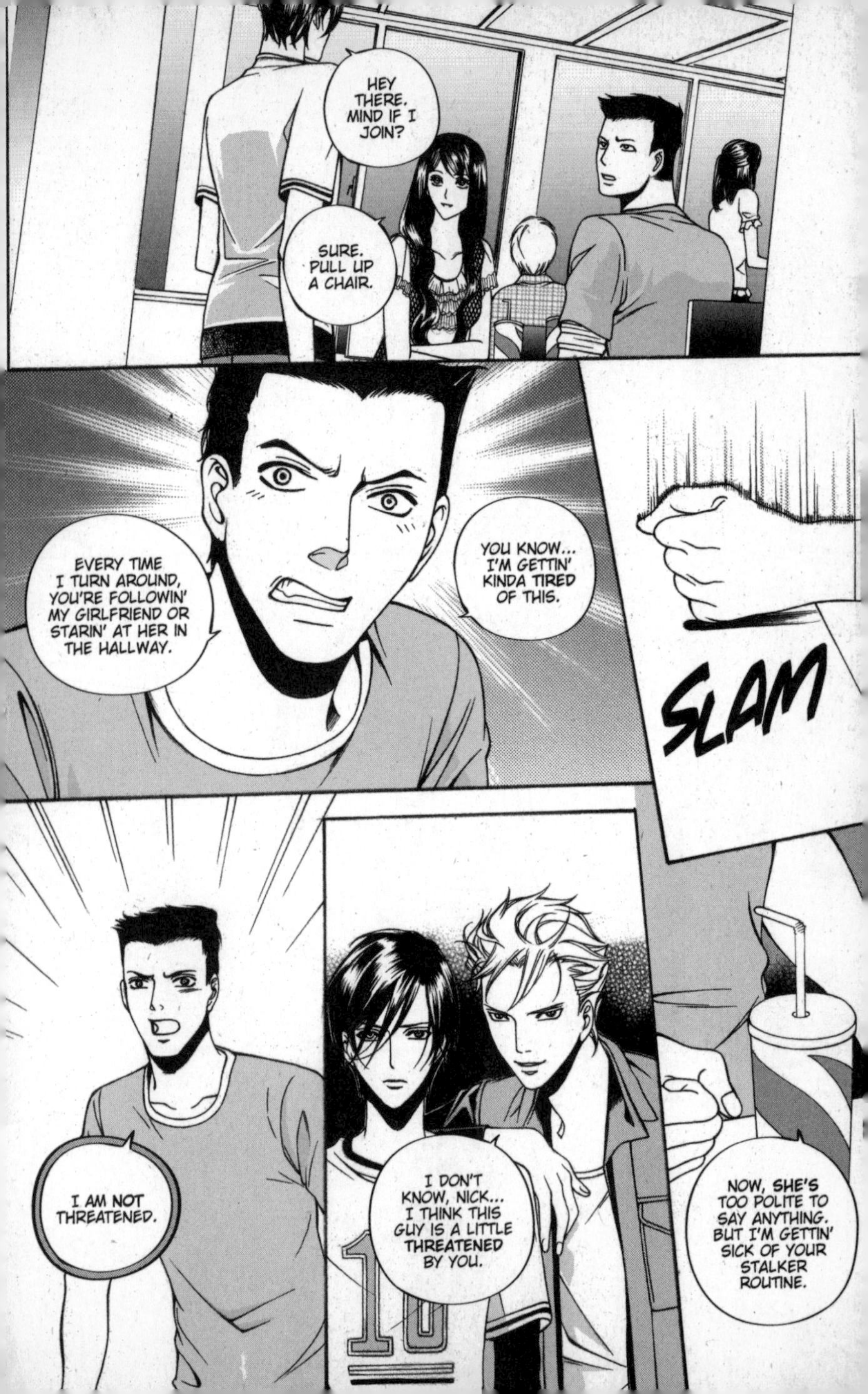
HEY THERE. MIND IF I JOIN?
SURE. PULL UP A CHAIR.
SLAM
YOU KNOW... I'M GETTIN' KINDA TIRED OF THIS.
EVERY TIME I TURN AROUND, YOU'RE FOLLOWIN' MY GIRLFRIEND OR STARIN' AT HER IN THE HALLWAY.
NOW, SHE'S TOO POLITE TO SAY ANYTHING. BUT I'M GETTIN' SICK OF YOUR STALKER ROUTINE.
I DON'T KNOW, NICK... I THINK THIS GUY IS A LITTLE THREATENED BY YOU.
I AM NOT THREATENED.

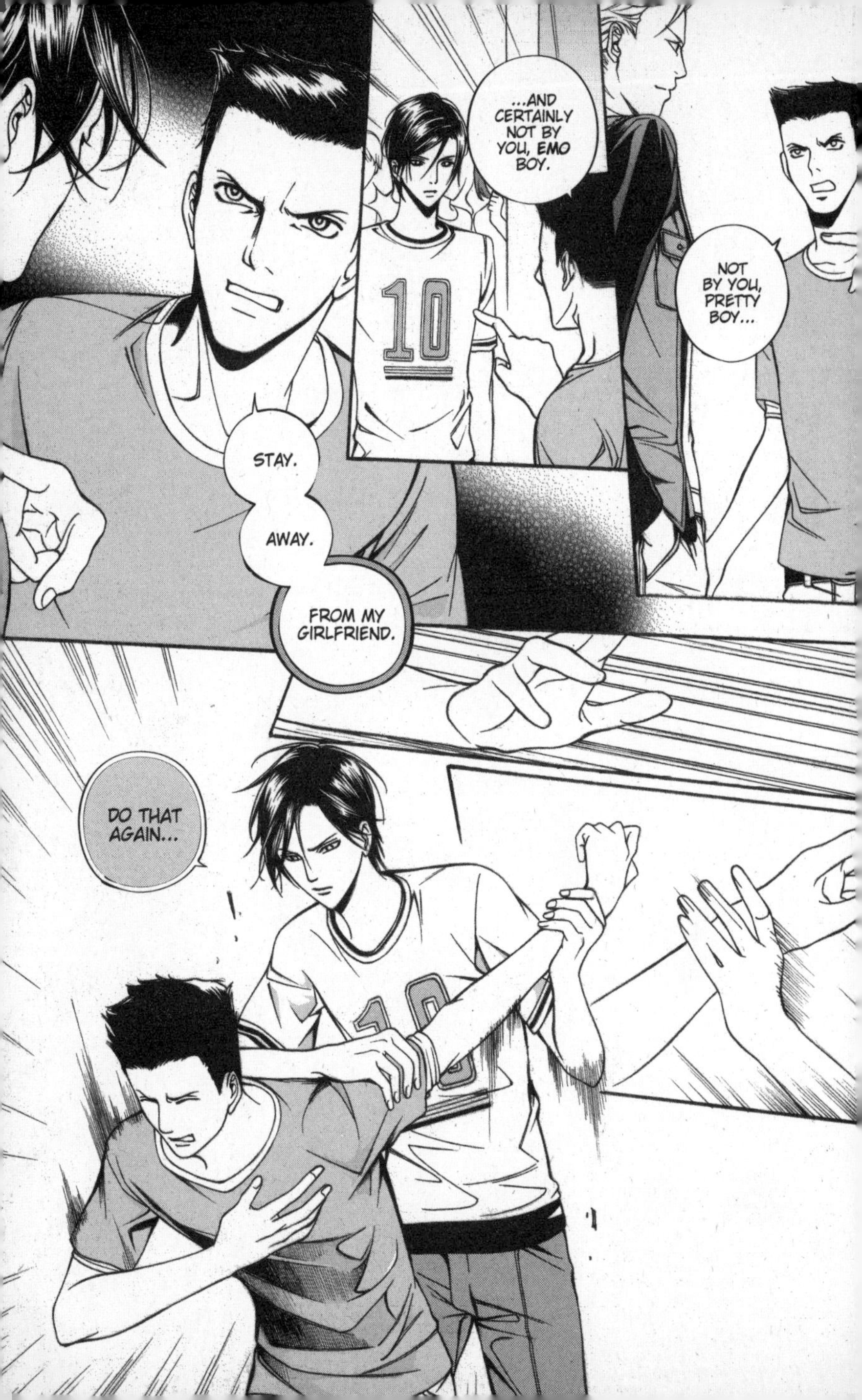
NOT BY YOU, PRETTY BOY...
...AND CERTAINLY NOT BY YOU, EMO BOY.
STAY.
AWAY.
FROM MY GIRLFRIEND.
DO THAT AGAIN...

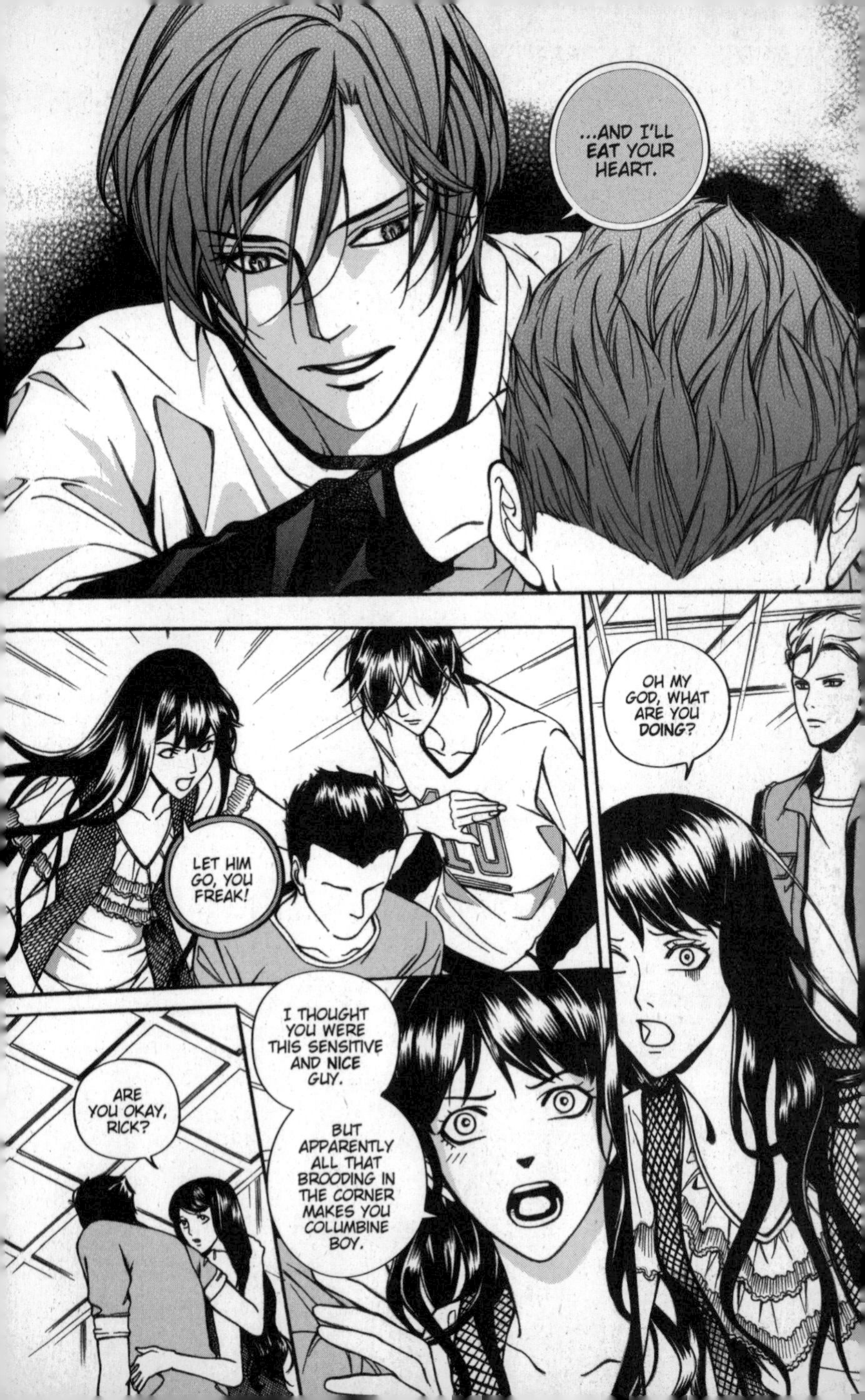
...AND I'LL EAT YOUR HEART.
OH MY GOD, WHAT ARE YOU DOING?
LET HIM GO, YOU FREAK!
I THOUGHT YOU WERE THIS SENSITIVE AND NICE GUY.
BUT APPARENTLY ALL THAT BROODING IN THE CORNER MAKES YOU COLUMBINE BOY.
ARE YOU OKAY, RICK?

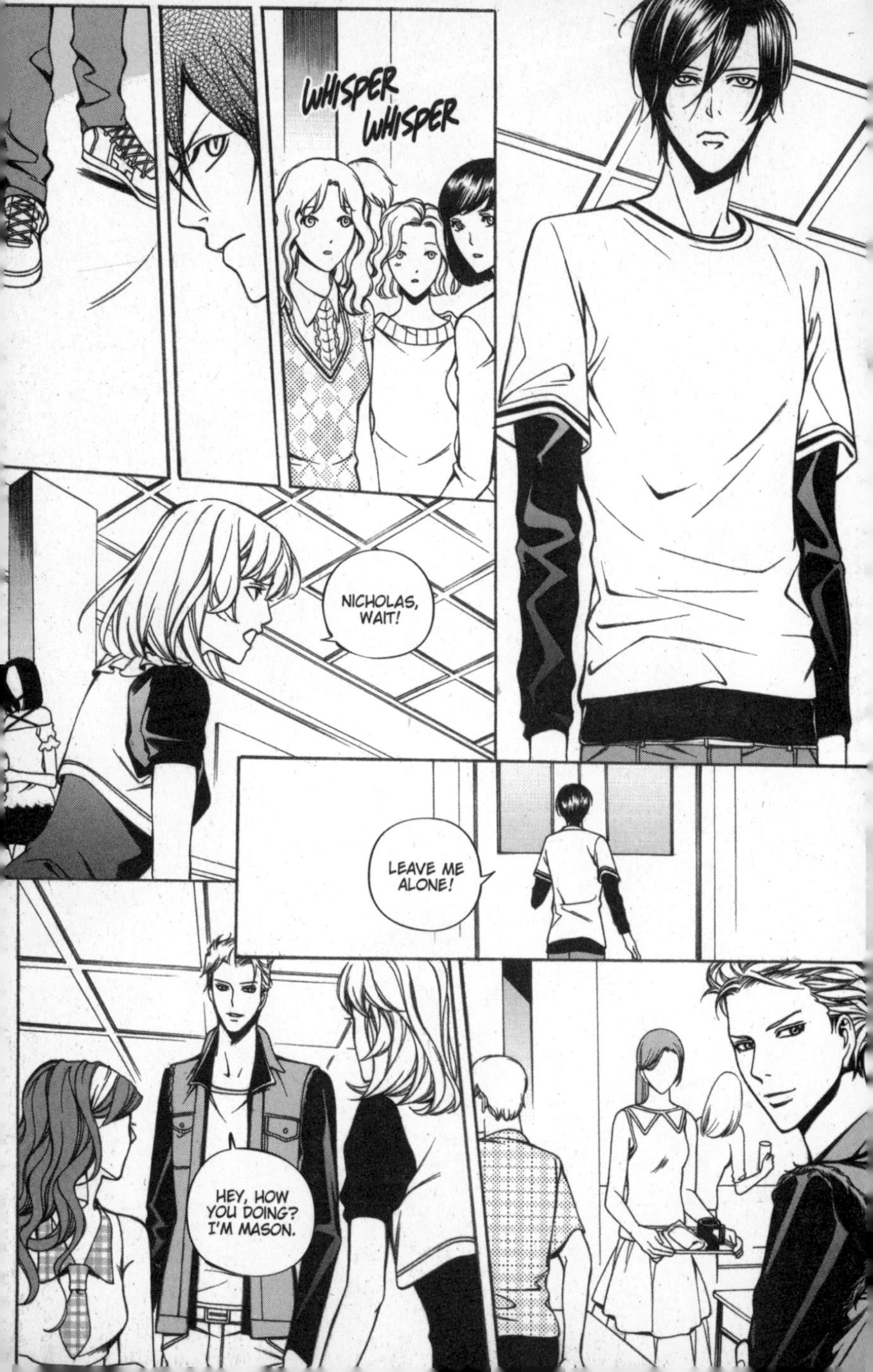
WHISPER WHISPER
NICHOLAS, WAIT!
LEAVE ME ALONE!
HEY, HOW YOU DOING? I'M MASON.

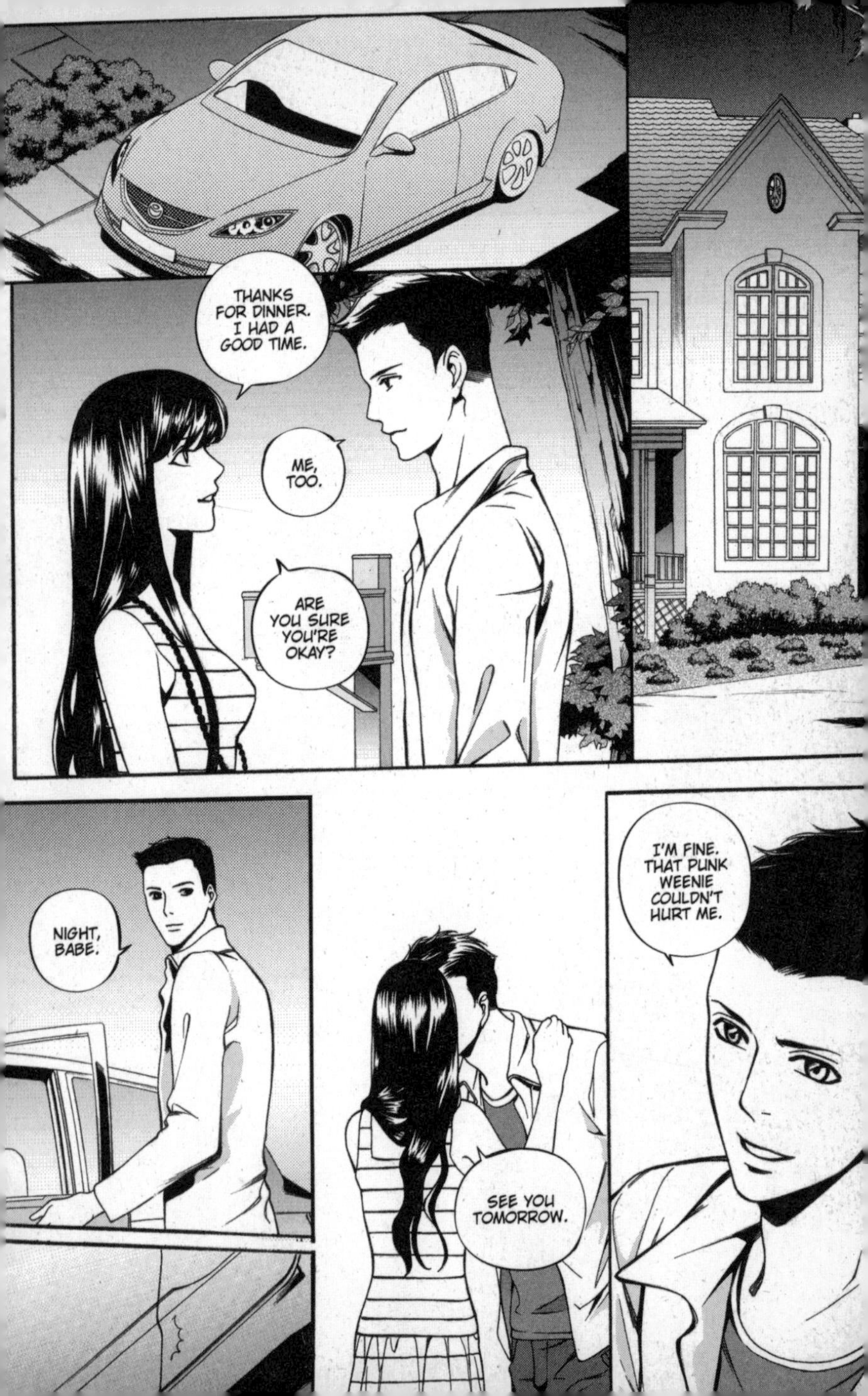
THANKS FOR DINNER. I HAD A GOOD TIME.
ME, TOO.
ARE YOU SURE YOU'RE OKAY?
I'M FINE. THAT PUNK WEENIE COULDN'T HURT ME.
SEE YOU TOMORROW.
NIGHT, BABE.

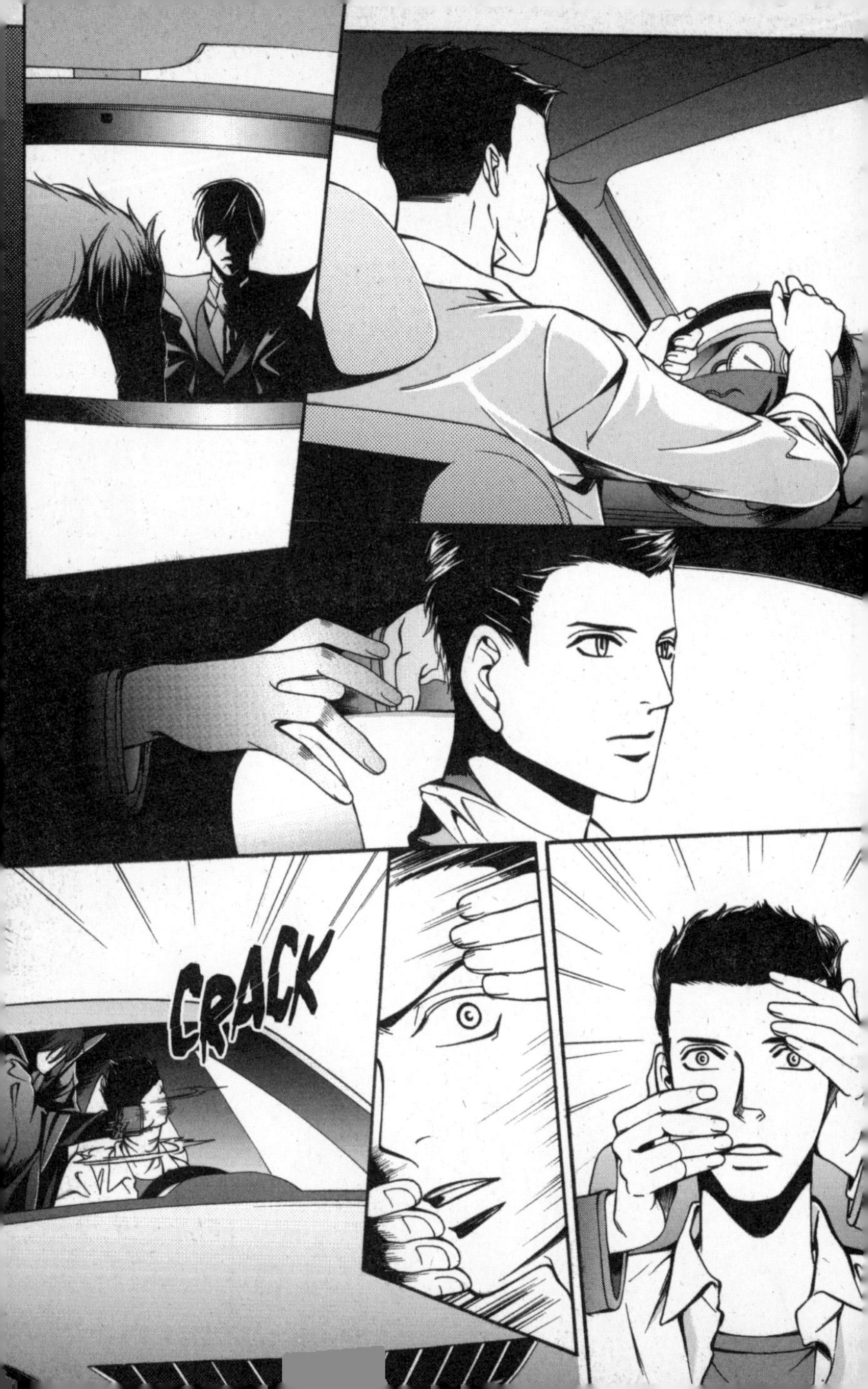
CRACK

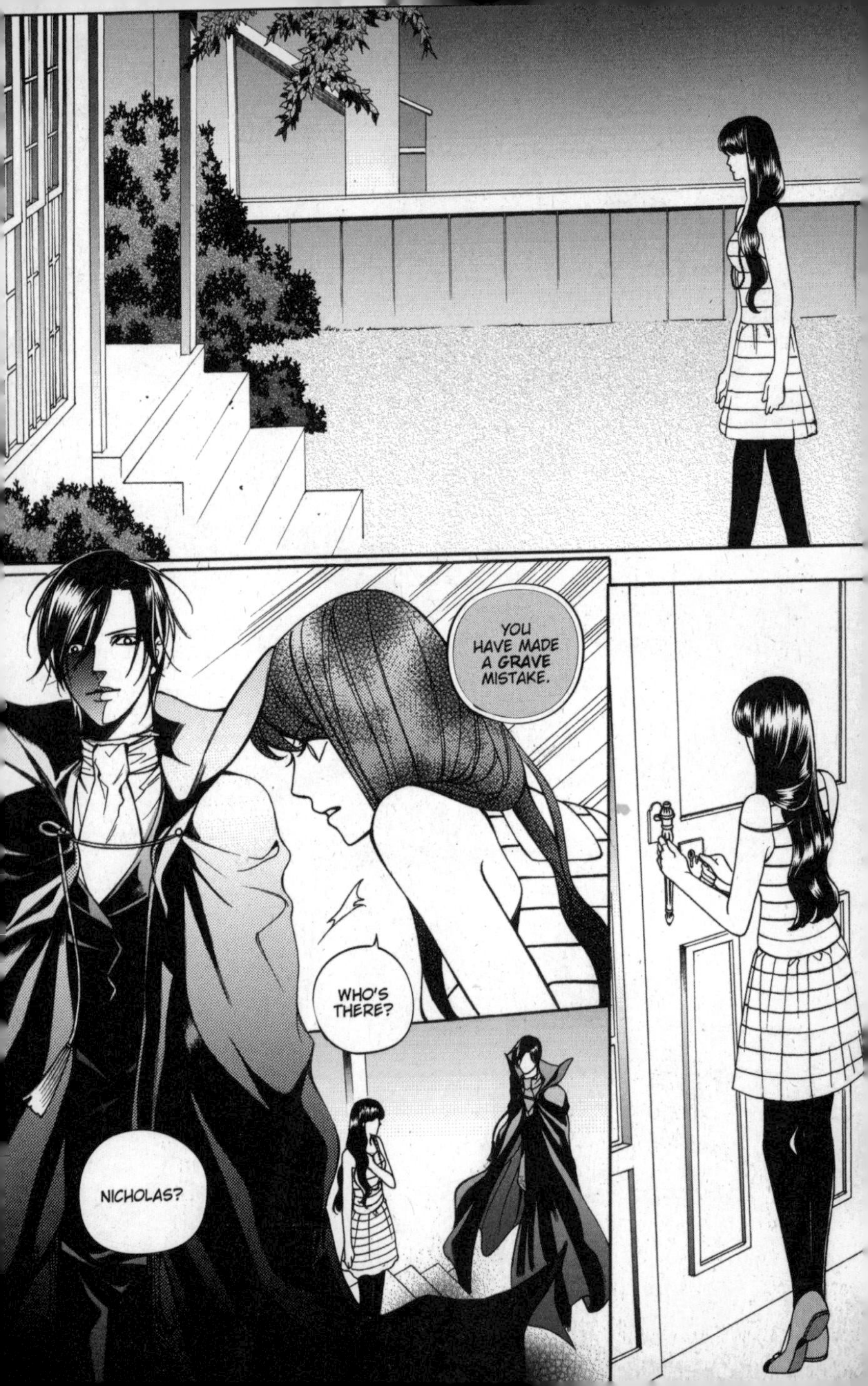
YOU HAVE MADE A GRAVE MISTAKE.
WHO'S THERE?
NICHOLAS?

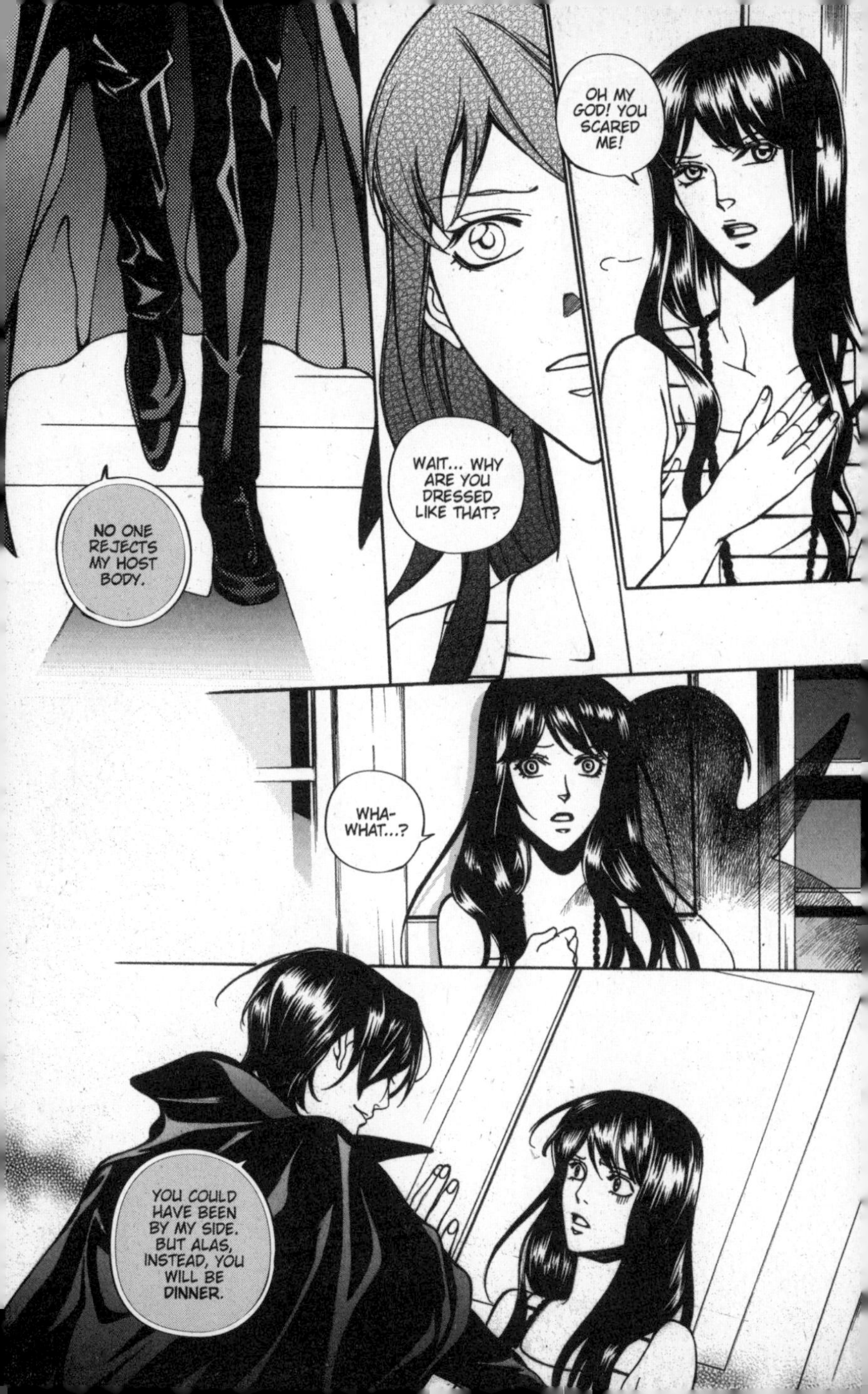
OH MY GOD! YOU SCARED ME!
WAIT... WHY ARE YOU DRESSED LIKE THAT?
NO ONE REJECTS MY HOST BODY.
WHA-WHAT...?
YOU COULD HAVE BEEN BY MY SIDE. BUT ALAS, INSTEAD, YOU WILL BE DINNER.

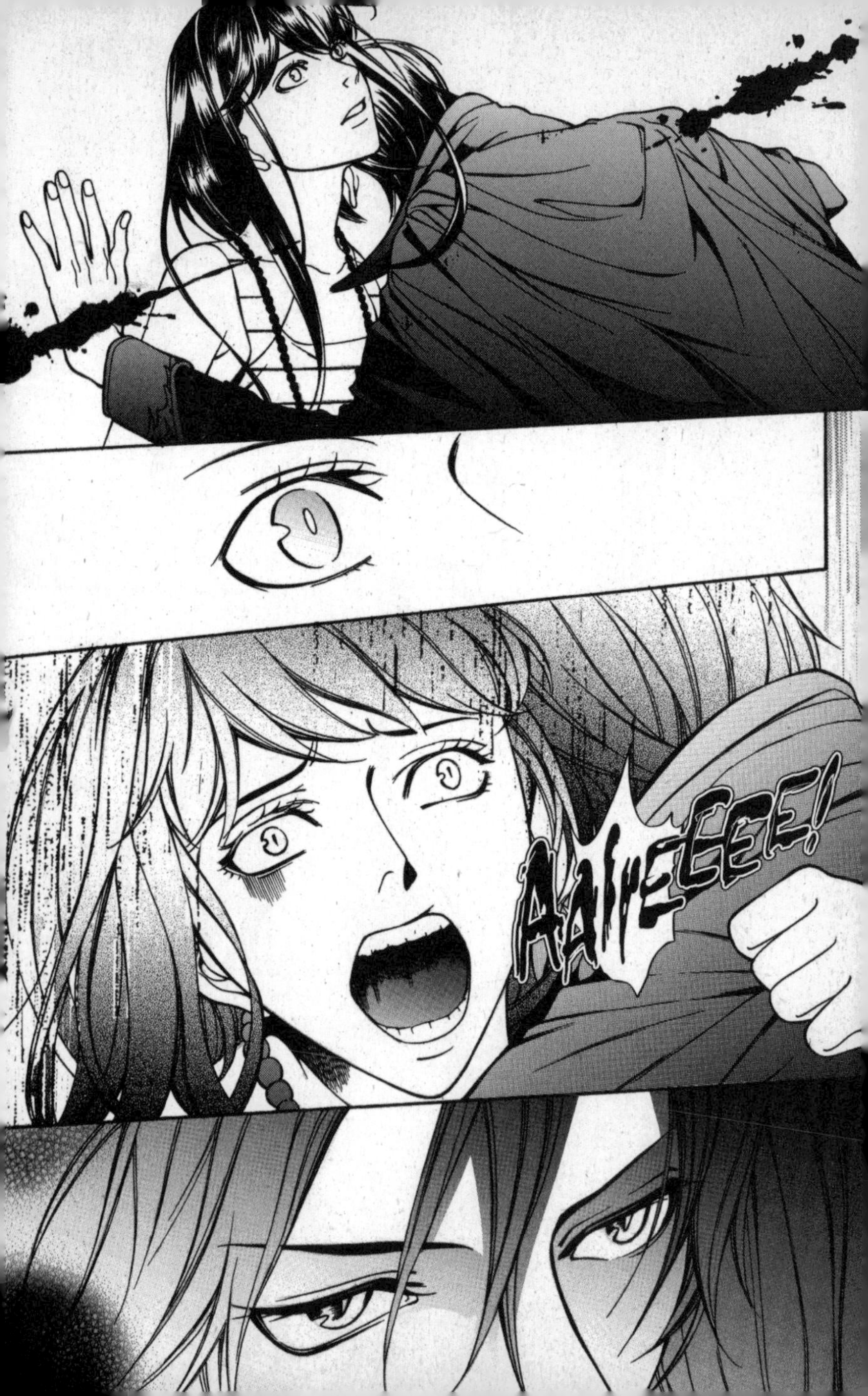
AAIEEEEE!

CHAPTER
5

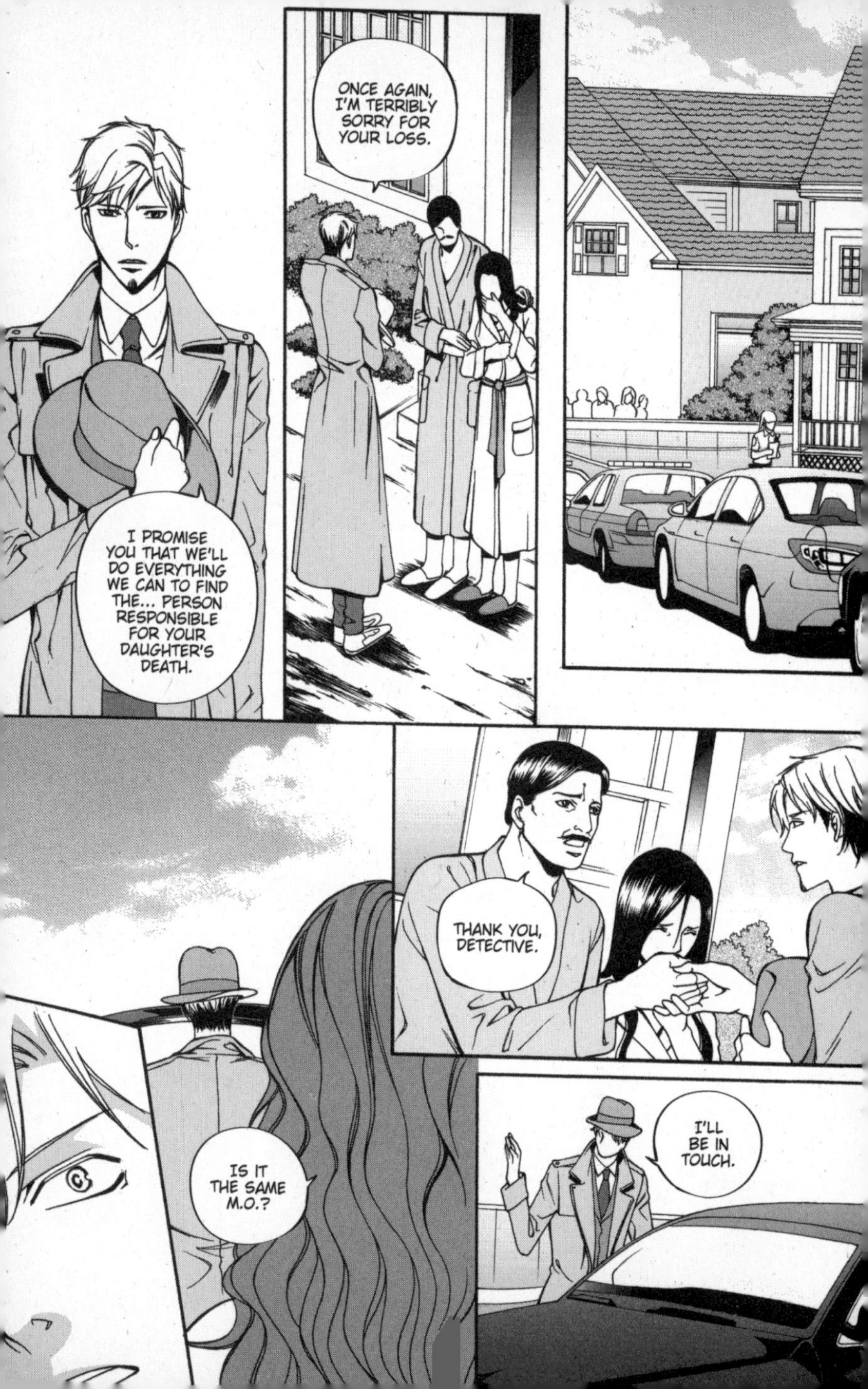
ONCE AGAIN, I'M TERRIBLY SORRY FOR YOUR LOSS.
I PROMISE YOU THAT WE'LL DO EVERYTHING WE CAN TO FIND THE... PERSON RESPONSIBLE FOR YOUR DAUGHTER'S DEATH.
THANK YOU, DETECTIVE.
I'LL BE IN TOUCH.
IS IT THE SAME M.O.?

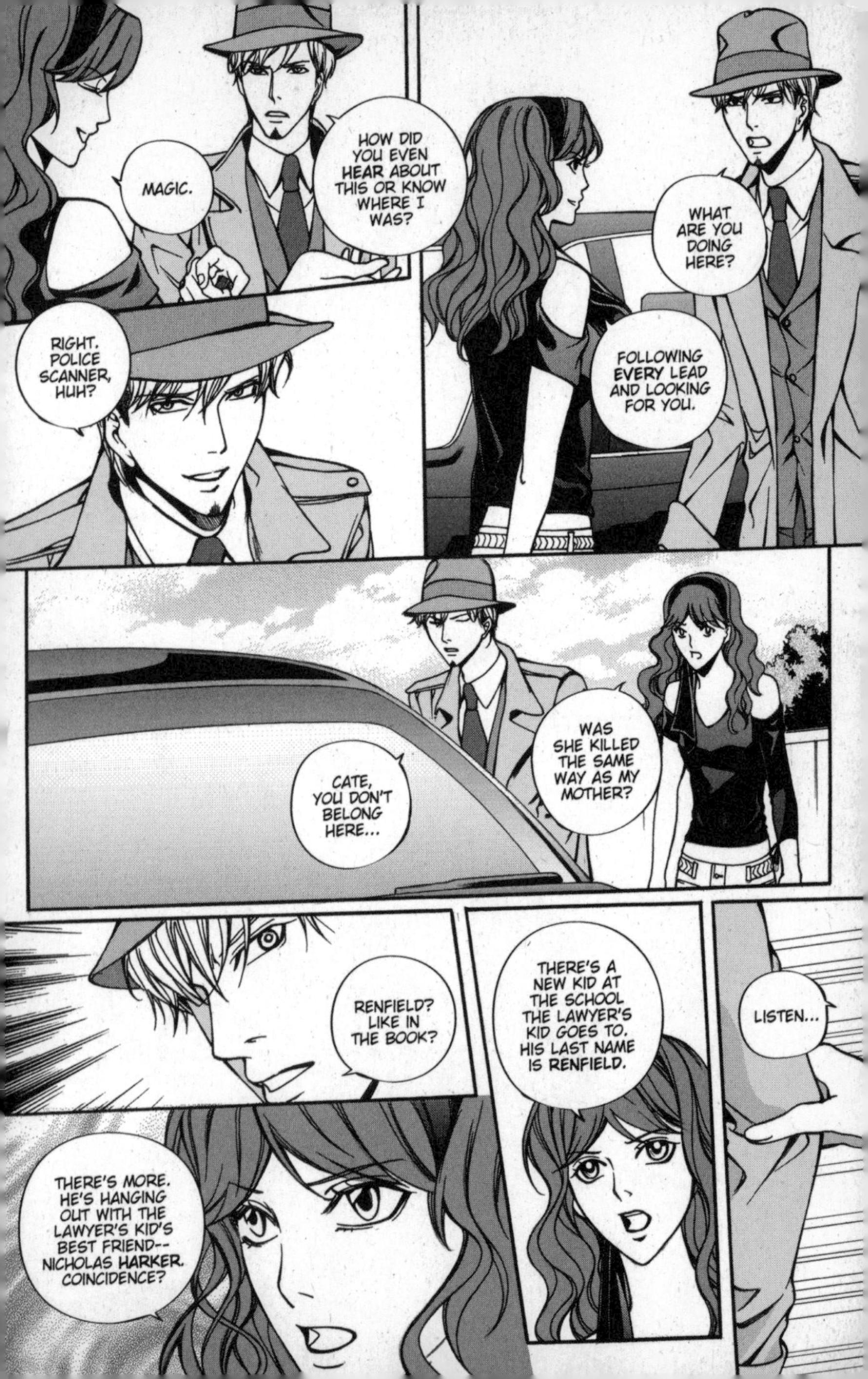
WHAT ARE YOU DOING HERE?
FOLLOWING EVERY LEAD AND LOOKING FOR YOU.
HOW DID YOU EVEN HEAR ABOUT THIS OR KNOW WHERE I WAS?
MAGIC.
RIGHT. POLICE SCANNER, HUH?
WAS SHE KILLED THE SAME WAY AS MY MOTHER?
CATE, YOU DON'T BELONG HERE...
LISTEN...
THERE'S A NEW KID AT THE SCHOOL THE LAWYER'S KID GOES TO. HIS LAST NAME IS RENFIELD.
RENFIELD? LIKE IN THE BOOK?
THERE'S MORE. HE'S HANGING OUT WITH THE LAWYER'S KID'S BEST FRIEND-- NICHOLAS HARKER. COINCIDENCE?

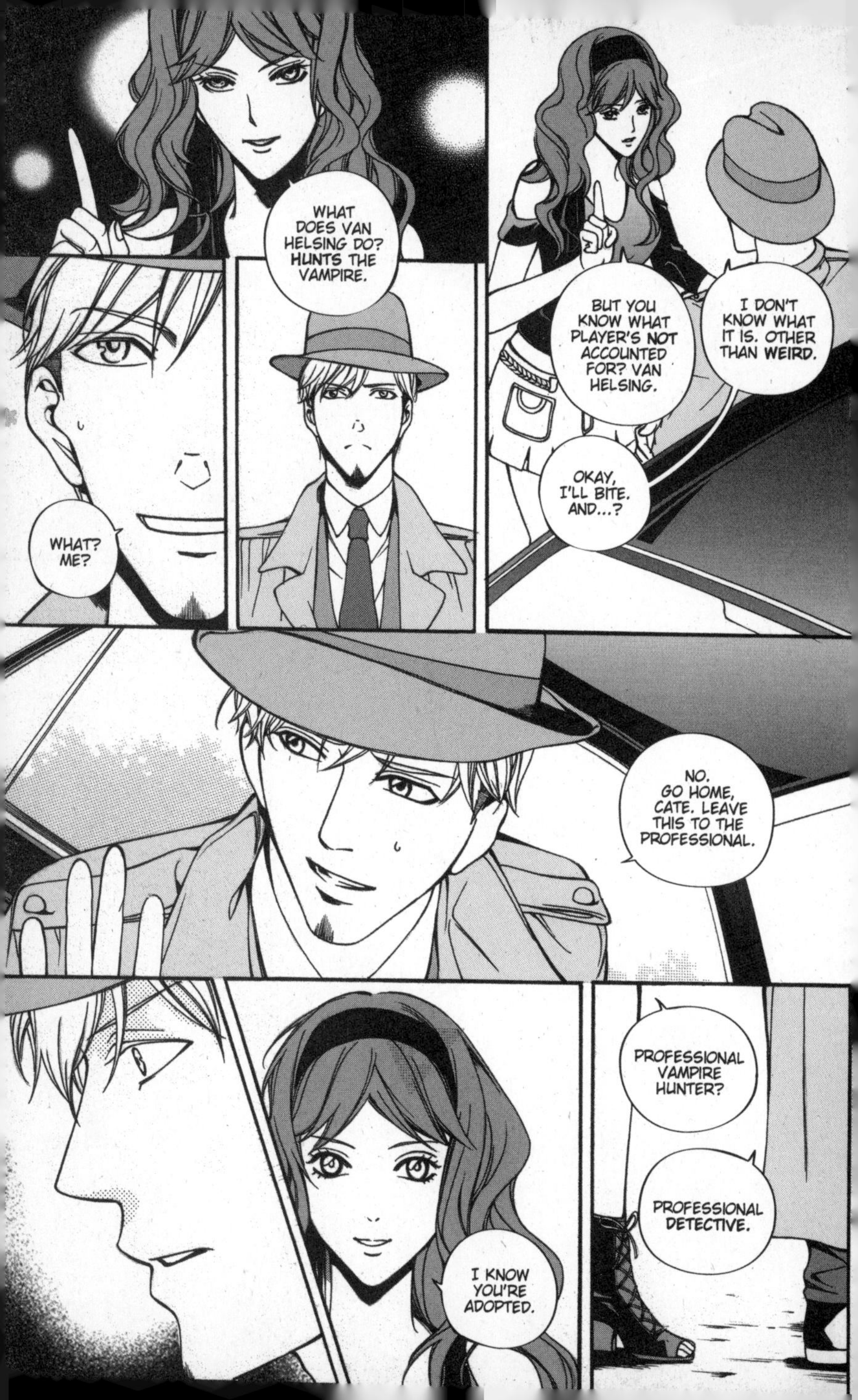
I DON'T KNOW WHAT IT IS. OTHER THAN WEIRD.
BUT YOU KNOW WHAT PLAYER'S NOT ACCOUNTED FOR? VAN HELSING.
OKAY, I'LL BITE. AND...?
WHAT DOES VAN HELSING DO? HUNTS THE VAMPIRE.
WHAT? ME?
NO. GO HOME, CATE. LEAVE THIS TO THE PROFESSIONAL.
PROFESSIONAL VAMPIRE HUNTER?
PROFESSIONAL DETECTIVE.
I KNOW YOU'RE ADOPTED.

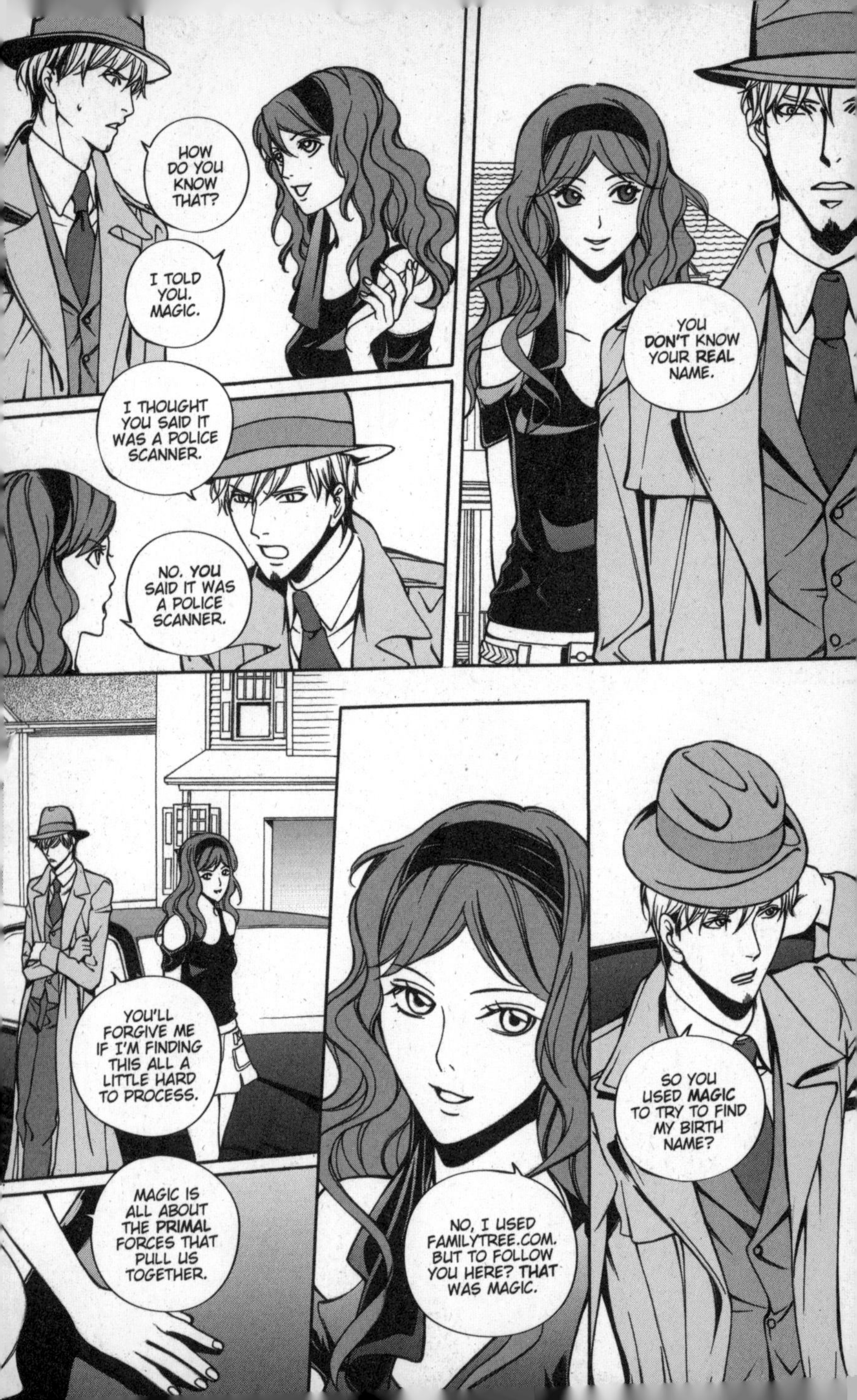
YOU DON'T KNOW YOUR REAL NAME.
HOW DO YOU KNOW THAT?
I TOLD YOU. MAGIC.
I THOUGHT YOU SAID IT WAS A POLICE SCANNER.
NO. YOU SAID IT WAS A POLICE SCANNER.
SO YOU USED MAGIC TO TRY TO FIND MY BIRTH NAME?
NO, I USED FAMILYTREE.COM. BUT TO FOLLOW YOU HERE? THAT WAS MAGIC.
YOU'LL FORGIVE ME IF I'M FINDING THIS ALL A LITTLE HARD TO PROCESS.
MAGIC IS ALL ABOUT THE PRIMAL FORCES THAT PULL US TOGETHER.

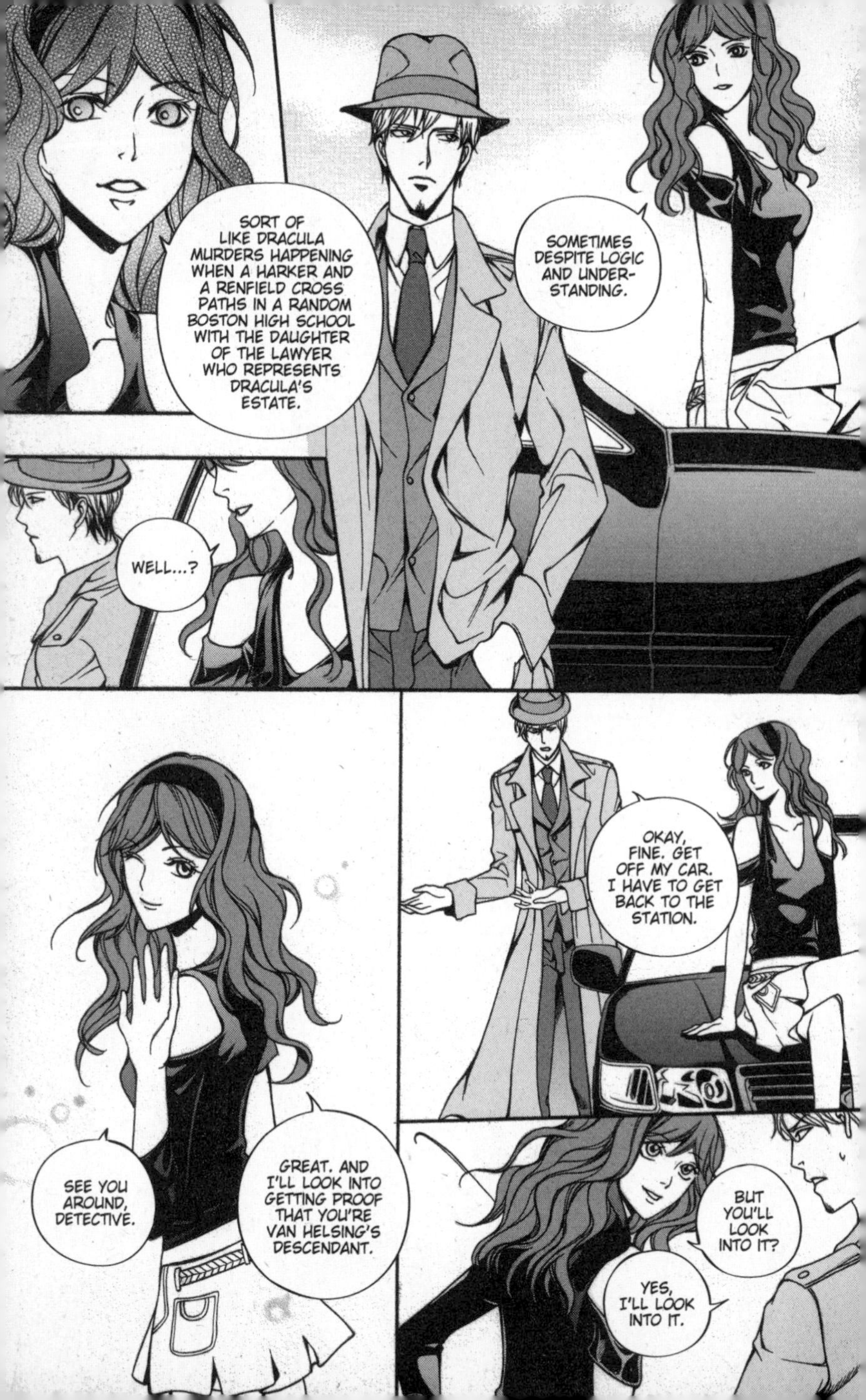
SOMETIMES DESPITE LOGIC AND UNDER-STANDING.
SORT OF LIKE DRACULA MURDERS HAPPENING WHEN A HARKER AND A RENFIELD CROSS PATHS IN A RANDOM BOSTON HIGH SCHOOL WITH THE DAUGHTER OF THE LAWYER WHO REPRESENTS DRACULA'S ESTATE.
WELL...?
OKAY, FINE. GET OFF MY CAR. I HAVE TO GET BACK TO THE STATION.
BUT YOU'LL LOOK INTO IT?
YES, I'LL LOOK INTO IT.
GREAT. AND I'LL LOOK INTO GETTING PROOF THAT YOU'RE VAN HELSING'S DESCENDANT.
SEE YOU AROUND, DETECTIVE.

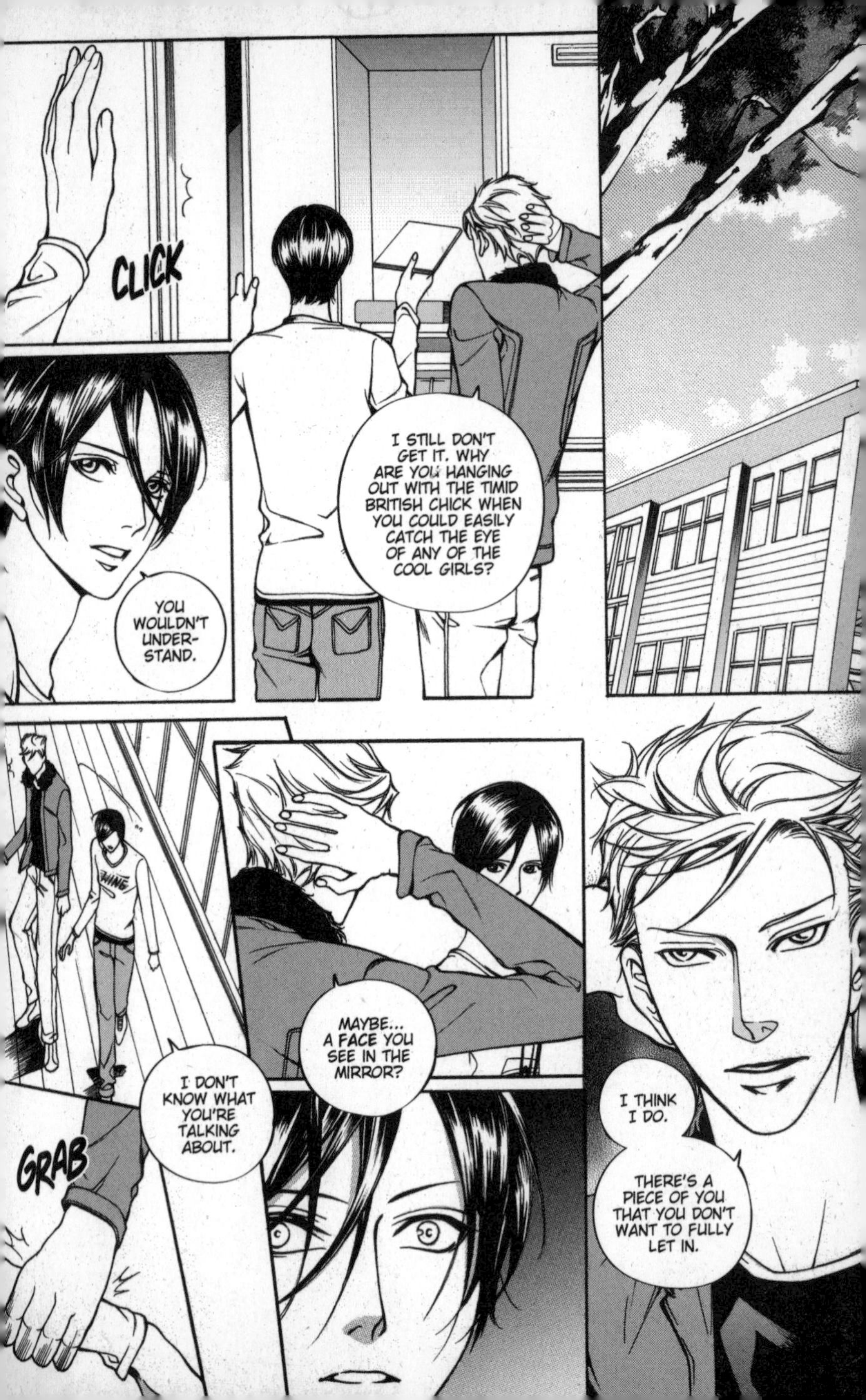
I STILL DON'T GET IT. WHY ARE YOU HANGING OUT WITH THE TIMID BRITISH CHICK WHEN YOU COULD EASILY CATCH THE EYE OF ANY OF THE COOL GIRLS?
CLICK
YOU WOULDN'T UNDER-STAND.
I THINK I DO.
THERE'S A PIECE OF YOU THAT YOU DON'T WANT TO FULLY LET IN.
MAYBE... A FACE YOU SEE IN THE MIRROR?
I DON'T KNOW WHAT YOU'RE TALKING ABOUT.
GRAB

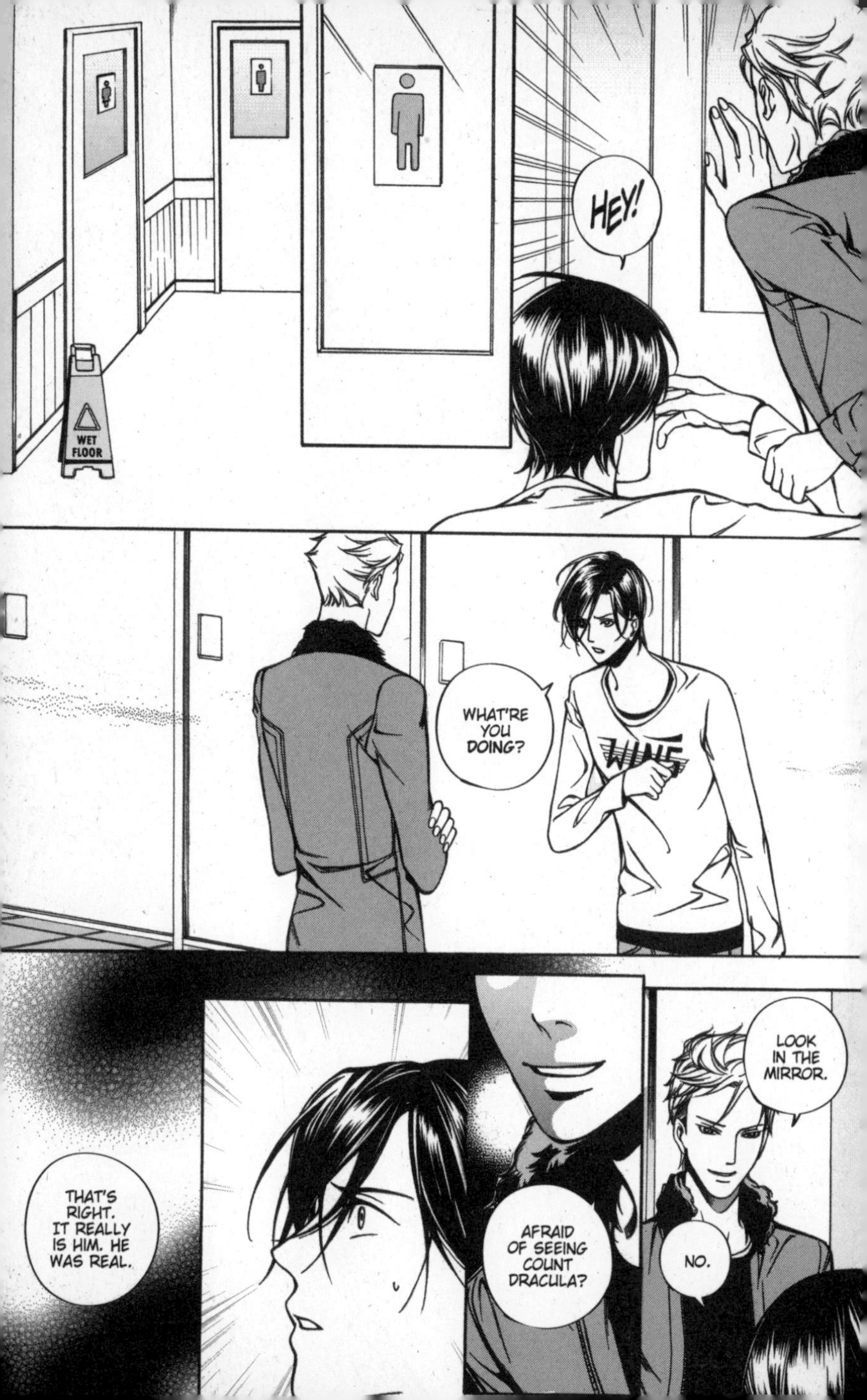
HEY!
WET FLOOR
WHAT'RE YOU DOING?
LOOK IN THE MIRROR.
NO.
AFRAID OF SEEING COUNT DRACULA?
THAT'S RIGHT. IT REALLY IS HIM. HE WAS REAL.

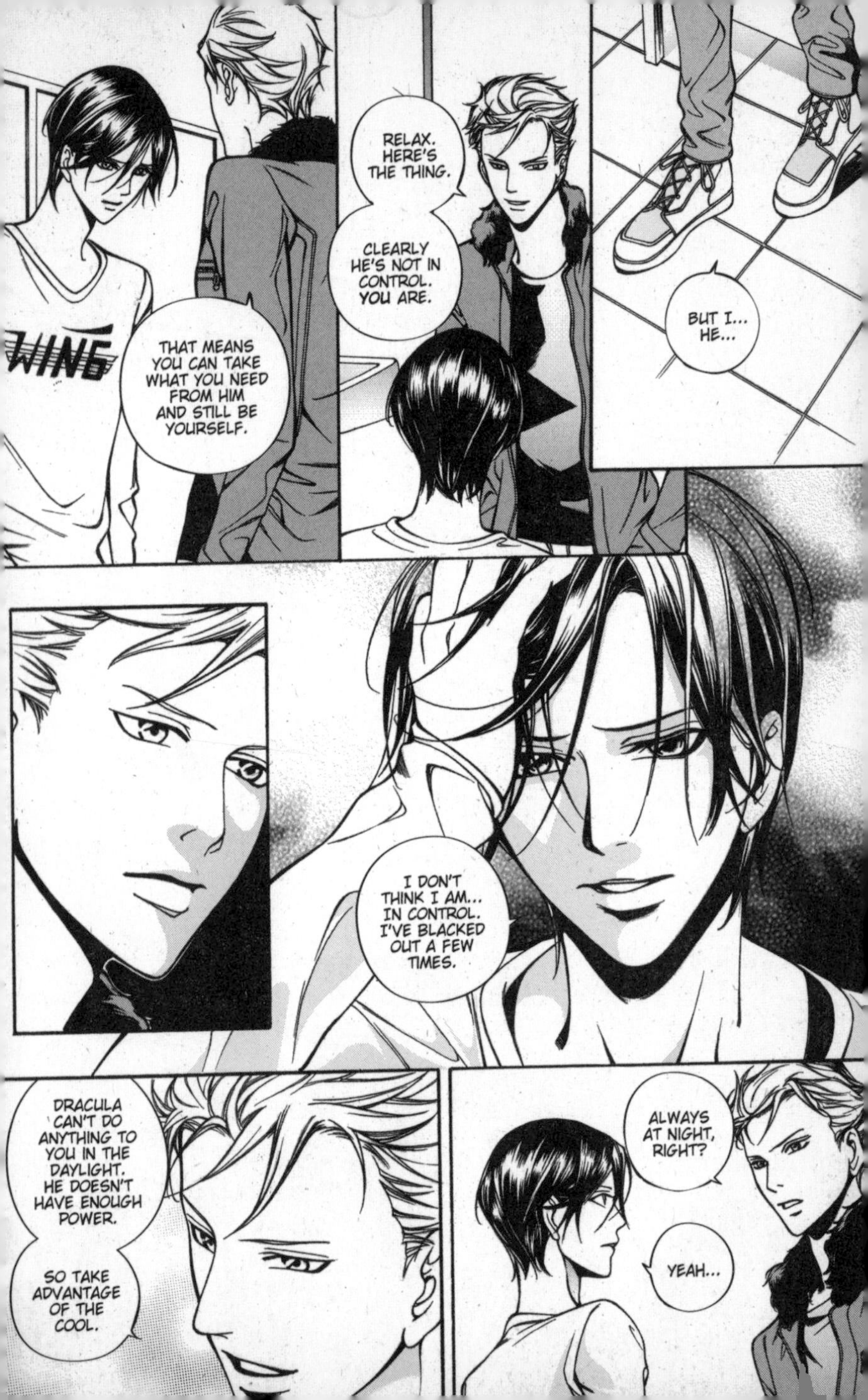
BUT I... HE...
RELAX. HERE'S THE THING.
CLEARLY HE'S NOT IN CONTROL. YOU ARE.
THAT MEANS YOU CAN TAKE WHAT YOU NEED FROM HIM AND STILL BE YOURSELF.
WING
I DON'T THINK I AM... IN CONTROL. I'VE BLACKED OUT A FEW TIMES.
ALWAYS AT NIGHT, RIGHT?
YEAH...
DRACULA CAN'T DO ANYTHING TO YOU IN THE DAYLIGHT. HE DOESN'T HAVE ENOUGH POWER.
SO TAKE ADVANTAGE OF THE COOL.

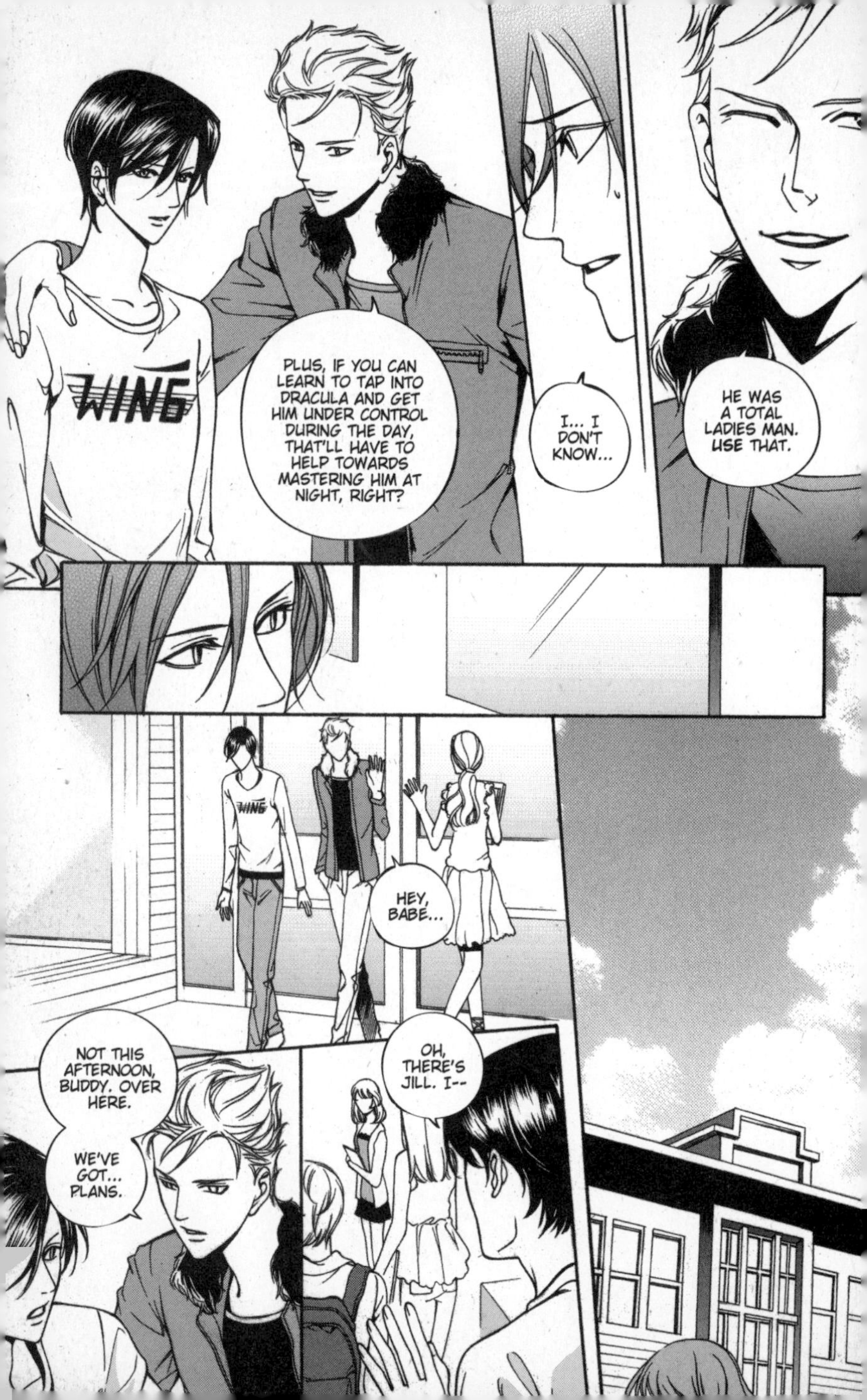
HE WAS A TOTAL LADIES MAN. USE THAT.
I... I DON'T KNOW...
PLUS, IF YOU CAN LEARN TO TAP INTO DRACULA AND GET HIM UNDER CONTROL DURING THE DAY, THAT'LL HAVE TO HELP TOWARDS MASTERING HIM AT NIGHT, RIGHT?
WING
WING
HEY, BABE...
OH, THERE'S JILL. I--
NOT THIS AFTERNOON, BUDDY. OVER HERE.
WE'VE GOT... PLANS.

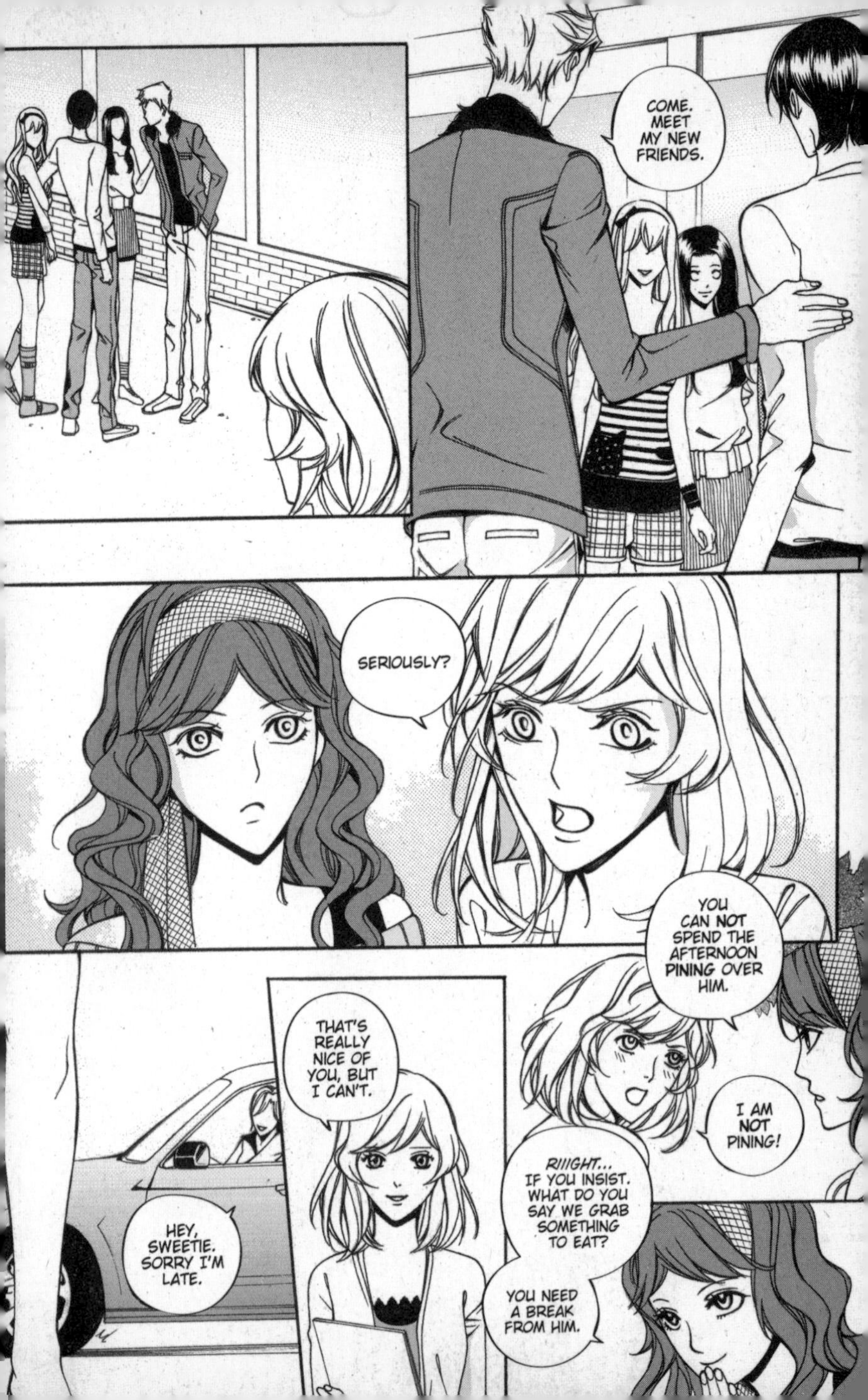
COME. MEET MY NEW FRIENDS.
SERIOUSLY?
YOU CAN NOT SPEND THE AFTERNOON PINING OVER HIM.
I AM NOT PINING!
RIIIGHT... IF YOU INSIST. WHAT DO YOU SAY WE GRAB SOMETHING TO EAT?
YOU NEED A BREAK FROM HIM.
THAT'S REALLY NICE OF YOU, BUT I CAN'T.
HEY, SWEETIE. SORRY I'M LATE.

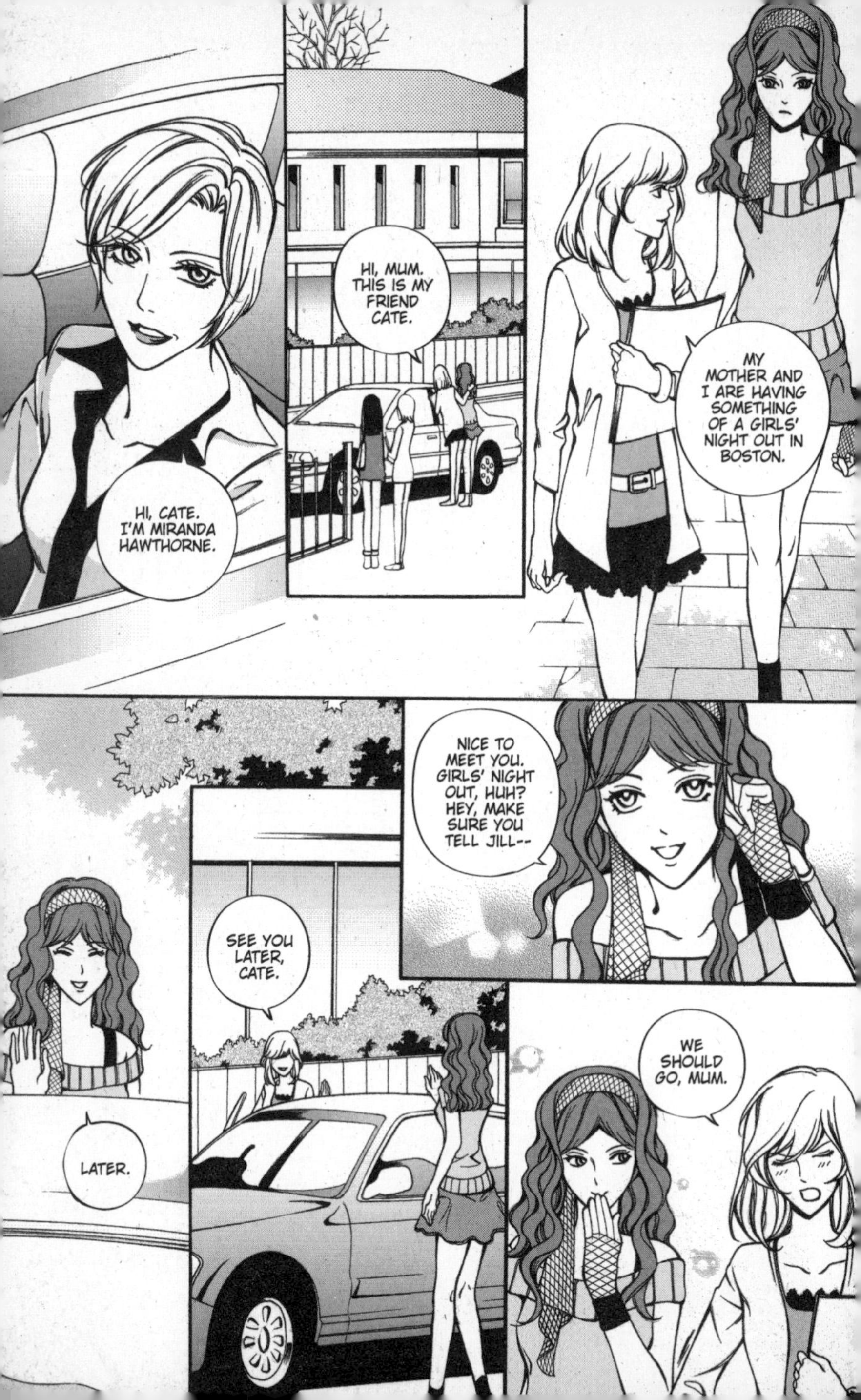
MY MOTHER AND I ARE HAVING SOMETHING OF A GIRLS' NIGHT OUT IN BOSTON.
HI, MUM. THIS IS MY FRIEND CATE.
HI, CATE. I'M MIRANDA HAWTHORNE.
NICE TO MEET YOU. GIRLS' NIGHT OUT, HUH? HEY, MAKE SURE YOU TELL JILL--
WE SHOULD GO, MUM.
SEE YOU LATER, CATE.
LATER.

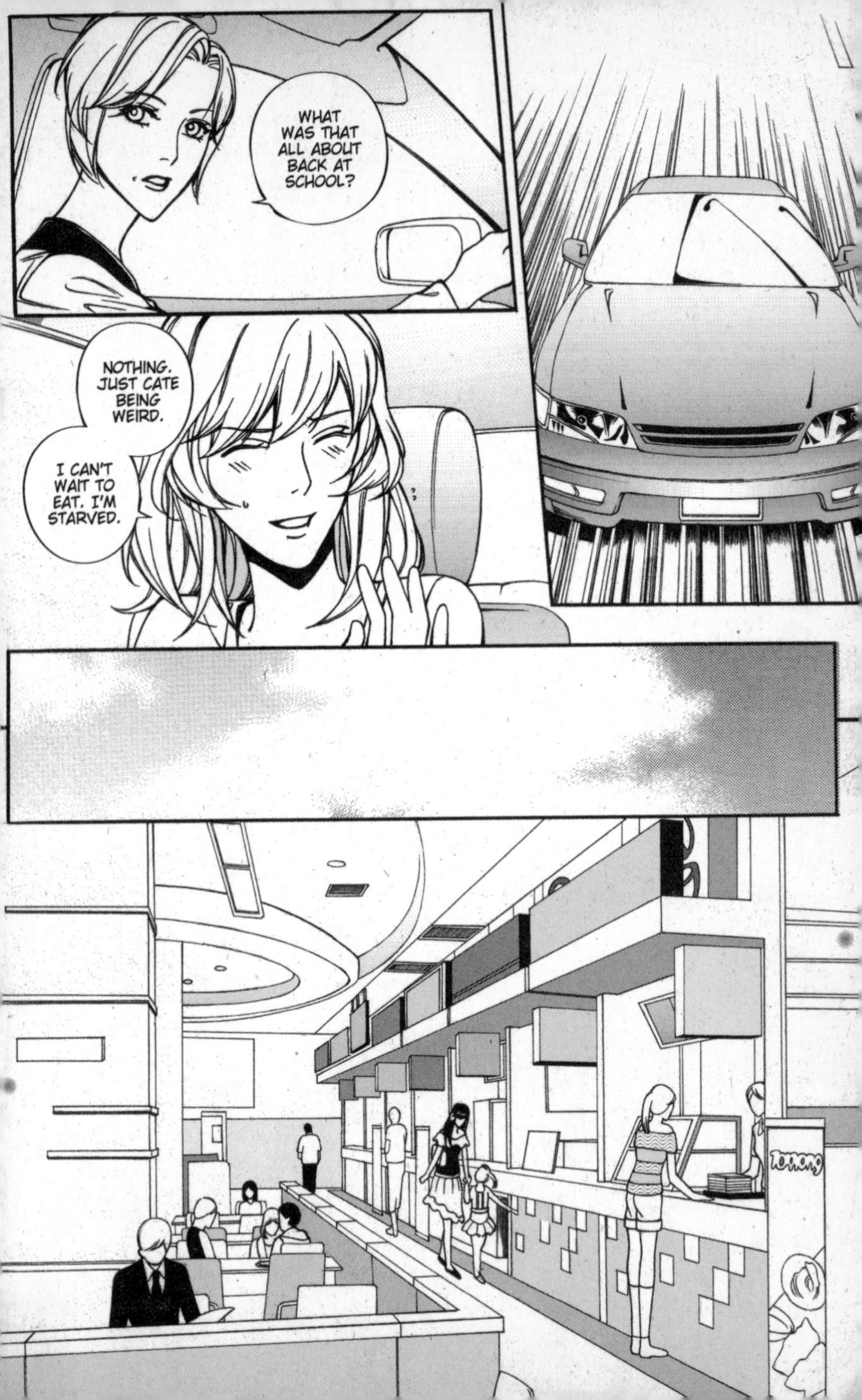
WHAT WAS THAT ALL ABOUT BACK AT SCHOOL?
NOTHING. JUST CATE BEING WEIRD.
I CAN'T WAIT TO EAT. I'M STARVED.

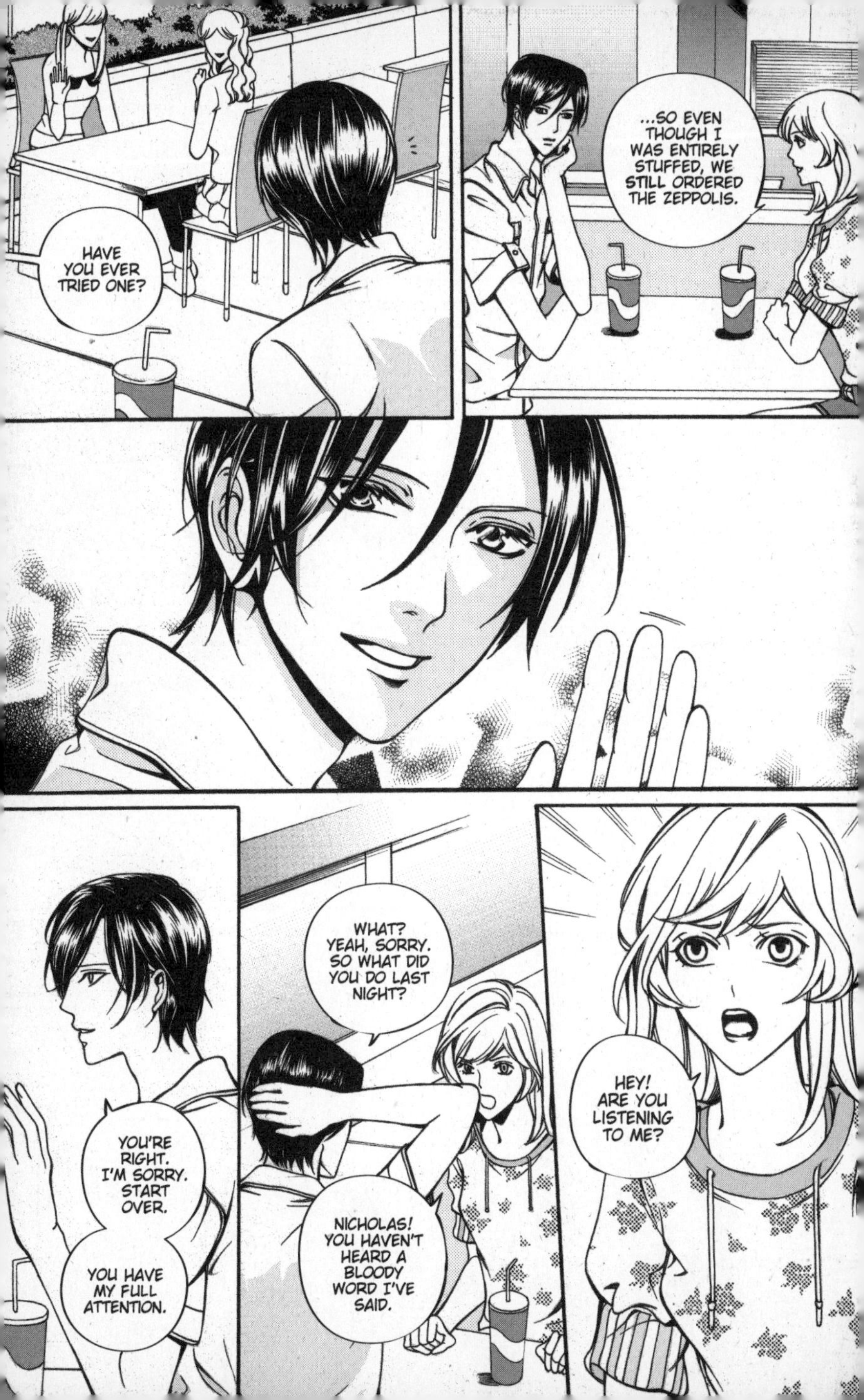
...SO EVEN THOUGH I WAS ENTIRELY STUFFED, WE STILL ORDERED THE ZEPPOLIS.
HAVE YOU EVER TRIED ONE?
HEY! ARE YOU LISTENING TO ME?
WHAT? YEAH, SORRY. SO WHAT DID YOU DO LAST NIGHT?
NICHOLAS! YOU HAVEN'T HEARD A BLOODY WORD I'VE SAID.
YOU'RE RIGHT. I'M SORRY. START OVER.
YOU HAVE MY FULL ATTENTION.

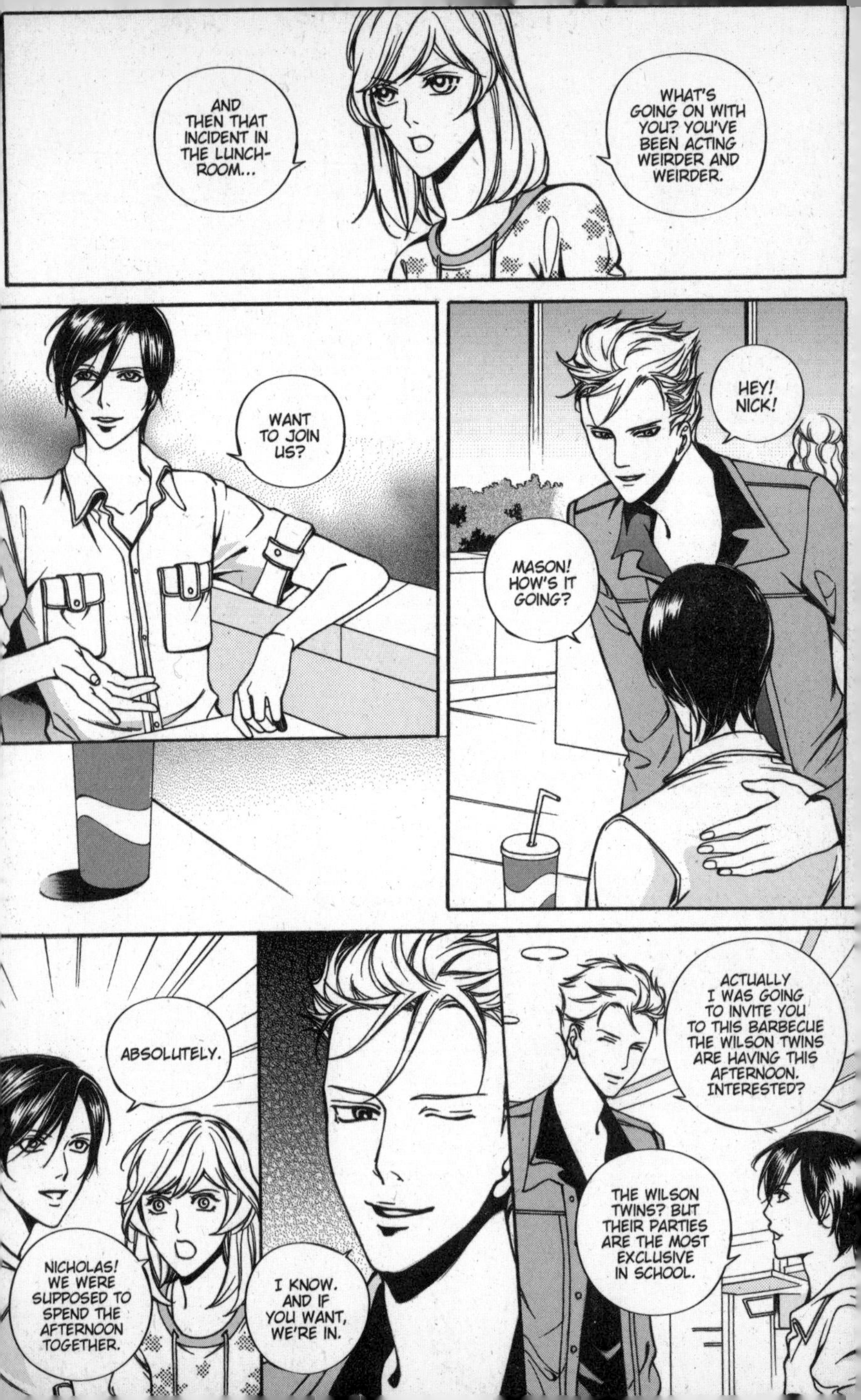
WHAT'S GOING ON WITH YOU? YOU'VE BEEN ACTING WEIRDER AND WEIRDER.
AND THEN THAT INCIDENT IN THE LUNCH-ROOM...
HEY! NICK!
MASON! HOW'S IT GOING?
WANT TO JOIN US?
ACTUALLY I WAS GOING TO INVITE YOU TO THIS BARBECUE THE WILSON TWINS ARE HAVING THIS AFTERNOON. INTERESTED?
THE WILSON TWINS? BUT THEIR PARTIES ARE THE MOST EXCLUSIVE IN SCHOOL.
I KNOW. AND IF YOU WANT, WE'RE IN.
ABSOLUTELY.
NICHOLAS! WE WERE SUPPOSED TO SPEND THE AFTERNOON TOGETHER.

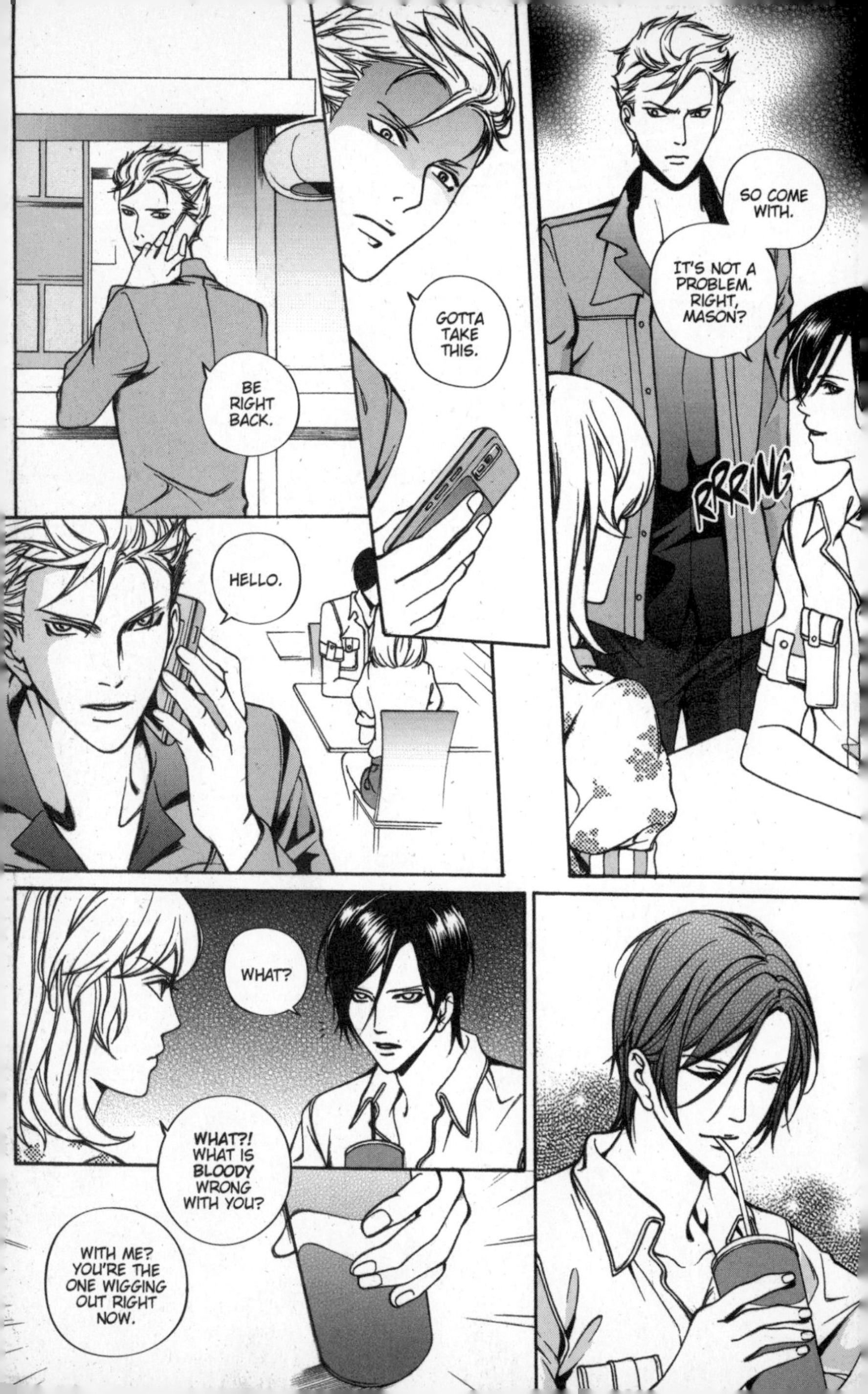
SO COME WITH.
IT'S NOT A PROBLEM. RIGHT, MASON?
RRRING
GOTTA TAKE THIS.
BE RIGHT BACK.
HELLO.
WHAT?
WHAT?! WHAT IS BLOODY WRONG WITH YOU?
WITH ME? YOU'RE THE ONE WIGGING OUT RIGHT NOW.

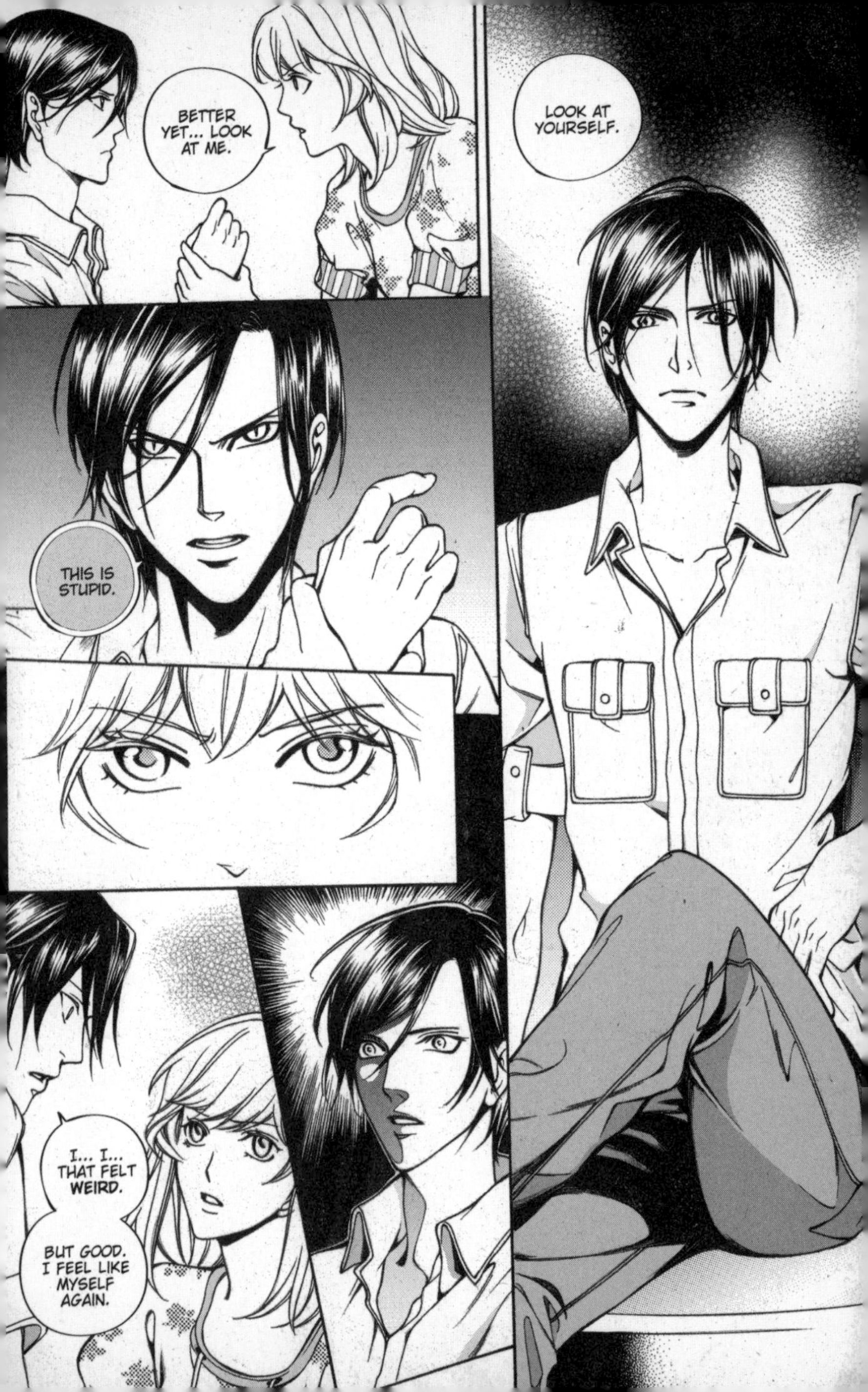
LOOK AT YOURSELF.
BETTER YET... LOOK AT ME.
THIS IS STUPID.
I... I... THAT FELT WEIRD.
BUT GOOD. I FEEL LIKE MYSELF AGAIN.

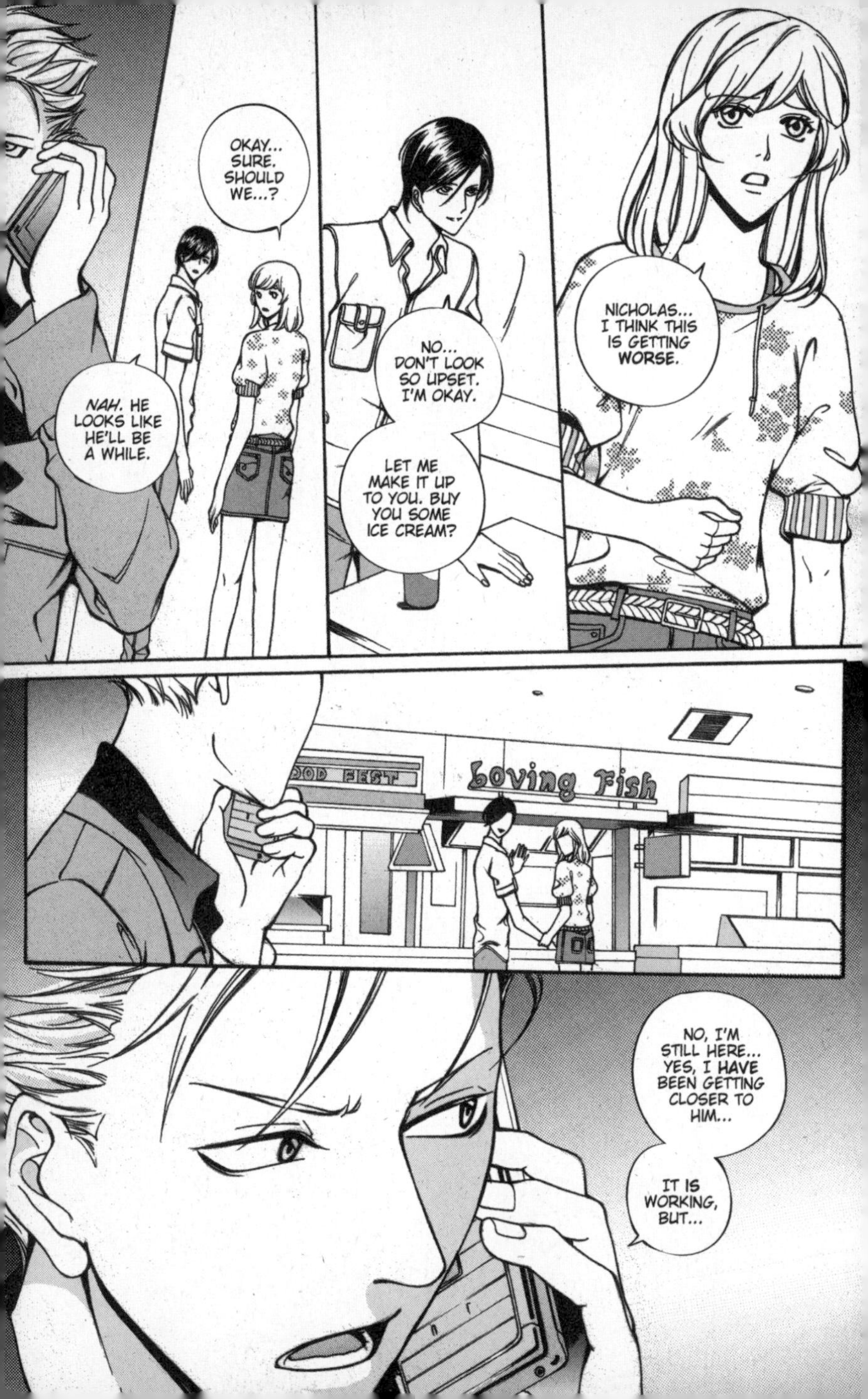
NICHOLAS... I THINK THIS IS GETTING WORSE.
NO... DON'T LOOK SO UPSET. I'M OKAY.
LET ME MAKE IT UP TO YOU. BUY YOU SOME ICE CREAM?
OKAY... SURE. SHOULD WE...?
NAH. HE LOOKS LIKE HE'LL BE A WHILE.
Loving Fish
NO, I'M STILL HERE... YES, I HAVE BEEN GETTING CLOSER TO HIM...
IT IS WORKING, BUT...

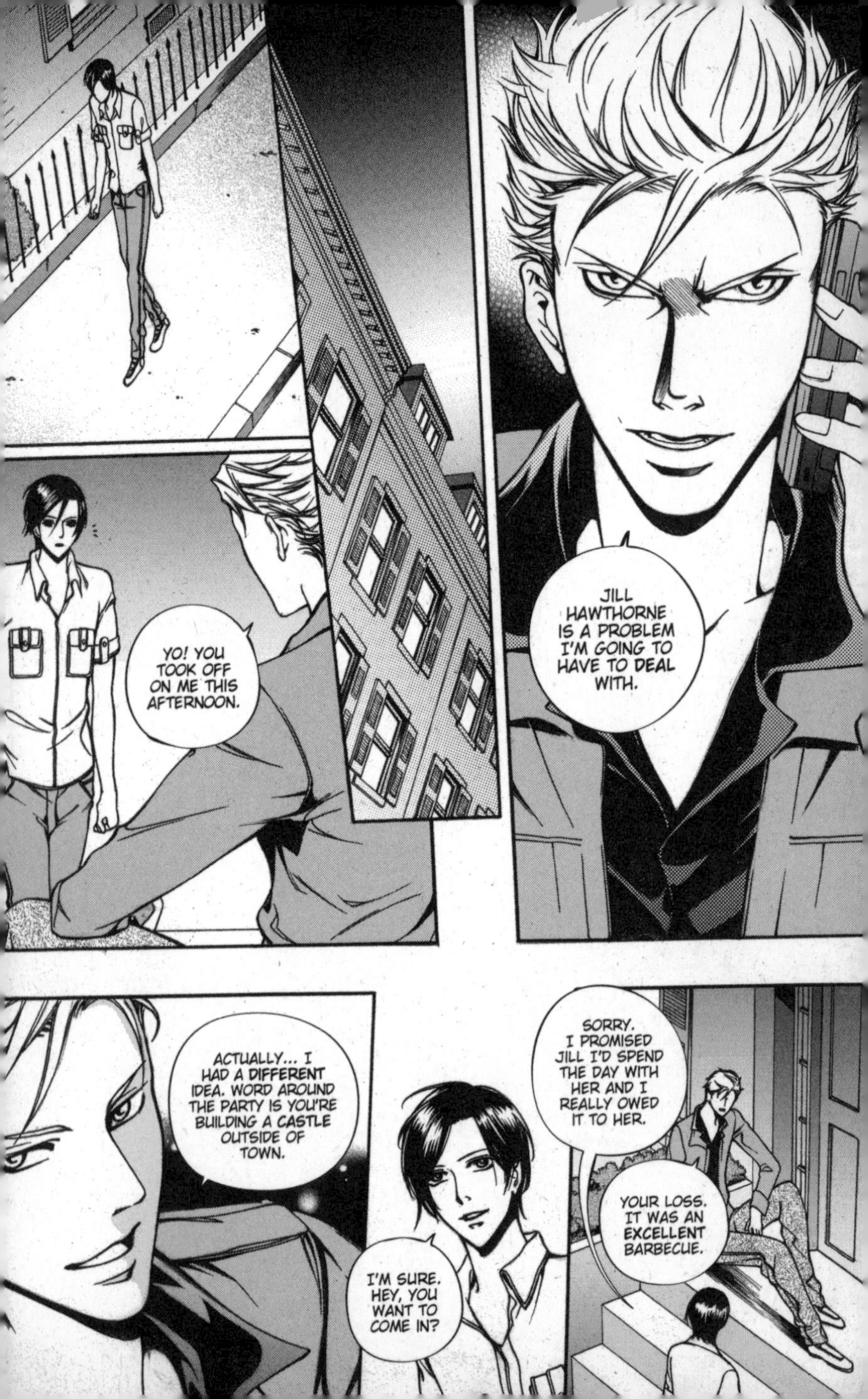
JILL HAWTHORNE IS A PROBLEM I'M GOING TO HAVE TO DEAL WITH.
YO! YOU TOOK OFF ON ME THIS AFTERNOON.
SORRY. I PROMISED JILL I'D SPEND THE DAY WITH HER AND I REALLY OWED IT TO HER.
YOUR LOSS. IT WAS AN EXCELLENT BARBECUE.
I'M SURE. HEY, YOU WANT TO COME IN?
ACTUALLY... I HAD A DIFFERENT IDEA. WORD AROUND THE PARTY IS YOU'RE BUILDING A CASTLE OUTSIDE OF TOWN.

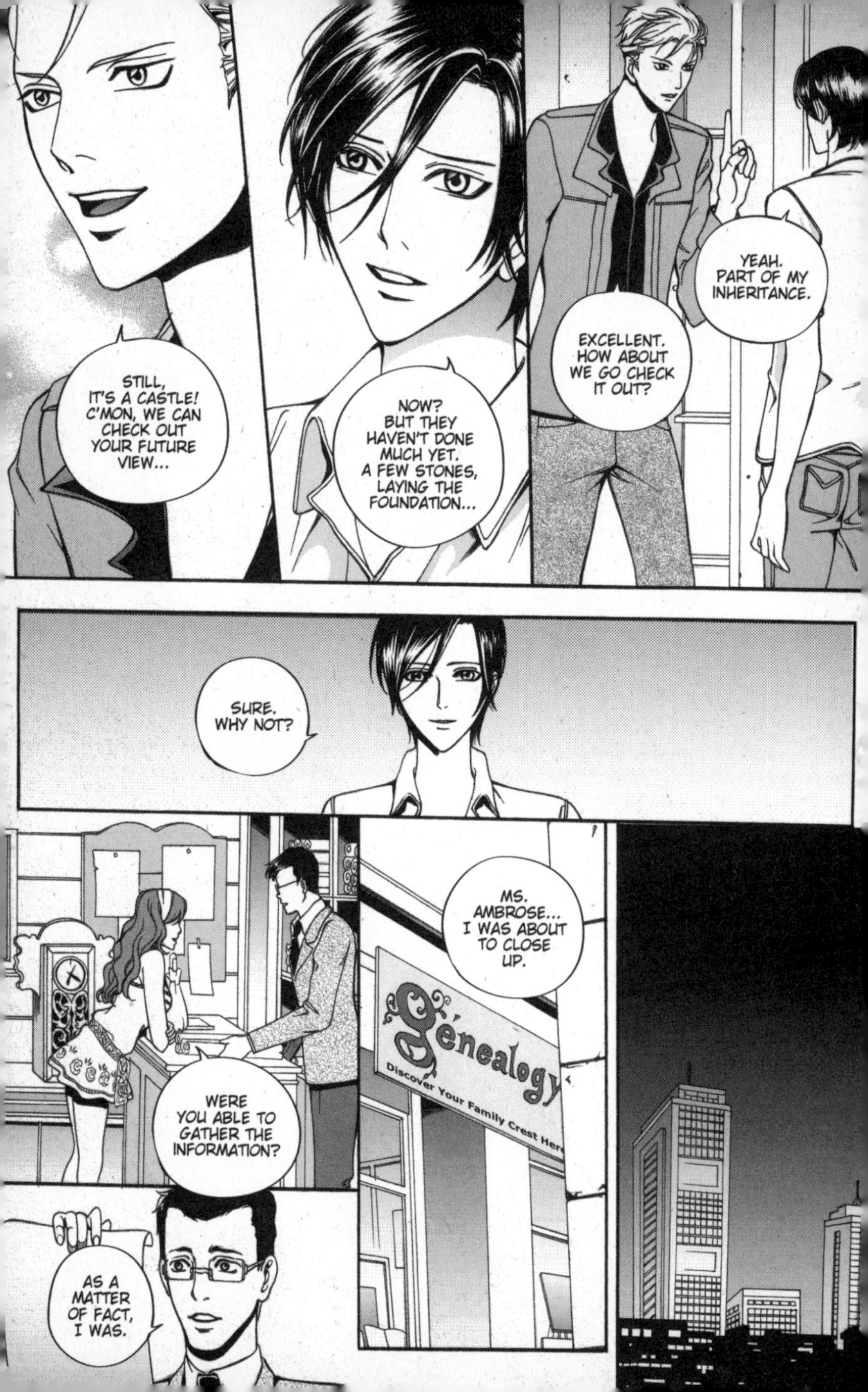
YEAH. PART OF MY INHERITANCE.
EXCELLENT. HOW ABOUT WE GO CHECK IT OUT?
NOW? BUT THEY HAVEN'T DONE MUCH YET. A FEW STONES, LAYING THE FOUNDATION...
STILL, IT'S A CASTLE! C'MON, WE CAN CHECK OUT YOUR FUTURE VIEW...
SURE. WHY NOT?
MS. AMBROSE... I WAS ABOUT TO CLOSE UP.
Génealogy
Discover Your Family Crest Her
WERE YOU ABLE TO GATHER THE INFORMATION?
AS A MATTER OF FACT, I WAS.

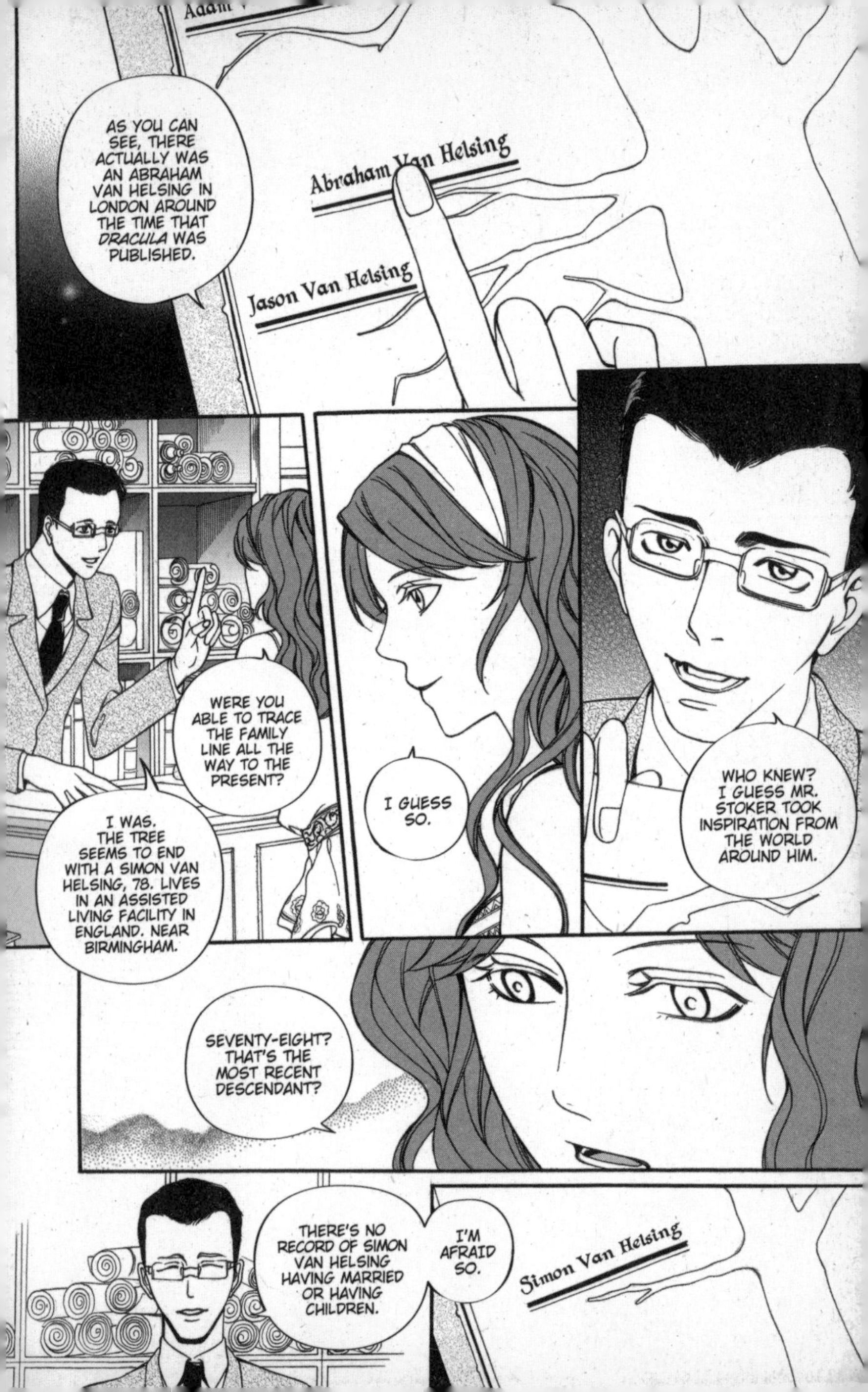
Adam
Abraham Van Helsing
Jason Van Helsing
AS YOU CAN SEE, THERE ACTUALLY WAS AN ABRAHAM VAN HELSING IN LONDON AROUND THE TIME THAT *DRACULA* WAS PUBLISHED.
WHO KNEW? I GUESS MR. STOKER TOOK INSPIRATION FROM THE WORLD AROUND HIM.
I GUESS SO.
WERE YOU ABLE TO TRACE THE FAMILY LINE ALL THE WAY TO THE PRESENT?
I WAS. THE TREE SEEMS TO END WITH A SIMON VAN HELSING, 78. LIVES IN AN ASSISTED LIVING FACILITY IN ENGLAND. NEAR BIRMINGHAM.
SEVENTY-EIGHT? THAT'S THE MOST RECENT DESCENDANT?
Simon Van Helsing
I'M AFRAID SO.
THERE'S NO RECORD OF SIMON VAN HELSING HAVING MARRIED OR HAVING CHILDREN.

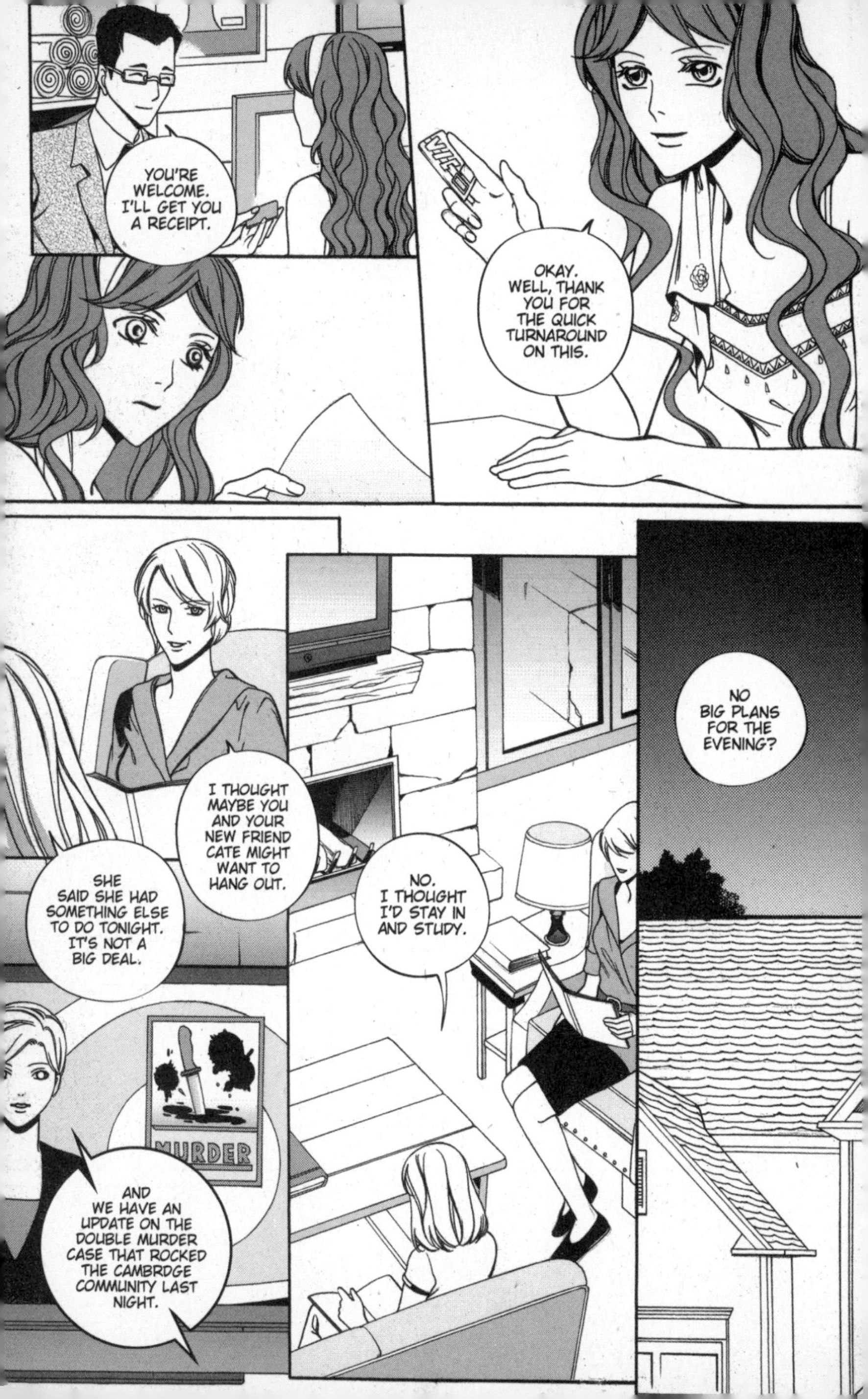
OKAY. WELL, THANK YOU FOR THE QUICK TURNAROUND ON THIS.
YOU'RE WELCOME. I'LL GET YOU A RECEIPT.
NO BIG PLANS FOR THE EVENING?
NO. I THOUGHT I'D STAY IN AND STUDY.
I THOUGHT MAYBE YOU AND YOUR NEW FRIEND CATE MIGHT WANT TO HANG OUT.
SHE SAID SHE HAD SOMETHING ELSE TO DO TONIGHT. IT'S NOT A BIG DEAL.
MURDER
AND WE HAVE AN UPDATE ON THE DOUBLE MURDER CASE THAT ROCKED THE CAMBRDGE COMMUNITY LAST NIGHT.

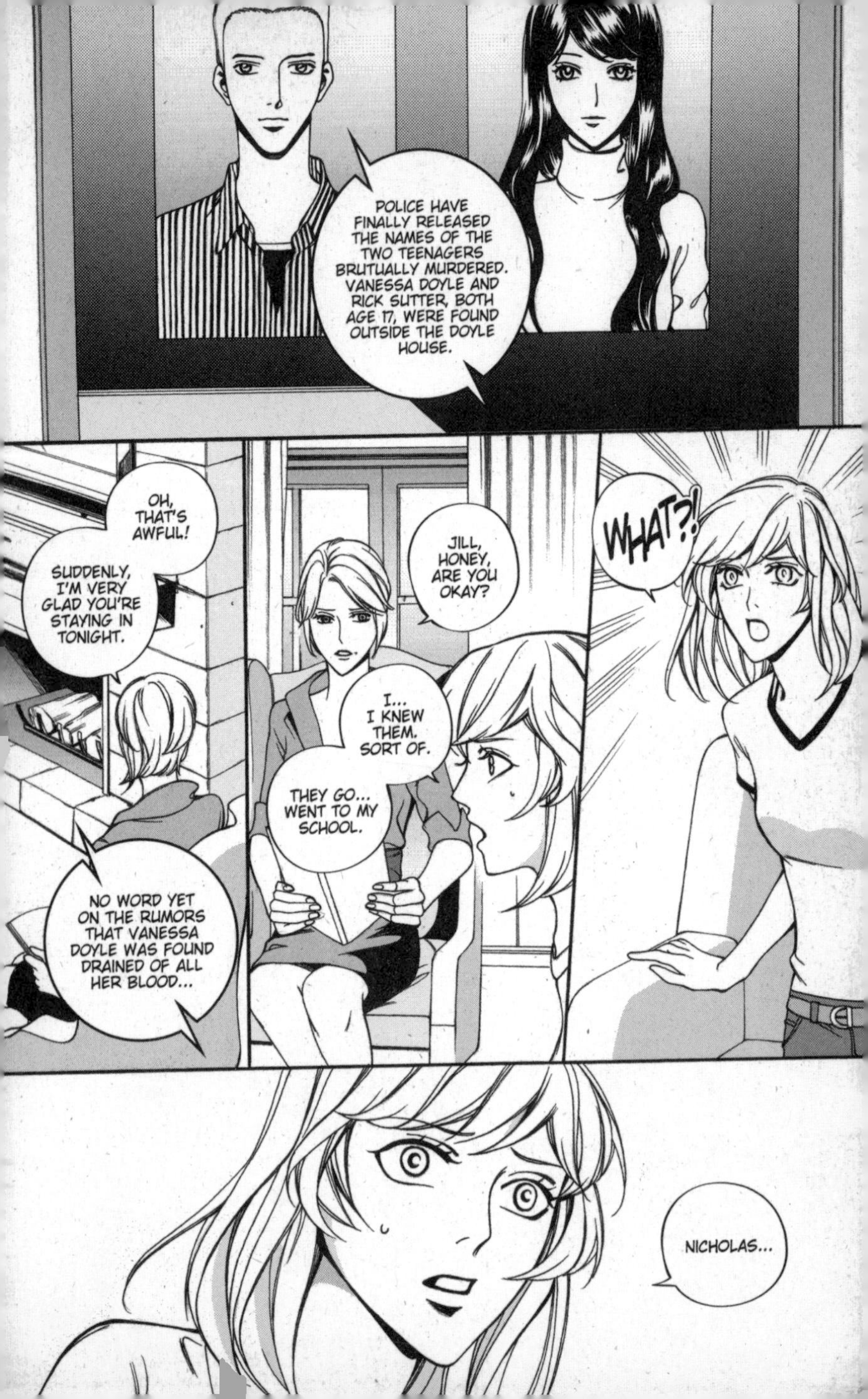
POLICE HAVE FINALLY RELEASED THE NAMES OF THE TWO TEENAGERS BRUTUALLY MURDERED. VANESSA DOYLE AND RICK SUTTER, BOTH AGE 17, WERE FOUND OUTSIDE THE DOYLE HOUSE.
WHAT?!
JILL, HONEY, ARE YOU OKAY?
I... I KNEW THEM. SORT OF.
THEY GO... WENT TO MY SCHOOL.
OH, THAT'S AWFUL!
SUDDENLY, I'M VERY GLAD YOU'RE STAYING IN TONIGHT.
NO WORD YET ON THE RUMORS THAT VANESSA DOYLE WAS FOUND DRAINED OF ALL HER BLOOD...
NICHOLAS...

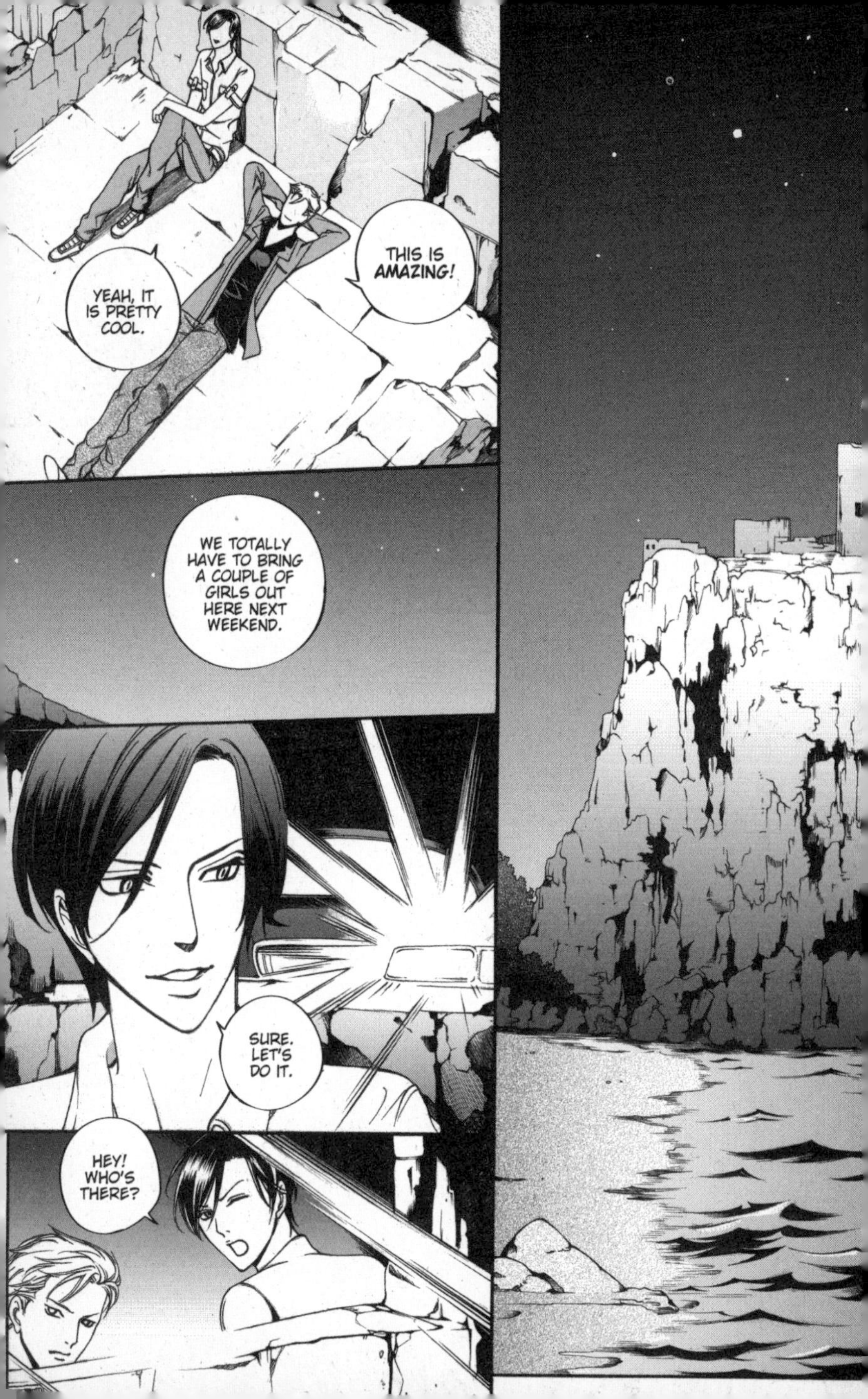
THIS IS AMAZING!
YEAH, IT IS PRETTY COOL.
WE TOTALLY HAVE TO BRING A COUPLE OF GIRLS OUT HERE NEXT WEEKEND.
SURE. LET'S DO IT.
HEY! WHO'S THERE?

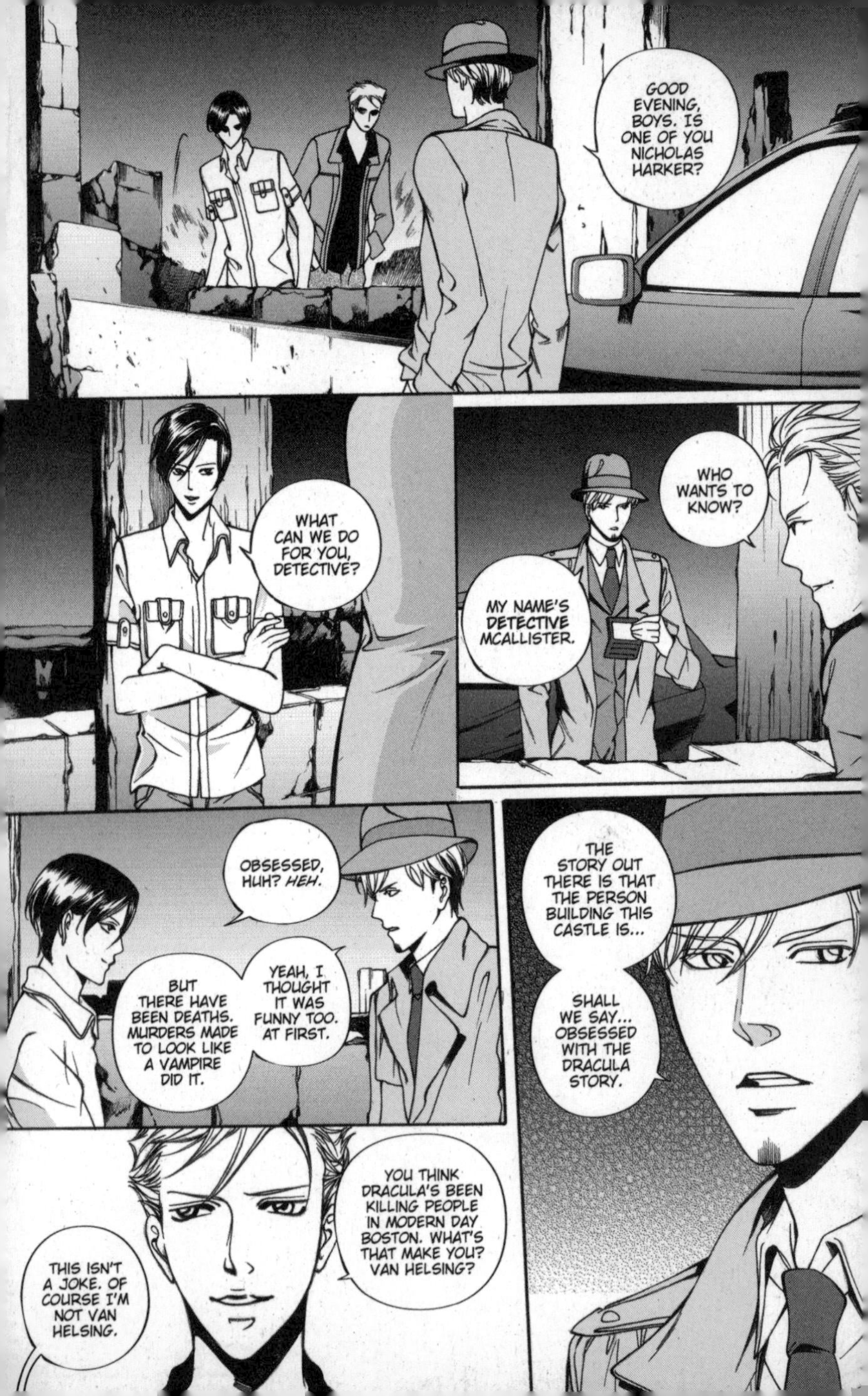
GOOD EVENING, BOYS. IS ONE OF YOU NICHOLAS HARKER?
WHO WANTS TO KNOW?
MY NAME'S DETECTIVE MCALLISTER.
WHAT CAN WE DO FOR YOU, DETECTIVE?
THE STORY OUT THERE IS THAT THE PERSON BUILDING THIS CASTLE IS...
SHALL WE SAY... OBSESSED WITH THE DRACULA STORY.
OBSESSED, HUH? *HEH.*
YEAH, I THOUGHT IT WAS FUNNY TOO. AT FIRST.
BUT THERE HAVE BEEN DEATHS. MURDERS MADE TO LOOK LIKE A VAMPIRE DID IT.
YOU THINK DRACULA'S BEEN KILLING PEOPLE IN MODERN DAY BOSTON. WHAT'S THAT MAKE YOU? VAN HELSING?
THIS ISN'T A JOKE. OF COURSE I'M NOT VAN HELSING.

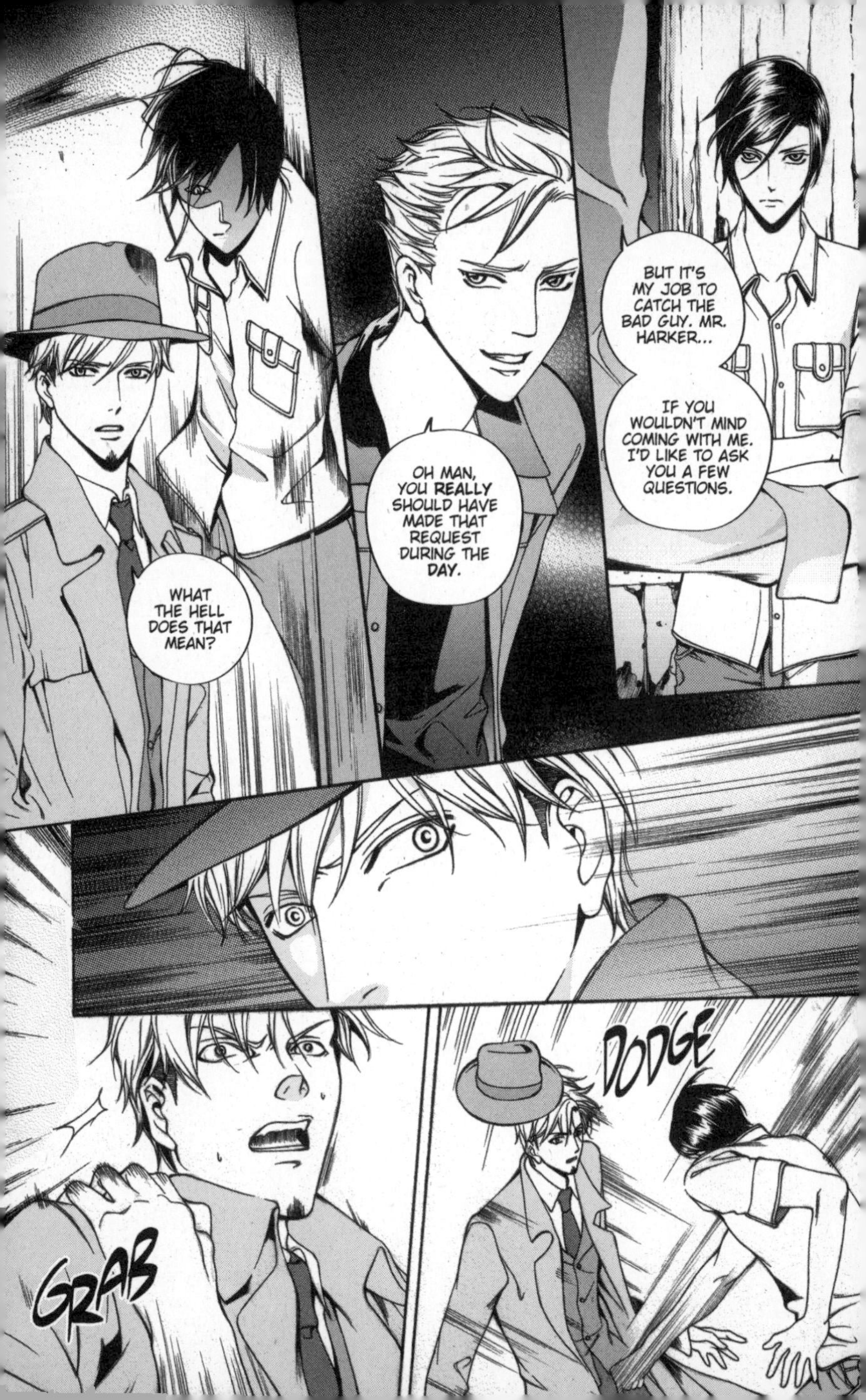
BUT IT'S MY JOB TO CATCH THE BAD GUY. MR. HARKER...
IF YOU WOULDN'T MIND COMING WITH ME. I'D LIKE TO ASK YOU A FEW QUESTIONS.
OH MAN, YOU **REALLY** SHOULD HAVE MADE THAT REQUEST DURING THE **DAY**.
WHAT THE HELL DOES THAT MEAN?
DODGE
GRAB

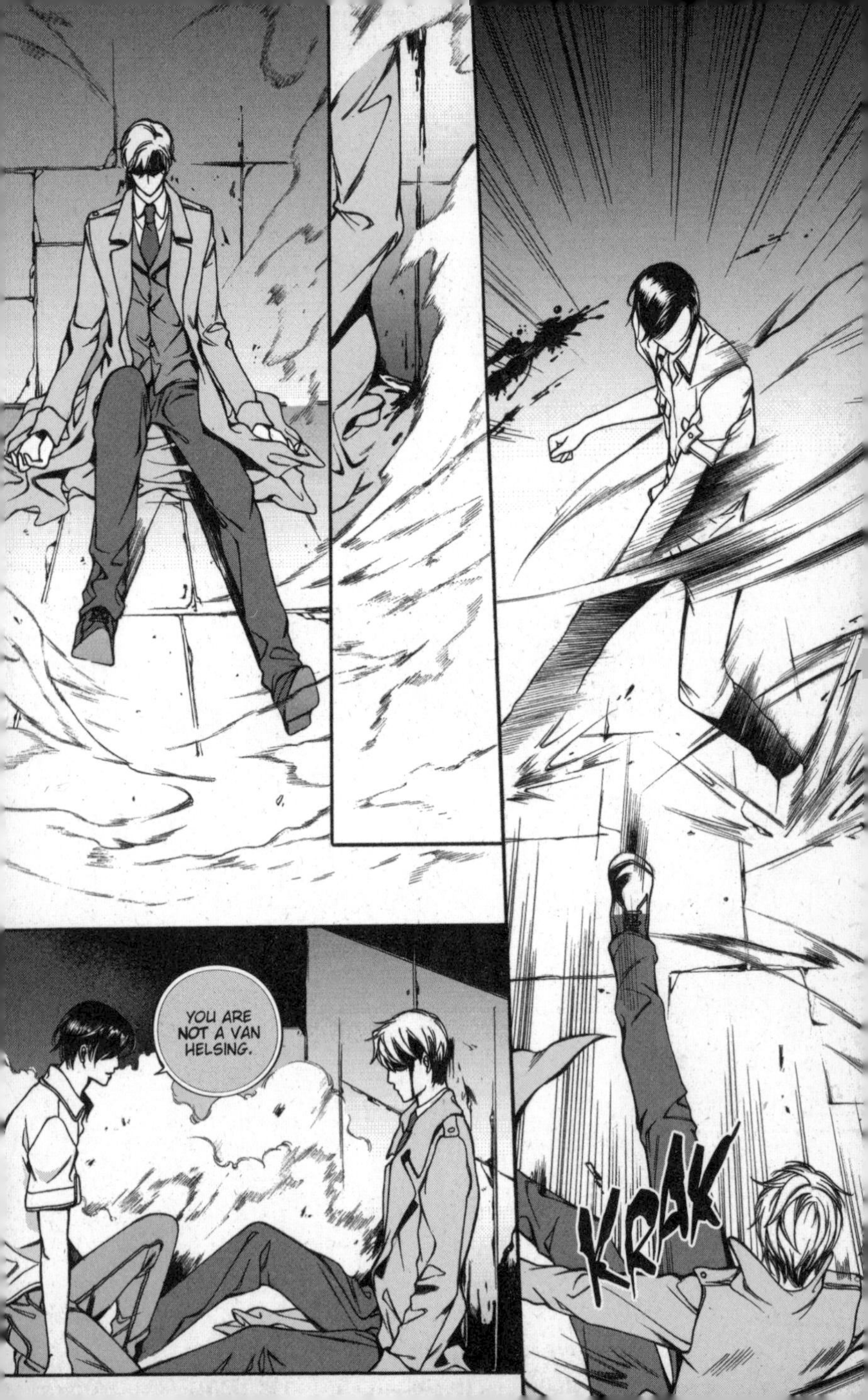
KRAK
YOU ARE NOT A VAN HELSING.

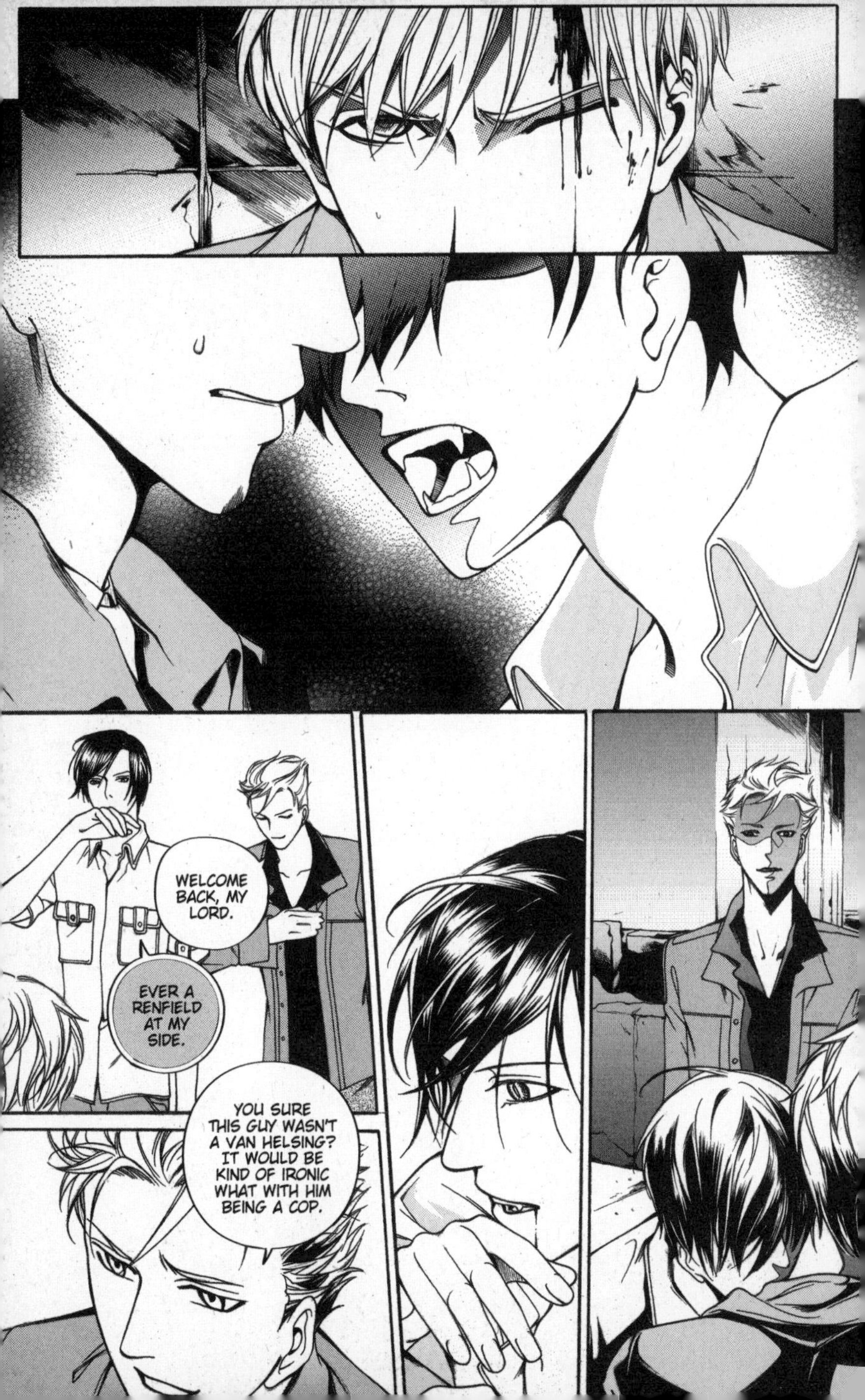
WELCOME BACK, MY LORD.
EVER A RENFIELD AT MY SIDE.
YOU SURE THIS GUY WASN'T A VAN HELSING? IT WOULD BE KIND OF IRONIC WHAT WITH HIM BEING A COP.

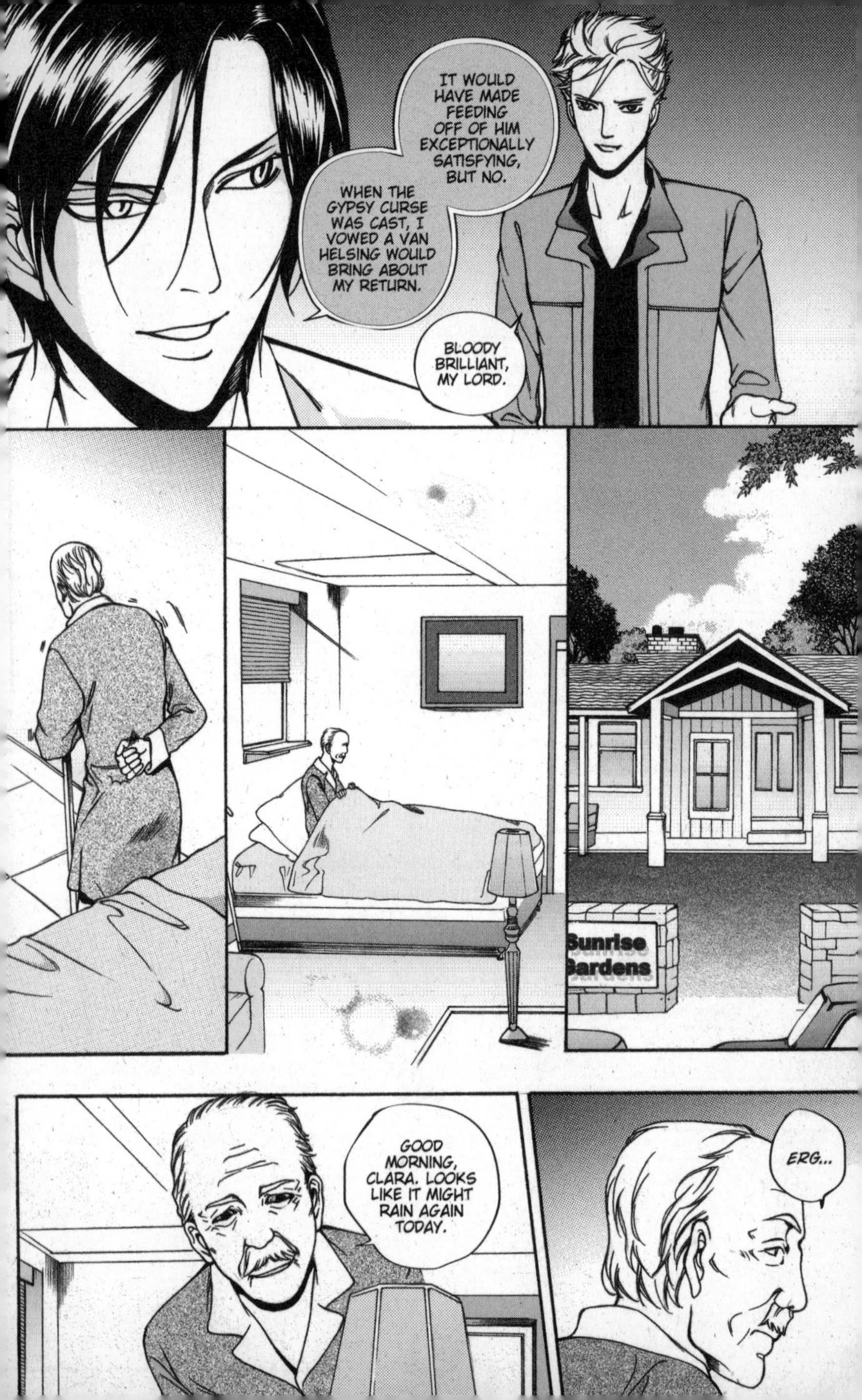
IT WOULD HAVE MADE FEEDING OFF OF HIM EXCEPTIONALLY SATISFYING, BUT NO.
WHEN THE GYPSY CURSE WAS CAST, I VOWED A VAN HELSING WOULD BRING ABOUT MY RETURN.
BLOODY BRILLIANT, MY LORD.
Sunrise Gardens
ERG...
GOOD MORNING, CLARA. LOOKS LIKE IT MIGHT RAIN AGAIN TODAY.

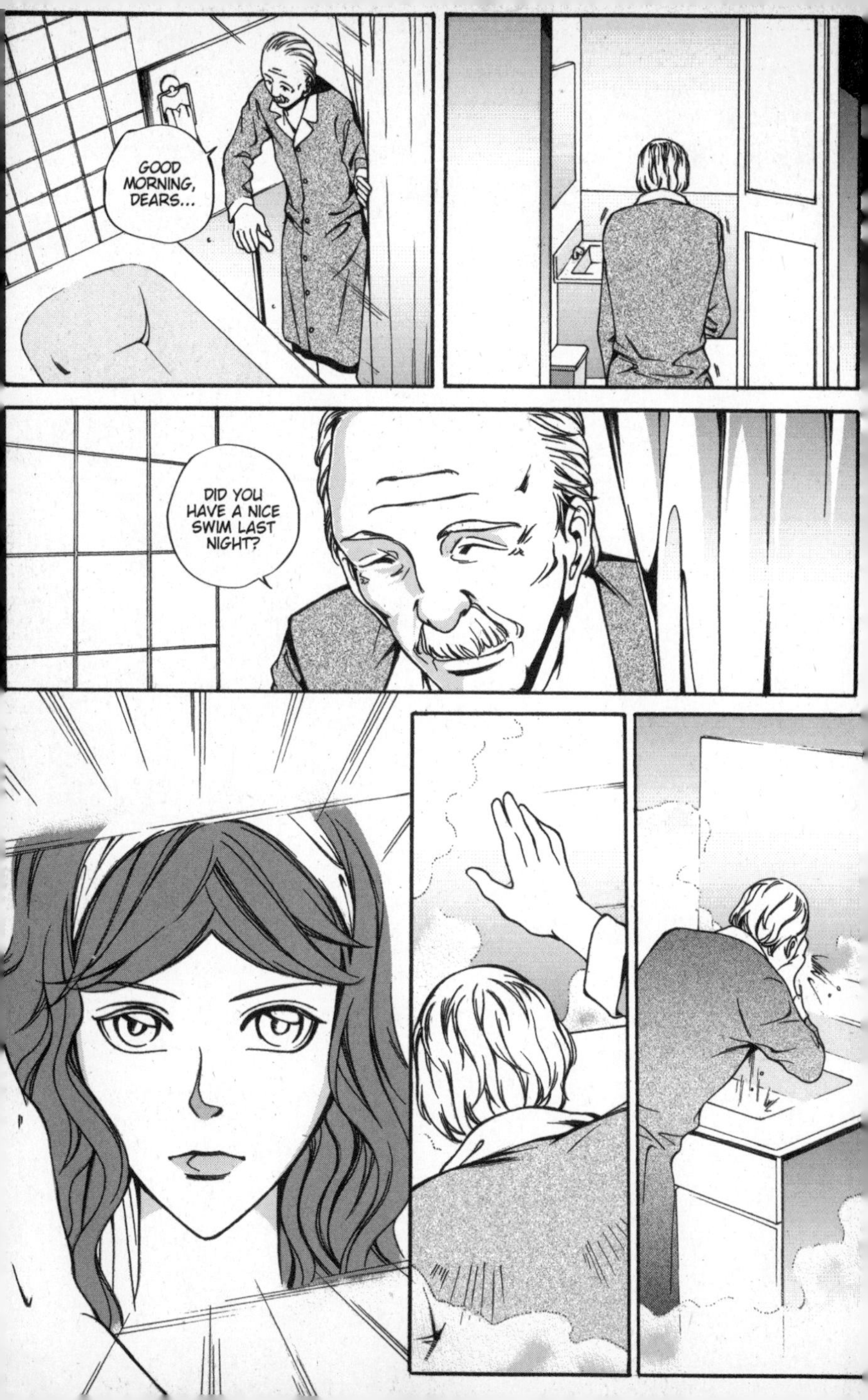
GOOD MORNING, DEARS...
DID YOU HAVE A NICE SWIM LAST NIGHT?

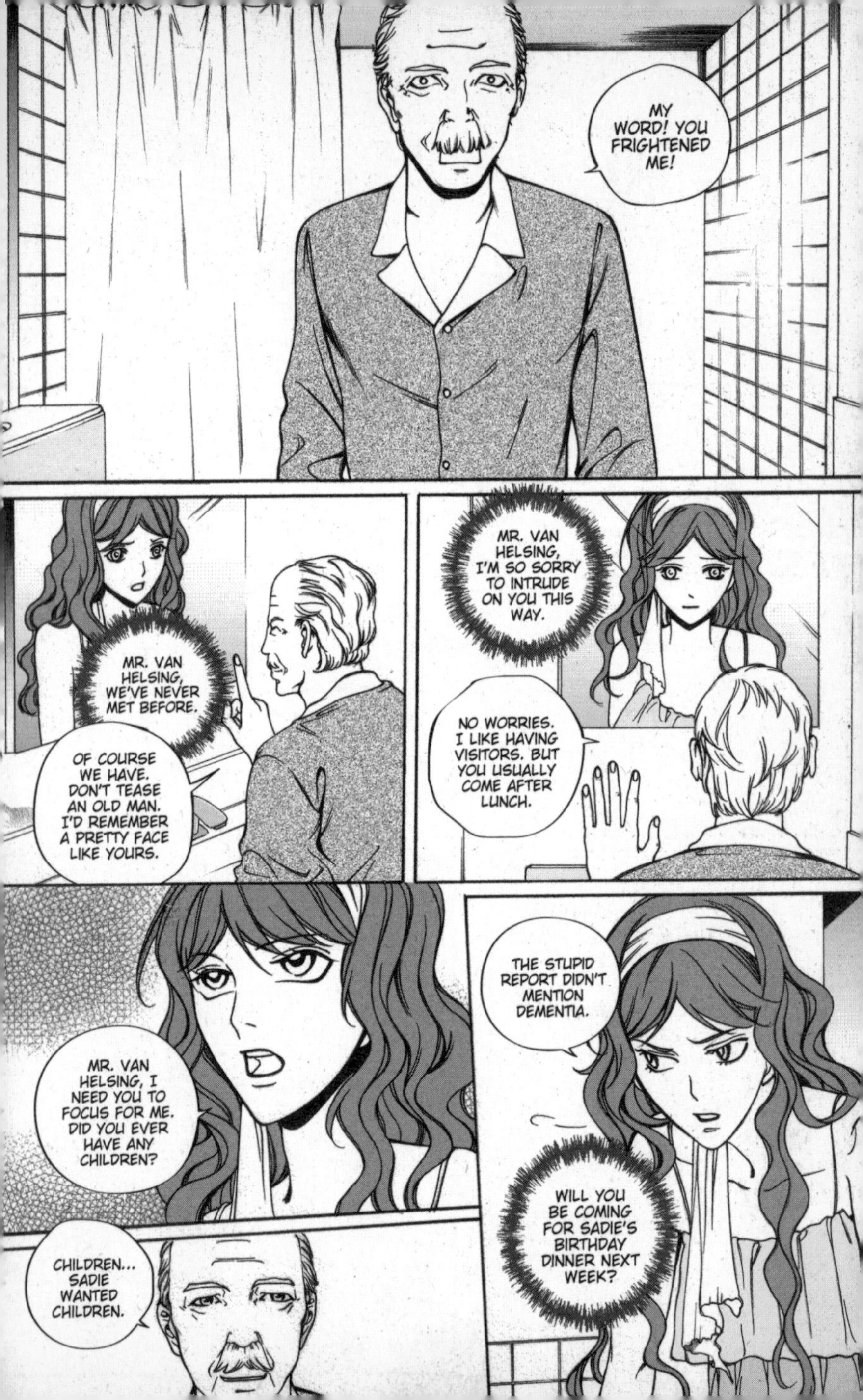
MY WORD! YOU FRIGHTENED ME!
MR. VAN HELSING, I'M SO SORRY TO INTRUDE ON YOU THIS WAY.
NO WORRIES. I LIKE HAVING VISITORS. BUT YOU USUALLY COME AFTER LUNCH.
MR. VAN HELSING, WE'VE NEVER MET BEFORE.
OF COURSE WE HAVE. DON'T TEASE AN OLD MAN. I'D REMEMBER A PRETTY FACE LIKE YOURS.
THE STUPID REPORT DIDN'T MENTION DEMENTIA.
WILL YOU BE COMING FOR SADIE'S BIRTHDAY DINNER NEXT WEEK?
MR. VAN HELSING, I NEED YOU TO FOCUS FOR ME. DID YOU EVER HAVE ANY CHILDREN?
CHILDREN... SADIE WANTED CHILDREN.

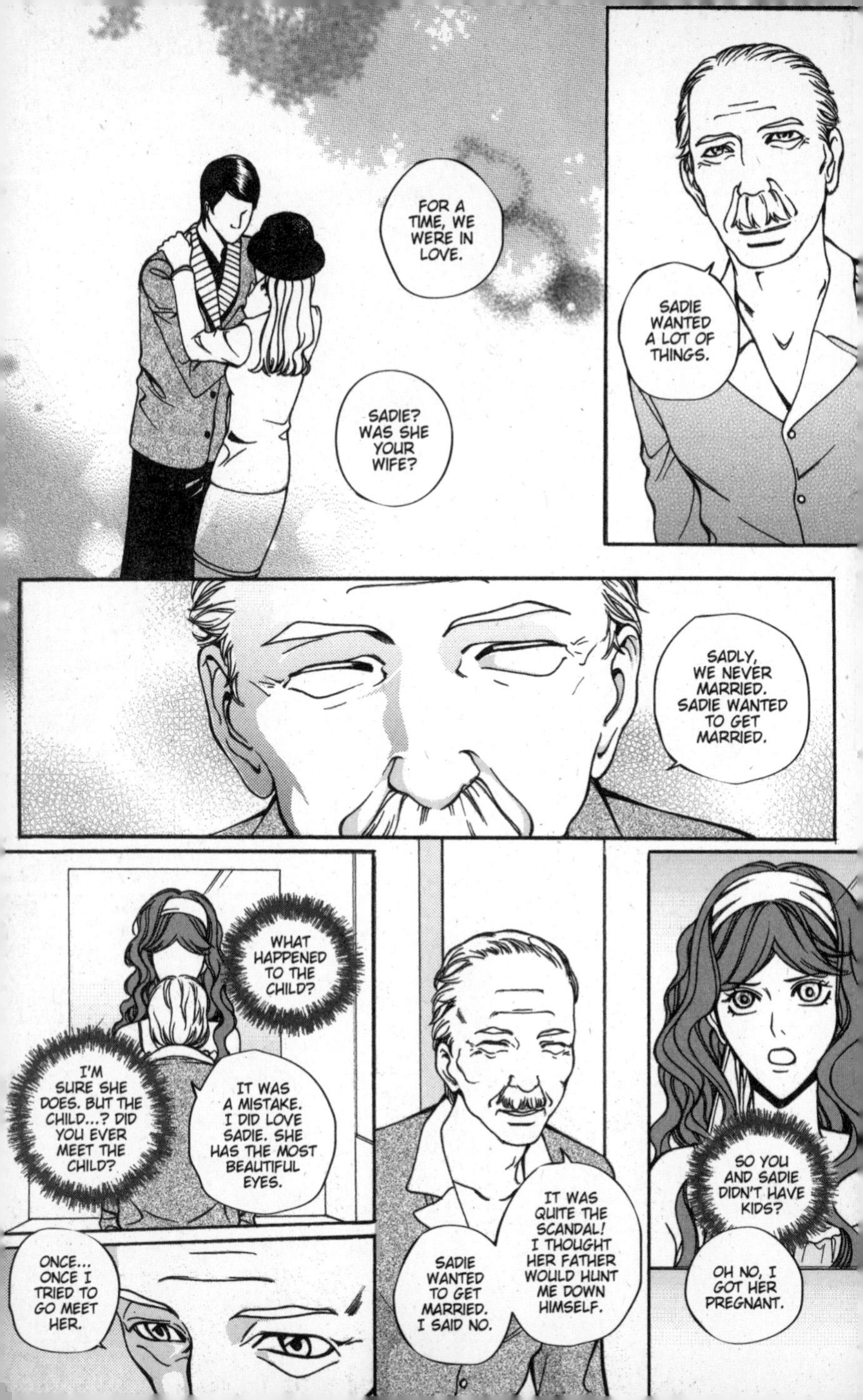
SADIE WANTED A LOT OF THINGS.
FOR A TIME, WE WERE IN LOVE.
SADIE? WAS SHE YOUR WIFE?
SADLY, WE NEVER MARRIED. SADIE WANTED TO GET MARRIED.
SO YOU AND SADIE DIDN'T HAVE KIDS?
OH NO, I GOT HER PREGNANT.
IT WAS QUITE THE SCANDAL! I THOUGHT HER FATHER WOULD HUNT ME DOWN HIMSELF.
SADIE WANTED TO GET MARRIED. I SAID NO.
WHAT HAPPENED TO THE CHILD?
IT WAS A MISTAKE. I DID LOVE SADIE. SHE HAS THE MOST BEAUTIFUL EYES.
I'M SURE SHE DOES. BUT THE CHILD...? DID YOU EVER MEET THE CHILD?
ONCE... ONCE I TRIED TO GO MEET HER.

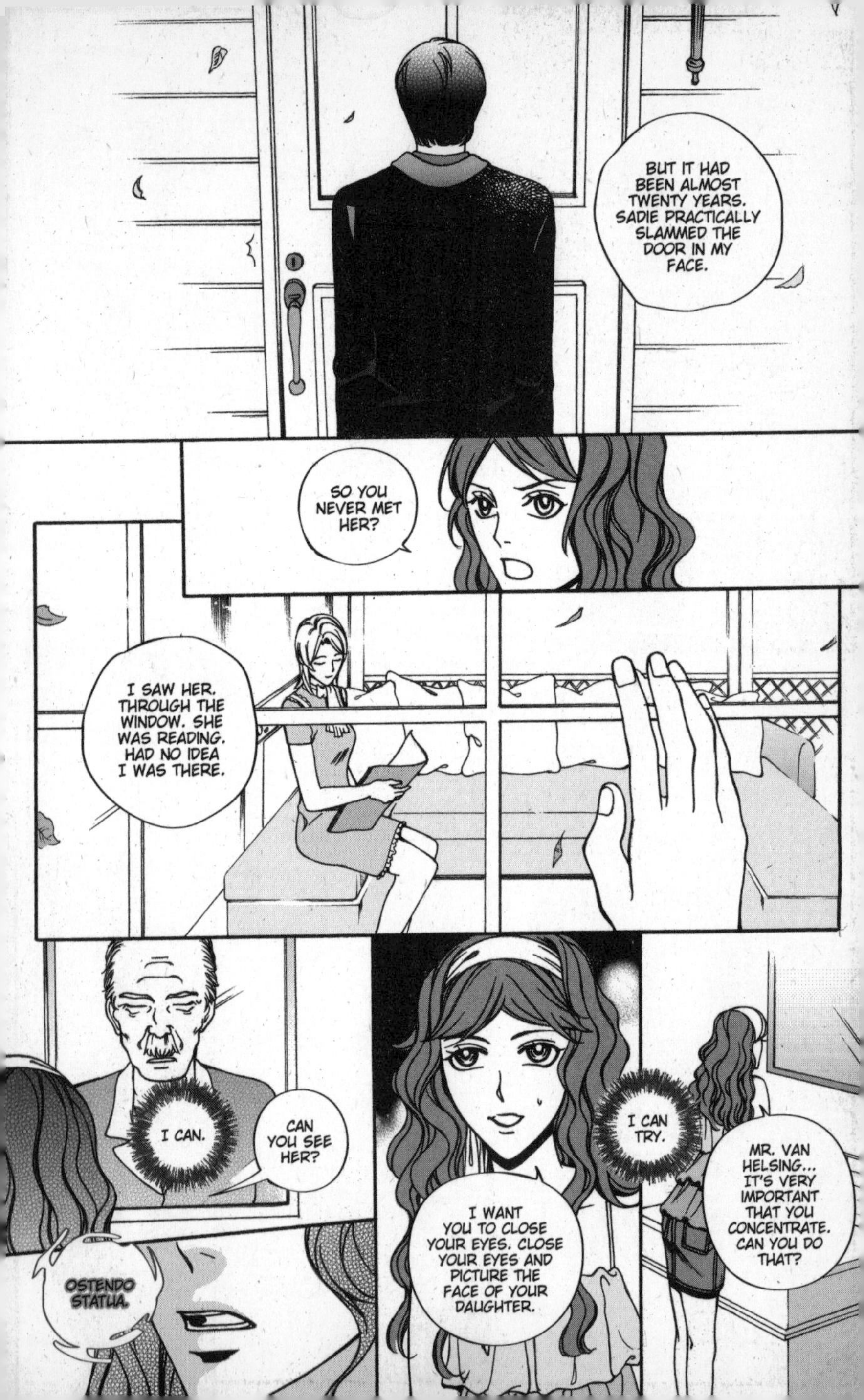

BUT IT HAD BEEN ALMOST TWENTY YEARS. SADIE PRACTICALLY SLAMMED THE DOOR IN MY FACE.
SO YOU NEVER MET HER?
I SAW HER. THROUGH THE WINDOW. SHE WAS READING. HAD NO IDEA I WAS THERE.
MR. VAN HELSING... IT'S VERY IMPORTANT THAT YOU CONCENTRATE. CAN YOU DO THAT?
I CAN TRY.
I WANT YOU TO CLOSE YOUR EYES. CLOSE YOUR EYES AND PICTURE THE FACE OF YOUR DAUGHTER.
CAN YOU SEE HER?
I CAN.
OSTENDO STATUA.

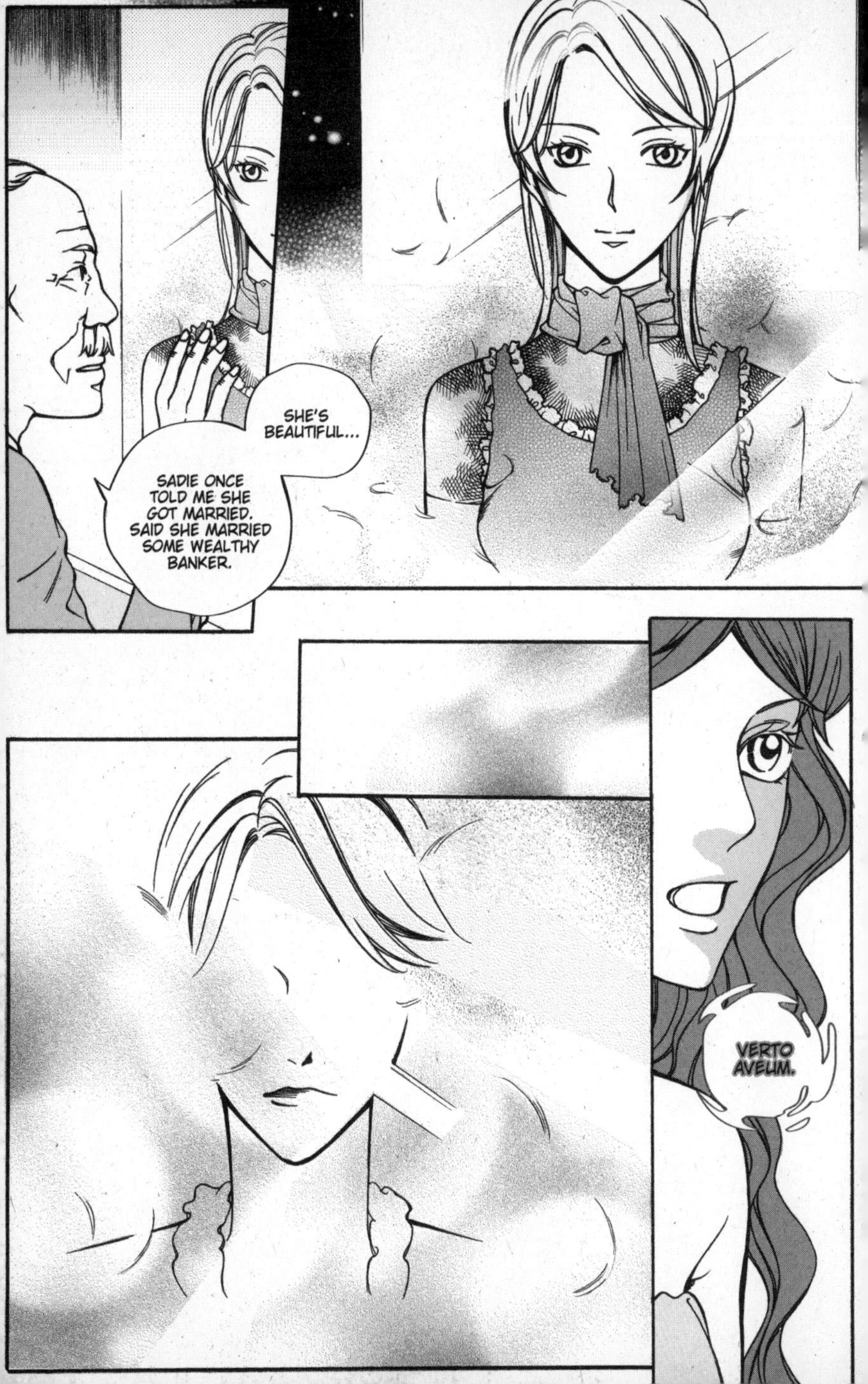
SHE'S BEAUTIFUL...
SADIE ONCE TOLD ME SHE GOT MARRIED. SAID SHE MARRIED SOME WEALTHY BANKER.
VERTO AVEUM.

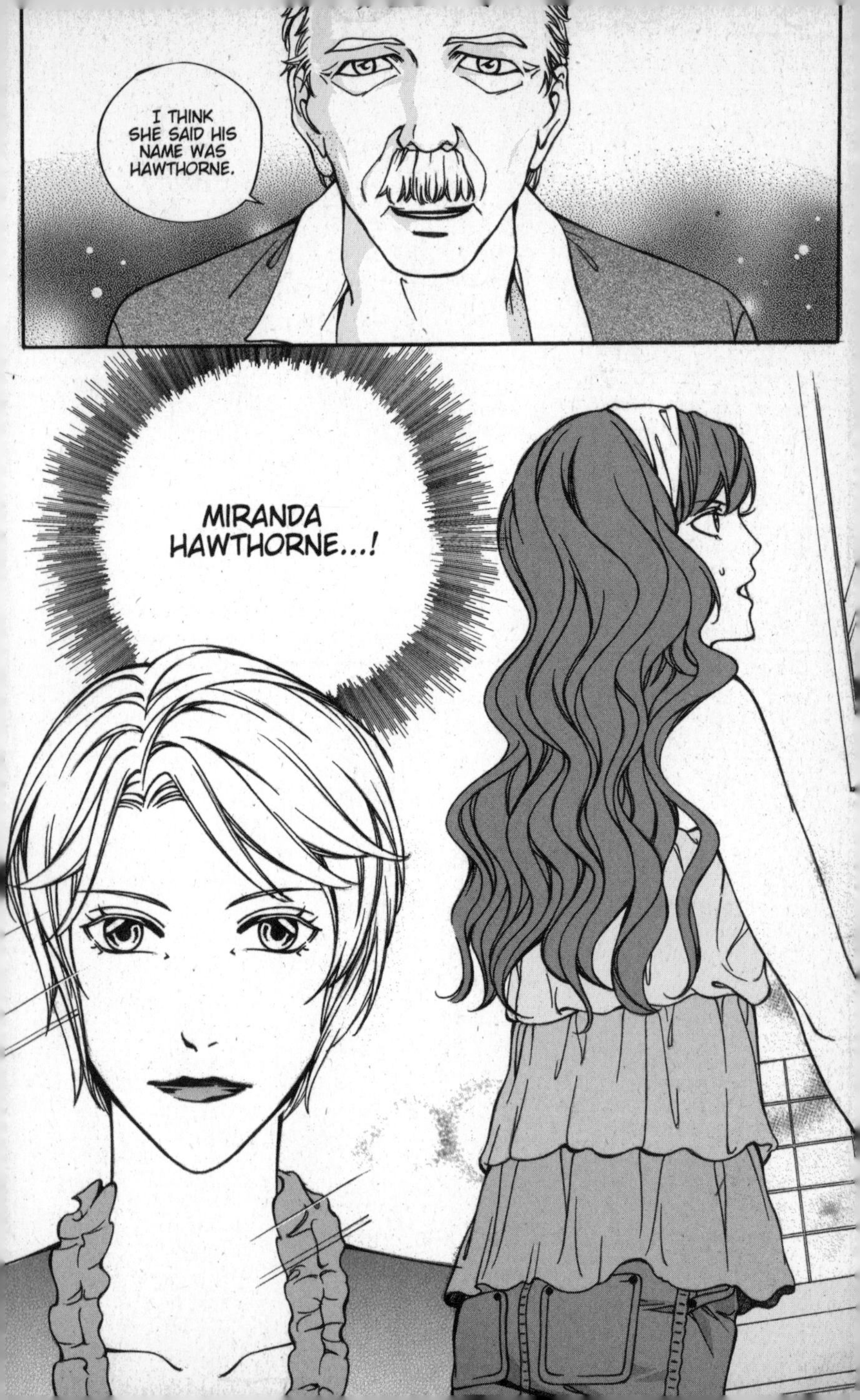
I THINK SHE SAID HIS NAME WAS HAWTHORNE.
MIRANDA HAWTHORNE...!

NOTE FROM THE AUTHORS:

When Bram Stoker wrote *Dracula*, he wrote in epistolary form. The book is a collection of letters and notes, which Stoker claimed he'd collected from real world sources.

Most people thought this a clever way to present his story, to make the horror of the vampire seem all the more real.

But what if they WERE real? What if Stoker had intercepted letters, interviewed subjects, gathered the truth about a Transylvanian Count, his English tutor, and his terrorizing trip to London?

Jason DeAngelis of Seven Seas is a great publisher. He lets us tell the stories we like to tell. But in researching the *Dracula* legend before presenting it to us, he found evidence. Evidence that Stoker's publisher was a bit more controlling. Evidence that suggested Stoker either genuinely DID base Dracula (or, as he originally titled it, *The Dead Un-Dead*) on real events, or—at the very least—that he believed them to be real.

Reproduced on the following page are notes and letters Stoker exchanged with his publisher, Archibald Constable and Company, in 1896, the year before Stoker's masterpiece was published.

They hint that there was much more to the story. Elements that, if true, could leave everyone in mortal danger. And if untrue, it would mean that Stoker had future stories in mind.

Either way, Jason brought these notes to our attention, and we extrapolated the events you see in this book and the volumes that will follow.

Was Stoker telling the truth? Were his characters real? Were the rumors he wanted to include in his manuscript warnings that the Dark Lord would rise again...?

Who can say for sure...?

David Auerbach
Archibald Constable & Company
2 Whitehall Gardens
London

Bram,

Enclosed please find your revised ending to The Dead Un-Dead. I am sending back these changes as I find them to leave the book in an unsatisfactory place. Readers will not want rumours and hints of Dracula's return. They will be seeking, I daresay, reassurance that the evil has been put to rest once and forever.

I find your manuscript to be satisfactory on every level in the previous draft. It is this company's intention to publish it in such condition.

Best,
David

Mr. Auerbach,

These rumours I have added to my book were not the last second choice of a writer seeking to alter a work on which he has spent considerable time. It was not a whim, nor a creative urge.

It was based on fact. There are rumours of gypsy magic. Rumours of the dark lord's return. We ignore these at our peril.

With great hope,

Bram

not going to change our mind on this, Bram. Your assertion that your book is based on facts is a charming façade that will help sell this book. But we are publishing it as fiction, and as such, it will be edited for the best possible story decisions.

Expect a May release in the coming year.

Sincerely,
David

CHARACTER DESIGNS

On the next few pages, we've included the character designs and notes for a large chunk of our cast.

We've included the original design notes that we sent to Rhea, and then her comments (after having drawn them) about the characters and their looks.

Hope you enjoy the inside view...

— Nunzio & Christina

NICHOLAS HARKER:

Original Character and Design notes sent to Rhea:

Nicholas is seventeen years old and just starting his senior year of high school. He is dark haired and at the start a little meek. He doesn't have as much confidence as he could and tends to blend into the background. When his parents die, he is left somewhat broken, an empty shell of himself. It is his friendship with Jill that gives him strength. And then he finds a Harker heirloom—a locket with the word "Everlasting" engraved on it. When he opens it, he is imbued with the Dracula essence and this transforms him. He gains confidence and consequently is a little better looking, suaver.

Nicholas changes over the course of Volume 1. It's not that Dracula's presence changes him physically, but it's as if he gets a male makeover. At the start, his body language, his clothes, his hair—everything about him—is unassuming. It allows him to blend in and not be noticed. He's very average in how he carries himself. But as Dracula inhabits him, his confidence starts to grow. His hair gets longer (passage of time, not magically) and his wardrobe and posture change. The conflict of being more assertive versus having a horrible dark side will make him broody and sexy and introspective. Lastly, you should feel free to design whatever effect is used to show that Dracula has taken control in this moment—that could be an aura, an eye-effect, maybe some kind of silhouette or outline—whatever you think works.

Rhea's Notes:

Nick: He's your typical pretty boy type, so that means he's the easiest to draw. I always have a good sense of drawing anything pretty :D He's starting out meek and his personality changes along the way. I love drawing and coloring his black hair; it's my favorite part of him. I'm wondering where he gets his Dracula outfit, though, which leads to one of the world's unresolved mysteries.

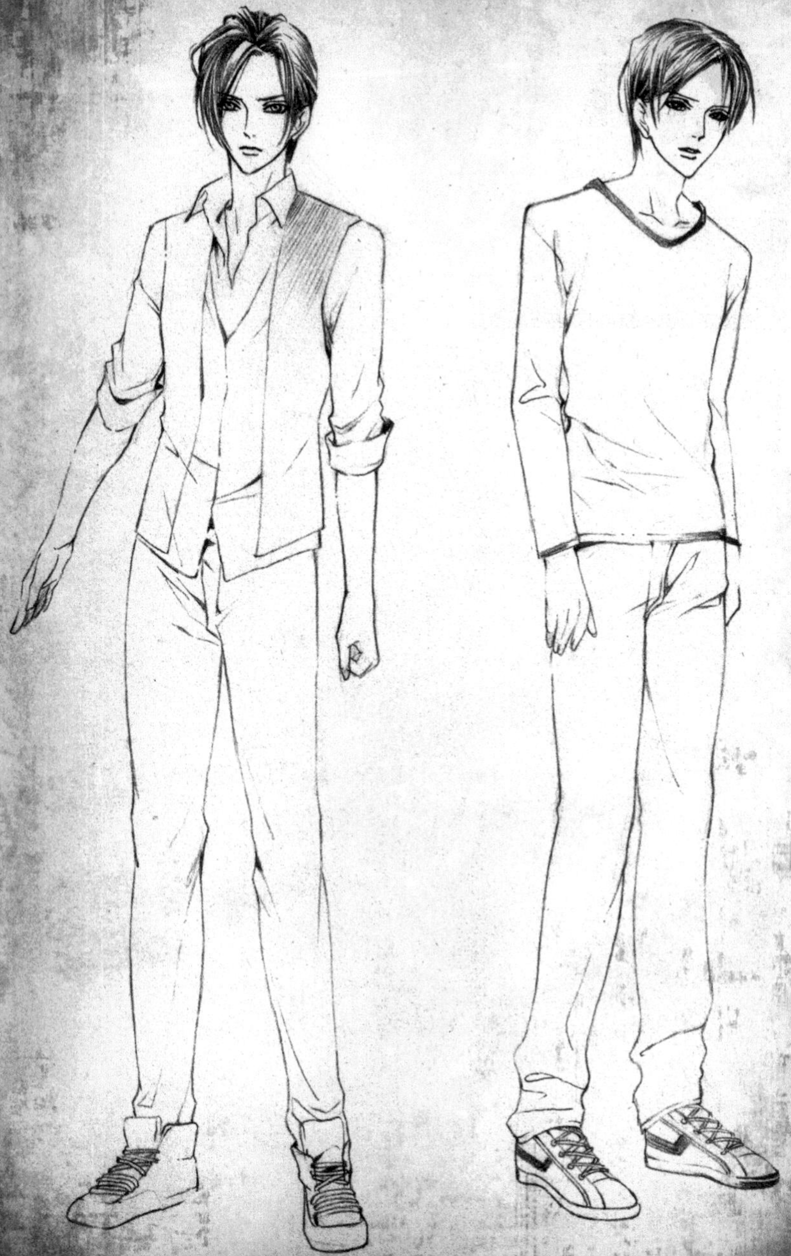

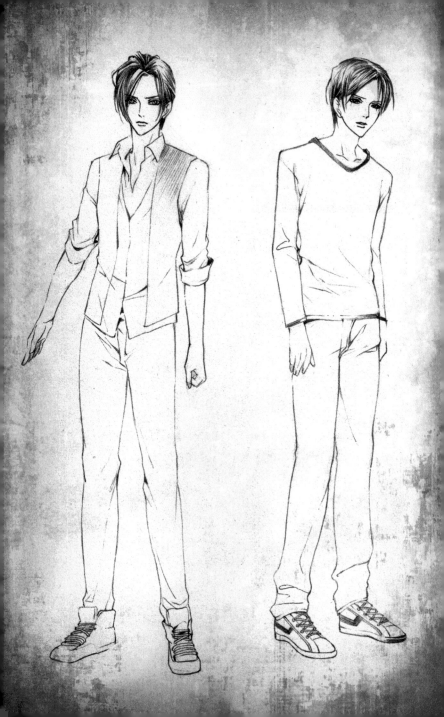

JILLIAN (JILL) HAWTHORNE

Original Character and Design notes sent to Rhea:

Jill is the prototypical girl next door. She's friendly and kind but also very introverted. Raised in London, she proves herself quite adaptable when her mother uproots them and moves to Boston. Shy herself, Jill is really good at being a best friend, but that makes it all the harder when she actually realizes that she quite "likes" her new best friend. She's an avid reader and loves fantasy. She has no idea about her family heritage.

Jill is blonde, cute but not flashy. Shy. Maybe glasses? Definitely the type who could be a romantic lead if only she were more confident. But even if she were, it would be an everygirl beauty, not a fashion model beauty. More cute than sexy.

Rhea's Notes:

Jill's design is simple enough. She's supposed to be cute, but not too eye-catching. She's also one of the most simple characters to draw. I hate the ends of her hair where it curls—it kills my hand when inking! *laugh*

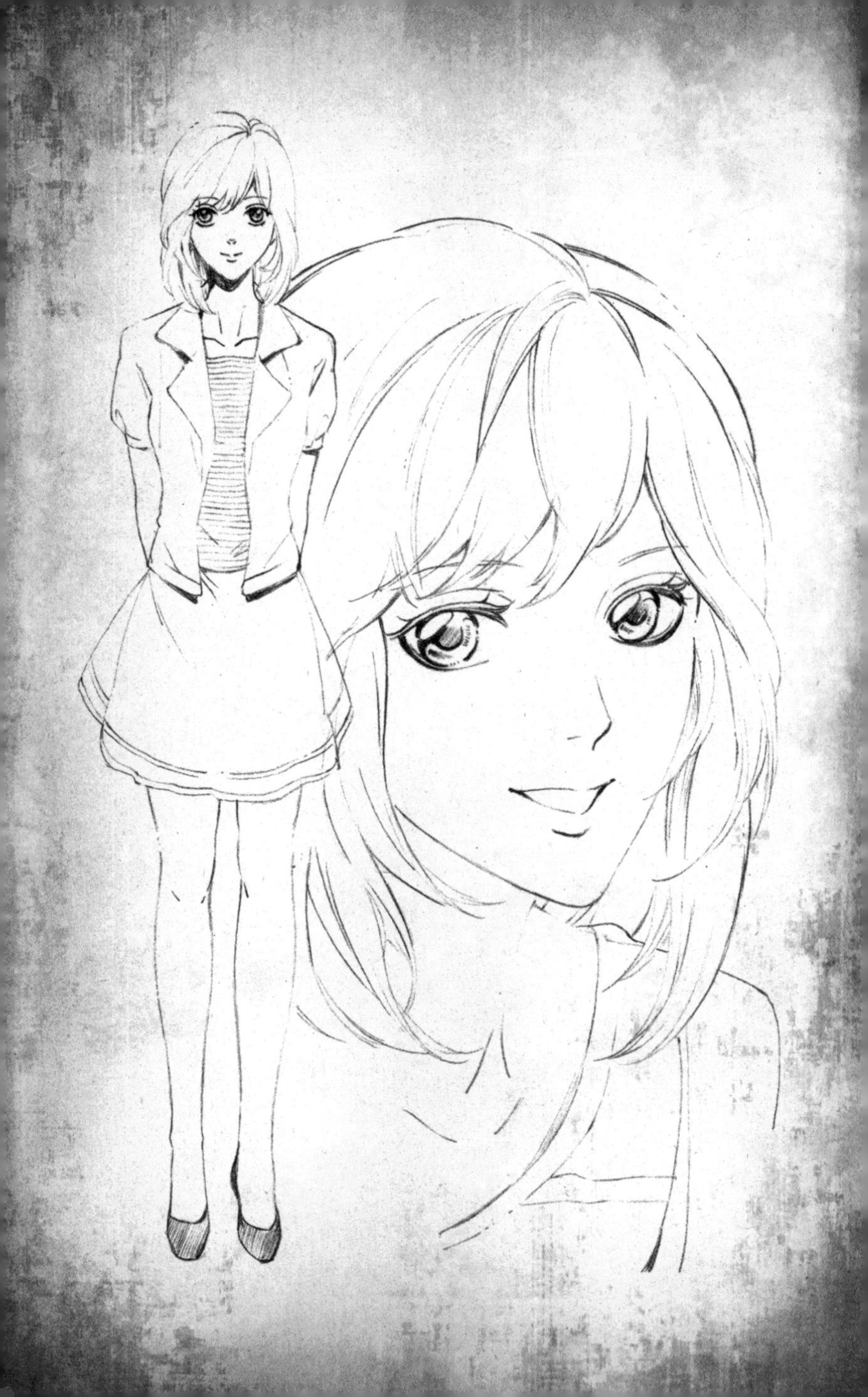

HECATE (CATE) AMBROSE

Original Character and Design notes sent to Rhea:

The daughter of Rayne. Rayne was young when she had Cate. Cate has fully embraced her witch powers and even tapped into some of the darker magics. Cate is all sass and attitude. She's the center of attention wherever she goes, because it's another way she can exert power over the world.

Cate should be far from the goth stereotype. She's stunning and sexy and wears short skirts and makes people take notice wherever she goes. Black hair maybe? Or red hair if we want to mix things up. As sexy and troublemaking as we want her to be, she should never look so harsh as to be unlikable. She's anti-hero material.

Rhea's Notes:

I love her. She has a cool personality and a sexy body. Definitely the type of the girl I want to be.

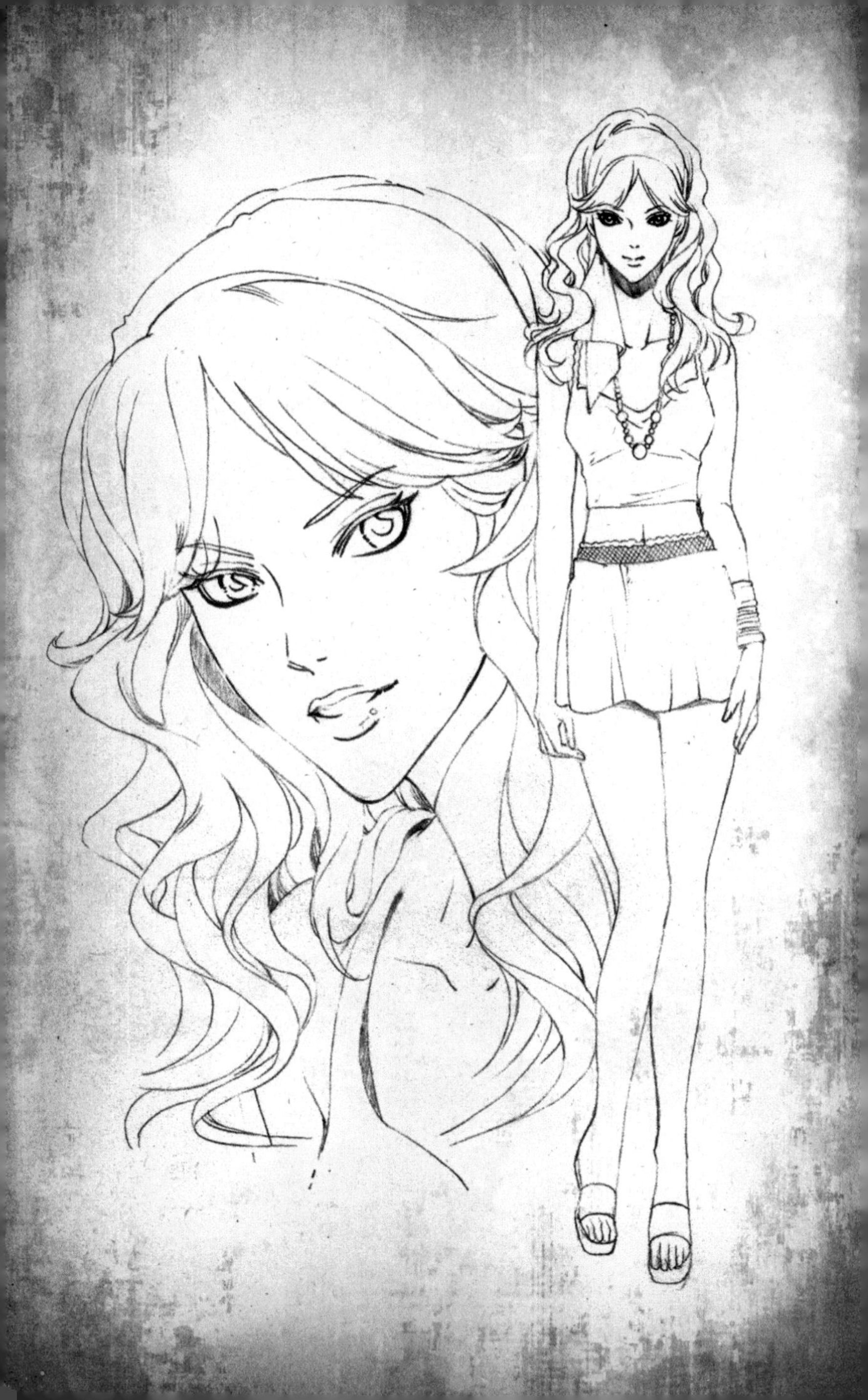

MIRANDA HAWTHORNE

Original Character and Design notes sent to Rhea:

A British barrister. She's Jill's mother and is Nicholas's lawyer, once he inherits the estate. She is elegant, well put together, and a very take-charge woman.

Ms. Hawthorne probably has a short, sleek haircut and wears lots of stylish pants suits, occasionally skirt suits. But always well dressed and professional. She's lean and athletic, and in great shape for her age—which is about 40.

Rhea's Notes:

She's a tough mom, being a single parent and all. But I think she's kind and motherly on the inside, so I try to show that in the design.

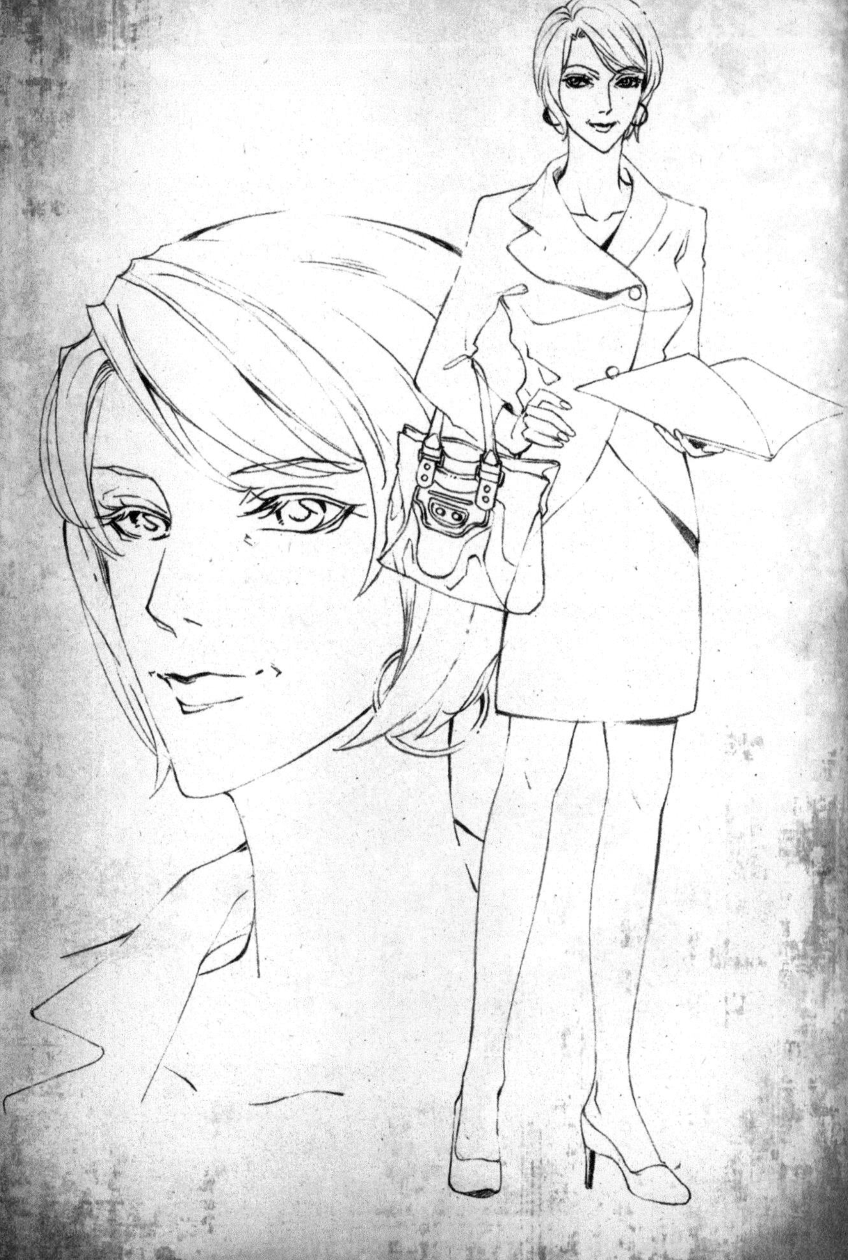

MASON RENFIELD

Original Character and Design notes sent to Rhea:

The youngest of the Renfield boys, he's not creepy and slimy and bug-eating like his brothers and father. He's a good-looking charmer. In his family, that makes him something of the black sheep. Mason feels like he has a lot to prove and is the one who sticks it out to befriend Nicholas so he can shepherd in the new era of Dracula.

Good looking, lean and well built. His good looks should probably be of the dangerous variety.

Rhea's Notes:

I changed his design twice. His first design was a calm looking guy who hides his deceit underneath. Later on, I thought he looked too much like Nick and I wanted him to show his dangerousness on the outside. So I redrew him and made him look more like a bad boy. He's my favorite character; I like his cool and imposing personality. If only he wasn't a bad guy...LOL.

VANESSA DOYLE

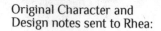

Original Character and Design notes sent to Rhea:

The popular girl in the senior class. Nicholas has had a crush on her since time began, but he is beneath her notice. Vanessa is gorgeous, bubbly, and popular.

Unlike Cate, whose persona is laced with sex appeal beyond her years, Vanessa is more of the typical rich girl/cheerleader/queen bee type. She's good looking, and dresses well, but never fully "slutty." She has red hair—or black hair if Cate's a redhead. Also, unlike Cate, feel free to make her look cold and snobby. The reader need not like her at all.

RAYNE AMBROSE

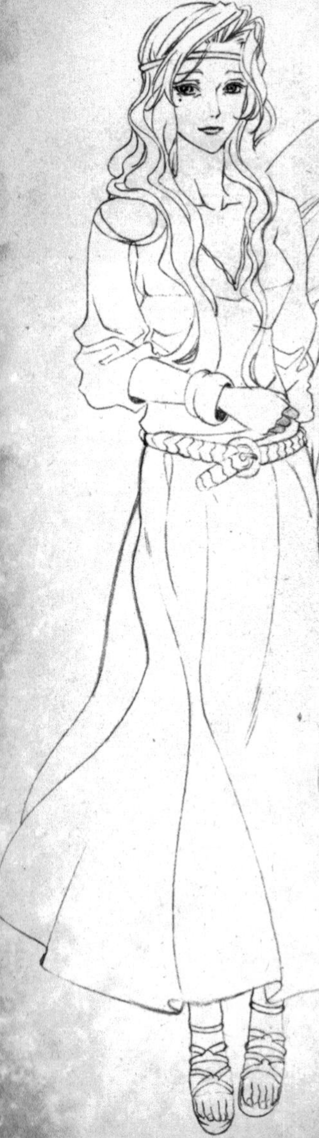

Original Character and Design notes sent to Rhea:

A hippie new-age wiccan. She's in her late thirties, had a child very young. She loves her crystals and discussions of positive energies.

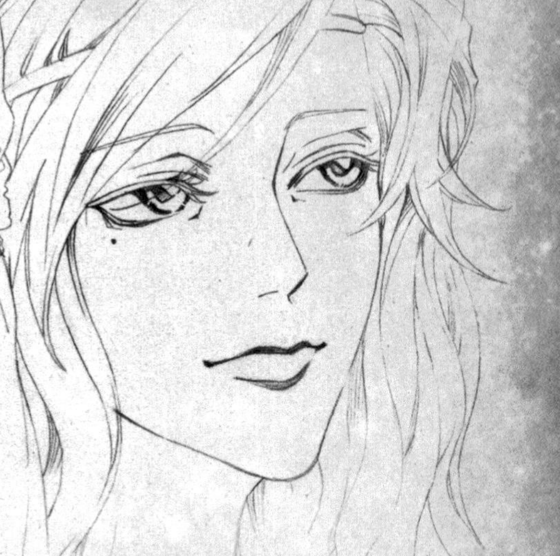

Rayne has real magic, but should still look like a bit of the cliché. Earthy looks, long flowing skirts, long hair. A combination of hippie and new-ager. She's, as mentioned above, in her late thirties.

Rhea's Notes:

She's Cate's mom, so they should look alike. They have the same red curly flowing hair.

Detective DAVIS MCALLISTER

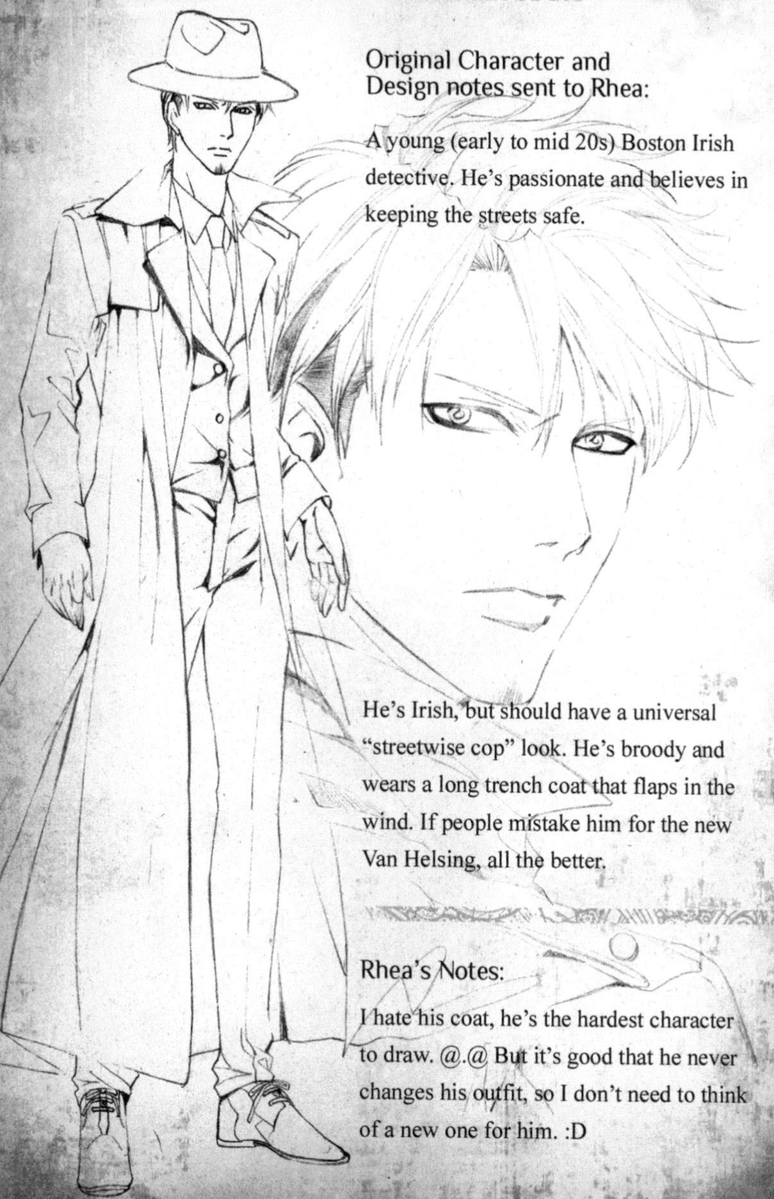

Original Character and Design notes sent to Rhea:

A young (early to mid 20s) Boston Irish detective. He's passionate and believes in keeping the streets safe.

He's Irish, but should have a universal "streetwise cop" look. He's broody and wears a long trench coat that flaps in the wind. If people mistake him for the new Van Helsing, all the better.

Rhea's Notes:

I hate his coat, he's the hardest character to draw. @.@ But it's good that he never changes his outfit, so I don't need to think of a new one for him. :D

KARL RENFIELD

Original Character and Design notes sent to Rhea:

The current head of the Renfield family. He is part of a long line that has been waiting generations for their Dark Master to rise again.

Karl is an oily, creepy looking sycophant. Kind of like a middle-aged Peter Lorre.

All of his sons, except Mason, are creepy, angry, disturbing looking.

Rhea's Notes:

Renfield and his three sons: They're a troupe of ugly-looking family members (except Mason, of course). Renfield is portrayed as the usual middle-aged man. The brothers...well, they're supposed to look ugly, so here they are.